Cliffs Advanced Placement™

CliffsAP™

Calculus AB and BC

3RD EDITION

by

Kerry J. King, M.S.
and
Dale W. Johnson, M.A.

Series Editor
Jerry Bobrow, Ph.D.

WILEY
Wiley Publishing, Inc.

Author's Acknowledgments

I would like to thank the following people for their invaluable assistance in proofreading and editing the manuscript for this book: Connie Day, mathematics editor; Don Gallaher, AP calculus teacher; and Dr. Jerry Bobrow, series editor. Finally, thanks to Alan Tussy for inspiration and guidance.

Editorial

Project Editor: Christina Van Camp

Acquisitions Editor: Sherry Gomoll

Technical Editor: Dale Johnson

Composition

Proofreader: Arielle Carole Mannelle

Wiley Indianapolis Composition Services

CliffsAP™ Calculus AB and BC, 3rd Edition

Published by:
Wiley Publishing, Inc.
111 River Street
Hoboken, NJ 07030
www.wiley.com

Copyright © 2001 Kerry J. King.

Published by Wiley Publishing, Inc., New York, NY
Published simultaneously in Canada

Library of Congress Control Number: 2001088756

ISBN: 0-7645-8683-1

Printed in the United States of America

10 9 8 7 6 5 4

3B/QW/QU/QR/IN

For general information on our other products and services or to obtain technical support, please contact our Customer Care Department within the U.S. at 800-762-2974, outside the U.S. at 317-572-3993, or fax 317-572-4002.

Wiley also publishes its books in a variety of electronic formats. Some content that appears in print may not be available in electronic books.

Table of Contents

PART I: INTRODUCTION

PART II: SPECIFIC TOPICS

PART III: AP CALCULUS AB AND BC PRACTICE TESTS

Preface

This book is intended as a study aid for the student who plans to take the Advanced Placement Calculus AB and BC examination. It is not meant to be a comprehensive guide to learning calculus or a replacement for an advanced placement course of study. It is simply a resource for you to draw on during your year of study — and especially during the last four to five weeks before the AP exam in May.

A specific graphing calculator was used to generate the screens shown in this book. Your calculator may produce different displays.

Study Guide Checklist

❑ **1.** Read the outline of topics given in the *Advanced Placement Course Description — Mathematics: Calculus AB, Calculus BC* (the "Acorn Book," available from your teacher or directly from Educational Testing Service). Be sure to look at the left column for AP Calculus AB.

❑ **2.** Read "Questions Commonly Asked About the AP Calculus AB and BC Exams" in this guide.

❑ **3.** Read "Topics Covered on a Recent AP Calculus AB or BC Exam."

❑ **4.** If you do not already have one, buy a graphing calculator before proceeding any further. Be sure you are familiar with the necessary functions and how to access them for your particular calculator.

❑ **5.** Go through each of the specific topics. Read or skim the explanations. Work through the examples in the text and then complete the questions at the end of each chapter. Practice writing out your answers to the free-response questions in thorough, precise form, as if they were a part of a real AP exam.

❑ **6.** Memorize important facts (see the list under "Strategies for the Exam"). A set of flash cards may be useful. Be sure to know the key terms listed in the appendix.

❑ **7.** Take the first full-length practice exam (the AB exam). Simulate actual test-taking conditions. Grade the practice test using the answer key and the grading rubric.

❑ **8.** Analyze your results from the first test. Identify subject areas that you seem to know well and those you need to practice more. Review the latter by rereading the appropriate section and/or working through the examples.

❑ **9.** Take the second full-length practice exam (the BC exam). Again, simulate testing conditions and grade the test.

❑ **10.** Analyze the results from the second test and review any weak areas.

❑ **11.** Just prior to the actual exam, review your memorized facts and put a fresh set of batteries in your calculator.

❑ **12.** Take the exam!

Format of a Recent Calculus AB and BC Exam			
Section I: Multiple-Choice Questions		**50% of total**	
IA:	55 minutes	28 questions	calculator not allowed
IB:	50 minutes	17 questions	must use calculator*
Section II: Free-Response Questions		**50% of total**	
IIA*	45 minutes	3 questions	graphing calculator required
IIB**	45 minutes	3 questions	NO calculator

*See page 11 for a list of approved calculators.

**During IIB, Students are allowed to continue work on questions 1–3 from IIA, but a calculator may NOT be used during this time.

The AP Calculus BC Grade report will also include an AB subscore (approximately 60% of the BC exam consists of AB topics).

PART I

INTRODUCTION

Questions Commonly Asked About the AP Calculus AB and BC Exams

Q: What is the AP calculus exam?

A: The three and one-quarter hour Advanced Placement calculus exam is given to high school students in May to determine how well each student has mastered the subject of calculus. Passing the AP calculus exam, which requires a grade of 3 or higher on a 5-point scale, allows a student to earn college credit for calculus at universities and colleges participating in the AP program. Students who pass the AP Calculus AB exam generally receive credit for one quarter or one semester of college calculus.

Q: What are the advantages of taking AP calculus?

A: The main advantage is that of earning college credit. Students who will be required to take calculus in college for their major field of study may be able to skip coursework in that subject entirely or enter the calculus sequence at a more advanced level.

Q: What's the difference between Calculus AB and Calculus BC? Which exam should I take?

A: The Calculus BC exam includes all of the material in the Calculus AB exam plus additional selected topics, notably on sequences and series. You should take the exam you have prepared for. Do not try to cram in the extra BC material on your own. Typically, students who pass the Calculus AB exam receive either a quarter's worth or a semester's worth of college credit, while students who pass the Calculus BC exam receive one semester's worth or two quarter's worth of college credit. Check with the admissions officer at the universities or colleges you are interested in attending for more specific information.

Q: Do all colleges accept AP exam grades for college credit?

A: No, but most universities and colleges do. For a complete list of schools that accept AP scores for credit, you can ask your teacher for the *Advanced Placement Course Description — Mathematics: Calculus AB, Calculus BC,* commonly known as the "Acorn Book." The College Board and Educational Testing Service (ETS) publish this booklet each year. If you need more information, call the institution you are interested in and speak to someone in the registrar's office.

Q: How is the AP exam graded and what do the scores mean?

A: The multiple-choice section is machine-scored, and the free-response section of the exam is graded by groups of AP calculus teachers and/or college calculus instructors. The total exam is scored on a point system (see the practice AP scoring worksheet in this book), and then the chief faculty consultants determine how these raw point totals correlate to the scores of 1 through 5. A score of 3, 4, or 5 is considered passing and generally earns college credit.

Q: Are there old exams out there that I can look at?

A: The free-response section of each test is released on the day of the exam each year, so see your AP teacher for copies of old free-response questions. Several multiple-choice question sets have also been released over the years. However, now that the use of graphing calculators is required, some new question types may vary significantly from old question types.

Q: What materials should I take to the exam?

A: You should take four or five sharpened number 2 pencils or mechanical pencils with HB or softer lead. Also take an eraser, a watch, a photo ID, and your graphing calculator. Be sure your calculator has brand-new batteries in it just prior to the exam.

Q: When will I get my score?

A: Scores are usually mailed out in the middle of July.

Q: Suppose I do terribly on the exam. May I cancel the test and/or the score?

A: Yes. By writing a letter to ETS, you can cancel all records of an exam. There is no fee for canceling a score, but the test fee will not be refunded.

Q: May I write on the test?

A: Yes. For the multiple-choice section, only the machine-scored answer sheet will be graded. You may use the test booklet for all your scratch work for this section, but be sure to mark your answer choice on the answer sheet. For the free-response section, all work must be shown in the pink test booklet. Work on the green question sheet will not be counted.

Q: How and when do I register?

A: Registration begins about one month before the exam, around the beginning of April. Check with the AP test coordinator at your school for more specific information, such as how to pay the fees. (Note: If your school does not offer an AP course in a subject, you may still take the exam by registering at a neighboring school that does give the exam.)

Q: What's on the exam?

A: The AP Calculus AB exam covers many topics in differential calculus and their applications, and many of the topics and applications in integral calculus. In addition to all of the AP Calculus AB topics, the AP Calculus BC exam covers additional methods and applications of integral calculus, as well as topics from series — their convergence or divergence — and power series approximation to some common functions. For more specifics, see the Table of Contents and "Topics Covered on a Recent AP Calculus AB or BC Exam" (page 13) in this book.

Q: When is the AP calculus exam administered?

A: AP exams are given throughout the country on designated days during the first two weeks in May. Ask your AP teacher or testing coordinator for the specific day of the calculus exam.

Q: Where can I get more information?

A: Your AP teacher should have a copy of the "Acorn Book" mentioned previously. This booklet contains an outline of the material that will be on the exam and some sample multiple-choice and free-response questions. It also contains some specific information about graphing calculators, including some important programs for certain less powerful calculators. *A Student Guide to the AP Mathematics Courses and Examinations* may be useful, but it does not contain much more than what you will find in the "Acorn Book." A list of publications and their prices, including the title mentioned above, can be obtained by writing the Advanced Placement Program, P.O. Box 6670, Princeton, NJ 08541-6670 for an order form.

Strategies for the Exam

Q: How should I prepare for the AP calculus exam?

A: First, keep up and do well in your AP calculus class. Then practice! Become comfortable with the test and its format. Take several practice exams to work on your timing. Carefully analyze your mistakes and review the material you have forgotten or don't know well.

Q: When should I study this book?

A: Read this book carefully about four weeks before the exam. With four weeks to go, you should have covered in class most of the material that will be on the exam, and you will be able to plan your final intensive study time. Refer to the "Study Guide Checklist" on page ix for suggestions on how to use the exercises and practice tests in this book.

Q: What topics should I study the most?

A: The 45 questions in Sections IA and IB cover a wide range of topics from calculus and precalculus. Balance your preparation accordingly. A list of topics covered on a recent exam appears on page 13. Don't overlook the precalculus material beginning on page 19. Several questions are derived from this material every year. Based on previous exams, some topics are guaranteed to appear: function theory, definition of the derivative, increasing/decreasing intervals and concavity, particle motion, optimization, related rates, area and volume, and continuity.

Q: Do I need to memorize a lot of formulas? Can't I just rely on my calculator?

A: Just as memorizing the multiplication tables was necessary to pass math tests in grade school, memorizing certain calculus facts is necessary to do well on the AP exam. Do not overlook this simple step when preparing for the exam. Count on a number of multiple-choice questions requiring memorized facts, such as

$$\int \sec^2 3x\, dx = \frac{1}{3}\tan 3x + C$$

A set of flashcards can help you memorize facts. These should include:

A. derivative formulas

B. antiderivative formulas (including integration by parts)

C. trig identities

D. theorems: Rolle's theorem, mean value theorem, L'Hôpital's rule, Newton's method, trapezoidal rule, integral pattern for volumes of solids of revolution

E. definitions: derivative, definite integral

In Sections IB and IIA, graphing calculators can be used to help with facts; however, since they are not allowed in Section IA, be careful about relying on your calculator too heavily.

Q: How do I handle difficult word problems?

A: One of the keys to success on the AP exam, especially on the more difficult word problems such as those on related rates and optimization, is being able to interpret both English and calculus appropriately. For example, if the phrase "particle moving right" appears in a rate-of-change problem, the only way to solve the problem is to translate the English to calculus:

"particle moving right" $\Leftrightarrow v(t) > 0$

Without this translation, it is simply impossible to solve the problem. Thus knowing how to translate English into calculus is essential to success on the AP exam. A list of phrases that you will typically encounter on the exam can be found in the Appendix. *Memorize it.*

Q: What should I do the night before the exam?

A: Review your list of derivative and antiderivative formulas, definitions, theorems, trig identities, and the calculus dictionary in the Appendix. This is all factual information that you need to have memorized for Section IA. Make sure you have a strong set of batteries in your calculator. *Then go to sleep.* Staying up until 4 A.M. will hurt your grade, not help it. You cannot learn calculus overnight. Trust in your year of preparation and spend the night before resting, so you will be fresh and wide awake at 8 A.M.

Multiple-Choice Questions

Q: Should I answer the multiple-choice questions in the order in which they appear?

A: Some students like to pick and choose questions, for example, by doing all the questions that require derivatives first. Other students prefer to work through the questions in order. Do whatever seems easiest for you; however, don't waste time on questions that seem exceptionally difficult. Consider using the +/– system to prevent you from getting stuck on one question and wasting time:

1. As you go through each section, answer all the easy questions first.

2. When you come to a question that seems impossible to answer, mark a large minus sign (–) next to it in your test booklet. You are penalized for wrong answers, so do not guess at this point. Move on to the next question.

3. When you come to a question that seems solvable but appears too time-consuming, mark a large plus sign (+) next to that question in your test booklet. Do not guess. Then move on to the next question.

Note: Don't waste time deciding whether a question gets a plus or minus. Act quickly. The intent of this strategy is to *save* you valuable time.

4. After you have worked all the easy questions, go back and work on your "+" problems.

5. If you finish working your "+" problems and still have time left, do one of two things:

   A. Attempt the "–" problems, but remember not to guess blindly.

   B. Forget the "–" problems and go back over your completed work to be sure you didn't make any careless mistakes on the questions you thought were easy to answer. You do not have to erase the pluses and minuses you made in your question booklet.

Q: If I don't know an answer, should I guess?

A: When your AP exam is graded, one-fourth of the number of questions answered incorrectly is subtracted from the number answered correctly, so guessing is penalized. However, if you can eliminate at least two answer choices, go ahead and guess.

Also, don't second-guess yourself by going back and changing a multiple-choice answer unless a specific error is evident. First choices are correct more often than not.

Q: Is there a method for helping me eliminate answer choices?

A: Take advantage of being able to mark in your test booklet. As you go through the questions, use quick sketches to help you eliminate possible choices. Visually eliminate choices from consideration by marking them out in your test booklet with a slash mark through the answer choice letter [(A̸)]. Place a question mark before any choices you wish to consider as possible answers [?(B)]. This technique will help you avoid reconsidering those choices that you have already eliminated and will thus save you time. It will also help you narrow down your possible answers. Remember that if you are able to eliminate two or more possible answers, you may want to guess. Under these conditions, you stand a better chance of raising your score by guessing than by leaving the answer sheet blank.

Q: What if I've had four answers in a row of C in the multiple-choice section, and I'm pretty sure the next one is C but could be a D? Should I pick D?

A: No, go ahead and choose C. Don't play games with the letter patterns.

Q: What if I don't finish all the multiple-choice questions?

A: Don't panic about finishing all of the questions. Many students do not finish all of the multiple-choice questions and still receive high scores on their exams. Take the time to answer all the "easy" questions *correctly*. Don't guess randomly if you find you are running short of time. Chances are that random guessing will hurt your score rather than help it.

Q: How many multiple-choice questions do I have to get right to pass the exam with a 3?

A: If you correctly answer about 60 percent of the questions in Section I, you will most likely receive a passing score, assuming you earn an equal percentage in the free-response section. So, you need to get about 27 of the 45 multiple-choice questions correct, along with 3 of the 6 free-response questions. You don't need to get 3 free-response questions totally right to pass, but you do need to earn about half of the total points available in Section II. The two sections of the test are weighted equally.

Q: Exactly what score do I get for a right answer, a wrong answer, and no answer on the multiple-choice section?

A: In figuring your score, a right answer is worth 1 point, no answer is worth 0, and a wrong answer is worth –0.25. See the scoring worksheet at the end of each practice test for a more detailed explanation.

Q: Are there any trick questions in the multiple-choice section?

A: No. In fact, you can expect some of the questions to be "freebies," that is, problems you can answer quickly with little or no writing. Don't worry that these simple questions might be trick questions. They're not.

Q: How fast do I have to work in order to complete the exam?

A: In Section I, watch the clock and pace yourself accordingly. In Section IA, *average* about one question every 2 minutes, and in Section IB, *average* about one question every 3 minutes. Some questions will take longer than average, of course, and some will take much less time. Don't obsess about exactly how long each question is taking; just keep an eye on the clock so you are not caught by surprise. Do not waste time on questions that seem impossible — use the +/– system to sort them out.

Free-Response Questions

Q: Should I do the six free-response questions in the order they appear?

A: The six free-response questions are separated into two sections, each containing three questions. Section IIA (questions 1–3) will contain some questions or parts of a question for which a graphing calculator is required. During IIA, look through the three questions and answer first the ones that seem to be the easiest. Number 3 is not necessarily harder than the other two questions, just different. In Section IIB, a calculator is NOT allowed. Once again, you should do the easier of the questions 4–6 first. During IIB, you will be allowed to continue working on questions from IIA, but the use of a calculator is NOT permitted.

Q: How fast do I have to work to finish the free-response questions?

A: Again, keep an eye on the clock. Ninety minutes for six questions means completing an *average* of one question every 15 minutes. Some questions will take less than 15 minutes, others may take longer. Don't panic; just watch the time. If a question is not working out, leave the work you have already completed (don't erase it) and come back to it later as time allows.

Q: How much work should I show on free-response questions?

A: Always show all your work in a detailed, logical, organized manner. A rule of thumb is that whatever math is happening in your brain should be put down on paper. The graders are not mind readers; they can grade only what they see in your answer booklet. It's better to have shown too much work than not enough.

Watch out for the words "justify your answer," "prove your answer," and other similar phrases. When these key words appear, provide the appropriate calculus in a clear, concise manner. For example, if the problem asks only for "any intervals where the function is increasing," a correct answer for full credit would appear simply as "increasing when $x > 3$." However, if the question also adds "justify your answer," the correct solution should include 1) the calculus to find the first derivative, 2) the algebra to derive the critical numbers from the first derivative, 3) some type of interval testing to find where the derivative is positive, and 4) the conclusion of "increasing when $x > 3$." "Justify your answer" is more likely to appear on the exam now that graphing calculators are allowed. Give precise, thorough explanations of your method and reasoning when taking information from a graphing calculator to help answer a question.

Q: What if I can't get part of a free-response question, and I need it for the next part of the question?

A: If Part A of a free-response question is proving difficult, don't give up on solving Parts B, C, and D. Part A may be irrelevant to finishing the rest of the question. If the latter parts of a free-response question do depend on an answer you can't get, simply make up a reasonable answer and proceed with it in the other parts. In such a case, don't just tell how the problem *could* be solved; do the actual work with a made-up answer.

Q: What form should I use for free-response answers?

A: Answer the question completely in whatever form is requested. For example, if the question asks for "any points of inflection of a graph," be sure to provide *both* coordinates, not just the x-coordinate. It may be helpful to circle key words or phrases in the question that indicate the type or form of the answer that is required. If you choose to give an approximation to an answer, be sure to follow the directions about rounding.

Q: Should I simplify my answers?

A: Don't waste time simplifying unnecessarily, especially with derivatives, linear equations, and definite integrals. Expressions such as

$$\frac{1}{2}\left[\left(3(5)^2 - 4(5)\right) - \left(3(-1)^2 - 4(-1)\right)\right]$$

can be left as is, unless a calculator approximation is requested. However, expressions such as $\cos 0$, $\ln 1$, and $e^{\ln 3}$ should be simplified.

Q: How are free-response questions scored?

A: The free-response questions are scored on a 9-point scale, although the point distribution is not printed in the exam. The more difficult parts of a question count for more points. Pay careful attention to any question parts that ask you to "justify your answer" because they are frequently worth more points. You need to demonstrate your knowledge of the subject in a clear, concise fashion to get all the points. See the grading rubric following each free-response question in the practice tests for more information.

Q: How many of the free-response questions do I have to get right to pass the exam with a 3?

A: If you can earn about 60 percent of the points available in the free-response section, you will most likely earn a 3, assuming an equal percentage are correct on the multiple-choice section. This does not mean that you must get at least three of the six problems completely and totally correct, just that you earn about 32 of the 54 total points. However, don't be preoccupied with how many points you're getting as you do the exam. Do your best, and let the readers worry about the points.

Calculator Questions

Q: Do I really need a calculator?

A: Since May 1995, use of a graphing calculator has been required for some questions on the AP exam. Calculators are *not* provided. Students must bring their own approved calculators (see the list on page 11). Sharing calculators is not allowed.

Q: What functions does my calculator have to perform?

A: Four basic functions are listed in the course outline:

- graphing a function within an arbitrary viewing window

- finding the zeros of a function

- computing the derivative of a function numerically, that is, finding the value of a derivative at a specific point

- computing definite integrals (with constant endpoints) numerically

Here is a comparison of the various features of the most commonly used calculators.

	Graph	*Zeros*	*Numerical Derivative*	*Definite Integral*
Cassio 700	yes	no	no	yes
HP-48	yes	yes	yes	yes
Sharp 9300	yes	yes	yes	yes
TI-81	yes	no	yes	no
TI-82	yes	yes	yes	yes
TI-85	yes	yes	yes	yes
TI-86	yes	yes	yes	yes

Q: I already have a graphing calculator, but it doesn't do all of the necessary functions. Now what?

A: The four required functions may either be built into the calculator or programmed prior to the exam. Calculator memories will not be cleared either prior to or after the exam. The "Acorn Book" contains a set of programs that may be installed into the less powerful graphing calculators to provide all the necessary functions.

Q: How many questions will require the use of a calculator?

A: Only about 7 of the 17 multiple-choice questions in Section IB and portions of the free-response section will require the use of a calculator. Be sure to get plenty of practice with your calculator well before the AP exam. Familiarity with the machine will allow for the most efficient use of time. Also, know the appropriate calculator syntax. Some types of calculators may require that functions be entered in a specific manner to graph completely.

Q: Which calculators are allowed at the AP calculus exam?

A: The following machines met the requirements for use on the 2000 exam.

Approved List of Graphing Calculators					
Casio	*Hewlett-Packard*	*Radio Shack*	*Sharp*	*Texas Instruments*	*Other*
FX-6000 series	HP-28 series	EC-4033	EL-5200	TI-73	Micronta
FX-6200 series	HP-38G series	EC-4034	EL-9200 series	TI-80	Smart[2]
FX-6300 series	HP-48 series	EC-4037	EL-9300 series	TI-81	
FX-6500 series			EL-9600 series	TI-82	
FX-7000 series				TI-83/TI-83 Plus	
FX-7300 series				TI-85	
FX-7400 series				TI-86	
FX-7500 series				TI-89	
FX-7700 series					
FX-7800 series					
FX-8000 series					
FX-8500 series					
FX-8700 series					
FX-8800 series					
FX-9700 series					
FX-9750 series					
CFX-9800 series					
CFX-9850 series					
CFX-9950 series					
CFX-9970 series					

Q: What calculators are not allowed at the AP exam?

A: Unacceptable machines include laptop computers, pocket organizers, electronic writing pads or pen input devices, and palmtop computers with QWERTY keyboards.

Q: What if I want to use a calculator that is not on the approved list?

A: If you wish to use a calculator not on the above list, your teacher must contact ETS prior to April 1 to receive written permission for you to use your calculator at the AP calculus exam.

Q: How will I know when to use a calculator?

A: Each of the seven review sections in this book contains sample questions requiring the use of a calculator. Familiarize yourself with them. Practice will help you identify the types of questions that require a calculator; however, such questions will not be indicated in any special manner on the actual exam. Knowing when to use a calculator and when not to use a calculator is part of what is being tested.

On multiple-choice questions, the format of the answer choices may indicate when a calculator should be used. If all of the choices are given in decimal form, a calculator is probably necessary.

Only the four basic functions previously identified will be required on the test. If a problem seems to require inordinate amounts of lengthy calculator work not mentioned on this list, stop. There may be a simple solution not requiring a calculator that you have overlooked.

Q: Won't a calculator be useful on all of the free-response questions?

A: You may only use a calculator on IIA (questions 1–3) of the free-response section. Sometimes the use of a graphing calculator is not effective or efficient. For example, if a question asks for "any points of inflection of a graph," it may be possible to find an appropriate window on a graphing calculator to visually find a change in concavity. However, due to limited resolution of the image on the screen, it may be impossible to find such a window. [If you don't believe it, try to find the point of inflection of $f(x) = x^{2/3}(x - 5)$ by looking at the graph on a calculator. (It's at $x = -1$.)]

Only one or two of the free-response questions will require the use of a graphing calculator, so don't rely on your calculator too heavily.

Q: How does the use of graphing calculators affect the types of questions that are asked on the exam?

A: The use of graphing calculators in the free-response section of the test may affect not only those parts which require a calculator but also the questions in other parts of the problems. For example, the type of problem that requires finding the graph of a function through the use of the first and second derivatives to find extrema and points of inflection becomes trivial when a graphing calculator is allowed. If you encounter this type of question, count on the words "justify your answer" to appear at every step of the problem. Or, the request to justify your answer may appear in an altered form. Rather than providing a specific algebraic equation to manipulate through first and second derivatives, the question may provide a graphical interpretation of the derivative and ask for conclusions regarding the function and/or second derivative. In another context, the problem may provide a chart showing the signs of the first and second derivatives over given intervals and ask for conclusions or sketches.

In Section IB of the multiple-choice section, only about 7 of the 17 questions will require a calculator. These could include simple processes, such as finding a decimal approximation for ln 2, and more complicated operations, like finding zeros or the intersection of two curves.

Topics Covered on a Recent AP Calculus AB or BC Exam

(* represents BC-only topic)

Precalculus
Functions

- Domain and range
- Zeros and intercepts
- Product, sum, quotient, composite of functions
- Inverse functions
- Odd and even functions, symmetry
- Asymptotes of rational functions
- Trig functions: amplitude, period and phase shifts, identities
- Shifts and distortions to graphs of functions: $y = af([b(s + c)] + d$
- Absolute value of functions: $y = |f(x)|$ and $y = f(|x|)$
- *Parametric equations
- *Polar curves
- *Vectors and vector valued functions

Calculus
Limits

- Limit theorems: constant, sum, product, quotient
- One-side limits
- Infinite limits and limits at infinity
- Non-existence limits
- L'Hôpital's rule for 0/0 and ∞/∞
- *L'Hôpital's rule for $(0)(\infty)$, $\infty - \infty$, 0^0, 1^∞, ∞^0

Continuity

- Formal definition, graphical interpretation
- Intermediate value theorem and extreme value theorem
- Relationship between continuity and differentiability

Differential Calculus

Limit definitions of the derivative: general and at a point

Derivative rules: power, product, quotient, chain, trig, inverse trig, exponential, and logarithmic

Derivation of two rules: $d/dx(\sin x) = \cos x$ and $d/dx(x^n) = nx^{n-1}$, n a positive integer

Implicit differentiation

Higher order derivatives

Logarithmic differentiation

Derivative theorems: Rolle's theorem and mean value theorem

*Derivatives of parametric, polar, and vector functions

Derivative Applications

Tangent and normal lines, slope of a curve

Average and instantaneous rates of change

Curve sketching: increasing, decreasing, relative extrema, concavity, inflection points

Differentials

Related rates

Optimization, absolute extrema

Position/velocity/acceleration (PVA) in linear motion

PVA with vectors

Integral Calculus

Antiderivatives

Integration formulas

Integration techniques: general power rule, substitution, trig, inverse trig

*Integration techniques: parts, partial fractions

Definition of the definite integral (limit of a Riemann sum)

Properties of the definite integral

Approximation for definite integrals: rectangles, trapezoids

Fundamental theorems

*Improper integrals

*Vector integration

Applications of Antiderivatives and the Definite Integral

Position*/velocity/acceleration (PVA) in linear motion

Differential equations (variables separable)

Area between curves

*Area with polar functions

Average value of a function over an interval

Volume: solids of revolution and solids with known cross sections

Exponential growth/decay and its derivation: $dy/dt = ky$, $y = Ce^{kt}$

*Logistic growth

*Arc length

*PVA with vectors

*Geometric interpretation of differential equations via slope fields

*Numerical solution of differential equations using Euler's method

*Power Series and Polynomial Approximations

*Sequences and Series

*Limit of a sequence

*Increasing/decreasing sequence

*Infinite series — harmonic, geometric, p-series, alternating series

*Tests of convergence/divergence of infinite series: comparison, limit comparison, integral, ratio root and alternating series test

*Alternating series with error bound

*Absolute and conditional convergence

*Radius and interval of convergence

*Power Series

*Taylor polynomial — with Lagrange form of the remainder

*Macclaurin polynomial

*Macclaurin series for functions

*Radius and interval of convergence of power series

*Differentiation and integration of power series

*Formation of new series from known series

PART II

SPECIFIC TOPICS

Familiarity with certain noncalculus topics is essential for success on the AP exam. Approximately 10 percent of the multiple-choice questions deal strictly with precalculus topics. The majority of the questions based on calculus also require a working knowledge of precalculus topics. Expect precalculus material to appear in part (a) or parts (a) and (b) of a free-response question. Because these parts may be essential to completing the calculus portion of the question, precalculus material should be reviewed thoroughly.

At the end of this chapter, you will find a set of multiple-choice questions that corresponds to the material presented here. If you feel confident in your ability with precalculus material, you may want to go to these questions. They will help you determine whether there are any areas that you need to review.

Functions and Function Notation

Calculus has been called the study of functions, so the formal definition of a function is an important one.

Definition of a Function

A **function** is a set of ordered pairs where no two ordered pairs have the same *x*-coordinate. Graphically, this definition means that any vertical line may intersect the graph only once if the relation is to be a function.

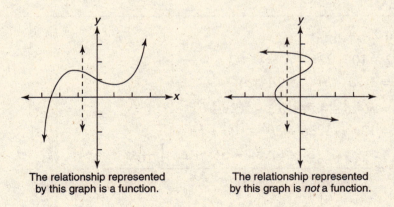

The relationship represented by this graph is a function.

The relationship represented by this graph is *not* a function.

Figure 1.1

Vocabulary

The x-coordinate is known as the independent variable. The entire set of x-coordinates of a function is known as its **domain.** The y-coordinate is the dependent variable. The set of y-coordinates is the **range** of the function. Finding the domain and range of specific functions is a common instruction on the AP exam.

Notation

Functions may be specified in a number of ways:

1. A list or roster: $\{(2, 1)\,(3, 2)\,(4, -5)\}$

2. Graphically: as shown on the previous page

3. An equation: $2x - 3y = 7$ or $y = 5x - 7$

4. Using function notation: $f(x) = 5x - 7$

Function notation is the method most commonly employed on the AP exam. Here are some typical uses:

Sample

Given that $f(x) = 3x^2 - 5x$, find

A. $f(-2)$

B. $f(2a - b)$

C. $\dfrac{f(x + \Delta x) - f(x)}{\Delta x}$

A. $f(-2) = 3(-2)^2 - 5(-2)$

$\qquad = 12 + 10 = 22$

B. $f(2a - b) = 3(2a - b)^2 - 5(2a - b)$

$\qquad = 3(4a^2 - 4ab + b^2) - 5(2a - b)$

$\qquad = 12a^2 - 12ab + 3b^2 - 10a + 5b$

C. $\dfrac{f(x + \Delta x) - f(x)}{\Delta x} = \dfrac{\left[3(x + \Delta x)^2 - 5(x + \Delta x)\right] - \left(3x^2 - 5x\right)}{\Delta x}$

$\qquad = \dfrac{\left[3\left(x^2 + 2x\Delta x + (\Delta x)^2\right) - 5x - 5\Delta x\right] - 3x^2 + 5x}{\Delta x}$

$\qquad = \dfrac{3x^2 + 6x\Delta x + 3(\Delta x)^2 - 5x - 5\Delta x - 3x^2 + 5x}{\Delta x}$

$\qquad = \dfrac{6x\Delta x + 3(\Delta x)^2 - 5\Delta x}{\Delta x}$

$\qquad = 6x + 3\Delta x - 5$

Part C in the foregoing problem will be used extensively later, in the definition of the derivative.

Zeros or Roots

Finding the **zeros,** or roots, of a function may be called for in a variety of contexts on the AP exam. To find zeros, or roots, find where $y = 0$ or $f(x) = 0$.

Sample

Find the zeros of $f(x) = 2x^2 - 12x$.

Find where
$$f(x) = 0$$
$$2x^2 - 12x = 0$$
$$2x(x - 6) = 0$$

$$2x = 0 \quad \text{or} \quad x - 6 = 0$$
$$x = 0 \qquad\qquad x = 6$$

To express the zeros accurately, write them as ordered pairs:

$$(0, 0) \quad \text{and} \quad (6, 0)$$

Symmetry

The most common types of symmetry on the AP exam are symmetry with respect to the y-axis and symmetry with respect to the origin, as shown in the following graphs. Proving that a function has a certain type of symmetry requires the definition that follows.

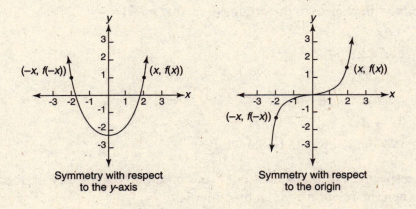

Figure 1.2

Definition of Symmetry

A function $f(x)$ is symmetric with respect to the y-axis if and only if $f(-x) = f(x)$.

A function $f(x)$ is symmetric with respect to the origin if and only if $f(-x) = -f(x)$.

A relation $g(y)$ is symmetric with respect to the x-axis if and only if $g(-y) = g(y)$.

Definition of Even and Odd Functions

A function $f(x)$ that is symmetric with respect to the y-axis is called an **even** function.

A function $f(x)$ that is symmetric with respect to the origin is called an **odd** function.

Sample

Show that $f(x) = x^2 - 2$ is symmetric with respect to the y-axis.

To show symmetry with respect to the y-axis, show that $f(-x) = f(x)$. Begin with the left side, $f(-x)$, and show that this equals the right side, $f(x)$.

$$
\begin{aligned}
f(-x) &= (-x)^2 - 2 \\
&= x^2 - 2 \\
&= f(x) \qquad \text{which was to be shown}
\end{aligned}
$$

Sample

Show that $g(x) = -7x^3 + 4x$ is symmetric with respect to the origin.

To show symmetry with respect to the origin, show that $g(-x) = -g(x)$.

$$
\begin{aligned}
g(-x) &= -7(-x)^3 + 4(-x) \\
&= -7(-x^3) - 4x \\
&= 7x^3 - 4x \\
&= -(-7x^3 + 4x) \\
&= -g(x) \qquad \text{which was to be shown}
\end{aligned}
$$

Symmetry with respect to the x-axis does not occur on the AP exam very frequently because it can occur only when the relation is *not* a function.

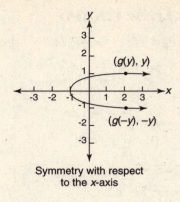

Symmetry with respect
to the *x*-axis

Figure 1.3

Sample

> Show that $x = y^2$ is symmetric with respect to the *x*-axis.

To show symmetry with respect to the *x*-axis, first express the *relation* using *y* as the independent variable, and then show that $g(-y) = g(y)$.

$$x = y^2 \Rightarrow g(y) = y^2$$
$$g(-y) = (-y)^2$$
$$= y^2$$
$$= g(y) \text{ which was to be shown}$$

Graphing a Function

Graphing or sketching a function is often a part of free-response problems on the AP exam. Even when not specifically requested, however, a sketch may be tremendously useful in helping solve the problem. The most common types of functions found on the AP exam are those outlined in this chapter: polynomials, trigonometric (including inverse), exponential, logarithmic, the conics, and rational functions. Expect these to appear regularly, both in basic forms and modified by shifts and distortions.

Shifts and Distortions of Graphs

Definition of Shift and Distortion

A **shift** of a function is merely a movement to a new location; the same size and shape are retained. A **distortion** changes the shape or size of a graph.

Theorem on Shifts and Distortions

If a basic function $y = F(x)$ is modified to $g(x) = aF[b(x + c)] + d$, then the constants a, b, c, and d have the following effects:

1. Shifts are caused by c and d.

c causes a horizontal shift $\begin{cases} c > 0 \Rightarrow \text{left} \\ c < 0 \Rightarrow \text{right} \end{cases}$

d causes a vertical shift $\begin{cases} d > 0 \Rightarrow \text{up} \\ d < 0 \Rightarrow \text{down} \end{cases}$

2. Distortions are caused by a and b.

a causes a vertical distortion $\begin{cases} a > 1 \Rightarrow \text{stretch} \\ a < 1 \Rightarrow \text{shrink} \end{cases}$

b causes a horizontal distortion $\begin{cases} b > 1 \Rightarrow \text{shrink} \\ b < 1 \Rightarrow \text{stretch} \end{cases}$

3. Reflections are caused when a or b is negative.

If a is negative, the graph is reflected about the x-axis.

If b is negative, the graph is reflected about the y-axis.

Sample

Sketch the graph of $g(x) = -(x + 3)^3 - 1$ by identifying the shifts, distortions, and reflections to the graph of $y = x^3$.

The basic graph of $y = x^3$ follows.

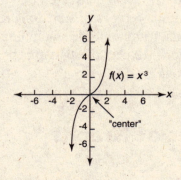

Figure 1.4

The graph of $g(x)$ has three changes:

1. A reflection about the x-axis due to a being negative
2. A shift 3 units to the left
3. A shift 1 unit down

These modifications produce the following graph:

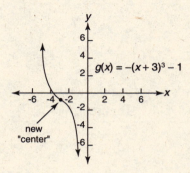

$g(x) = -(x + 3)^3 - 1$

new "center"

Figure 1.5

Absolute-Value Distortions

Two special types of distortions are created with absolute values. To sketch an absolute-value modification of the basic graph of $y = F(x)$, follow these guidelines:

1. $g(x) = |F(x)|$ affects the range (y-coordinates) of the graph.

   Leave Quadrants 1 and 2 completely alone. Then move the portion of the graph that is in Quadrants 3 and 4 into Quadrants 1 and 2 by reflecting it around the x-axis. The resulting graph is found only in Quadrants 1 and 2; Quadrants 3 and 4 are empty.

2. $g(x) = F(|x|)$ affects the domain (x-coordinates) of the graph.

   Erase whatever part of the graph is in Quadrants 2 and 3, and then reflect Quadrants 1 and 4 into Quadrants 2 and 3 while leaving the Quadrant 1 and 4 portions intact.

Sample

For the graph of $y = F(x)$ shown here, sketch $|F(x)|$ and $F(|x|)$.

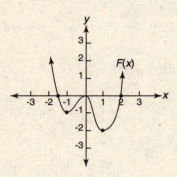

Figure 1.6

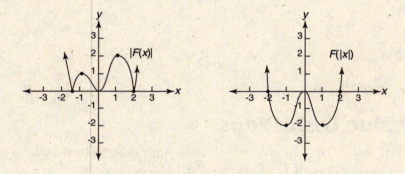

Figure 1.7

Inverse Functions

Inverse functions are functions that, in effect, cancel each other out. For example, given the two inverse functions

$$f(x) = 7 - 4x \text{ and } g(x) = \frac{7 - x}{4}$$

it is easy to show that $f(g(2)) = 2$ and that $g(f(2)) = 2$.

$$
\begin{aligned}
f(g(2)) = f(\tfrac{5}{4}) && g(f(2)) = g(-1) \\
= 7 - 4(\tfrac{5}{4}) && = \frac{7 - (-1)}{4} \\
= 7 - 5 && = \tfrac{8}{4} \\
= 2 && = 2
\end{aligned}
$$

Definition of Inverse Functions

Two functions $f(x)$ and $g(x)$ are said to be **inverses** if and only if $f(g(x)) = g(f(x)) = x$. The inverse of a function *may or may not* be a function. Examination of the domain and range of the function and/or its inverse may be needed to determine whether the inverse is really a function.

Notation

The notation most commonly used to define inverses is the "exponent" -1; thus the inverse of $f(x)$ is indicated as $f^{-1}(x)$. *Do not get this mixed up with the reciprocal of $f(x)$.* The most common applications of inverse on the AP exam are to find the inverse of a given function and to sketch the inverse. To find an inverse function:

1. Eliminate function notation; that is, replace $f(x)$ with y.

2. Interchange x and y.

3. Solve for y.

4. Return to function notation; that is, replace y with $f^{-1}(x)$.

Sample

es por q' resvelves

> Find the inverse of $f(x) = 3x - 7$.

1. Eliminate function notation. $y = 3x - 7$

2. Interchange x and y. $x = 3y - 7$

3. Solve for y. $x + 7 = 3y$

    $\dfrac{x + 7}{3} = y$

$$x = 3y - 7$$
$$+7 \qquad +7$$
$$\dfrac{x + 7}{3} = \dfrac{3y}{3}$$
$$\dfrac{x+7}{3} = y$$

$$f^{-1}(x)\dfrac{x+7}{3}$$

4. Return to function notation. $f^{-1}(x)\dfrac{x+7}{3}$

The graphs of inverse functions are symmetric with respect to the line $y = x$. To graph an inverse:

1. Sketch the line $y = x$.

2. Reflect the given graph around $y = x$.

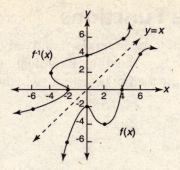

Figure 1.8

Polynomial Functions

Polynomial functions are one of the most common types of functions used on the AP exam. Here are a few examples of polynomial functions:

$$f(x) = 3x^2 - 2x + 7$$

$$g(x) = -6x^5 + \sqrt{2}\,x - \sqrt{3}$$

$$h(x) = 15x - \frac{2}{3}x^4$$

Polynomial functions are "well-behaved" functions that have no domain restrictions, no discontinuities, no asymptotes, and not even any sharp turns. Their graphs are smooth, pretty curves that are easy to sketch and work with.

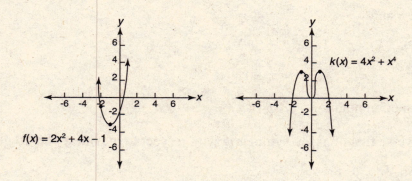

Figure 1.9

Two simple tests, the degree test and the leading coefficient test, will help you determine the behavior of polynomials.

Degree Test

If a polynomial function $f(x)$ has degree n, then the number of times the graph of $f(x)$ changes direction is equal to $n - 1$ or $n - 3$ or $n - 5 \ldots a$, where $a \geq 0$. Note that this means that even-powered functions must have an odd number of changes in direction, whereas odd-powered functions must have an even number of changes in direction.

Sample

> For $f(x) = 7x - 3x^3 + x^4 - 8$, how many changes in direction could the graph of $f(x)$ have?

$f(x)$ is a fourth-degree polynomial, so $n = 4$. Therefore, its graph could have three changes or one change in direction. Graphically, changes in direction appear as "bumps" on the graph. In the pictures that follow, note again that the even-powered functions have an odd number of bumps, and the odd-powered functions have an even number of bumps.

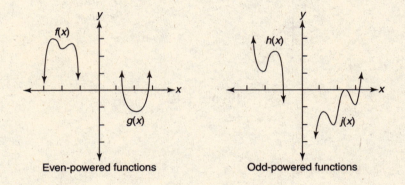

Figure 1.10

Leading Coefficient Test

The sign of the coefficient on the highest-degree term of a polynomial indicates the left and right behavior of the polynomial according to the following chart:

	Even degree	Odd degree
Leading coefficient positive	left: up right: up	left: down right: up
Leading coefficient negative	left: down right: down	left: up right: down

Figure 1.11

Trigonometric Functions

The six trig functions will appear frequently on the AP exam, so be prepared to work with them in a variety of contexts.

Graphs, Domain and Range, Periods

Know the graphs of all six functions, together with their domains and ranges and periods. You should be able to sketch trig functions that have a shift and/or distortion associated with them.

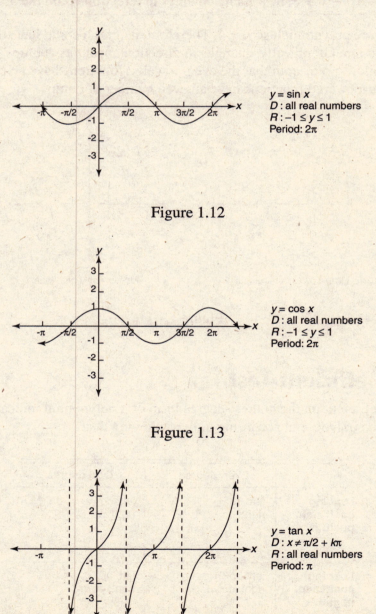

$y = \sin x$
D : all real numbers
R : $-1 \le y \le 1$
Period: 2π

Figure 1.12

$y = \cos x$
D : all real numbers
R : $-1 \le y \le 1$
Period: 2π

Figure 1.13

$y = \tan x$
D : $x \ne \pi/2 + k\pi$
R : all real numbers
Period: π

Figure 1.14

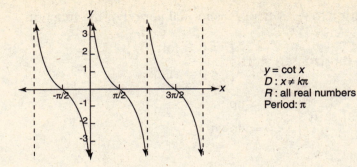

$y = \cot x$
$D: x \neq k\pi$
$R:$ all real numbers
Period: π

Figure 1.15

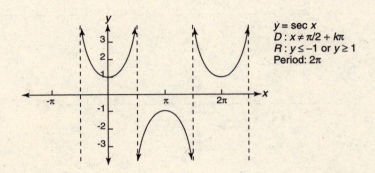

$y = \sec x$
$D: x \neq \pi/2 + k\pi$
$R: y \leq -1$ or $y \geq 1$
Period: 2π

Figure 1.16

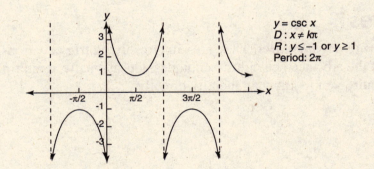

$y = \csc x$
$D: x \neq k\pi$
$R: y \leq -1$ or $y \geq 1$
Period: 2π

Figure 1.17

Shifts and Distortions for Trig Functions

Given that $y = a \sin b(x + c) + d$, a, b, c, and d have the following effects:

$$a \begin{cases} \text{changes the amplitude (A);} \\ A = \dfrac{\text{max} - \text{min}}{2} \text{ for sine and cosine} \\ \text{modifies the range for secant and cosecant} \\ \text{causes a vertical distortion for tangent and cotangent} \end{cases}$$

b changes the period to $\dfrac{P}{|b|}$ where P = normal period of the function

c causes a phase (horizontal) shift $\begin{cases} c > 0 \Rightarrow \text{left} \\ c < 0 \Rightarrow \text{right} \end{cases}$

d causes a vertical shift $\begin{cases} d > 0 \Rightarrow \text{up} \\ d < 0 \Rightarrow \text{down} \end{cases}$

Sample

Graph $y = \dfrac{1}{2}\sin 2\left(x + \dfrac{\pi}{2}\right) - 1$.

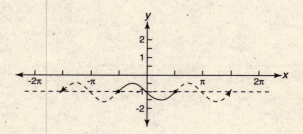

Figure 1.18

Trig Identities

Memorize the following trig identities. They are vital to solving trig equations, as well as to performing many of the advanced calculus techniques. Occasionally, a multiple-choice question may simply require you to know an identity directly.

Pythagorean

$\sin^2 x + \cos^2 x = 1$
$\tan^2 x + 1 = \sec^2 x$
$1 + \cot^2 x = \csc^2 x$

Double Angle

$\sin 2x = 2\sin x \cos x$
$\cos 2x = \cos^2 x - \sin^2 x$
$\qquad = 1 - 2\sin^2 x$
$\qquad = 2\cos^2 x - 1$

Power Reducing

$$\sin^2 x = \tfrac{1}{2}(1 - \cos 2x)$$
$$\cos^2 x = \tfrac{1}{2}(1 + \cos 2x)$$

Sum or Difference

$$\sin(x \pm y) = \sin x \cos y \pm \cos x \sin y$$
$$\cos(x \pm y) = \cos x \cos y \mp \sin x \sin y$$
$$\tan(x \pm y) = \frac{\tan x \pm \tan y}{1 \mp \tan x \tan y}$$

Negative Angle

$$\sin(-x) = -\sin x$$
$$\cos(-x) = \cos x$$
$$\tan(-x) = -\tan x$$

Product to Sum

$$\sin mx \sin nx = \tfrac{1}{2}[\cos(m - n)x - \cos(m + n)x]$$
$$\sin mx \cos nx = \tfrac{1}{2}[\sin(m + n)x + \sin(m - n)x]$$
$$\cos mx \cos nx = \tfrac{1}{2}[\cos(m - n)x + \cos(m + n)x]$$

Solving Trig Equations

Solving trig equations is always required on the AP exam. You may have to find an algebraic representation of an entire set of solutions, or you may have to find the solutions contained in a specified interval such as $[0, 2\pi)$. For calculator problems, be sure your calculator is in the correct mode (radians or degrees) to match the choices. Be wary of relying solely on a calculator to solve trig equations. A calculator will typically provide only the first-quadrant or fourth-quadrant solution. Use a unit-circle diagram and reference angle for the others.

To solve a trig equation:

1. Use identities and algebraic techniques to isolate one or more trig equations such as $\sin x = 1/2$.

2. Use a calculator or the special function values to finish solving.

3. Write out the generic solution first, and then find the solutions in the specified interval (if any).

Sample

> Find all the solutions of $3 \sin x \cos x = 2 \sin x$.

$3 \sin x \cos x - 2 \sin x = 0$

$\sin x(3 \cos x - 2) = 0$

$\sin x = 0 \quad$ or $\quad 3 \cos x - 2 = 0$

$x = k\pi \qquad\qquad \cos x = \frac{2}{3}$

$x \approx 0.84 + 2k\pi \ $ or $\ x \approx 5.44 + 2k\pi$

The first part of the solution ($k\pi$) should come from a known trig fact. The other two parts require the use of a calculator (use the $\cos^{-1}$ key, the "INV" key, the "2nd" key, or the "arc" key). The calculator will provide only the 0.84 solution; use a unit-circle diagram for the other.

You must also be able to deal with multiple-angle equations.

Sample

> Find all solutions of $\tan 2x = 4.3$ in the interval $(\pi, 2\pi]$.

$2x = \tan^{-1}(4.3)$

$2x \approx 1.34 + k\pi \quad$ from your calculator

$x \approx \dfrac{1.34 + k\pi}{2}$

$= 0.67 + \dfrac{k\pi}{2} \ \leftarrow$ these are all the solutions

$\approx 0.67 + k(1.57)$

$(\pi, 2\pi]$ is equivalent to $(3.14, 6.28]$, so $x = 3.81$ and $x = 5.38$ are the solutions in the given interval.

Inverse Trig Functions

You will need to know the graphs and properties of the inverse trig functions. The domains and ranges are of particular importance, because the ranges are restricted to result in inverses that are truly functions. The inverse trig functions may be indicated using several equivalent notations:

$y = \arcsin x$

$y = \text{Arcsin } x$

$y = \sin^{-1} x$

Recent AP exams have used the first two of these; most calculators use the last.

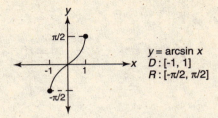

Figure 1.19

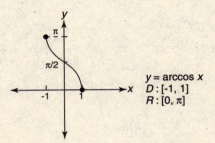

Figure 1.20

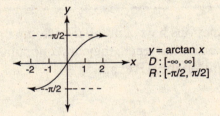

Figure 1.21

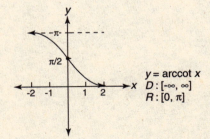

Figure 1.22

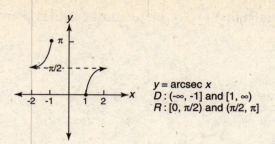

$y = \text{arcsec } x$
$D : (-\infty, -1]$ and $[1, \infty)$
$R : [0, \pi/2)$ and $(\pi/2, \pi]$

Figure 1.23

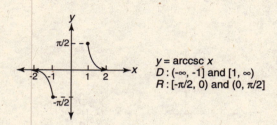

$y = \text{arccsc } x$
$D : (-\infty, -1]$ and $[1, \infty)$
$R : [-\pi/2, 0)$ and $(0, \pi/2]$

Figure 1.24

Exponential and Logarithmic Functions

Exponential and logarithmic functions have a number of unique properties that make them interesting without being overly difficult. Hence, they are a popular choice for free-response as well as multiple-choice questions on the AP exam.

Exponential Functions

Form: $y = b^x$, $b > 0$

Domain: all real numbers

Range: all positive real numbers

y-intercept: $(0, 1)$

Zero(s): none

Asymptote: x-axis

Examples

$y = 2^x$ and $y = (0.4)^x$ are examples of exponential functions. Of course, exponential functions can be shifted and distorted to produce new and different forms such as $y = -3(2)^x - 1$.

Graphs

The two typical graphs are a result of whole-number bases (shown on the left) and fractional bases (shown on the right). Note that the graph on the right can also be written with a whole-number base and with a negative exponent.

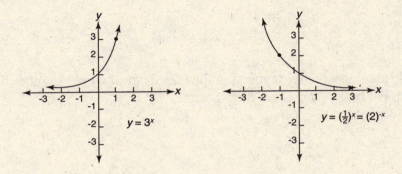

Figure 1.25

A Special Exponential Function

One particular exponential function is so common that it is often referred to as *the* exponential function: $y = e^x$. The number e is a transcendental number and a nonterminating, nonrepeating decimal. It is frequently approximated as $e \approx 2.71828$. Remember that e is *a constant number, not a variable.* One way to be more comfortable with e is to think of it as a cousin of π. A more formal definition of e will be given in the next chapter. The graph of $y = e^x$ looks similar to the one on the left in Figure 1.25, except that $y = e^x$ contains the point $(1, e)$, or $(1, 2.71828)$, rather than the point $(1, 3)$.

Logarithmic Functions

Form: $y = \log_b x, b > 0$

Domain: all positive real numbers

Range: all real numbers

y-intercept: none

Zero(s): $(1, 0)$

Asymptote: y-axis

Examples

$y = \log_3 x$ and $y = \log x$ (base-10 logarithm) are two examples of log functions. And again, log functions can be shifted and distorted: $y = -\log 2(x - 5) + 3$.

Log and Exponential Forms

It is sometimes convenient to work with log functions in exponential form. The change can be made according to the equation

$$y = \log_b x \Leftrightarrow b^y = x$$

Graphs

As in exponential functions, the two typical graphs result from whole-number bases (shown on the left) and fractional bases (shown on the right).

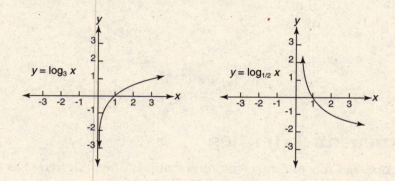

Figure 1.26

Special Log Functions

There are two special logarithmic functions.

$y = \ln x$ a base-e logarithm read as the "natural log."

$y = \log x$ a base-10 logarithm known as the "common log."

Both graphs have the same general shape as the one on the left in Figure 1.26.

Properties of Logarithms

There are several handy properties of logarithms that you must know and be able to apply. These are frequently used in simplifying or modifying expressions with logs in them. Watch out for these to appear, especially on multiple-choice problems: Your answer may be present as one of the choices but in a disguised form via the log properties.

Log Properties

$$\log_b(xy) = \log_b x + \log_b y$$

$$\log_b\left(\frac{x}{y}\right) = \log_b x - \log_b y$$

$$\log_b(x^y) = y \log_b x$$

$$\log_b\left(\sqrt[y]{x}\right) = \frac{1}{y} \log_b x$$

Exponential Equations

The log properties are also used extensively in solving exponential equations. To solve exponential equations:

1. Isolate the b^x part of the equation.
2. Take the "log" of both sides, usually the natural log.

Sample

> Solve $2^{x-4} - 3 = 12$.

Isolate the b^x expression.	$2^{x-4} = 15$
Take the natural log of both sides.	$\ln(2^{x-4}) = \ln 15$
Apply the third log property.	$(x-4)\ln 2 = \ln 15$
Solve for x.	$x - 4 = \dfrac{\ln 15}{\ln 2}$
	$x = \dfrac{\ln 15}{\ln 2} + 4$
Calculator approximation	$x \approx 7.907$

Logarithmic Equations

To solve logarithmic equations:

1. Isolate the log expression.
2. Switch to exponential form.
3. Use a calculator if necessary.

Sample

Solve $3 \log_4 (2x - 1) = 5$.

Isolate the log expression. $\log_4 (2x - 1) = {}^5\!/_3$

Switch to exponential form. $4^{5/3} = 2x - 1$

Solve for x. $4^{5/3} + 1 = 2x$

$$x = \tfrac{1}{2}(4^{5/3} + 1)$$

Calculator approximation $x \approx 5.540$

Relationship Between Logs and Exponentials

Exponential and logarithmic functions are inverses, as shown by the following:

$f(x) = e^x$ and $g(x) = \ln x \Rightarrow$

$f(g(x)) = g(f(x)) = x$ since

$e^{\ln x} = x$ and $\ln (e^x) = x$

You may occasionally need the last line above to simplify expressions.

Rational Functions

Rational functions provide excellent material for free-response questions on asymptotes and on increasing and decreasing functions. These types of questions can be answered quickly by graphing the function, although calculus support may be required (see Chapter 3, "Derivatives").

Definition of a Rational Function

A **rational function** is a function of the form

$$r(x) = \frac{p(x)}{q(x)}$$

where $p(x)$ and $q(x)$ are polynomial functions and $q(x) \neq 0$.

Examples of rational functions include

$$f(x) = \frac{2x - 3}{x^2 - 9} \text{ and } g(x) = \frac{3x^2 - 4x + 9}{x^3 - 27}$$

Graphing a Rational Function

To graph a rational function, do not simply plot a bunch of points and then try to "connect the dots." Rational functions typically have one or more discontinuities in the forms of asymptotes or "holes," and plotting a large number of points is often tedious or too time-consuming. The best plan of attack is as follows:

1. Simplify, if possible.
2. Find zeros (if any).
3. Find the y-intercept (if any).
4. Find all asymptotes, including vertical, horizontal, and slant.
5. Check for symmetry.
6. Plot a few points.

Except for finding the asymptotes, these six steps are self-explanatory. To find vertical asymptotes, let the denominator = 0. To find horizontal or slant asymptotes, compare the degree of the numerator with the degree of the denominator:

$$\left.\begin{array}{c} \text{deg num} \le \text{deg denom} \Rightarrow \\ \text{horizontal, divide} \\ \text{deg num} = 1 + \text{deg denom} \Rightarrow \\ \text{slant, divide} \end{array}\right\} y = \text{quotient without the remainder is the asymptote}$$

$$\text{deg num} > 1 + \text{deg denom} \Rightarrow \text{no asymptote}$$

Sample

Graph the function $f(x) = \dfrac{3x^2 - 6x}{3x^3 - 27x}$

1. Simplify.

$$f(x) = \frac{3x^2 - 6x}{3x^3 - 27x} = \frac{3x(x-2)}{3x(x^2-9)}$$

$$= \frac{3x(x-2)}{3x(x-3)(x+3)}$$

$$= \frac{x-2}{(x-3)(x+3)} \quad x \ne 0$$

Note the restriction on x that results from your having canceled a factor. This restriction will produce a "hole" in the final graph.

2. Zeros: Let $f(x) = 0$.

$$x - 2 = 0$$
$$x = 2 \qquad \text{so } (2, 0) \text{ is the zero}$$

3. y-intercept: Let $x = 0$.

$$f(0) = \frac{0 - 2}{(0 - 3)(0 + 3)} = \frac{2}{9}, \text{ so } \left(0, \frac{2}{9}\right) \text{ is the } y\text{-intercept}$$

But the restriction $x \neq 0$ means that $(0, \frac{2}{9})$ is a "hole," not a y-intercept.

4. Asymptotes

Vertical: Let the denominator $= 0$.

$$(x - 3)(x + 3) = 0$$
$$x = 3 \qquad \text{or} \qquad x = -3$$

Horizontal: degree of numerator $\leq$ degree of denominator $\Rightarrow$ divide

$$x^2 - 9 \overline{)x - 2}^{\,0}, \text{ so } y = 0 \text{ is the asymptote}$$

5. For symmetry, check $f(-x)$.

$$f(-x) = \frac{(-x) - 2}{(-x)^2 - 9} = \frac{-x - 2}{x^2 - 9}$$

$f(-x) \neq f(x)$, and

$f(-x) \neq -f(x)$ so there is no symmetry

6. Find extra points.

x	y
-4	$\frac{-6}{7}$
-1	$\frac{3}{8}$
4	$\frac{2}{7}$

7. Graph the function.

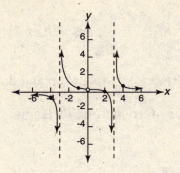

Figure 1.27

Conic Sections

The four conic sections — the parabola, circle, ellipse, and hyperbola — are so named because they are defined as the intersection of a cone and a plane. Of the four, only the parabola may be a function. The others sometimes occur as semi-conics and so may be treated as functions. For all the conics, know the standard forms and how to sketch the graph. Here are the standard forms and the principle properties.

Parabolas

$y = a(x - h)^2 + k$ vertex (h, k) opens: up if $a > 0$
down if $a < 0$

$x = a(y - k)^2 + h$ vertex (h, k) opens: right if $a > 0$
left if $a < 0$

Circles

$(x - h)^2 + (y - k)^2 = r^2$ center (h, k) radius $= r$

Ellipses

$\dfrac{(x - h)^2}{a^2} + \dfrac{\left(y - k^2\right)}{b^2} = 1$ center (h, k) extreme points: $(h \pm a, k)$ and $(h, k \pm b)$

Hyperbolas

$$\frac{(x-h)^2}{a^2} - \frac{(y-k)^2}{b^2} = 1 \quad \text{center } (h, k) \qquad \text{opens: left and right}$$

$$\frac{(y-k)^2}{b^2} - \frac{(x-h)^2}{a^2} = 1 \quad \text{center } (h, k) \qquad \text{opens: up and down}$$

Vertices of asymptotic rectangle: $(h \pm a, k \pm b)$ (both forms)

Completing the Square

If a conic section is not in standard form, force it into standard form by completing the square on one or both variables. The term needed to complete a square is

($\frac{1}{2}$ linear coefficient)^2

Also, remember that the quadratic coefficient must be 1 before the square can be completed.

Sample

Put the following conic section in standard form:

$2x^2 - 8x + 2y^2 + 6y = 0$

$$2x^2 - 8x + 2y^2 + 6y = 0$$

Divide by 2 to make quadratic coefficients 1. $\quad x^2 - 4x + y^2 + 3y = 0$

Complete the squares: $\qquad (x^2 - 4x + 4) + (y^2 + 3y + \frac{9}{4}) = 0 + 4 + \frac{9}{4}$

Because $\quad [\frac{1}{2}(-4)]^2 = 4 \quad$ and $\quad [\frac{1}{2}(3)]^2 = \frac{9}{4}$

$(x - 2)^2 + (y + \frac{3}{2})^2 = \frac{25}{4}$

Thus the conic is a circle, the center is $(2, -\frac{3}{2})$, and the radius is $r = \frac{5}{2}$.

For the graphs, here are some examples to study.

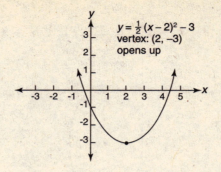

Figure 1.28

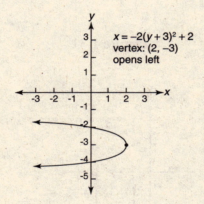

Figure 1.29

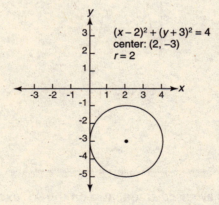

Figure 1.30

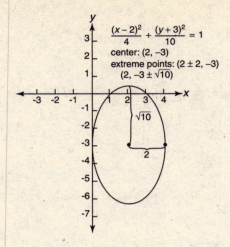

Figure 1.31

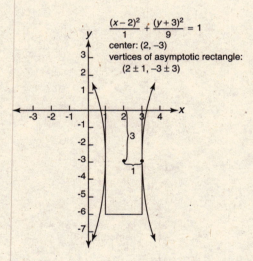

Figure 1.32

Algebra

Several basic algebra techniques are used frequently on the AP exam.

Interval Notation

The following notations are equivalent. Either may be used on the exam.

$$(a, b) \Leftrightarrow \{x : a < x < b\}$$
$$[a, b] \Leftrightarrow \{x : a \leq x \leq b\}$$
$$[a, b) \Leftrightarrow \{x : a \leq x < b\}$$

$(a, b] \Leftrightarrow \{x : a < x \le b\}$

$(a, \infty) \Leftrightarrow \{x : x > a\}$

$[a, \infty) \Leftrightarrow \{x : x \ge a\}$

$(-\infty, b) \Leftrightarrow \{x : x < b\}$

$(-\infty, b] \Leftrightarrow \{x : x \le b\}$

Lines

On the AP exam, lines and related subjects could be a part of almost any type of question. Know the following:

Slope: $m = \dfrac{y_2 - y_1}{x_2 - x_1} = \dfrac{\text{rise}}{\text{run}} = \dfrac{\Delta y}{\Delta x}$

Slope/intercept form: $y = mx + b$

Point/slope form: $y - y_1 = m(x - x_1)$

Two-point form: $y - y_1 = \left(\dfrac{y_2 - y_1}{x_2 - x_1} \right)(x - x_1)$

Parallel lines: $m_1 = m_2$

Perpendicular lines: $m_1 \cdot m_2 = -1$

Interval Testing

Finding intervals where a higher degree inequality takes on positive or negative values can be accomplished in several ways. The easiest of these follows.

1. Change the inequality to the form $f(x) > 0$ [or $f(x) \ge 0$, $f(x) < 0$, or $f(x) \le 0$].
2. Find the zeros of $f(x)$ by factoring.
3. Label a number line with the zeros you found in step 2.
4. Choose a value in each interval from the number line, and test the value of $f(x)$ to see if the inequality holds true.

Sample

Solve $7x^3 + 3x^4 \le 6x^2$.

$7x^3 + 3x^4 \le 6x^2$

$3x^4 + 7x^3 - 6x^2 \le 0$

$x^2(3x - 2)(x + 3) \le 0$

zeros: $x = 0, \frac{2}{3}, -3$

$$\xleftarrow[\;\;-3\quad\;\;0\quad\;\;\frac{2}{3}\;\;]{\text{pos}\;|\;\text{neg}\;|\;\text{neg}\;|\;\text{pos}}$$

Therefore, this inequality is true for $[-3, \frac{2}{3}]$.

Absolute Value

You may need to be familiar with the definition of absolute value in order to rewrite an absolute-value function as a piece function.

$$|x| = \begin{cases} x \text{ if } x \geq 0 \\ -x \text{ if } x < 0 \end{cases}$$

Sample

Write $y = |3x^2 - 2x - 1|$ as a piece function.

Find where the argument is equal to zero, and do interval testing.

$3x^2 - 2x - 1 = 0$

$(3x + 1)(x - 1) = 0$

$x = -\frac{1}{3}$ or $x = 1$

$$\xleftarrow[\;\;\frac{-1}{3}\quad\;\;1\;\;]{\text{pos}\;|\;\text{neg}\;|\;\text{pos}}$$

$$y = \begin{cases} 3x^2 - 2x - 1 & \text{if } x \geq 1 \\ -\left(3x^2 - 2x - 1\right) & \text{if } \dfrac{-1}{3} < x < 1 \\ 3x^2 - 2x - 1 & \text{if } x \leq \dfrac{-1}{3} \end{cases}$$

Parametric Equations (BC Only)

Some types of curves that are difficult to graph and manipulate in the Cartesian system can be dealt with more effectively and efficiently using parametric equations. Parametric equations use a third variable, the parameter t, in representing separate functions for the x- and y-coordinates. Parametric problems on the AP exam will frequently require the use of a calculator.

If f and g are continuous functions of t, then the set of parametric equations

$x = f(t)$ and $y = g(t)$

represent the set of points (x, y) or $(f(t), g(t))$ in the Cartesian system.

Sample

Use a graphing calculator to sketch the curve below for $0 \le t \le 5$.

$x = 3\cos(t)$ and $y = 3t^2 - 10$

Set the mode for parametric equations and type in the equations for x and y in the editor. The window needs to reflect the minimum and maximum values for t, which are given here as 0 and 5. The increment value for t needs to be set around 0.1. A larger t-step can speed up the graphing process, but may result in the parametric graph appearing as a strange set of line segments. For the minimum and maximum values for x and y, analyze the range of the x and y equations on the domain of $0 \le t \le 5$. Since the x equation includes a cosine function, there is a restriction on the range, so the x values will be between –3 and 3. The y equation represents a parabola, which will be increasing for $0 \le t \le 5$, so the y values will be between –10 and 65. The window below shows the resulting graph.

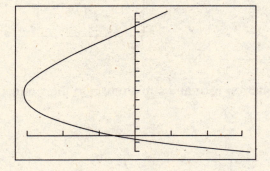

```
WINDOW
  Tmin =0
  Tmax =5
  Tstep =.1
  Xmin =-3
  Xmax =3
  Xscl =1
  Ymin=-10
  Ymax=65
  Yscl=5
```

Domain of *t*

If no particular domain is given for t, do NOT assume $t \ge 0$. For some application problems, where t represents time, such a restriction may be needed, but it is not generally true that t must be positive. Other restrictions on t may come from "built in" domain restrictions from the specific functions. For example, if $x = 5\sqrt{(t-2)}$, t must be greater than or equal to 2 for the radical expression to be real.

Eliminating the Parameter

AP exam problems will probably not require elimination of the parameter. In fact, most problems will be written so that eliminating the parameter is either very difficult or impossible, so that work must all be accomplished in the parametric system.

Sample

Sketch the graph of

$$x = 5 - t^2 \text{ and } y = t^2 + 3t$$

both in parametric form and by eliminating the parameter.

A graphing calculator yields:

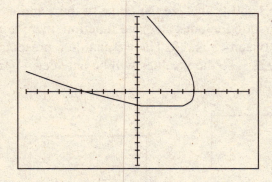

```
WINDOW
  Tmin =-10
  Tmax =10
  Tstep =1
  Xmin =-10
  Xmax =10
  Xscl =1
  Ymin=-10
  Ymax=10
  Yscl=1
```

To eliminate the parameter, solve the *x* equation for *t* and substitute into the *y* equation.

$$x = 5 - t^2$$
$$\Rightarrow t^2 = 5 - x$$
$$t = \pm\sqrt{5-x}$$
$$so, y = (5-x) + 3(\pm\sqrt{5-x})$$
$$= 5 - x \pm 3\sqrt{5-x}$$

This Cartesian equation, when graphed, yields the same graph as above.

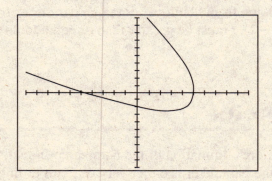

```
WINDOW
  Xmin =-10
  Xmax =10
  Xscl =1
  Ymin =-10
  Ymax =10
  Yscl =1
  Xres=1
```

For each set of parametric equations, eliminate the parameter *t*, and then describe the graph represented by the resulting equation.

1. $x = \dfrac{t}{2}$ and $y = t^2 - 4$

$\downarrow$

$2x = t \rightarrow \ y = t^2 - 4$

$\qquad\qquad\quad y = (2x)^2 - 4$

$\qquad\qquad\quad y = 4x^2 - 4$

(parabola)

2. $x = 2t - 3$ and $y = 2 + 3t$

$\downarrow$

$x + 3 = 2t$

$\dfrac{x+3}{2} = t \rightarrow y = 2 + 3\left(\dfrac{x+3}{2}\right)$

$\qquad\qquad\quad y = 2 + \dfrac{3x}{2} + \dfrac{9}{2}$

$\qquad\qquad\quad y = \dfrac{3x}{2} + \dfrac{13}{2}$

(line)

3. $x = t - 1$ and $y = \dfrac{t}{t-1}$

$\downarrow$

$x + 1 = t \rightarrow y = \dfrac{x+1}{(x+1)-1}$

$\qquad\qquad\quad y = \dfrac{x+1}{x}$

(diagonal hyperbola)

Sometimes a trigonometric identity can be used to eliminate the parameter.

4. $x = \sec\theta$ and $y = \cos\theta$

$xy = (\sec\theta)(\cos\theta)$

$\quad = \dfrac{1}{\cos\theta}(\cos\theta)$

$xy = 1$

$y = \dfrac{1}{x}$

(diagonal hyperbola)

5. $x = 3 \cos \theta$ and $y = 4 \sin \theta$

$\dfrac{x}{3} = \cos \theta \qquad \dfrac{y}{4} = \sin \theta$

since $(\cos \theta)^2 + (\sin \theta)^2 = 1$

$$\left(\frac{x}{3}\right)^2 + \left(\frac{y}{4}\right)^2 = 1$$

$$\frac{x^2}{9} + \frac{y^2}{16} = 1$$

(ellipse)

6. $x = 2 + 3 \cos \theta$ and $y = -3 + 2 \sin \theta$

$x - 2 = 3 \cos \theta \qquad y + 3 = 2 \sin \theta$

$\dfrac{x-2}{3} = \cos \theta \qquad \dfrac{y+3}{2} = \sin \theta$

since $(\cos \theta)^2 + (\sin \theta)^2 = 1$

$$\left(\frac{x-2}{3}\right)^2 + \left(\frac{y+3}{2}\right)^2 = 1$$

$$\frac{(x-2)^2}{9} + \frac{(y+3)^2}{4} = 1$$

(ellipse)

Particle Problems

Parametric equations can be used to describe the motion of a particle in a plane. In this case, the parameter t is frequently taken to represent time.

Sample

> Two particles move along parametric curves as defined below for any time $t, t \geq 0$.
>
> | Particle A | Particle B |
> |---|---|
> | $x = t - 4$ | $x = \dfrac{3t}{2} - 7$ |
> | $y = (t-3)^2$ | $y = \dfrac{3t}{2}$ |
>
> At what time(s), if any, do the two particles collide?

A graphing calculator sketch of the motion of the two particles shows the following:

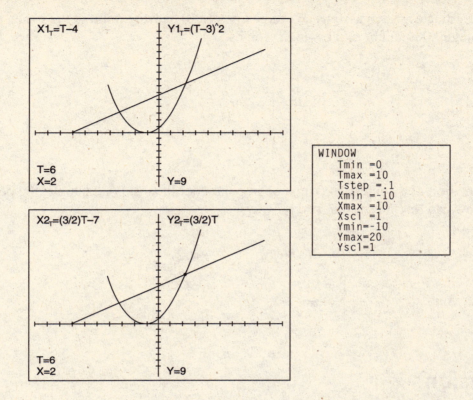

```
WINDOW
  Tmin =0
  Tmax =10
  Tstep =.1
  Xmin =-10
  Xmax =10
  Xscl =1
  Ymin=-10
  Ymax=20
  Yscl=1
```

From this graph, it would appear that the particles collide twice; however, this is not the case. The PATHS of the two particles do intersect twice, but for an actual collision, the particles must be at the same location AT THE SAME TIME. To find this algebraically, set BOTH the x and y equations equal to each other and solve.

$x_A = x_B$

$t - 4 = 3t/2 - 7$

$2t - 8 = 3t - 14$

$6 = t$

$y_A = y_B$

$(t - 3)^2 = 3t/2$

$t^2 - 6t + 9 = 3t/2$

$2t^2 - 12t + 18 = 3t$

$2t^2 - 15t + 18 = 0$

$(2t - 3)(t - 6) = 0$

$t = 3/2$ or $t = 6$

Therefore, particles A and B collide when $t = 6$. At this time, $x = t - 4 = 6 - 4 = 2$ and $y = (t - 3)^2 = (6 - 3)^2 = 9$. When $t = 6$, particles A and B will both be at the point $(2,9)$.

Only one solution is apparent here, where $t = 6$. To see this demonstrated graphically, use a graphing calculator in "simultaneous" mode, and set the t-step to 0.05 to slow down the motion.

Polar Coordinates and Graphs (BC Only)

A basic understanding of polar coordinates and graphs is necessary for the calculus required on the BC exam.

Notation

The polar coordinate system assigns an ordered pair (r, θ) to every point in the plane, as shown below. The angle θ should be expressed in radians.

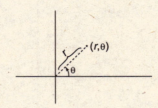

The representation of a point is NOT unique in polar coordinates. For example, the point P graphed below can be expressed in several ways:

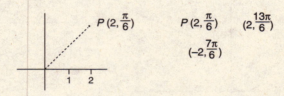

Conversion

Changing a point or equation from polar to rectangular coordinates will probably not be necessary on the AP exam; it is expected that work would be done entirely in the polar system. However, it may be helpful to convert occasionally if you are unable to, say, determine the quadrant of a point.

polar to rectangular

$$x = r \cos \theta$$

$$y = r \sin \theta$$

rectangular to polar

$$r = \sqrt{x^2 + y^2}$$

$$\theta = \tan^{-1} \frac{y}{x}$$

Calculators

When using a graphing calculator in polar, ALWAYS be sure to set the "mode" to RADIANS. For some calculators, it may be necessary to set the display of coordinates to polar (not rectangular). Also check the window settings: the minimum and maximum values for θ typically default to 0 and 2π, with a θ increment value of $\pi/24$ (approximately 0.131). It may be necessary to modify these depending on a given domain for a function, or its periodicity. Be careful not to set the θ increment too large, however. A larger θ step WILL speed up the graphing process, but may result in the polar graph appearing as a strange set of line segments. Generally, a θ step of about 0.1 will give a good graph in a short amount of time.

Polar Graphs

Familiarity with several basic types of graphs will assist in understanding the calculus later on. While using a calculator will speed the process of graphing, knowing the general types of equations may help avoid errors. The general types are: lines, circles, spirals, rose curves, limacons, and lemniscates. To see how polar graphs are generated, it may be useful to graph each of these types on a graphing calculator and then use the trace function to see how the points are swept out.

Symmetry

The symmetry tests in polar form can be quite tedious to apply, and probably are not worth memorizing. However, it may be worth noting polar equations which use ONLY the sine function are automatically symmetric with respect to the y axis (the line $\theta = \pi/2$ in polar). Similarly, if an equation contains only the cosine function, the graph is symmetric to the x axis (polar axis).

Intersections

To find the area of a polar region, it is sometimes necessary to find the point(s) of intersection of two polar curves. Generally, this requires equating the r expressions for the two curves and solving the resulting trig equation. Also, the pole (origin) may be an intersection point of two curves but with different θ values: $(0, \pi/2)$ and $(0, \pi/4)$ are both representations of the same point, i.e., the pole or origin. Finding intersection points using a graphing calculator may also be required on the exam.

Sample

Find all intersection points of $r = 1 + \cos\theta$ and $r = 1 - \sin\theta$.

Begin by graphing the two curves.

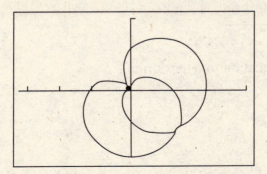

The intersection point in Quadrant 3 seems clear, but the number of intersection points (if any) in Quadrant 2 is not as obvious. A closer window sheds some light on this area, revealing a second intersection point in Quadrant 2. In addition, it seems that both curves contain the pole, where $r = 0$.

To find all of these points, set the two r expressions equal to each other.

$$1 + \cos\theta = 1 - \sin\theta$$

$$\cos\theta = -\sin\theta$$

$$\theta = \frac{3\pi}{4} + 2k\pi, \frac{7\pi}{4} + 2k\pi$$

To check the pole,

$0 = 1 + \cos\theta$	$0 = 1 - \sin\theta$
$\cos\theta = -1$	$\sin\theta = 1$
$\theta = \pi + 2k\pi$	$\theta = \frac{\pi}{2} + 2k\pi$
$(0, \pi)$	$(0, \frac{\pi}{2})$

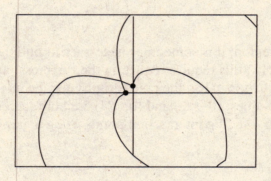

Converting Equations from Rectangular to Polar Form

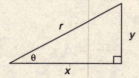

$$x^2 + y = r^2 \qquad x = r\cos\theta$$

$$\tan\theta = \frac{y}{x} \qquad y = r\sin\theta$$

(x,y) rectangular coordinates

(r, θ) polar coordinates

Convert each rectangular equation to polar form:

1. $x^2 + y^2 = 16$

$$r^2 = 16$$

$$r = 4$$

2. $x = 3$

$r \cos \theta = 3$

$r = \dfrac{3}{\cos \theta}$

$r = \sec \theta$

3. $y = \left(\sqrt{3}\right) x$

$r \sin \theta = \sqrt{3} \left(r \cos \theta\right)$

$\sin \theta = \sqrt{3} \cos \theta$

$\dfrac{\sin \theta}{\cos \theta} = \sqrt{3}$

$\tan \theta = \sqrt{3}$

$\theta = \dfrac{\pi}{3}$

Converting Equations from Polar to Rectangular Form

Convert each polar equation below to rectangular form:

1. $r = 3 \cos \theta$

$r(r) = 3r \cos \theta$

$r^2 = 3 \cos \theta$

$x^2 + y^2 = 3x$

$x^2 - 3x + y^2 = 0$

(circle)

2. $r = 5 \csc \theta$

$r = \dfrac{5}{\sin \theta}$

$r \sin \theta = 5$

$y = 5$

(horizontal line)

3.

$$\theta = \frac{\pi}{6}$$

$$\tan\theta = \tan\left(\frac{\pi}{6}\right)$$

$$\tan\theta = \frac{\sin\left(\frac{\pi}{6}\right)}{\cos\left(\frac{\pi}{6}\right)}$$

$$\tan\theta = \frac{\frac{1}{2}}{\frac{\sqrt{3}}{2}}$$

$$\frac{y}{x} = \frac{1}{\sqrt{3}}$$

$$y = \left(\frac{1}{\sqrt{3}}\right)x$$

$$y = \left(\frac{\sqrt{3}}{3}\right)x$$

(line)

4.

$$r = \frac{5}{3 + 2\cos\theta}$$

$$r(3 + 2\cos\theta) = 5$$

$$3r + 2r\cos\theta = 5$$

$$3r = 5 - 2r\cos\theta$$

$$3\sqrt{x^2 + y^2} = 5 - 2x$$

$$\left(3\sqrt{x^2 + y^2}\right)^2 = (5 - 2x)^2$$

$$9(x^2 + y^2) = 25 - 20x + 4x^2$$

$$9x^2 + 9y^2 = 25 - 20x + 4x^2$$

$$5x^2 + 9y^2 + 20x - 25 = 0$$

(ellipse)

5.

$$r = \frac{3}{5\cos\theta - 2\sin\theta}$$

$$r(5\cos\theta - 2\sin\theta) = 3$$

$$5r\cos\theta - 2r\sin\theta = 3$$

$$5x - 2y = 3$$

(line)

Special Polar Graphs

Many times we encounter certain types of graphs whose equations are much simpler in polar rather than in rectangular form. For example, the graph at the equation $x^2 + y^2 = 16$ is a circle. In polar form, the equation $x^2 + y^2 = 16$ becomes $r^2 = 16$, so $r = 4$. Below are examples of some graphs and their popular equations.

A. Limacons: one of the forms $r = a \pm b \cos\theta$ or $r = a \pm b \sin\theta$ **where** $a > 0$ **and** $b > 0$.

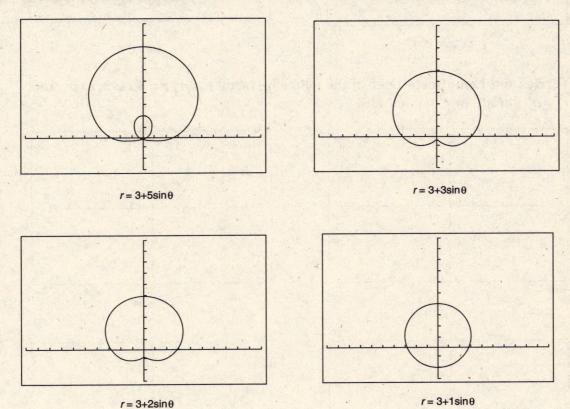

$r = 3 + 5\sin\theta$

$r = 3 + 3\sin\theta$

$r = 3 + 2\sin\theta$

$r = 3 + 1\sin\theta$

B. Rose Curves: one of the forms $r = a \cos(n\theta)$ or $r = a \sin(n\theta)$

These curves will have n petals, if n is odd, but they will have $2n$ petals if n is even (for $n \geq 2$).

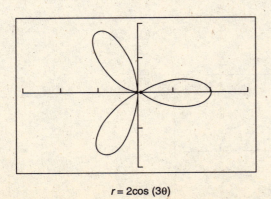

$r = 2\cos(3\theta)$

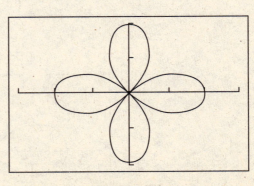

$r = 2\cos(2\theta)$

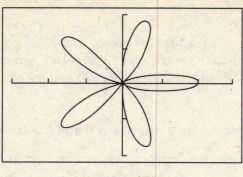

$r = 2\cos(5\theta)$

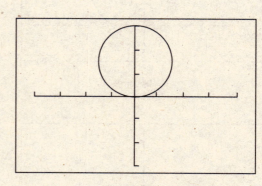

$r = 2\cos(4\theta)$

C. Circles and Lemniscates: one of the following forms $r = a$, $r = a\cos\theta$, $r = a\sin\theta$, $r^2 = a^2\sin(2\theta)$, **or** $r^2 = a^2\cos(2\theta)$

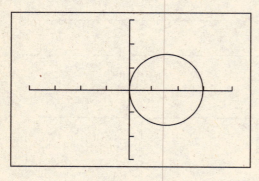

$r = 3\cos\theta$

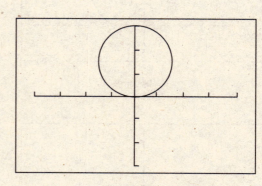

$r = 3\sin\theta$

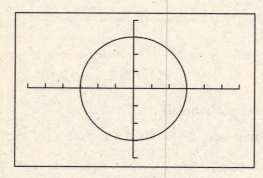

$r = 3$

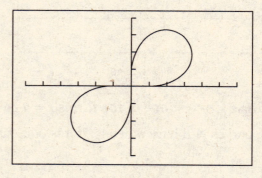

$r^2 = 16\sin(2\theta)$

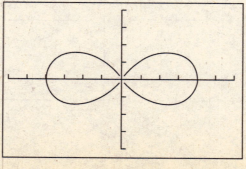

$r^2 = 16\cos(2\theta)$

D. Miscellaneous Curves: of the form $r = \theta$ **or** $\theta = a$

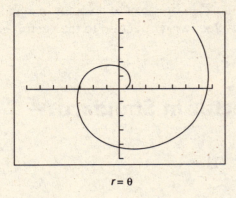

$r = \theta$

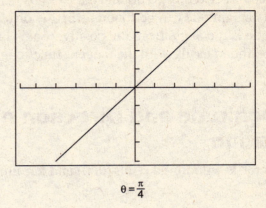

$\theta = \dfrac{\pi}{4}$

Vectors and Vector-Valued Functions (BC Only)

A vector can be thought of informally as a ray or a directed line segment: It has a beginning (or initial) point and an ending (or terminal) point, thus giving it a direction. Some vectors are graphed below. One of the most common notations used to represent vectors is $\vec{PQ}$, where the vector has P as its initial point and Q as its terminal point as shown in the graph below. In texts, vectors may also be indicated by a lower or upper case bold single letter such as **u** or **V.**

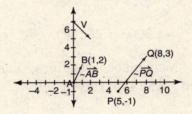

Vectors are frequently represented with their initial point at the origin, often referred to as standard position, as with $\vec{AB}$ in the graph above.

The component form of a vector gives the horizontal and vertical components of the vector, in that order, and is represented as an ordered pair with "pointy" parentheses: $< 3,4 >$. Thus, vector PQ above would have component form $< 3,4 >$, which can be found by subtracting the x and y coordinates, $8 - 5 = 3$ and $3 - (-1) = 4$. Note that since $\vec{AB}$ is in standard position above, the component form of $\vec{AB}$, $< 1,2 >$, can easily be found by examining the coordinates of the point B, $(1, 2)$.

Component Form of a Vector

If a vector **V** has initial point (x_1, y_1) and terminal point (x_2, y_2), then its component form is given by $<x_2 - x_1, y_2 - y_1>$. A vector **V** in standard position with terminal point (x, y) has component form $<x, y>$.

The length of a vector is referred to as its magnitude, and is represented by placing the name of the vector between two double bars: $\|V\|\ or\ \|\overline{AB}\|$. Given the initial and terminal points of a vector, its magnitude can be found using the distance formula. The direction of a vector in standard position is the angle from the positive x axis in a counter-clockwise direction to the vector, and can be found easily with the tangent function.

Magnitude and Direction of a Vector in Standard Position

A vector $\mathbf{V}$ with initial point $(0, 0)$ and terminal point (x, y) has

component form $\mathbf{V} = <x, y>$

magnitude $\|V\| = \sqrt{x^2 + y^2}$

and direction $\theta = \tan^{-1}(y/x)$ where $0 \leq \theta \leq 2\pi$ or $0 \leq \theta \leq 360°$

Sample

Find the magnitude and direction of the vector $\mathbf{V} = <5, -2>$

The magnitude is $\|V\| = \sqrt{(5)^2 + (-2)^2} = \sqrt{29} \approx 5.3852$

For the direction, $\theta = \tan^{-1}(5/-2) \approx -1.1903 + 2k\pi \approx 5.0929$ (where $k = 1$)

When working with vectors, single real number quantities, such as 3, are referred to as scalars. Several operations with scalars and vectors are shown below.

Vectors Operations

Let $\mathbf{V} = <x_1, y_1>$ and $\mathbf{U} = <x_2, y_2>$ be given vectors, and k by a given scalar quantity.

The vector sum of the vectors is $\mathbf{V} + \mathbf{U} = <x_1 + x_2, y_1 + y_2>$.

The scalar multiple of k and $\mathbf{V}$ is the vector $k\mathbf{V} = <kx_1, ky_1>$.

The opposite (of negative) of $\mathbf{V}$ is $-\mathbf{V} = <-x_1, -y_1>$.

The difference of $\mathbf{U}$ and $\mathbf{V}$ is $\mathbf{U} - \mathbf{V} = \mathbf{U} + (-\mathbf{V}) = <x_2 - x_1, y_2 - y_1>$.

The sum, or resultant, of two vectors can also be found graphically. To find the sum of $\mathbf{U}$ and $\mathbf{V}$ graphically, recopy $\mathbf{V}$ so that its initial point coincides with the terminal point of $\mathbf{U}$. The vector which is the sum of the $\mathbf{U}$ and $\mathbf{V}$ has the same initial point as $\mathbf{U}$ and the same terminal point as the new, recopied version of $\mathbf{V}$. This process is illustrated below.

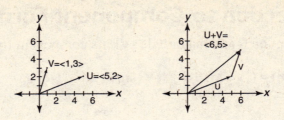

Yet another way to represent vectors uses scalar multiplication and vector addition, along with two unit vectors. For this notation, two special unit vectors (a vector with a magnitude of 1) are given particular names: **i** is the unit vector in the direction of the x axis, and **j** is the unit vector in the direction of the y axis, as shown in the graph below. Notice that **i** has no vertical component and **j** has no horizontal component.

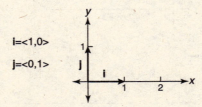

Now, any vector can be written as the vector sum of scalar multiples of **i** and **j**.

Sample

> Write the vector with initial point R(3, –1) and terminal point S(5, 2) in component form using **i** and **j**.

In component form, $\vec{RS}$ = <2 – (–1), 5 – 3> = <3, 2>.

So, $\vec{RS}$ can be written as the sum of the vectors 3**i** and 2**j** as shown in the graph below.

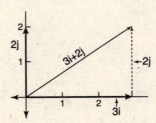

Alternate Component Form

The vector **V** = <x, y> can also be written in component form as **V** = $x\mathbf{i} + y\mathbf{j}$.

Vectors can only be added when they are in component form. So, to find the resultant of two vectors, it may be necessary to change from magnitude/direction to component form. These formulas are a direct result of the definition of sin and cos.

Magnitude/Direction to Component Form

Given a vector $\mathbf{V}$ with direction θ and magnitude $\|\mathbf{V}\|$, its component form is given by

$$\mathbf{V} = \|\mathbf{V}\|(\cos\theta\mathbf{i} + \sin\theta\mathbf{j}) = (\|\mathbf{V}\|\cos\theta)\mathbf{i} + (\|\mathbf{V}\|\sin\theta)\mathbf{j}$$

or

$$\mathbf{V} = <\|\mathbf{V}\|\cos\theta, \|\mathbf{V}\|\sin\theta>$$

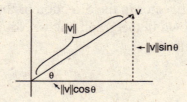

Sample

> A force of 20 pounds makes an angle of 60° with the positive x axis, while a force of 30 pounds has a direction of 135°. Find the component form of the forces, find the resultant in component form, and find its direction and magnitude.

The magnitude of the first force is given as 20 and the direction $\theta = 60°$.

$$\mathbf{F} = 20\cos 60°\,\mathbf{i} + 20\sin 60°\,\mathbf{j}$$
$$= 20\left(\frac{1}{2}\right)\mathbf{i} + 30\left(\frac{\sqrt{3}}{2}\right)\mathbf{j}$$
$$= 10\mathbf{i} + 10\sqrt{3}\,\mathbf{j}$$

For the second force,

$$\mathbf{G} = 30\cos 135°\,\mathbf{i} + 30\sin 135°\,\mathbf{j}$$
$$= 30\left(\frac{\sqrt{2}}{2}\right)\mathbf{i} + 30\left(\frac{\sqrt{2}}{2}\right)\mathbf{j}$$
$$= -15\sqrt{2}\,\mathbf{i} + 15\sqrt{2}\,\mathbf{j}$$

For the resultant,

$$\mathbf{R} = \mathbf{F} + \mathbf{G} = (10\mathbf{i} + 10\sqrt{3}\,\mathbf{j}) + (-15\sqrt{2}\,\mathbf{i} + 15\sqrt{2}\,\mathbf{j})$$
$$= (10 - 15\sqrt{2})\mathbf{i} + (10\sqrt{3} + 15\sqrt{2})\mathbf{j}$$
$$\approx -11.2132\mathbf{i} + 38.5337\mathbf{j}$$

$$\|\mathbf{R}\| = \sqrt{(-11.2132)^2 + (38.5337)^2}$$
$$\approx 40.1321\,lbs$$

$$\theta_R = \tan^{-1}\left(\frac{38.5337}{-11.2132}\right) + 180$$
$$\approx 106.22°$$

Vector-Valued Functions

Vectors can also be analyzed by considering a special set of functions that has the set of real numbers as the domain, and a set of vectors as the range. These are known as vector-valued functions.

$\mathbf{R}(t) = f(t)\,\mathbf{i} + g(t)\,\mathbf{j}$ is a vector-valued function where $f(t)$ and $g(t)$ are real-valued functions.

t is any number in the domain of both $f(t)$ and $g(t)$

Note: In the above function, the x and y components of the vectors are obviously given by $x = f(t)$ and $y = g(t)$. This should make it easy to see the relationship between parametric equations and vector-valued functions. For vector AP problems, it may be possible to solve them by considering the corresponding set of parametric equations, and vice versa. If a problem seems confusing or complicated as one type, vector or parametric, try considering it the other way.

For convenience, the graph of a vector-valued function is usually shown as just the terminal points of the vectors, rather than with all the vectors (rays) included. To graph a vector-valued function with a calculator, use parametric mode, with $x = f(t)$ and $y = g(t)$.

The calculus that goes with vectors is probably easiest to perform using the vector-valued function notation, since most people are already comfortable taking limits, and finding derivatives and anti-derivatives with standard function notation.

Sample Multiple-Choice Questions: Precalculus

1. $\arcsin\left(\dfrac{7\pi}{6}\right) =$

   A. $\dfrac{11\pi}{6}$

   B. $\dfrac{7\pi}{6}$

   C. $\dfrac{5\pi}{6}$

   D. $\dfrac{\pi}{6}$

   E. $\dfrac{-\pi}{6}$

2. If the zeros of $f(x)$ are $x = -1$ and $x = 2$, then the zeros of $f(x/2)$ are $x =$

   A. $-1, 2$

   B. $-\frac{1}{2}, \frac{5}{2}$

   C. $-\frac{3}{2}, \frac{3}{2}$

   D. $-\frac{1}{2}, 1$

   E. $-2, 4$

3. How is $g(x)$ related to $f(x)$?

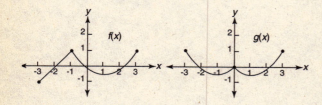

   A. $g(x) = f(|x|)$

   B. $g(x) = |f(x)|$

   C. $g(x) = f(-x)$

   D. $g(x) = -f(x)$

   E. $g(x) = f(x)$

4. $\cos 2\theta =$

   A. $\cos^2\theta + \sin^2\theta$

   B. $1 - 2\sin^2\theta$

   C. $1 - 2\cos^2\theta$

   D. $\sin^2\theta - \cos^2\theta$

   E. none of these

5. The graphs of all of the following are asymptotic to the x-axis EXCEPT

   A. $y = \dfrac{2}{x^2 - 1}$

   B. $y = e^{x-2}$

   C. $y = \dfrac{4x}{x^2 + 1}$

   D. $y = -\log(x + 1)$

   E. $xy = 1$

6. Suppose that $f(x) = \ln x$ and $g(x) = 9 - x^2$. The domain of $f(g(x))$ is

   A. $x \le 3$

   B. $|x| \le 3$

   C. $|x| > 3$

   D. $|x| < 3$

   E. $0 < x < 3$

7. The domain of the function $f(x) = 1/\sqrt{1-x}$ is

   A. $x \ge 0$

   B. $x \le 1$

   C. $x \ge 1$

   D. $x < 1$

   E. $x > 1$

8. $\log_b\left(\dfrac{m\sqrt{n}}{p}\right) =$

   A. $\log_b m - \frac{1}{2}\log_b n - \log_b p$

   B. $\log_b m + \frac{1}{2}\log_b n - \log_b p$

   C. $\log_b m - \frac{1}{2}\log_b n + \log_b p$

   D. $\frac{1}{2}\log_b m - \log_b n - \log_b p$

   E. $\frac{1}{2}\log_b m + \log_b n - \log_b p$

9. If the amplitude of $y = (1/k)\cos(k^2\theta)$ is 2, then its period must be

   A. π

   B. 2π

   C. 4π

   D. 8π

   E. 16π

10. Find the most general set of solutions of $2\sin^2\theta = \sin\theta$.

   A. $\dfrac{\pi}{6} + 2k\pi, \dfrac{5\pi}{6} + 2k\pi, k\pi$

   B. $\dfrac{\pi}{3} + 2k\pi, \dfrac{2\pi}{3} + 2k\pi, k\pi$

   C. $\dfrac{\pi}{3} + 2k\pi, \dfrac{5\pi}{3} + 2k\pi, \dfrac{\pi}{2} + k\pi$

   D. $\dfrac{\pi}{6} + 2k\pi, \dfrac{5\pi}{6} + 2k\pi, \dfrac{\pi}{2} + k\pi$

   E. $\dfrac{\pi}{6} + k\pi, \dfrac{5\pi}{6} + k\pi, k\pi$

11. For $f(x) = 1 - x$ and $g(x) = \sqrt{x - 3}, g\big(f(-2)\big)$ is

   A.   undefined

   B. $1 - \sqrt{5}$

   C.   0

   D. $\sqrt{2}$

   E. $\sqrt{5}$

12. The graph of $y^2 - 3y - 2 = x^2$ is a(n)

   A.   parabola

   B.   circle

   C.   hyperbola

   D.   ellipse

   E.   line

13. The vertex of the graph of $y^2 - 4y = 3x - 6$ is

   A. $(2, \frac{2}{3})$

   B. $(2, 2)$

   C. $(\frac{2}{3}, -2)$

   D. $(\frac{2}{3}, 2)$

   E. $(-2, \frac{2}{3})$

14. For $f(x) = \log_3(x - 2)$, find $f^{-1}(x)$.

   A. $f^{-1}(x) = 3^x + 2$

   B. $f^{-1}(x) = 3^{x+2}$

   C. $f^{-1}(x) = 3^x - 2$

   D. $f^{-1}(x) = \dfrac{1}{\log_3(x+2)}$

   E. $f^{-1}(x) = \log_3\left(\dfrac{1}{x-2}\right)$

15. If $f(x) = \dfrac{e^{\ln x}}{x}$, then $f(1)$ is

   A.   0

   B.   1

   C. $\frac{e}{2}$

   D. e

   E.   not defined

16. Which of the following is an odd function?

A. $y = x^3 + 1$

B. $y = \cos x$

C. $y = \sin x$

D. $y = \ln x$

E. $y = e^{-x}$

17. If the curve of $f(x)$ is symmetric with respect to the origin, then it follows that

A. $f(0) = 0$

B. $f(-x) = -f(x)$

C. $f(-x) = f(x)$

D. $f(x)$ is also symmetric with respect to the x- and y-axes

E. $f(-x) = -f(-x)$

18. If $9e^{3t} = 27$, then $t =$

A. $\dfrac{\ln 27}{27}$

B. $\ln\sqrt[3]{3}$

C. 1

D. $\ln 3$

E. $\ln 9$

19. $\ln a = b$ is equivalent to

A. $e^a = b$

B. $\ln b = a$

C. $a^e = b$

D. $b^e = a$

E. $e^b = a$

20. The graph of $y^2 = x^2 + 9$ is symmetric with respect to

I.   the x-axis

II. the y-axis

III. the origin

A. I only

B. II only

C. III only

D. I and II only

E. I, II, and III

21. Which of the following graphs are graphs of functions?

A. I only

B. II only

C. III only

D. I and II only

E. I, II, and III

22. For what values of x is $(3x^2 + 6x)(2x - 5) < 0$?

A. $(-\infty, -2) \cup (0, \frac{5}{2})$

B. $(-2, 0)$

C. $(-2, \frac{5}{2})$

D. $(-2, 0) \cup (\frac{5}{2}, \infty)$

E. $(-2, \infty)$

Answers to Multiple-Choice Questions

1. E. $\arcsin\left(\sin\frac{7\pi}{6}\right) = \arcsin\left(\frac{-1}{2}\right) = \frac{-\pi}{6}$

Remember that the range of inverse sine is $[-\pi/2, \pi/2]$. Because of this, the two functions do not "cancel" exactly. However, if the question had asked for sin (arcsin 2/3), the two functions would have "canceled," because the only restriction on the function is $-1 \le \sin x \le 1$. You can also use your calculator for these questions.

2. E. The coefficient of 1/2 inside the function creates a horizontal stretch, in effect moving the zeros twice as far out to $x = -2$ and $x = 4$.

x	$f(x)$		x	$\dfrac{x}{2}$	$f\left(\dfrac{x}{2}\right)$
-1	0		-2	-1	0
2	0		4	2	0

3. A. The second and third quadrants in the original graph of $f(x)$ play no part in the graph of $g(x)$, whereas the first and fourth quadrants have been reflected into the second and third quadrants, so $g(x) = f(|x|)$.

4. B. *Know the identities.*

5. D. The graphs of A, C and E are all asymptotic to the x-axis because they are rational functions with the degree of the numerator less than the degree of the denominator. B is asymptotic to the x-axis because it is simply a shift 2 to the right of $y = e^x$, which is itself asymptotic to the x-axis. D is a version of a log curve, with a reflection around the x-axis and a shift 1 to the left. Log curves are not asymptotic to the x-axis.

6. D. $f(x) = \ln x$ and $g(x) = 9 - x^2 \Rightarrow$

$f(g(x)) = f(9 - x^2) = \ln(9 - x^2)$

For the domain of any logarithmic function, the argument must be strictly positive.

$(9 - x^2) > 0$
$(3 - x)(3 + x) > 0$

Using interval testing to solve this inequality yields

neg | pos | neg
-3 3

so $-3 < x < 3$, or $|x| < 3$.

7. D. For a radical expression, the domain must be restricted to numbers that make the expression under the radical greater than or equal to zero. But here the radical is also in the denominator of a fraction, which means the radical cannot equal zero.

$$1 - x > 0 \Rightarrow x < 1$$

8. B. $\log_b \left(\dfrac{m\sqrt{n}}{p} \right) = \log_b m + \log_b n^{1/2} - \log_b p$

$$= \log_b m + \tfrac{1}{2} \log_b n - \log_b p$$

9. D. The amplitude of $y = (1/k)\cos (k^2 \theta)$ is given by the expression $1/k$.

$$\tfrac{1}{k} = 2 \Rightarrow k = \tfrac{1}{2}$$

The period of $y = (1/k)\cos (k^2\theta)$ is given by the expression $2\pi/k^2$.

$$P = \frac{2\pi}{k^2} = \frac{2\pi}{\left(\frac{1}{2}\right)^2} = \frac{2\pi}{\frac{1}{4}} = 8\pi$$

10. A. $\qquad\qquad 2\sin^2 \theta = \sin \theta$

$$2\sin^2 \theta - \sin \theta = 0$$
$$\sin \theta (2\sin \theta - 1) = 0$$
$$\sin \theta = 0 \text{ or } 2\sin \theta - 1 = 0$$
$$\theta = k\pi \qquad \sin \theta = 1/2$$
$$\theta = \frac{\pi}{6} + 2k\pi \quad \text{or} \quad \theta = \frac{5\pi}{6} + 2k\pi$$

11. C. Work from the inside to the outside: $f(-2) = 1 - (-2) = 3$. Thus

$$g\big(f(2)\big) = g(3) = \sqrt{3-3} = 0$$

12. C. $y^2 - 3y - 2 = x^2 \Leftrightarrow y^2 - 3y - x^2 = 2$

You should be able to tell that this is a hyperbola because of the -1 coefficient on the x^2. Complete the square if you're not convinced.

13. D. Complete the square on $y^2 - 4y = 3x - 6$.

$$3x - 6 + \underline{4} = y^2 - 4y + \underline{4}$$
$$3x - 2 = (y - 2)^2$$
$$x = \tfrac{1}{3}(y - 2)^2 + \tfrac{2}{3} \Rightarrow \text{vertex is } (\tfrac{2}{3}, 2)$$

14. A. $f(x) = \log_3 (x-2) \Leftrightarrow y = \log_3 (x-2)$

Now switch the x and y to create the inverse, and solve for y.

$x = \log_3(y-2)$
$3^x = y - 2$
$y = 3^x + 2 \Rightarrow f^{-1}(x) = 3^x + 2$

15. B. Simplify by using the log properties on the numerator.

$f(x) = \dfrac{e^{\ln x}}{x} = \dfrac{x}{x} = 1$

16. C. Odd functions are symmetric with respect to the origin, so look for a function where

$f(-x) = -f(x)$
$f(-x) = \sin(-x)$
$\quad = -\sin x = -f(x)$ which shows symmetry with respect to the origin

17. B. *Know the symmetry tests*.

18. B. $9e^{3t} = 27 \Leftrightarrow e^{3t} = 3$

Take the natural log of both sides.

$\ln (e^{3t}) = \ln 3$
$\qquad 3t = \ln 3$
$\qquad t = \frac{1}{3} \ln 3$

And by the natural log properties,

$t = \ln 3^{1/3} = \ln\sqrt[3]{3}$

19. E. In general, $\log_m n = p$ is equivalent to $m^p = n$. For this problem, the base is e because it is a natural log (ln). Therefore,

$\ln a = b \Leftrightarrow \log_e a = b \Leftrightarrow e^b = a$

20. E. This can be verified with the symmetry tests:

$$y^2 = x^2 + 9 \Rightarrow y = \pm\sqrt{x^2+9} \text{ or } f(x) = \pm\sqrt{x^2+9}$$

$$f(-x) = \pm\sqrt{(-x)^2+9} = f(x) \Rightarrow \text{symmetric with respect to } y\text{-axis}$$

$$f(-x) = -f(x) \text{ because } \pm \text{ "changes" to } \pm \Rightarrow \text{symmetric with respect to the origin}$$

As a relation in y,

$$g(y) = \pm\sqrt{y^2-9}$$

$g(-y) = g(y) \Rightarrow$ symmetric with respect to y-axis

Alternately, use conics:

$$y^2 = x^2 + 9 \Leftrightarrow y^2 - x^2 = 9$$

$$\Leftrightarrow \frac{y^2}{9} - \frac{x^2}{9} = 1$$

This last equation is recognizable as a hyperbola centered at the origin with a square asymptotic rectangle. Thus it is symmetric with respect to both axes and to the origin.

21. D. Use the vertical-line test. In the first two graphs, all vertical lines will intersect the graph only once, whereas in the third graph, many vertical lines will hit the circle twice.

22. A. Solve by the number line method and interval testing.

$$(3x^2 + 6x)(2x - 5) < 0$$

$$3x(x + 2)(2x - 5) < 0$$

Thus $x < -2$ or $0 < x < 5/2$. Change to interval notation.

Sample Free-Response Question: Precalculus

1. Consider the function $f(x) = \dfrac{2x^2 - x^3}{x^3 - 3x^2 - 4x + 12}$

    A. Give the zeros of $f(x)$.

    B. Give the equations of any vertical asymptotes.

    C. Give the equations of any horizontal asymptotes.

    D. Make a sketch of the graph.

Answer to Free-Response Question

1. Always simplify first. By factoring the numerator first, you may be able to find a potential factor of the third-degree numerator and thus make the factoring simpler (see the synthetic division that follows).

$$f(x) = \frac{2x^2 - x^3}{x^3 - 3x^2 - 4x + 12}$$

$$= \frac{-x^2(x-2)}{(x-2)(x^2 - x - 6)}$$

$$= \frac{-x^2(x-2)}{(x-2)(x+2)(x-3)}$$

$$= \frac{-x^2}{(x+2)(x-3)}, \quad x \neq 2$$

$$
\begin{array}{r|rrrr}
2 & 1 & -3 & -4 & 12 \\
  &   & 2 & -2 & -12 \\
\hline
  & 1 & -1 & -6 & 0
\end{array}
$$

    A. Zeros: Let $f(x) = 0 \Rightarrow x = 0$

        Thus $(0, 0)$ is the only zero.

    B. Vertical asymptotes: Let denominator $= 0 \Rightarrow (x + 2)(x - 3) = 0$

        Thus $x = -2$ and $x = 3$ are vertical asymptotes.

C. Horizontal asymptotes: Compare degrees.

degree of numerator = degree of denominator $\Rightarrow$ divide

$$f(x) = \frac{-x^2}{(x+2)(x-3)}, x \neq 2$$

$$
\begin{array}{r}
-1 \\
x^2 - x - 6 \overline{\smash{\big)}\, -x^2 } \\
\underline{-x^2 + x + 6} \\
-x - 6
\end{array}
$$

Thus $y = -1$ is the horizontal asymptote.

D. Sketch:

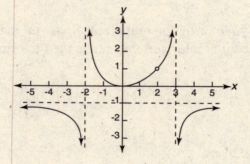

The single major concept that separates precalculus math from calculus is that of the limit of a function. Although none of the formal definitions of limits are on the AP exam, you must have a solid, intuitive understanding of how a limit works in order to be able to apply limits to concepts such as continuity. You must also master a variety of different techniques used to find limits, because the AP exam will include multiple-choice questions that deal directly with finding limits.

Intuitive Definition of a Limit

Perhaps the simplest way to understand the concept of the limit of a function is through a graphical interpretation and in terms of the following translation from calculus to English:

Calculus	$\Leftrightarrow$	English
$\lim\limits_{x \to 2}(2x-1)=?$	$\Leftrightarrow$	Read: "What is the limit of $2x-1$ as x approaches 2?"
		Think: As the x-coordinates get closer and closer to 2 what values (if any) are the y-coordinates getting closer to?

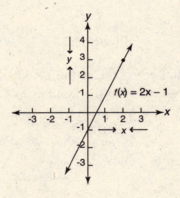

Figure 2.1

From the graph, it should be clear that as the x-coordinates get closer and closer to 2, the y-coordinates get closer and closer to 3. The calculus notation for this is

$$\lim\limits_{x \to 2}(2x-1)=3$$

The value of the function at the exact point where $x = 2$ is irrelevant to answering the limit question. The limit question is answered by determining what value the y-coordinates are approaching as x gets *closer and closer* to 2. Examine the following table of values.

x	1	1.5	1.6	1.8	1.9	1.99	2.01	2.1	2.2	2.3	2.5	3
$f(x)$	1	2	2.2	2.6	2.8	2.98	3.02	3.2	3.4	3.6	4	5

On the top line, x-coordinates have been selected as a series of values approaching 2 from both directions — that is, increasing from 1 and decreasing from 3. Note that the corresponding y-values on the bottom line are approaching 3 from both directions, that is, increasing from 1 and decreasing from 5. The ordered pair (2, 3) is not included in the chart because it is not relevant to determining the limit. In fact, if a function $g(x)$ is created that has the same values as $f(x)$ above, but is defined differently (or even undefined) at $x = 2$, the limit of $g(x)$ is the same as for $f(x)$:

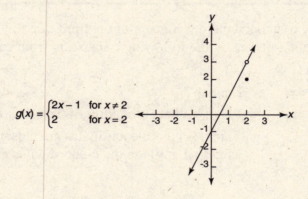

$$g(x) = \begin{cases} 2x - 1 & \text{for } x \neq 2 \\ 2 & \text{for } x = 2 \end{cases}$$

Figure 2.2

From the graph it should be clear that here, too, as the x-coordinates get closer and closer to 2, the y-coordinates get closer and closer to 3. In the language of calculus

$$\lim_{x \to 2} g(x) = 3$$

Here are some other examples of limits:

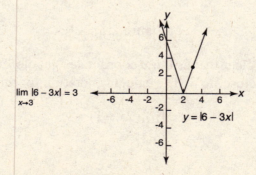

$$\lim_{x \to 3} |6 - 3x| = 3$$

$$y = |6 - 3x|$$

Figure 2.3

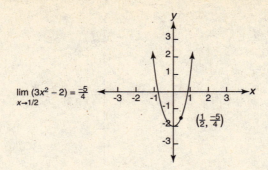

$$\lim_{x \to 1/2} (3x^2 - 2) = \frac{-5}{4}$$

Figure 2.4

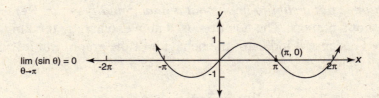

$$\lim_{\theta \to \pi} (\sin \theta) = 0$$

Figure 2.5

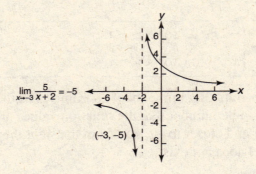

$$\lim_{x \to -3} \frac{5}{x + 2} = -5$$

Figure 2.6

Generally, finding the limit of a continuous function requires straightforward substitution. Even the limits of certain types of discontinuous functions, such as $g(x)$ above, can be found by direct substitution. However, some types of discontinuities may dramatically affect the limit of the function at the point of discontinuity, as shown in the examples that follow.

Sample

What is $\displaystyle\lim_{x \to 1} \frac{2}{(x - 1)^2}$?

Begin by sketching the graph. The graph shows that as the x-coordinates get closer and closer to 1, the function values (y-coordinates) simply get bigger and bigger. The calculus notation used to symbolize this is

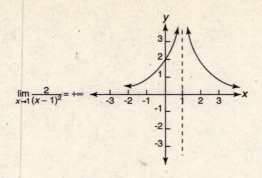

$$\lim_{x \to 1} \frac{2}{(x-1)^2} = +\infty$$

Figure 2.7

Caution: This notation is not meant to imply that a limit actually exists. Remember that ∞ (infinity) is a concept, not a number. The notation used above, whereby the limit "equals infinity," is generally preferred because it indicates the behavior of the graph. But it is also correct to write

$$\lim_{x \to 1} \frac{2}{(x-1)^2} \text{ does not exist}$$

Sample

Find $\lim_{x \to -1} h(x)$ if $h(x) = \begin{cases} -2x - 4 & \text{for } x \leq -1 \\ x^2 & \text{for } x > -1 \end{cases}$

Again, begin by sketching the graph. Examine the y-coordinates as the x-coordinates get closer and closer to –1. There is no single number that the function values are getting closer to: From the left the y-values get closer and closer to –2, and from the right they get closer and closer to 1. This implies that $\lim_{x \to -1} h(x)$ does not exist.

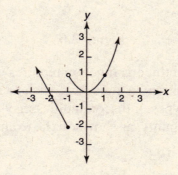

Figure 2.8

The limit notation can be modified to symbolize the situation where the lefthand and righthand limits are different.

$$\lim_{x \to -1^-} h(x) = -2 \text{ and } \lim_{x \to -1^+} h(x) = 1$$

Such **one-sided limits** will be explained in greater detail later in this chapter.

Algebraic Techniques for Finding Limits

Finding the limit of a continuous function requires the simple algebraic technique of substitution. For more complicated functions, other algebraic techniques are required. These techniques include

1. Substitution

2. Simplifying expressions

3. Rationalizing the numerator or denominator

These last two techniques are used when direct substitution yields the **indeterminate form,** wherein both numerator and denominator are zero (0/0). When the indeterminate form arises from direct substitution, some type of algebra must be done to change the form of the function. *Caution: Do not make the mistake of assuming that the indeterminate form of 0/0 somehow "cancels out" and is equal to 1.* This is not true, as shown by the following examples.

Sample

> What is $\lim\limits_{x \to 1} \dfrac{x^2 + x - 2}{x^2 - 1}$?

Substituting $x = 1$ in directly gives

$$\lim\limits_{x \to 1} \frac{x^2 + x - 2}{x^2 - 1} = \frac{1 + 1 - 2}{1 - 1} = \frac{0}{0}$$

This is the indeterminate form, which implies that algebra needs to be done — in this case, factoring.

$$\lim\limits_{x \to 1} \frac{x^2 + x - 2}{x^2 - 1} = \lim\limits_{x \to 1} \frac{(x + 2)(x - 1)}{(x + 1)(x - 1)} \qquad \text{by factoring}$$

$$= \lim\limits_{x \to 1} \left(\frac{x + 2}{x + 1} \right) \qquad \text{by canceling}$$

$$= \tfrac{3}{2} \qquad \text{by substitution}$$

The graph of $f(x)$, a rational function, shows a hole at $(1, \tfrac{3}{2})$. Recall that the limit is not affected by an undefined or unusual value at the limit site.

$$f(x) = \frac{x^2 + x - 2}{x^2 - 1}$$

$$= \frac{x + 2}{x + 1} \quad x \neq 1$$

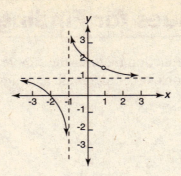

Figure 2.9

Sample

> What is $\displaystyle\lim_{x \to 4}\frac{\sqrt{x}-2}{x-4}$?

Again, direct substitution yields the indeterminate form.

$$\lim_{x \to 4}\frac{\sqrt{x}-2}{x-4} = \frac{\sqrt{4}-2}{4-4} = \frac{0}{0}$$

Therefore, you must do algebra to change the form.

Rationalizing the numerator, $\displaystyle\lim_{x \to 4}\frac{\sqrt{x}-2}{x-4}\left(\frac{\sqrt{x}+2}{\sqrt{x}+2}\right)$

Simplifying, $= \displaystyle\lim_{x \to 4}\frac{x-4}{(x-4)\left(\sqrt{x}+2\right)}$

Canceling factors, $= \displaystyle\lim_{x \to 4}\left(\frac{1}{\sqrt{x}+2}\right)$

Substituting, $= \dfrac{1}{\sqrt{4}+2} = \dfrac{1}{4}$

One-Sided Limits

One-sided limits are used most frequently with piece functions, functions with domain restrictions, or infinite limits. One-sided limits can be interpreted similarly to general limits:

Calculus		English
$\displaystyle\lim_{x \to 1^{+}}(x^{2}) = ?$	$\Leftrightarrow$	Think: As the x-coordinates get closer and closer to 1 from the right side, what values (if any) are the y-coordinates getting closer to?

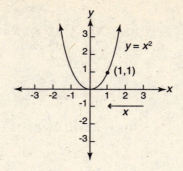

Figure 2.10

From the graph, it should be clear that the y-coordinates are approaching 1 as the x-coordinates approach 1 from the right. The calculus notation is

$$\lim_{x \to 1^+}\left(x^2\right) = 1$$

Similarly,

$$\lim_{x \to 1^-}\left(x^2\right) = 1$$

One-sided limits are not often used with continuous functions such as this one because it is simpler just to use a general limit:

$$\lim_{x \to 1}\left(x^2\right) = 1$$

In piece functions, however, one-sided limits are needed, as in the next example.

Sample

Let g be defined as follows: $g(x) = \begin{cases} \sin x & \text{for } x \geq 0 \\ \cos\dfrac{x}{2} & \text{for } x < 0 \end{cases}$

Find $\lim_{x \to 0^+} g(x)$ and $\lim_{x \to 0^-} g(x)$.

Begin by graphing the function.

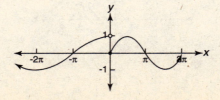

Figure 2.11

For the limit from the right

$$\lim_{x \to 0^+} g(x) = \lim_{x \to 0^+} (\sin x)$$
$$= 0$$

And for the limit from the left

$$\lim_{x \to 0^-} g(x) = \lim_{x \to 0^-} \left(\cos \frac{x}{2} \right)$$
$$= 1$$

As mentioned before, if the one-sided limits are not equal, then the general limit does not exist.

$$\left. \begin{array}{l} \lim_{x \to 0^+} g(x) = 0 \\ \lim_{x \to 0^-} g(x) = 1 \end{array} \right\} \Rightarrow \lim_{x \to 0} g(x) \text{ does not exist}$$

In general, if $\lim_{x \to a^+} f(x) \neq \lim_{x \to a^-} f(x)$, then $\lim_{x \to a} f(x)$ does not exist.

This method provides one method that is commonly used on free-response questions to justify the answer that a limit does not exist.

Functions with implied domain restrictions are a second case where one-sided limits are required.

Sample

> What is $\lim_{x \to 2^+} \sqrt{x - 2}$?

As a result of the domain of $y = \sqrt{x - 2}$ a one-sided limit must be used for this problem. Because x can only be greater than or equal to 2, it would be impossible to approach 2 from the left. The function is continuous on its domain, however, so just substitute:

$$\lim_{x \to 2^+} \sqrt{x - 2} = \sqrt{2 - 2} = 0$$

A graph may also be useful. The graph for this problem is the top half of a parabola.

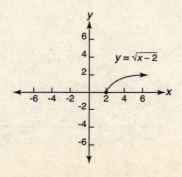

Figure 2.12

$$y = \sqrt{x-2} \Leftrightarrow y^2 = x - 2 \text{ where } y \geq 0$$

$$x = (y-0)^2 + 2 \text{ where } y \geq 0$$

$$\text{vertex}(2,0), \text{opens right}$$

Infinite Limits

Another type of nonexistent limit that can require the use of one-sided limits is the **infinite limit** mentioned previously. The formal definition of an infinite limit is not on the AP exam.

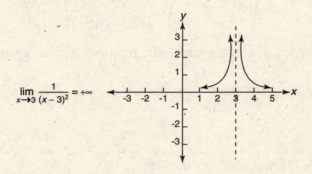

Figure 2.13

There are essentially two ways to find infinite limits:

1. Graph the function and look for vertical asymptotes.

2. Apply the theorem for infinite limits (given below).

Graphing the function is effective when the function is not terribly complicated. For example, with simple rational functions, locating the vertical asymptotes requires only finding any points where the denominator equals zero. For the foregoing function,

$$f(x) = \frac{1}{(x-3)^2} \Rightarrow \text{vertical asymptote where } (x-3)^2 = 0$$

Thus there is a vertical asymptote where $x = 3$, so

$$\lim_{x \to 3} \frac{1}{(x-3)^2} = +\infty$$

Some functions may not even have to be graphed, but only visualized. Examples include

$$\lim_{x \to (\pi/2)^+} (\tan x) = -\infty \text{ and } \lim_{x \to (\pi/2)^-} (\tan x) = +\infty$$

Note the application of one-sided limits here. See the section on trig functions if no visualization suggests itself.

Graphing can be impractical, so sometimes it may be easier to apply the following theorem.

Theorem for Infinite Limits

$$\lim_{x \to a} \frac{f(x)}{g(x)} = \pm \infty \text{ if } \begin{cases} \lim_{x \to a} f(x) = \text{any cons} \tan t \\ \quad\quad and \\ \lim_{x \to a} g(x) = 0 \end{cases}$$

The validity of this theorem can be demonstrated by examining a set of fractions where the numerator is held constant while the denominator approaches 0:

$$\frac{2}{4}, \frac{2}{3}, \frac{2}{2}, \frac{2}{1}, \frac{2}{\frac{1}{2}}, \frac{2}{\frac{1}{3}}, \frac{2}{\frac{1}{4}}, \frac{2}{\frac{1}{10}}, \frac{2}{\frac{1}{100}}, \frac{2}{\frac{1}{1000}}, \text{etc.}$$

As the denominator becomes arbitrarily small, the fractions are increasing without bound; that is, the limit is infinite.

Sample

Use the theorem for infinite limits to show that

$$\lim_{x \to 3} \frac{1}{(x-3)^2} = +\infty$$

(from the original example in this section).

$$\lim_{x \to 3} \frac{1}{(x-3)^2} = +\infty \text{ because } \begin{cases} \lim_{x \to 3} 1 = 1 \, (\text{a constant}) \\ \quad\quad and \\ \lim_{x \to 3} (x-3)^2 = 0 \end{cases}$$

A simpler notation that may be helpful is

$$\lim_{x \to 3} \frac{1}{(x-3)^2} = \left(\frac{1}{0}\right) = +\infty$$

Note that (1/0) is enclosed in parentheses. (1/0) is, of course, an undefined expression; it is used here as a convenient notation for infinite limits. Determining the sign of the answer, $+\infty$ or $-\infty$, requires three steps:

1. Find the sign of the numerator by substitution.

2. Find how the denominator approaches zero, from negative numbers or positive numbers, by choosing a value from the correct side (if it's a one-sided limit) and substituting.

3. Apply the usual division rules to your results from the first two steps.

Sample

Find $\lim\limits_{x \to 2^+} \dfrac{x-3}{x-2}$ by applying the theorem for infinite limits.

Because the limit of the numerator is a constant and the limit of the denominator is 0, the limit of the quotient is $\pm\infty$.

$$\left.\begin{array}{l} \lim\limits_{x \to 2^+}(x-3)=-1 \\[2mm] \lim\limits_{x \to 2^+}(x-2)=0 \end{array}\right\} \Rightarrow \lim\limits_{x \to 2^+}\dfrac{x-3}{x-2}=\pm\infty$$

But is it $+\infty$ or $-\infty$? Use the three steps listed above.

1. The sign of the numerator is negative: $\lim\limits_{x \to 2^+}(x-3)=-1$

2. Choose $x = 3$, a number to the *right* of 2, because that is the indicated direction on the limit, and substitute this into the denominator. Because $3 - 2 = 1$, a positive number, the denominator approaches 0 from positive values.

3. Applying the division rule

   $$\dfrac{\text{negative}}{\text{positive}} = \text{negative}$$

   reveals that the limit is $-\infty$.

Modifying the simplified notation from above, the symbol 0^+ or 0^- can be used to indicate the behavior of the denominator:

$$\lim\limits_{x \to 2^+}\dfrac{x-3}{x-2}=\left(\dfrac{-1}{0^+}\right)=-\infty$$

and for the other side of the limit:

$$\lim\limits_{x \to 2^-}\dfrac{x-3}{x-2}=\left(\dfrac{-1}{0^-}\right)=+\infty$$

On a free-response problem, you may have to find the vertical asymptotes of a function and then use calculus to show, or "justify," that they are truly vertical asymptotes. If so, just show that the function increases or decreases without bound by demonstrating that the limit is $\pm\infty$:

$$x = a \text{ is a vertical asymptote of the function } f(x) \Leftrightarrow \lim\limits_{x \to a^{+\text{ or }-}} f(x)=+\infty \text{ or } -\infty$$

Limits at Infinity

An interesting variation on the concept of a limit involves taking the limit as the x-coordinates increase or decrease without bound, rather than as the x-coordinates approach a specific value. The best way to interpret this is graphically:

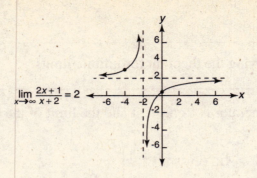

$$\lim_{x \to \infty} \frac{2x+1}{x+2} = 2$$

Figure 2.14

As the x-coordinates increase without bound ($x \to +\infty$), the y-coordinates (function values) get closer and closer to 2, which implies that the limit, or limiting value, of the function is 2. The function values never actually have to equal 2 for the limit to be 2, as long as they get closer and closer to 2, as shown in the following chart:

x	−1	0	1	2	3	4	10	100	1,000
$f(x)$	−1	0.5	1	1.25	1.4	1.5	1.75	1.97	1.997

From the graph, it should be obvious that as x decreases without bound ($x \to -\infty$), the function values approach 2. It should be obvious that horizontal asymptotes are thus also justified by limits.

$y = a$ is a horizontal asymptote of the function $f(x) \Leftrightarrow \lim\limits_{x \to \pm\infty} f(x) = a$

As with infinite limits, there are two basic methods for finding limits at infinity:

1. Graph the function and look for horizontal asymptotes.

2. Use the theorem on page 84.

Graphing or visualizing the function in order to determine its horizontal asymptotes is probably the quickest and easiest method for finding limits at infinity. To find the horizontal asymptotes of a rational function, recall that you need to examine the degree of the numerator and denominator (see page 41) as shown in the next two examples.

Sample

What is $\lim\limits_{x \to \infty}\left(\dfrac{3x^2 - 27}{8 - 2x^2}\right)$?

degree of numerator = degree of denominator

$\Rightarrow$ divide to find asymptote

$$-2x^2 + 8 \overline{\smash{\big)}\, 3x^2 - 27} \quad \overset{-\frac{3}{2}}{} \Rightarrow y = -\frac{3}{2} \text{ is the horizontal asymptote as shown on the graph}$$
$$\underline{3x^2 - 12}$$
$$-15$$

Therefore,

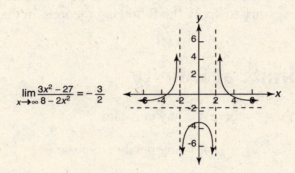

$$\lim_{x \to \infty} \frac{3x^2 - 27}{8 - 2x^2} = -\frac{3}{2}$$

Figure 2.15

A shortcut: When the degree of the numerator equals the degree of the denominator, the limit is equal to the quotient of the leading coefficients of the numerator and denominator. In this example, the leading coefficient of the numerator is 3 and that of the denominator is –2, so

$$\lim_{x \to \infty} \frac{3x^2 - 27}{8 - 2x^2} = \frac{3}{-2} = -\frac{3}{2}$$

Sample

What is $\lim_{x \to \infty} \dfrac{x - 3}{4 - 2x^2}$?

degree of numerator < degree of denominator

$\Rightarrow$ divide to find asymptote

$$-2x^2 + 4 \overline{\smash{\big)}\, x - 3} \quad \overset{0}{}$$

$\Rightarrow$ $y = 0$ (the x-axis) is the horizontal asymptote

Thus

$$\lim_{x \to \infty} \frac{x - 3}{4 - 2x^2} = 0$$

A shortcut: When the degree of the numerator is less than the degree of the denominator, the x-axis is the asymptote, so the limit is always 0.

Sample

> What is $\lim\limits_{x \to \infty}(\arctan x)$?

Some horizontal asymptotes should be known, and in these cases you may be able to avoid any graphing:

$$\lim_{x \to \infty}(\arctan x) = \frac{\pi}{2}$$

A graph will not suffice for justifying limits at infinity or horizontal asymptotes on a free-response problem. It is necessary to apply the following theorem in that case.

Theorem for Limits at Infinity

$$\lim_{x \to \pm\infty} \frac{a}{x^n} = 0 \text{ where } a = \text{any constant}$$

$$n = \text{any positive constant}$$

Here are some examples of the application of that theorem.

$$\lim_{x \to -\infty} \frac{2}{x^2} = 0 \qquad \lim_{x \to \infty} \frac{-4}{\sqrt{x}} = 0$$

An appealing reason for the validity of this theorem is found by examining a sequence of fractions where the numerator stays constant and the denominator increases without bound:

$$\frac{3}{\frac{1}{2}} \quad \frac{3}{1} \quad \frac{3}{2} \quad \frac{3}{4} \quad \frac{3}{6} \quad \frac{3}{10} \quad \frac{3}{100} \quad \frac{3}{1000} \quad \frac{3}{1,000,000}$$

This series is obviously approaching zero.

The theorem for limits at infinity is very useful when applied in conjunction with a simple rule: Rewrite the function in a new form by multiplying the numerator and denominator by the fraction $1/(x^h)$ where h is the highest power of any term in the function.

Sample

> What is $\lim\limits_{x \to \infty} \dfrac{3x - 2x^2}{7x^2 + 5}$?

The highest power in the function is 2, so multiply the numerator and denominator by $1/(x^2)$.

$$\lim_{x \to \infty} \frac{(3x - 2x^2)\left(\frac{1}{x^2}\right)}{(7x^2 + 5)\left(\frac{1}{x^2}\right)} = \lim_{x \to \infty} \left(\frac{\frac{3}{x} - 2}{7 + \frac{5}{x^2}} \right)$$

$$= \frac{0 - 2}{7 + 0} = \frac{-2}{7}$$

In the solution above, notice the theorem is used twice:

$$\lim_{x \to \infty} \frac{3}{x} = 0 \text{ and } \lim_{x \to \infty} \frac{5}{x^2} = 0$$

A sneaky version of limits at infinity often arises on the AP exam:

Sample

Find $\lim\limits_{x \to +\infty} \dfrac{\sqrt{x^2+2}}{2x-5}$ and $\lim\limits_{x \to -\infty} \dfrac{\sqrt{x^2+2}}{2x-5}$.

For both of these problems, the highest power is actually first degree. But, in order to be able to simplify the expression, you must multiply the numerator and denominator by $1/\sqrt{x^2}$ rather than $1/x$.

$$\lim_{x \to +\infty} \left(\frac{\sqrt{x^2+2}}{2x-5} \right) \left(\frac{\frac{1}{\sqrt{x^2}}}{\frac{1}{\sqrt{x^2}}} \right) = \lim_{x \to +\infty} \frac{\sqrt{\frac{x^2}{x^2} + \frac{2}{x^2}}}{(2x-5)\frac{1}{\sqrt{x^2}}}$$

$$= \lim_{x \to +\infty} \frac{\sqrt{\frac{x^2}{x^2} + \frac{2}{x^2}}}{(2x-5)\frac{1}{x}}$$

$$= \lim_{x \to +\infty} \frac{\sqrt{1 + \frac{2}{x^2}}}{\left(2 - \frac{5}{x}\right)} = \frac{\sqrt{1}}{2} = \frac{1}{2}$$

For the limit as x decreases without bound, all the previous work applies except for the simplification of the multiplier in the denominator (from the first to the second lines below). For the limit as x decreases without bound, x is a negative number, so $\sqrt{x^2} = -x$.

$$\lim_{x \to -\infty} \frac{\sqrt{x^2+2}}{2x-5} = \lim_{x \to -\infty} \left(\frac{\sqrt{x^2+2}}{2x-5} \right) \left(\frac{\frac{1}{\sqrt{x^2}}}{\frac{1}{\sqrt{x^2}}} \right)$$

$$= \lim_{x \to -\infty} \frac{\sqrt{\frac{x^2}{x^2} + \frac{2}{x^2}}}{(2x-5)\left(\frac{1}{-x}\right)}$$

$$= \lim_{x \to -\infty} \frac{\sqrt{1 + \frac{2}{x^2}}}{\left(-2 + \frac{5}{x}\right)} = \frac{\sqrt{1}}{-2} = -\frac{1}{2}$$

Special Trig Limits

Two special trig limits occur frequently on the AP exam, both in standard forms and with subtle variations. They are

$$\lim_{x \to 0} \frac{\sin x}{x} = 1 \quad \text{and} \quad \lim_{x \to 0} \frac{1 - \cos x}{x} = 0$$

Both of these limits can be proved in a variety of ways, including L'Hôpital's rule, which is covered in the chapter on applications of the derivative. For now, memorize both limits, and learn how to apply them. Do not try direct substitution of 0 into either function; substituting yields the indeterminate form 0/0.

Sample

Find $\lim_{\theta \to 0} \dfrac{\sin 2\theta}{\theta}$.

In order for you to apply the special trig limits directly, the arguments must match. This can be achieved by multiplying the numerator and denominator by 2.

$$\lim_{\theta \to 0} \frac{\sin 2\theta}{\theta}\left(\frac{2}{2}\right) = \lim_{\theta \to 0}\left(\frac{\sin 2\theta}{2\theta}\right)2$$
$$= 1 \cdot 2 = 2$$

Sample

Find $\lim_{\alpha \to 0} \dfrac{\cos \alpha - 1}{\alpha}$.

$$\lim_{\alpha \to 0} \frac{\cos \alpha - 1}{\alpha} = \lim_{\alpha \to 0} -\left(\frac{1 - \cos \alpha}{\alpha}\right) = -1\,(0) = 0$$

Continuity

Continuity is an important calculus concept that is closely related to limits. An intuitive understanding of continuity is easy. If you can draw a function without having to lift your pencil, then the function is continuous. Conversely, if you have to lift your pencil for any reason, you have found a point of discontinuity. Study the graph of the following function and see if you can identify the points where it is discontinuous.

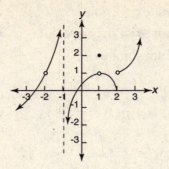

Figure 2.16

$f(x)$ is discontinuous at $x = -2, -1, 1$, and 2.

In many cases, simply examining a graph may be sufficient to determine whether a function is continuous and to find any points of discontinuity. However, on free-response problems, proving or justifying continuity (or discontinuity) at a point may be required. You can do this by using the following three-part definition.

Definition of Continuity at a Point

A function $f(x)$ is said to be continuous at a point $x = a$ if

1. $f(a)$ exists
2. $\lim\limits_{x \to a} f(x)$ exists
3. $\lim\limits_{x \to a} f(x) = f(a)$

All three conditions must be true for the function to be continuous at *a*.

Discontinuities such as those shown in Figure 2.16 at $x = -2$ (a hole) and $x = 1$ (a hole with an "extra" point) are called **removable discontinuities.** Those at $x = -1$ (an asymptote) and $x = 2$ (a break or skip) are called **nonremovable discontinuities.**

Sample

Use the definition of continuity to prove that $f(x)$ as graphed in Figure 2.16 is discontinuous at $x = -2, -1, 1$, and 2.

In order to show that a function is discontinuous at a point, show that at least one of the three parts of the definition of continuity is not satisfied. It is not necessary (nor is it always possible) to show that all three parts of the definition are not satisfied.

At $x = -2$	$f(-2)$ does not exist (hole)	discontinuous
At $x = -1$	$f(-1)$ does not exist (asymptote)	discontinuous
	or $\lim\limits_{x \to -1} f(x)$ does not exist	discontinuous

At $x = 1$
$$\left. \begin{array}{l} f(1) = 2 \\ \lim\limits_{x \to 1} f(x) = 1 \end{array} \right\} \Rightarrow \lim\limits_{x \to 1} f(x) \neq f(1) \qquad \text{discontinuous}$$

At $x = 2$
$$\left. \begin{array}{l} \lim\limits_{x \to 2^-} f(x) = 0 \\ \lim\limits_{x \to 2^+} f(x) = 1 \end{array} \right\} \Rightarrow \begin{array}{l} \lim\limits_{x \to 2} f(x) \\ \text{does not exist} \end{array} \qquad \text{discontinuous}$$

Continuity on an interval is defined by considering the interval to be a group of points and applying the definition of continuity at a point to each point in the interval.

Definition of Continuity on an Open Interval

$f(x)$ is continuous on the interval (a, b) if $f(x)$ is continuous for every point c where $c \in (a, b)$.

Definition of Continuity on a Closed Interval

For closed intervals, a slight modification of this definition is required in order to ensure continuity at the two endpoints. $f(x)$ is continuous on the interval $[a, b]$ if

1. $f(x)$ is continuous for every point c where $c \in (a, b)$
2. $\lim\limits_{x \to a^+} f(x) = f(a)$
3. $\lim\limits_{x \to b^-} f(x) = f(b)$

Justifying continuity often arises in the context of piece functions. One type of problem commonly found on the AP exam requires that you determine a value of a variable to guarantee continuity of a piece function and then justify the answer by applying the definition. This is illustrated in the next example.

Sample

Let f be defined as follows:
$$f(x) = \begin{cases} -x - 3 & \text{for } x \leq -2 \\ ax + b & \text{for } -2 < x < 1 \\ x^2 & \text{for } x \geq 1 \end{cases}$$

Find a and b such that the function is continuous. Justify your answer using the definition of continuity.

If this problem were to appear as a multiple-choice question, it would simply be a matter of forcing the line $y = ax + b$ to contain the points $(-2, -1)$ and $(1, 1)$.

$$(-2, -1) \text{ and } (1, 1) \Rightarrow m = \frac{-1-1}{-2-1} = \frac{2}{3}$$

$$\text{point/slope form} \Rightarrow y - (-1) = \frac{2}{3}(x - (-2))$$

$$y = \frac{2}{3}x + \frac{1}{3}$$

Therefore, $a = \frac{2}{3}$ and $b = \frac{1}{3}$.

But if this is a free-response question, you must now justify this choice of a and b via the definition of continuity. $f(x)$ is now

$$f(x) = \begin{cases} -x - 3 & \text{for } x \le -2 \\ \frac{2}{3}x + \frac{1}{3} & \text{for } -2 < x < 1 \\ x^2 & \text{for } x \ge 1 \end{cases}$$

Thus, at $x = -2$

1. $f(-2) = -1$, so $f(-2)$ exists

2. $\left.\begin{array}{l} \lim\limits_{x \to -2^-} f(x) = \lim\limits_{x \to -2^-} (-x - 3) = -1 \\ \lim\limits_{x \to -2^+} f(x) = \lim\limits_{x \to -2^+} \left(\frac{2}{3}x + \frac{1}{3}\right) = -1 \end{array}\right\} \Rightarrow \begin{array}{l} \lim\limits_{x \to -2} f(x) = -1 \\ \text{so a limit exists} \end{array}$

3. $\lim\limits_{x \to -2} f(x) = f(-2) = -1$

Therefore, $f(x)$ is continuous at $x = -2$, since all three parts of the definition are satisfied.

Now, at $x = 1$,

1. $f(1) = 1$, so $f(1)$ exists

2. $\left.\begin{array}{l} \lim\limits_{x \to 1^-} f(x) = \lim\limits_{x \to 1^-} (\frac{2}{3}x + \frac{1}{3}) = 1 \\ \lim\limits_{x \to 1^+} f(x) = \lim\limits_{x \to 1^+} (x^2) = 1 \end{array}\right\} \Rightarrow \begin{array}{l} \lim\limits_{x \to 1} f(x) = 1 \\ \text{so a limit exists} \end{array}$

3. $\lim\limits_{x \to 1} f(x) = f(1) = 1$

Therefore, $f(x)$ is continous at $x = 1$.

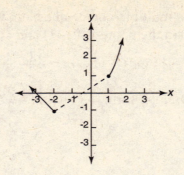

Figure 2.17

Sample Multiple-Choice Questions: Limits and Continuity

1. What is $\lim\limits_{x \to 2^+} \dfrac{x^3 - 8}{x - 2}$?

   A. 0

   B. 12

   C. $+\infty$

   D. $-\infty$

   E. none of these

2. Let f be defined as follows:

   $$f(x) = \begin{cases} 12 - 3x & \text{for } x \le 3 \\ 15 - x & \text{for } x > 3 \end{cases}$$

   What is $\lim\limits_{x \to 3^+} f(x)$?

   A. 3

   B. 12

   C. 15

   D. 21

   E. The limit does not exist.

3. What is $\lim\limits_{x \to 4} \sqrt[3]{\dfrac{7x}{x - 3}}$?

   A. 1

   B. $\sqrt[3]{7}$

   C. 3

   D. $\sqrt[3]{28}$

   E. The limit does not exist.

4. Find $\lim\limits_{x \to 1/2} \lVert x \rVert$ (where $\lVert \ \rVert$ indicates the greatest-integer function).

   A. 0

   B. $\dfrac{1}{2}$

   C. 1

   D. 2

   E. The limit does not exist.

5. What is $\lim\limits_{x \to \infty} \dfrac{3 - \sqrt{x}}{2\sqrt{x} + 5}$?

   A. $-\dfrac{1}{2}$

   B. $-\dfrac{1}{5}$

   C. $\dfrac{3}{5}$

   D. $\dfrac{3}{2}$

   E. undefined

6. What is $\lim\limits_{x \to \infty} \dfrac{2x-1}{3x+2}$?

- **A.** $+\infty$
- **B.** $-\infty$
- **C.** $\dfrac{1}{3}$
- **D.** $\dfrac{2}{3}$
- **E.** 1

7. What is $\lim\limits_{x \to \infty} \dfrac{4x^2}{x^2+10,000x}$?

- **A.** 0
- **B.** $\dfrac{1}{2500}$
- **C.** 1
- **D.** 4
- **E.** The limit does not exist.

8. Which of the following statements is or are true?

- I. $\lim\limits_{x \to 2}(x^2+2x-1)=7$
- II. $\lim\limits_{x \to -3}\dfrac{x^2+5x+6}{x^2-x-12}=\dfrac{1}{7}$
- III. $\lim\limits_{x \to 9}\dfrac{3-\sqrt{x}}{9-x}=\pm\infty$

- **A.** I and II only
- **B.** I and III only
- **C.** II and III only
- **D.** III only
- **E.** I, II, and III

9. What is $\lim\limits_{x \to 2^-}\dfrac{5}{x-2}$?

- **A.** 0
- **B.** $-\dfrac{5}{4}$
- **C.** $+\infty$
- **D.** $-\infty$
- **E.** none of these

10. What is $\lim\limits_{x \to 2^+}\dfrac{2x}{x^2-4}$?

- **A.** $\dfrac{-1}{2}$
- **B.** 0
- **C.** 2
- **D.** $+\infty$
- **E.** $-\infty$

11. What is $\lim\limits_{x \to 0}\dfrac{\tan x}{2x}$?

- **A.** 0
- **B.** $\dfrac{1}{2}$
- **C.** 1
- **D.** 2
- **E.** undefined

12. What is $\lim\limits_{\phi \to 0}\dfrac{\cos\phi-1}{\phi}$?

- **A.** -1
- **B.** 0
- **C.** 1
- **D.** ∞
- **E.** none of these

13. Which of the following is NOT necessary to establish in order to show that a function $f(x)$ is continuous at the point $x = c$?

- **A.** $f(c)$ exists
- **B.** domain of $f(x)$ is all real numbers
- **C.** $\lim\limits_{x \to c}f(x)=f(c)$
- **D.** $\lim\limits_{x \to c}f(x)$ exists
- **E.** All of these are necessary.

14. Let f be defined as follows:

$$f(x) = \begin{cases} \dfrac{x^2 - 1}{x - 1} & \text{for } x \neq 1 \\ 4 & \text{for } x = 1 \end{cases}$$

Which of the following statements is or are true?

I. $\lim\limits_{x \to 1} f(x)$ exists

II. $f(1)$ exists

III. $f(x)$ is continuous at $x = 1$

A. I only

B. II only

C. I and II only

D. I and III only

E. I, II, and III

15. Determine a value of k such that $f(x)$ is continuous, where

$$f(x) = \begin{cases} 3kx - 5 & \text{for } x > 2 \\ 4x - 5k & \text{for } x \leq 2 \end{cases}$$

A. 1

B. $\dfrac{13}{11}$

C. $\dfrac{3}{11}$

D. $\dfrac{-3}{11}$

E. -3

16. Find the value of k such that the following function is continuous for all real numbers.

$$f(x) = \begin{cases} kx - 1 & \text{for } x < 2 \\ kx^2 & \text{for } x \geq 2 \end{cases}$$

A. 1

B. $\dfrac{1}{2}$

C. $-\dfrac{1}{6}$

D. $-\dfrac{1}{2}$

E. none of these

17. The function $f(x) = \dfrac{x^2 + 5x + 6}{x^2 - 4}$ has

A. only a removable discontinuity at $x = -2$

B. only a removable discontinuity at $x = 2$

C. a removable discontinuity at $x = -2$ and a nonremovable discontinuity at $x = 2$

D. removable discontinuities at $x = -2$ and $x = -3$

E. nonremovable discontinuities at $x = 2$ and $x = -3$

Answers to Multiple-Choice Questions

1. B. $\lim\limits_{x \to 2^+} \dfrac{x^3 - 8}{x - 2} = \lim\limits_{x \to 2^+} \dfrac{(x-2)(x^2 + 2x + 4)}{x - 2}$

$\qquad\qquad = \lim\limits_{x \to 2^+} (x^2 + 2x + 4) = 12$

2. B. The problem asks for the limit from the right, so use the part of the piece function where, $x > 3$ — that is, $y = 15 - x$.

$$\lim\limits_{x \to 3^+} f(x) = \lim\limits_{x \to 3^+} (15 - x) = 12$$

3. D. $y = \sqrt[3]{\dfrac{7x}{x - 3}}$ is discontinuous only at $x = 3$, so just substitute:

$\lim\limits_{x \to 4} = \sqrt[3]{\dfrac{7x}{x - 3}} = \sqrt[3]{\dfrac{7(4)}{4 - 3}} = \sqrt[3]{28}$

4. A. The greatest-integer function is $\|x\|: x \to$ greatest integer less than or equal to x. It looks like this:

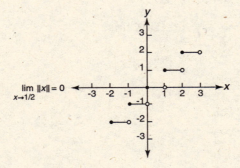

5. A. $\lim\limits_{x \to \infty} \dfrac{3 - \sqrt{x}}{2\sqrt{x} + 5} = \lim\limits_{x \to \infty} \left(\dfrac{3 - \sqrt{x}}{2\sqrt{x} + 5} \right) \left(\dfrac{\frac{1}{\sqrt{x}}}{\frac{1}{\sqrt{x}}} \right)$

$\qquad\qquad = \lim\limits_{x \to \infty} \dfrac{\frac{3}{\sqrt{x}} - 1}{2 + \frac{5}{\sqrt{x}}} = \dfrac{0 - 1}{2 + 0} = \dfrac{-1}{2}$

6. D. $\lim\limits_{x \to \infty} \dfrac{2x - 1}{3x + 2} = \lim\limits_{x \to \infty} \left(\dfrac{2x - 1}{3x + 2} \right) \left(\dfrac{\frac{1}{x}}{\frac{1}{x}} \right)$

$\qquad\qquad = \lim\limits_{x \to \infty} \dfrac{2 - \frac{1}{x}}{3 + \frac{2}{x}} = \dfrac{2 - 0}{3 + 0} = \dfrac{2}{3}$

7. D. $\lim\limits_{x \to \infty} \dfrac{4x^2}{x^2 + 10,000x} = \lim\limits_{x \to \infty} \left(\dfrac{4x^2}{x^2 + 10,000x} \right) \dfrac{\frac{1}{x^2}}{\frac{1}{x^2}}$

$$= \lim\limits_{x \to \infty} \dfrac{4}{1 + \dfrac{10,000}{x}} = \dfrac{4}{1 + 0} = 4$$

8. A. Examine each statement individually:

I. $\lim\limits_{x \to 2} (x^2 + 2x - 1) = 2^2 + 2(2) - 1 = 7$, so I is true.

II. $\lim\limits_{x \to -3} \dfrac{x^2 + 5x + 6}{x^2 - x - 12} = \lim\limits_{x \to -3} \dfrac{(x + 2)(x + 3)}{(x - 4)(x + 3)}$

$$= \lim\limits_{x \to -3} \dfrac{x + 2}{x - 4} = \dfrac{-1}{-7} = \dfrac{1}{7}, \text{ so II is true.}$$

III. $\lim\limits_{x \to 9} \dfrac{3 - \sqrt{x}}{9 - x} = \lim\limits_{x \to 9} \left(\dfrac{3 - \sqrt{x}}{9 - x} \right) \left(\dfrac{3 + \sqrt{x}}{3 + \sqrt{x}} \right)$

$$= \lim\limits_{x \to 9} \dfrac{9 - x}{(9 - x)(3 + \sqrt{x})}$$

$$= \lim\limits_{x \to 9} \dfrac{1}{3 + \sqrt{x}} = \dfrac{1}{6}, \text{ so III is false.}$$

9. D. $\lim\limits_{x \to 2^-} \dfrac{5}{x - 2} = \left(\dfrac{5}{0^-} \right) = -\infty$

10. D. $\lim\limits_{x \to 2^+} \dfrac{2x}{x^2 - 4} = \left(\dfrac{4}{0^+} \right) = +\infty$

11. B. $\lim\limits_{x \to 0} \dfrac{\tan x}{2x} = \lim\limits_{x \to 0} \left(\dfrac{\sin x}{x} \right) \left(\dfrac{1}{2} \right) \left(\dfrac{1}{\cos x} \right)$

$$= (1) \left(\dfrac{1}{2} \right) (1) = \dfrac{1}{2}$$

12. B. $\lim\limits_{\phi \to 0} \dfrac{\cos \phi - 1}{\phi} = \lim\limits_{\phi \to 0} \dfrac{-1(1 - \cos \phi)}{\phi} = (-1)(0) = 0$

13. B. The definition of continuity at a point is made up of A, C, and D, so all three are necessary. Because the problem requires continuity only at a point, not on the set of real numbers, the domain does *not* need to be the real numbers.

14. C. The first part of the function can be simplified:

$$\frac{x^2-1}{x-1} = \frac{(x+1)(x-1)}{x-1} = x+1, x \neq 1$$

Now $f(x) = \begin{cases} x+1 & \text{for } x \neq 1 \\ 4 & \text{for } x = 1 \end{cases}$

which is graphed below.

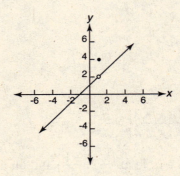

Statement I is true because $\lim\limits_{x \to 1} f(x) = 2$.

Statement II is also true, because the second part of the piece function yields $f(1) = 4$.

Statement III is false. For $f(x)$ to be continuous at 1, $\lim\limits_{x \to 1} f(x)$ must equal $f(1)$.

15. B. The function needs to "hook up" at $x = 2$.

$$f(x) = \begin{cases} 3kx - 5 & \text{for } x > 2 \\ 4x - 5k & \text{for } x \leq 1 \end{cases}$$

For the left piece: $f(2) = 3k(2) - 5 = 6k - 5$
For the right piece: $f(2) = 4(2) - 5k = 8 - 5k$

$\Rightarrow 6k - 5 = 8 - 5k$ for continuity

$\qquad 11k = 13$

$\qquad\quad k = \dfrac{13}{11}$

16. D. The function needs to "hook up" at $x = 2$.

$$f(x) = \begin{cases} kx - 1 & \text{for } x < 2 \\ kx^2 & \text{for } x \geq 2 \end{cases}$$

For the left piece: $f(2) = k(2) - 1 = 2k - 1$ }
For the right piece: $f(2) = k(2)^2 = 4k$ }

$\Rightarrow 2k - 1 = 4k$ for continuity

$\quad -2k = 1$

$\quad\quad k = \dfrac{-1}{2}$

17. C. $f(x) = \dfrac{x^2 + 5x + 6}{x^2 - 4} = \dfrac{(x+2)(x+3)}{(x+2)(x-2)} = \dfrac{x+3}{x-2}, x \neq -2$

$f(x)$ is a rational function with a hole at $\left(-2, \dfrac{-1}{4}\right)$ and an asymptote at $x = 2$. Therefore, there is a removable discontinuity at $x = -2$ and a nonremovable discontinuity at $x = 2$.

Sample Free-Response Questions: Limits and Continuity

1. Let f be defined as follows:

$$f(x) \begin{cases} 2x + 1 & \text{for } x \leq -2 \\ ax^2 + b & \text{for } -2 < x < 1 \\ \ln x & \text{for } x \geq 1 \end{cases}$$

Find values for a and b such that the function is continuous and use the definition of continuity to justify your answer.

2. Consider the function $f(x) = \dfrac{x^2 - 2x}{x^3 - 9x}$ on the interval $[-5, 5]$.

A. Give any zeros of $f(x)$.

B. Give equations of *all* asymptotes. Justify your answer.

C. List all points where $f(x)$ is discontinuous. Use the definition of continuity to justify your answer.

D. Sketch $f(x)$.

Answers to Free-Response Questions

1. First, find a and b. The function must contain the points $(-2, -3)$ and $(1, 0)$ because these are the "ends" of the known pieces. A quick sketch may help.

$(-2, -3)$ on $y = ax^2 + b \Rightarrow -3 = 4a + b$

$(1, 0)$ on $y = ax^2 + b \Rightarrow \underline{0 = a + b}$

$$-3 = 3a$$

$$-1 = a \quad \Rightarrow b = 1, \text{ so } y = -x^2 + 1 \text{ for continuity}$$

Thus $f(x) = \begin{cases} 2x + 1 & \text{for } x \le 2 \\ -x^2 + 1 & \text{for } -2 < x < 1 \\ \ln x & \text{for } x \ge 1 \end{cases}$

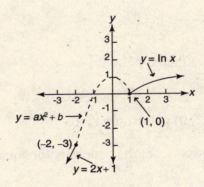

Now show that these values for a and b imply continuity by using the definition.

Justification by using the definition of continuity:

$f(x)$ is continuous at $x = a$ if:

1. $f(a)$ exists,
2. $\lim\limits_{x \to a} f(x)$ exists, and
3. $\lim\limits_{x \to a} f(x) = f(a)$

At $x = -2$: $f(-2) = -3$

$\left. \begin{array}{l} \lim\limits_{x \to -2^-} f(x) = \lim\limits_{x \to -2^-} (2x + 1) = -3 \\ \lim\limits_{x \to -2^+} f(x) = \lim\limits_{x \to -2^+} (-x^2 + 1) = -3 \end{array} \right\} \Rightarrow \lim\limits_{x \to -2} f(x) = -3$

$\lim\limits_{x \to -2} f(x) = f(-2) = -3$

Therefore, $f(x)$ is continuous by definition at $x = -2$ for $a = -1$ and $b = 1$.

At $x = 1: f(1) = 0$

$$\left.\begin{array}{l}\lim_{x \to 1^+} f(x) = \lim_{x \to 1^+}(\ln x) = 0 \\[2mm] \lim_{x \to 1^-} f(x) = \lim_{x \to 1^-}(-x^2 + 1) = 0\end{array}\right\} \Rightarrow \lim_{x \to 1} f(x) = 0$$

$$\lim_{x \to 1} f(x) = f(1) = 0$$

Therefore, $f(x)$ is continuous by definition at $x = 1$ for $a = -1$ and $b = 1$.

2. Always begin by simplifying.

$$f(x) = \frac{x^2 - 2x}{x^3 - 9x} = \frac{x(x-2)}{x(x^2-9)} = \frac{x-2}{x^2-9} \quad x \neq 0$$

Therefore, $f(x) = \dfrac{x-2}{(x+3)(x-3)} \quad x \neq 0$

   (a) For zeros, set the numerator equal to zero.

   $$x - 2 = 0$$
   $$x = 2, \text{ so } (2, 0) \text{ is the only zero}$$

   (b) For vertical asymptotes, set the denominator equal to zero.
   $$(x+3)(x-3) = 0$$

So $x = -3$ and $x = 3$ are the vertical asymptotes.

To justify the vertical asymptotes, show $\lim_{x \to a^+} f(x) = \pm \infty$ or $\lim_{x \to a^-} f(x) = \pm \infty$.

   For $x = -3$: $\quad \lim_{x \to -3^+} \dfrac{x-2}{x^2-9} = \left(\dfrac{-5}{0^-}\right) = +\infty$

   For $x = 3$: $\quad \lim_{x \to 3^-} \dfrac{x-2}{x^2-9} = \left(\dfrac{1}{0^-}\right) = -\infty$

For the horizontal asymptote, recall that

degree of numerator < degree of denominator

$\Rightarrow x - \text{axis is asymptote}$

Therefore, $y = 0$ is the horizontal asymptote.

To justify the horizontal asymptote, show $\lim\limits_{x \to +\infty} f(x) = a$ or $\lim\limits_{x \to -\infty} f(x) = a$.

$$\lim_{x \to +\infty} \frac{x-2}{x^2-9} = \lim_{x \to +\infty} \left(\frac{x-2}{x^2-9}\right)\left(\frac{\frac{1}{x^2}}{\frac{1}{x^2}}\right)$$

$$= \lim_{x \to +\infty} \frac{\frac{1}{x} - \frac{2}{x^2}}{1 - \frac{9}{x^2}} = \frac{0-0}{1-0} = 0$$

(c) $f(x)$ is discontinuous at $x = -3, 0,$ and 3.

Justification by using the definition of continuity:

$f(x)$ is continuous at $x = a$ if:

1. $f(a)$ exists,

2. $\lim\limits_{x \to a} f(x)$ exists, and

3. $\lim\limits_{x \to a} f(x) = f(a)$

At $x = -3$:

$f(-3)$ does not exist

or

$\lim\limits_{x \to -3} f(x)$ does not exist, $\left.\rule{0pt}{2.5em}\right\}$ ⇒ discontinuous at $x = -3$
because there is a vertical

asymptote at $x = -3$

At $x = 0$:

$f(0)$ does not exist ⇒ discontinuous at $x = 0$

At $x = 3$:

$f(3)$ does not exist

or

$\lim\limits_{x \to 3} f(x)$ does not exist, $\left.\rule{0pt}{2.5em}\right\}$ ⇒ discontinuous at $x = 3$
because there is a vertical

asymptote at $x = 3$

(d) Sketch. *Don't forget the hole at* $\left(0, \dfrac{2}{9}\right)$ *that results from the cancellation.*

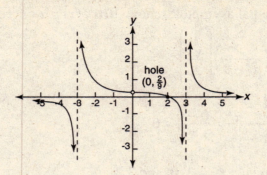

Calculus can be divided into two main branches: differential calculus and integral calculus, each based on a different major concept. The first of these is the concept of the derivative. In general terms, the derivative can be thought of as the instantaneous rate of change of one variable with respect to another variable. For the AP exam, you should know the limit definition of the derivative as well as the rules for finding the derivatives of polynomials, rational functions, the trig and inverse trig functions, and logarithmic and exponential functions. Two proofs of differentiation rules are also listed on the AP outline.

Definition of the Derivative

Differential calculus relies on the definition of the derivative. This definition can appear in two basic forms, both of which involve limits. The definition of the derivative will appear in some context on the AP exam; be sure to know both forms.

The **derivative of a function** $f(x)$, indicated by $f'(x)$, is given by

$$f'(x) = \lim_{\Delta x \to 0} \frac{f(x + \Delta x) - f(x)}{\Delta} \text{ if the limit exists}$$

The derivative of $f(x)$ at a particular point $x = c$ is given by

$$f'(c) = \lim_{x \to c} \frac{f(x) - f(c)}{x - c} \text{ if the limit exists}$$

One easy way to get a firm grip on the definition of the derivative is through the context of slope. In precalculus math, the slope of a line is defined as the ratio of the vertical change to the horizontal change, or sometimes the ratio of rise to run:

$$\text{slope of a line} = m = \frac{\text{vertical change}}{\text{horizontal change}} = \frac{\text{rise}}{\text{run}} = \frac{\Delta y}{\Delta x}$$

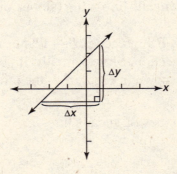

Figure 3.1

In calculus, the **slope of a curve** at any point is defined as the slope of the line tangent to the curve at that point.

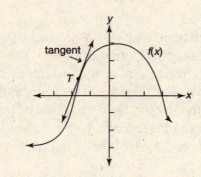

Figure 3.2

To find mathematically the value of the slope of the tangent line at a point T, examine a series of secant lines that contain T, shown in Figure 3.3 as lines $h, j, k,$ and l, intersecting the curve $f(x)$ at points $P_1, P_2, P_3,$ and P_4, respectively.

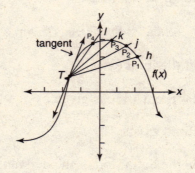

Figure 3.3

The numerical values of the slopes of the secant lines are getting closer and closer to that of the slope of the tangent line. In the language of limits, this idea can be expressed as follows:

$$\text{slope of tangent line} = \lim_{P \to T} (\text{slopes of secant lines})$$

This informal limit is being taken as P approaches T — that is, as the second point of intersection gets closer to the first point of intersection. More formally, if point T has coordinates $(c, f(c))$ and point P has coordinates $(x, f(x))$, as shown in Figure 3.4, the informal limit changes to

$$\text{slope of tangent line} = \lim_{P \to T} (\text{slopes of secant lines})$$

$$\text{slope of tangent line} = \lim_{x \to c} \frac{\Delta y}{\Delta x}$$

$$\text{slope of tangent line} = \lim_{x \to c} \frac{f(x) - f(c)}{x - c} = f'(c)$$

The third of these three equations is the definition of the derivative of $f(x)$ at $x = c$.

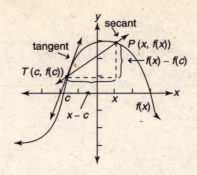

Figure 3.4

The first form of the definition of derivative can be found by means of a simple change in notation. If point T has coordinates $(x, f(x))$, and point P has an x-coordinate that is Δx units to the right of T, then P has coordinates $(x + \Delta x, f(x + \Delta x))$, as shown in Figure 3.5.

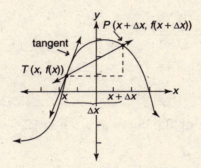

Figure 3.5

Now the slope becomes

$$\lim_{x \to c} \frac{\Delta y}{\Delta x} = \lim_{\Delta x \to 0} \frac{f(x + \Delta x) - f(x)}{\Delta x}$$

Several different notations are used to indicate the derivative.

derivative of $f(x)$: $f'(x) = \dfrac{dy}{dx} = \dfrac{d}{dx}(f(x)) = D_x y = D_x f(x)$

And, for the derivative of a function at a point,

derivative of $f(x)$ at $x = c \Rightarrow f'(c) = \dfrac{dy}{dx}\bigg|_{x = c}$

The general derivative, $f'(c)$ or dy/dx, results in a function of x, whereas the derivative at a point,

$f'(c)$ or $\dfrac{dy}{dx}\bigg|_{x = c}$

results in a constant number. The notation above can be modified to fit functions with different independent variables. For example, for the function $s(t) = 5t - 3t^3$, the derivative at $t = 3$ would be indicated as

$s'(3)$ or $\dfrac{ds}{dt}\bigg|_{t = 3}$

Sample

Find the derivative of $f(x) = 2x^2 + 3$ at the point where $x = 3$, and then use it to find the slope of the curve at this point.

$$\lim_{x \to c} \frac{f(x) - f(c)}{x - c} = \lim_{x \to 3} \frac{f(x) - f(3)}{x - 3}$$

$$= \lim_{x \to 3} \frac{(2x^2 + 3) - (2(3)^2 + 3)}{x - 3}$$

$$= \lim_{x \to 3} \frac{2x^2 + 3 - 21}{x - 3}$$

$$= \lim_{x \to 3} \frac{2x^2 - 18}{x - 3}$$

$$= \lim_{x \to 3} \frac{2(x^2 - 9)}{x - 3}$$

$$= \lim_{x \to 3} \frac{2(x + 3)(x - 3)}{(x - 3)}$$

$$= \lim_{x \to 3} 2(x + 3) = 12$$

Therefore, $f'(3) = 12 \Rightarrow$ the slope of the curve at $x = 3$ is 12.

Sample

Find the general derivative of $f(x) = 5x - 3x^2$, and then use it to find the slope of the line tangent to $f(x)$ at $x = 4$.

$$\lim_{\Delta x \to 0} \frac{f(x + \Delta x) - f(x)}{\Delta x} = \lim_{\Delta x \to 0} \frac{\left[5(x + \Delta x) - 3(x + \Delta x)^2\right] - \left(5x - 3x^2\right)}{\Delta x}$$

$$= \lim_{\Delta x \to 0} \frac{\left[5x + 5\Delta x - 3x^2 - 6x(\Delta x) - 3(\Delta x)^2\right] - 5x + 3x^2}{\Delta x}$$

$$= \lim_{\Delta x \to 0} \frac{5\Delta x - 6x(\Delta x) - 3(\Delta x)^2}{\Delta x}$$

$$= \lim_{\Delta x \to 0} (5 - 6x - 3(\Delta x)) = 5 - 6x$$

Therefore, $f'(x) = 5 - 6x$.

This expression gives the value of the derivative at any point x. For the slope of the tangent (m_t) at $x = 4$, find $f'(4)$.

$$f'(4) = 5 - 6(4) = -19 \text{ so } m_t = -19$$

Finding the slope of the tangent line or the slope of the curve at a point is just one of many, many applications of the derivative. The next chapter in this book covers all the different applications you are likely to encounter on the AP exam. However, all of these derivative applications can be generalized into a verbal definition of the derivative: The **derivative** gives the **instantaneous rate of change** of one variable with respect to another variable.

Differentiation Rules

Differentiating functions by using the definition is generally time-consuming and tedious. Fortunately, the definition can be used to derive many basic rules for differentiating various types of functions, and these roles are much simpler to apply. Only two of the derivations are listed as potential material on the outline that the College Board provides: $d(x^n)/dx = nx^{n-1}$, for n a positive integer, and $d(\sin x)/dx = \cos x$. These two derivations are given here; the rest of the differentiation rules are explained through examples.

The first three differentiation rules are straightforward and appealing.

Constant Rule

Given that c is a constant, $\frac{d}{dx}(c) = 0$

Translation: The derivative of any constant number is zero.

Example: $f(x) = 6 \Rightarrow f'(x) = 0$ or $\frac{d}{dx}(6) = 0$

Constant Multiple Rule

$\frac{d}{dx}(cf(x)) = c\frac{d}{dx}(f(x))$

Translation: You may factor out constants before doing the derivative.

Example: $y = 5x \Rightarrow \frac{dy}{dx} = 5\frac{d}{dx}(x) = 5$

Sum and Difference Rule

$$\frac{d}{dx}(f(x) \pm g(x)) = \frac{d}{dx}(f(x)) \pm \frac{d}{dx}(g(x))$$

Translation: The derivative of a sum or difference is the sum or difference of the individual derivatives.

Example: $y = x^2 + 2x \Rightarrow y' = \frac{d}{dx}(x^2) + \frac{d}{dx}(2x) = 2x + 2$

Power Rule

The power rule is one of the most frequently used differentiation rules. The simplest form of the power rule is one of the required proofs.

If n is any rational number, then $\frac{d}{dx}(x^n) = nx^{n-1}$.

Translation: To find the derivative of a power, the exponent becomes the coefficient. The new exponent is 1 less than the old exponent.

Proof of the Power Rule

Although the theorem holds for any rational number, the following proof deals only with the case where n is an integer.

$$\frac{d}{dx}(x^n) = \lim_{\Delta x \to 0} \frac{(x + \Delta x)^n - x^n}{\Delta x}$$

Expand by the binomial theorem.

$$= \lim_{\Delta x \to 0} \frac{x^n + nx^{n-1}(\Delta x) + \left(\frac{n(n-1)}{2}\right)x^{n-2}(\Delta x)^2 + \cdots + (\Delta x)^n - x^n}{\Delta x}$$

Simplify.

$$= \lim_{\Delta x \to 0} \frac{nx^{n-1}(\Delta x) + \left(\frac{n(n-1)}{2}\right)x^{n-2}(\Delta x)^2 + \cdots + (\Delta x)^n}{\Delta x}$$

Cancel the Δx.

$$= \lim_{\Delta x \to 0} \left(nx^{n-1} + \left(\frac{n(n-1)}{2}\right)x^{n-2}(\Delta x) + \cdots + (\Delta x)^{n-1}\right)$$

$$= nx^{n-1} \text{ which was to be shown}$$

The final limit results in only one term, because all the other terms have at least one factor of Δx in them and thus become 0 when the limit is taken.

This derivation could potentially show up as a free-response problem.

Sample

Find $\frac{d}{dx}(3x^2 - 2x^5 + 8x - 3)$.

You need to apply all the rules of differentiation here.

$$\frac{d}{dx}(3x^2 - 2x^5 + 8x - 3) = 3\frac{d}{dx}(x^2) - 2\frac{d}{dx}(x^5) + 8\frac{d}{dx}(x) - \frac{d}{dx}(3)$$
$$= 3(2x^1) - 2(5x^4) + 8(1x^0) - 0$$
$$= 6x - 10x^4 + 8$$

Usually, the second and third steps above are done mentally and not written down.

Sample

For $f(x) = 6\sqrt{x} - \frac{5}{\sqrt{x}} + 6x - 13$, find $f'(4)$.

First, rewrite the radicals as rational exponents; then proceed as above.

$$f(x) = 6\sqrt{x} - \frac{5}{\sqrt{x}} + 6x - 13 \Rightarrow f(x) = 6x^{1/2} - 5x^{-1/2} + 6x - 13$$

$$\Rightarrow f'(x) = 6(\tfrac{1}{2}x^{-1/2}) - 5(\tfrac{-1}{2}x^{-3/2}) + 6(1x^0) - 0$$

$$= \frac{3}{x^{1/2}} + \frac{5}{2x^{3/2}} + 6$$

$$\Rightarrow f'(4) = \frac{3}{4^{1/2}} + \frac{5}{2(4)^{3/2}} + 6$$

$$= \frac{3}{2} + \frac{5}{16} + 6 = 7\frac{13}{16} = \frac{125}{16} = 7.8125$$

Trigonometric Rules

$$\frac{d}{dx}(\sin x) = \cos x$$

$$\frac{d}{dx}(\cos x) = -\sin x$$

$$\frac{d}{dx}(\tan x) = \sec^2 x$$

$$\frac{d}{dx}(\sec x) = \sec x \tan x$$

$$\frac{d}{dx}(\csc x) = -\csc x \cot x$$

$$\frac{d}{dx}(\cot x) = -\csc^2 x$$

The proof of the derivative of sin x is not specifically listed on the AP outline. The derivation of the derivative of cos x is very similar to the one for sin x. The proofs for the other four trig rules use the derivatives of sin x and cos x and the quotient rule that follows.

Prove: $\quad\quad\quad \dfrac{d}{dx}(\sin x) = \cos x$

Proof: $\quad\quad\quad \dfrac{d}{dx}(\sin x) = \lim_{\Delta x \to 0} \dfrac{\sin(x + \Delta x) - \sin x}{\Delta x}$

$$= \lim_{\Delta x \to 0} \frac{\sin x \cos(\Delta x) + \cos x \sin(\Delta x) - \sin x}{\Delta x}$$

$$= \lim_{\Delta x \to 0} \frac{\cos x \sin(\Delta x) + [\sin x \cos(\Delta x) - \sin x]}{\Delta x}$$

$$= \lim_{\Delta x \to 0} \left[\cos x \frac{\sin(\Delta x)}{\Delta x} + \sin x \frac{\cos(\Delta x) - 1}{\Delta x} \right]$$

By the special trig limits:

$$= (\cos x)(1) + (\sin x)(0)$$

$$= \cos x \text{ which was to be shown}$$

Product Rule

If $f(x) = g(x)h(x)$, then $f'(x) = g(x)h'(x) + h(x)g'(x)$.

Translation: The derivative of a product of two functions equals (first)(derivative of the second) + (second)(derivative of the first)

Quotient Rule

If $f(x) = \dfrac{g(x)}{h(x)}$, where $h(x) \neq 0$, then

$$f'(x) = \frac{h(x)g'(x) - g(x)h'(x)}{[h(x)]^2}$$

Translation: The derivative of a quotient of two functions equals

$$\frac{(\text{bottom})(\text{derivative of the top}) - (\text{top})(\text{derivative of the bottom})}{(\text{bottom})^2}$$

To date, the proofs of these two rules have not been listed on the outline for the AP exam. However, it may be worthwhile to look at examples of problems done two ways, first without the use of the rules and then with them, to verify their validity.

First, for the product rule, find the derivative of the function $f(x) = (4x^2)(3x^5)$. Obviously, this function can first be simplified, and the derivative taken with the power rule.

$$f(x) = (4x^2)(3x^5) \Rightarrow f(x) = 12x^7$$
$$\Rightarrow f'(x) = 12(7x^6) = 84x^6$$

This is the logical method to use if presented with such a problem. Now, without simplifying, use the product rule to find the derivative.

$$f(x) = (4x^2)(3x^5)$$
$$f'(x) = (4x^2)(15x^4) + (3x^5)(8x)$$
$$= 60x^6 + 24x^6 = 84x^6 \text{ which is the same result as above}$$

Second, for the quotient rule, find $f'(x)$ for the function $f(x) = 12x^5/2x^3$.

Again, simplifying first gives

$$f(x) = \frac{12x^5}{2x^3} = 6x^2 \Rightarrow f'(x) = 12x$$

And applying the quotient rule with the original version yields

$$f(x) = \frac{12x^5}{2x^3} \Rightarrow f'(x) = \frac{(2x^3)(60x^4) - (12x^5)(6x^2)}{(2x^3)^2}$$

$$= \frac{120x^7 - 72x^7}{4x^6}$$

$$= \frac{48x^7}{4x^6} = 12x \text{ which is the same result as above}$$

Although these two examples are by no means valid as proofs of the product and quotient rules, they do serve as convincing evidence of the validity of both techniques. With many problems, it may be impossible to simplify first, and use of the product or quotient rules will be required, as in the next example.

Sample

For $f(x) = 3x^2 \sin x$, find $f'(\pi)$.

It may help to put parentheses around the first function and the second function before differentiating.

$$f(x) = 3x^2 \sin x = (3x^2)(\sin x)$$
$$f'(x) = (3x^2)(\cos x) + (\sin x)(6x)$$
$$f'(\pi) = 3(\pi)^2 \cos \pi + (\sin \pi) 6(\pi)$$
$$= 3\pi^2(-1) + (0) 6\pi$$
$$= -3\pi^2$$

A variation on this approach is to factor out a 3 to begin with and then choose the first and second functions.

$$f(x) = 3x^2 \sin x = 3[(x^2)(\sin x)]$$
$$f'(x) = 3[(x^2)(\cos x) + (\sin x)(2x)]$$
$$= (3x^2)(\cos x) + (\sin x)(6x) \text{ which is the same as } f'(x) \text{ above}$$

Sample

Find $\dfrac{d}{dt}\left(\dfrac{2\sqrt{t}}{\tan t}\right)$.

First rewrite the numerator with a rational exponent. Then apply the quotient rule.

$$\frac{d}{dt}\left(\frac{2\sqrt{t}}{\tan t}\right) = \frac{d}{dt}\left(\frac{2t^{1/2}}{\tan t}\right)$$

$$= \frac{(\tan t)\left(2 \cdot \frac{1}{2} t^{-1/2}\right) - \left(2t^{1/2}\right)\left(\sec^2 t\right)}{(\tan t)^2}$$

$$= \frac{\dfrac{1}{\sqrt{t}}\tan t - 2\sqrt{t}\sec^2 t}{\tan^2 t}\left(\frac{\sqrt{t}}{\sqrt{t}}\right)$$

$$= \frac{\tan t - 2t\sec^2 t}{\sqrt{t}\tan^2 t}$$

This answer could be rewritten in other forms by using trig identities.

$$= \frac{\left(\frac{\sin t}{\cos t}\right) - 2t\left(\frac{1}{\cos t}\right)^2}{\sqrt{t}\left(\frac{\sin t}{\cos t}\right)^2}\left(\frac{\cos^2 t}{\cos^2 t}\right)$$

$$= \frac{\sin t \cos t - 2t}{\sqrt{t}\sin^2 t}$$

Some students try to avoid the quotient rule by rewriting quotients as products with negative exponents. This is a perfectly valid technique to use.

Sample

Find $\dfrac{d}{dt}\left(\dfrac{2\sqrt{t}}{\tan t}\right)$ by using the product rule.

$$\frac{d}{dt}\left(\frac{2\sqrt{t}}{\tan t}\right) = \frac{d}{dt}[(2\sqrt{t})(\tan t)^{-1}]$$

$$= \frac{d}{dt}\left[(2t^{1/2})(\cot t)\right]$$

$$= (2t^{1/2})(-\csc^2 t) + (\cot t)\left(2 \cdot \tfrac{1}{2}t^{-1/2}\right)$$

$$= -2t^{1/2}\csc^2 t + t^{-1/2}\cot t$$

$$= t^{-1/2}\left[-2t\csc^2 t + \cot t\right]$$

$$= t^{-1/2}\left[\frac{-2t}{\sin^2 t} + \frac{\cos t}{\sin t}\right]$$

$$= t^{-1/2}\left[\frac{-2t + \sin t \cos t}{\sin^2 t}\right]$$

$$= \frac{\sin t \cos t - 2t}{\sqrt{t}\sin^2 t} \text{ which is the same result as above}$$

The Chain Rule

Many functions have arguments that are in themselves functions, such as

$$y = \sin(2x) \text{ or } y = \ln(3x^2)$$

To differentiate composite functions such as these requires the use of the chain rule.

Chain Rule

$$\frac{d}{dx}[f(g(x))] = f'(g(x))\,g'(x)$$

Translation: To find the derivative of a composite function, take the derivative of the exterior function, retaining the interior function inside this derivative, and then multiply by the derivative of the interior function.

Although the proof of the chain rule is not required for the AP exam, an example of a problem that can be differentiated both with and without the chain rule may help convince you that it really works. Say you are given $y = (3x^2)^4$, and asked to find dy/dx. First, simplify and apply the power rule.

$$y = (3x^2)^4 \Rightarrow y = 81x^8$$
$$\Rightarrow y' = 648x^7$$

Now, without simplifying, apply the chain rule to find the derivative. Identify the interior and exterior functions by writing it as a composition.

$$f(x) = x^4 \text{ and } g(x) = 3x^2 \Rightarrow f(g(x)) = (3x^2)^4$$
$$\Rightarrow f'(x) = 4x^3 \qquad g'(x) = 6x$$

Thus $f'(g(x))\,g'(x) = f'(3x^2)(6x)$
$$= 4(3x^2)^3(6x)$$
$$= 4(27x^6)6x = 648x^7 \text{ which is the same result as above}$$

When doing a problem with the chain rule, it is usually too much work to actually write out the individual functions and their derivatives. More typically, the solution appears this way:

$$y = (3x^2)^4 \Rightarrow y' = 4(3x^2)^3(6x)$$
$$= 4(27x^6)6x = 648x^7$$

Simplifying first may be impossible or impractical, and you may be required to use the chain rule, as in the next example.

Sample

For $y = 4\sin(3x)$, find $\left. \dfrac{dy}{dx} \right|_{x = \pi}$.

Identify the exterior and interior functions, either mentally or by writing out the composition.

$$y = 4\sin(3x) = f(g(x)) \text{ where } f(x) = 4\sin x \text{ (exterior function)}$$
$$\text{and } g(x) = 3x \text{ (interior function)}$$

$$\Rightarrow \frac{dy}{dx} = 4\cos(3x)(3)$$
$$= 12\cos(3x)$$
$$\Rightarrow \frac{dy}{dx}\bigg|_{x=\pi} = 12\cos(3\pi) = 12(-1) = -12$$

Sample

For $f(x) = 3x^4\sqrt{2x^2 + 10x}$, find $f'(1)$.

First rewrite $f(x)$ with a fractional exponent, and then use the product rule, along with the chain rule. The chain rule portion of the derivative is underlined.

$$f(x) = 3x^4\sqrt{2x^2 + 10x} = 3x^4(2x^2 + 10x)^{1/2}$$

$$f'(x) = (3x^4)\left[\tfrac{1}{2}(2x^2 + 10x)^{-1/2}\left(\underline{4x + 10}\right)\right] + (2x^2 + 10x)^{1/2}(12x^3)$$

$$= 3x^4(2x^2 + 10x)^{-1/2}(2x + 5) + 12x^3(2x^2 + 10x)^{1/2}$$

Because the question asks for the derivative at a specific point, it is probably easier to substitute now, rather than spending a great deal of time simplifying the general derivative.

$$f'(1) = 3\frac{1}{\sqrt{12}}(7) + 12\sqrt{12} = \frac{21}{2\sqrt{3}} + 24\sqrt{3} = \frac{21\sqrt{3}}{6} + 24\sqrt{3}$$

$$= \frac{165\sqrt{3}}{6} = \frac{55\sqrt{3}}{2}$$

You should be aware of the forms in which multiple-choice answers typically appear on the AP exam. In the foregoing problem, the general derivative $f'(x)$ would probably have appeared in factored form, where one term is a polynomial with integral coefficients:

$$f'(x) = 3x^4(2x^2 + 10x)^{-1/2}(2x + 5) + 12x^3(2x^2 + 10x)^{1/2}$$

$$= \left[3x^3(2x^2 + 10x)^{-1/2}\right]\left[x(2x + 5) + 4(2x^2 + 10x)\right]$$

$$= \left[3x^3(2x^2 + 10x)^{-1/2}\right]\left[10x^2 + 45x\right]$$

$$= \frac{15x^3(2x^2 + 9x)}{\sqrt{2x^2 + 10x}} = \frac{15x^4(2x + 9)}{\sqrt{2x^2 + 10x}}$$

The chain rule is sometimes also written in a different notation, which is useful for listing differentiation rules for composite functions.

Alternative Form of the Chain Rule

$\frac{dy}{dx} = \left(\frac{dy}{dx}\right)\left(\frac{du}{dx}\right)$ where y is a differentiable function of u and u is a differentiable function of x

This results in new forms of the familiar differentiation rules.

Power Rule with Chain

If u is a differentiable function of x, then $\dfrac{d}{dx}(u^n) = nu^{n-1}\dfrac{du}{dx}$.

Trig Rules with Chain

$$\frac{d}{dx}(\sin u) = \cos u \frac{du}{dx}$$

$$\frac{d}{dx}(\cos u) = -\sin u \frac{du}{dx}$$

$$\frac{d}{dx}(\tan u) = \sec^2 u \frac{du}{dx}$$

$$\frac{d}{dx}(\sec u) = \sec u \tan u \frac{du}{dx}$$

$$\frac{d}{dx}(\csc u) = -\csc u \cot u \frac{du}{dx}$$

$$\frac{d}{dx}(\cot u) = -\csc^2 u \frac{du}{dx}$$

All differentiation rules from now on will be given in their chain rule forms, u being a differentiable function of x. Occasionally, when there are functions that are "nested" three or more deep, you may need to use the chain rule more than once.

Sample

> If $y = \sec^3(5t)$, find $\dfrac{dy}{dt}$.

Rewrite the power with brackets, and then use the power rule to differentiate.

$$y = \sec^3(5t) = [\sec(5t)]^3$$
$$\Rightarrow \frac{dy}{dt} = 3[\sec(5t)]^2 \frac{d}{dt}(\sec(5t))$$
$$= 3[\sec(5t)]^2[\sec(5t)\tan(5t)\,5]$$
$$= 15\sec^3(5t)\tan(5t)$$

Note that in the second line above, the chain rule is indicated with derivative notation, rather than by immediately writing the derivative of the interior function. This technique may be helpful when the interior function has its own interior function. If you prefer, skip this second line. In any event, do not forget about the "extra" factor of 5. The 5 comes from a second use of the chain rule, where you are finding the derivative of the innermost function ($5t$).

Higher-Order Derivatives

Higher-order derivatives result from taking derivatives of derivatives. For example,

$$\text{if} \qquad f(x) = 3x^5 + 5x^2 - 2x + 12$$
$$\text{then} \qquad f'(x) = 15x^4 + 10x - 2$$
$$\text{and} \qquad f''(x) = 60x^3 + 10$$

Here the prime notation has been extended to include a double prime, indicating the second derivative — that is, the derivative of the first derivative. Taking the derivative of the second derivative yields the third derivative, which is indicated with a triple prime:

$$f'''(x) = 180x^2$$

This process and notation can be extended to include derivatives of any order. However, to avoid the need to count many primes, small Roman or Arabic numerals are used in the prime position for fourth-order derivatives and higher:

$$f^{iv}(x) = 360x \text{ or } f^4(x) = 360x$$

The differential notation can also be modified to allow for higher derivatives:

$$y = f(x)$$

$$\frac{dy}{dx} = f'(x)$$

$$\frac{d^2y}{dx^2} = f''(x)$$

$$\frac{d^3y}{dx^3} = f'''(x)$$

$$\frac{d^4y}{dx^4} = f^{iv}(x) = f^4(x)$$

etc.

Derivatives of Exponential Functions

The easiest derivative rule in calculus involves the exponential function, because the function $y = e^x$ is its own derivative. (The proof that $y = e^x$ is its own derivative is based on the definition of the natural log function and the properties of inverses. It is not on the AP exam.) Derivative rules for the other exponential functions, such as $y = a^x$, are also quite easy. Exponential functions appear quite regularly on both the multiple-choice and free-response sections of the AP exam.

Exponential Rule

$$\frac{d}{dx}(e^u) = e^u \frac{du}{dx}$$

Translation: The derivative of the exponential function is the exponential function (with the chain rule when applicable).

Sample

Find $\frac{d}{dx}(e^{2-3x^2})$

Begin by simply recopying the function, and then put in the chain rule.

$$\frac{d}{dx}(e^{2-3x^2}) = (e^{2-3x^2})(-6x)$$
$$= -6xe^{2-3x^2}$$

Sample

For $s(t) = \frac{5e^{3t}}{\cos 4t}$, find $s'(0)$.

This problem requires use of the quotient rule, plus the trig and exponential rules. Both the exponential function and the trig function will require use of the chain rule.

$$s(t) = \frac{5e^{3t}}{\cos 4t} \Rightarrow s'(t) = \frac{(\cos 4t)(5e^{3t} \cdot 3) - (5e^{3t})(-\sin 4t \cdot 4)}{(\cos 4t)^2}$$

$$= \frac{15e^{3t}\cos 4t + 20e^{3t}\sin 4t}{\cos^2 4t}$$

$$= \frac{5e^{3t}(3\cos 4t + 4\sin 4t)}{\cos^2 t}$$

Thus $s'(0) = \frac{5e^0(3\cos 0 + 4\sin 0)}{\cos^2 0}$

$$= \frac{5(3+0)}{1} = 15$$

Base-*a* Exponentials Rule

$$\frac{d}{dx}(a^u) = (\ln a)(a^u)\left(\frac{du}{dx}\right)$$

Translation: To find the derivatives of base-*a* exponential functions, put in an "extra" factor of ln *a*, recopy the function, and then use the chain rule if needed.

Although the derivation of this rule is not on the AP exam, it can be used as a pattern for finding these types of derivatives if you don't want to bother memorizing the rule. The derivation is based on rewriting the exponential base of e and then using the previous rule.

$$y = a^u \Leftrightarrow y = (e^{\ln a})^u \qquad \text{because } e^{\ln a} = a$$
$$\Leftrightarrow y = e^{(\ln a)(u)}$$

Now differentiate.

$$\frac{dy}{dx} = [e^{(\ln a)(u)}](\ln a)\left(\frac{du}{dx}\right)$$
$$= (a^u)(\ln a)\left(\frac{du}{dx}\right)$$

Be aware that in the foregoing differentiation, $\ln a$ is a constant. When the chain rule is applied, the factor of $\ln a$ shows up just the same way that $-6x$ shows up in the first example above.

Sample

> Find the derivative of $y = 10^{\cos 2x}$.

This derivative can be found in either of two ways: by applying the role directly or by following the pattern used in the derivation of the role. Using the rule yields

$$y = 10^{\cos 2x} \Rightarrow \frac{dy}{dx} = (\ln 10)(10^{\cos 2x})(-\sin 2x \cdot 2)$$
$$= -2 \ln 10 \sin 2x \cdot 10^{\cos 2x}$$

Following the pattern of the derivation yields

$$y = 10^{\cos 2x} \Rightarrow y = (e^{\ln 10})^{(\cos 2x)}$$
$$y = e^{(\ln 10)(\cos 2x)}$$
$$\frac{dy}{dx} = [e^{(\ln 10)(\cos 2x)}](\ln 10)(-\sin 2x \cdot 2)$$
$$= (10^{\cos 2x})(\ln 10)(-\sin 2x \cdot 2)$$
$$= -2 \ln 10 \sin x \cdot 10^{\cos 2x}$$

Derivatives of Logarithmic Functions

Derivatives of the natural logarithm function, and those of other logarithms of other bases, are often used as free-response problems on the AP exam. You should already be familiar with the properties of logarithms, as well as with the graphs of log functions.

Natural Log Rule

$$\frac{d}{dx}(\ln u) = \frac{1}{u}\frac{du}{dx} \qquad \text{or, alternatively} \qquad \frac{d}{dx}(\ln u) = \frac{u'}{u}$$

Translation: The derivative of the natural log is found by taking the reciprocal of the argument and then applying the chain rule if needed.

Notice that the natural log function does not appear anywhere in the derivative. Although this may seem strange, it is easily proved by examining the definition of the natural log function (see pages 273–274).

Sample

Find the slope of the line tangent to $f(x) = \ln(4x + 3x^2)$ at the point where $x = 2$.

For slope, find the value of the derivative at $x = 2$ — that is, $f'(2)$.

$$f(x) = \ln(4x + 3x^2) \Rightarrow f'(x) = \left(\frac{1}{4x + 3x^2}\right)(4 + 6x)$$

$$= \frac{4 + 6x}{4x + 3x^2}$$

So
$$f'(2) = \frac{4 + 12}{8 + 12} = \frac{16}{20} = \frac{4}{5}$$

Therefore, the slope of the tangent line at $x = 2$ is $\frac{4}{5}$.

Base-*a* Logarithms Rule

$$\frac{d}{dx}(\log_a u) = \left(\frac{1}{\ln a}\right)\left(\frac{1}{u}\right)\left(\frac{du}{dx}\right) = \frac{1}{(\ln a)u}\left(\frac{du}{dx}\right)$$

Translation: To find the derivative of base-*a* logarithms, put in an "extra" factor of $1/\ln a$, the reciprocal of the argument, and then apply the chain rule if needed.

As with the base-*a* exponentials, it may be prudent to know the derivation of this rule, rather than simply memorizing it. The derivation uses the change-of-base formula from precalculus math,

$$\log_a m = \frac{\ln m}{\ln a}$$

(In fact, the change-of-base formula holds true for any base, not just base e. Base e is chosen to allow use of the previous derivative rule.)

Prove: $\qquad \frac{d}{dx}(\log_a u) = \left(\frac{1}{\ln a}\right)\left(\frac{1}{u}\right)\left(\frac{du}{dx}\right)$

Proof: $\qquad y = \log_a u \Leftrightarrow y = \frac{\ln u}{\ln a} = \left(\frac{1}{\ln a}\right)(\ln u)$

$$\Rightarrow \frac{dy}{dx} = \left(\frac{1}{\ln a}\right)\left(\frac{1}{u}\right)\left(\frac{du}{dx}\right)$$

the change-of-base formula which was to be shown

Sample

Find the derivative of $p(r) = \log_4(\tan 3r)$.

Applying the rule directly yields

$$p(r) = \log_4(\tan 3r) \Rightarrow p'(r) = \left(\frac{1}{\ln 4}\right)\left(\frac{1}{\tan 3r}\right)(\sec^2 3r \cdot 3)$$
$$= \left(\frac{3}{\ln 4}\right)\left(\frac{\sec^2 3r}{\tan 3r}\right)$$

Sometimes the answer may appear in a different form in the multiple-choice section, as shown here:

$$= \left(\frac{3}{\ln 4}\right)\left(\frac{\frac{1}{\cos^2 3r}}{\frac{\sin 3r}{\cos 3r}}\right)$$
$$= \left(\frac{3}{\ln 4}\right)\left(\frac{1}{\cos 3r \sin 3r}\right)$$
$$= \left(\frac{3}{\ln 4}\right)(\sec 3r \csc 3r)$$

Alternatively, following the pattern of the derivation yields

$$p(r) = \log_4(\tan 3r) \Leftrightarrow p(r) = \frac{\ln(\tan 3r)}{\ln 4} = \left(\frac{1}{\ln 4}\right)\ln(\tan 3r)$$
$$\Rightarrow p'(r) = \left(\frac{1}{\ln 4}\right)\left(\frac{1}{\tan 3r}\right)(\sec^2 3r \cdot 3)$$

Finish as above.

Derivatives of Inverse Trigonometric Functions

The derivatives of the inverse trig functions do not contain any trig functions, let alone any inverse trig functions. The proofs of all six formulas are very similar, and even though they have not been listed on the outline for the AP exam to date, the proof for the derivative of $y = \arcsin x$ is included here. The property of the derivatives of inverses that is used in this proof could be on the AP exam.

Comment on notation: As mentioned previously, several equivalent notations for the inverse trig functions can be used:

$$y = \arcsin x \qquad y = \text{Arc}\sin x \qquad y = \sin^{-1} x$$

Recent AP exams have used the first two; most calculators use the third.

Inverse Trig Rules

$$\frac{d}{dx}(\arcsin u) = \frac{1}{\sqrt{1-u^2}}\left(\frac{du}{dx}\right)$$

$$\frac{d}{dx}(\arccos u) = \frac{-1}{\sqrt{1-u^2}}\left(\frac{du}{dx}\right)$$

$$\frac{d}{dx}(\arctan u) = \frac{1}{1+u^2}\left(\frac{du}{dx}\right)$$

$$\frac{d}{dx}(\operatorname{arc cot} u) = \frac{-1}{1+u^2}\left(\frac{du}{dx}\right)$$

$$\frac{d}{dx}(\operatorname{arc sec} u) = \frac{1}{|u|\sqrt{u^2-1}}\left(\frac{du}{dx}\right)$$

$$\frac{d}{dx}(\operatorname{arc csc} u) = \frac{-1}{|u|\sqrt{u^2-1}}\left(\frac{du}{dx}\right)$$

Memorization hint: The derivatives of co-functions are exact opposites. For example, the derivative of arccos u (a co-function) differs from the derivative of arcsin u only by the -1 in the numerator.

Sample

> Find the derivative of $y = \operatorname{arc sec}(e^{3x})$.

Apply the appropriate rule, with $u = e^{3x}$.

$$y = \operatorname{arc sec}(e^{3x}) \Rightarrow \frac{dy}{dx} = \frac{1}{\left|e^{3x}\right|\sqrt{(e^{3x})^2 - 1}}\frac{d}{dx}(e^{3x})$$

$$= \frac{1}{e^{3x}\sqrt{e^{6x}-1}}(e^{3x}\cdot 3)$$

$$= \frac{3}{\sqrt{e^{6x}-1}}$$

The chain rule in the first line of the derivative is written in derivative notation to begin with. This is better than attempting too much mental work in one step. Also note that the absolute-value bars in the third line were dropped because $e^{3x}x$ is positive for any value of x.

Derivatives of Inverses

If $f(x)$ and $g(x)$ are inverses, then $g'(x) = \dfrac{1}{f'(g(x))}$.

Proof: Because $f(x)$ and $g(x)$ are inverses, $f(g(x)) = x$.

Differentiate this last line with respect to x.

$$f'(g(x))g'(x) = 1 \Rightarrow g'(x) = \frac{1}{f'(g(x))} \text{ which was to be shown}$$

The following proof is for the basic derivative of arcsin x, without the chain rule.

Prove: $\dfrac{d}{dx}(\arcsin x) = \dfrac{1}{\sqrt{1-x^2}}$

Proof: First, let

$$f(x) = \sin x \text{ and } g(x) = \arcsin x$$
$$\Rightarrow f'(x) = \cos x \text{ and } g'(x) = \dfrac{d}{dx}(\arcsin x)$$

Because $f(x)$ and $g(x)$ are inverses, apply the foregoing result.

$$g'(x) = \dfrac{1}{f'(g(x))} = \dfrac{1}{\cos(\arcsin x)}$$

To simplify this expression, label a triangle, as shown here, with acute angle θ.

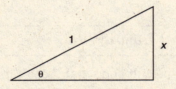

Figure 3.6

$$\sin\theta = x \Rightarrow \arcsin x = \theta$$
$$\Rightarrow \cos(\arcsin x) = \cos\theta$$

Using the Pythagorean theorem, label the rest of the triangle as shown.

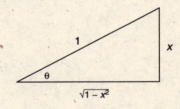

Figure 3.7

$$\Rightarrow \cos\theta = \sqrt{1-x^2}$$

Returning to the proof,

$$\dfrac{d}{dx}(\arcsin x) = g'(x) = \dfrac{1}{f'(g(x))} = \dfrac{1}{\cos(\arcsin x)}$$
$$= \dfrac{1}{\cos\theta} = \dfrac{1}{\sqrt{1-x^2}}$$

which was to be shown.

Implicit Differentiation

Implicit differentiation is not so much a differentiation rule to memorize as a technique to use in conjunction with the other differentiation rules. Implicit differentiation is used when it is either difficult or impossible to express the function or relation explicitly — that is, as a function of a single independent variable. Under these conditions, simply differentiate both sides of the equation one term at a time, using whatever rules are needed (product, quotient, trig, and so on). The important thing to remember, however, is the chain rule. You will be differentiating with respect to a specific variable (say x). Thus, whenever you differentiate an expression that is not strictly in terms of x (say an expression with y in it), you must be sure to include the appropriate chain expression: dy/dx. Be sure to do this every time you differentiate such an expression, but only at that time.

Sample

> Given that $y^2 - 6x^2 = 3x + 5y - 12$, find dy/dx.

Solving for y explicitly would be difficult and would result in a rather messy expression to try to differentiate, so use implicit differentiation. Differentiate term by term with respect to x, putting in dy/dx when differentiating a term with y in it.

$$y^2 - 6x^2 = 3x + 5y - 12$$
$$\Rightarrow 2y\frac{dy}{dx} - 12x = 3 + 5\frac{dy}{dx} - 0$$

Now solve this equation for the expression dy/dx.

$$2y\frac{dy}{dx} - 5\frac{dy}{dx} = 12x + 3$$
$$\frac{dy}{dx}(2y - 5) = 12x + 3$$
$$\frac{dy}{dx} = \frac{12x + 3}{2y - 5}$$

The final answer is in terms of both x and y. This is fairly typical of problems done with implicit differentiation. If you are asked to evaluate such a derivative, you may need to take the preliminary step of finding other values first, as shown in the next example.

Sample

> Evaluate $\left.\dfrac{dy}{dx}\right|_{x=1}$ where $y^2 - 6x^2 = 3x + 5y - 12$.

From above, $\dfrac{dy}{dx} = \dfrac{12x + 3}{2y - 5}$

Because x and y are both required to evaluate this expression, substitute $x = 1$ into the original equation and solve for y.

$$y^2 - 6x^2 = 3x + 5y - 12$$
$$x = 1 \Rightarrow y^2 - 6 = 3 + 5y - 12$$
$$y^2 - 5y + 3 = 0 \Rightarrow y = \frac{5 \pm \sqrt{13}}{2}$$

Therefore, $\left. \dfrac{dy}{dx} \right|_{x=1} = \dfrac{12(1) + 3}{2\left(\dfrac{5 \pm \sqrt{13}}{2}\right) - 5} = \dfrac{15}{\pm\sqrt{13}} = \pm\dfrac{15\sqrt{13}}{13}$

Sample

> For $\sin(2x + 3y) = e^{4x} - 2y + 7$, find dy/dx.

It would be nearly impossible to solve this equation for y, so differentiate term by term with respect to x, and then solve for dy/dx.

$$\sin(2x + 3y) = e^{4x} - 2y + 7$$
$$\Rightarrow [\cos(2x + 3y)]\left[2 + 3\frac{dy}{dx}\right] = e^{4x} \cdot 4 - 2\frac{dy}{dx} + 0$$
$$2\cos(2x + 3y) + 3\frac{dy}{dx}\cos(2x + 3y) = 4e^{4x} - 2\frac{dy}{dx}$$
$$3\frac{dy}{dx}\cos(2x + 3y) + 2\frac{dy}{dx} = -2\cos(2x + 3y) + 4e^{4x}$$
$$\frac{dy}{dx}[3\cos(2x + 3y) + 2] = -2\cos(2x + 3y) + 4e^{4x}$$

Therefore
$$\frac{dy}{dx} = \frac{-2\cos(2x + 3y) + 4e^{4x}}{3\cos(2x + 3y) + 2}$$

It is also possible to find higher-order derivatives by using implicit differentiation.

Sample

> Find d^2y/dx^2 implicitly, where $x^2 - y^2 = 8$.

Begin by finding the first derivative.

$$x^2 - y^2 = 8$$
$$\Rightarrow 2x - 2y\frac{dy}{dx} = 0$$
$$\frac{dy}{dx} = \frac{-2x}{-2y} = \frac{x}{y}$$

Now differentiate both sides of this last line with respect to x. The left side becomes the second derivative. Use a quotient rule for the right side.

$$\frac{d^2 y}{dx^2} = \frac{(y)(1) - (x)\left(\dfrac{dy}{dx}\right)}{y^2}$$

Now substitute for dy/dx.

$$\frac{d^2 y}{dx^2} = \frac{(y)(1) - (x)\left(\dfrac{dy}{dx}\right)}{y^2} = \frac{y - x\left(\dfrac{x}{y}\right)}{y^2}$$

$$= \frac{y - \dfrac{x^2}{y}}{y^2}\left(\frac{y}{y}\right)$$

$$= \frac{y^2 - x^2}{y^3}$$

This is a perfectly acceptable answer. However, if it does not appear as one of the choices on a multiple-choice problem, check to see whether it is possible to substitute from the original equation. In this case,

$$x^2 - y^2 = 8 \Rightarrow y^2 - x^2 = -8$$
$$\Rightarrow \frac{d^2 y}{dx^2} = \frac{y^2 - x^2}{y^3} = \frac{-8}{y^3}$$

Logarithmic Differentiation

Like implicit differentiation, log differentiation is a technique to be used in conjunction with other derivative rules, rather than a rule itself. When a function has the independent variable in both base and exponent, such as $y = x^{3x+1}$, you cannot use the power rule or the exponential rule, although it is tempting to do so. You need to take the log of both sides in order to apply the log properties and bring the exponent "down" to the base position. To successfully apply log differentiation, remember the following important properties from previous sections:

$$\ln a^b = b \ln a \quad \text{and} \quad \frac{d}{dx}(\ln y) = \frac{1}{y}\frac{dy}{dx}$$

Sample

> Given $f(x) = x^{3x^2 - 5}$, find $f'(x)$.

Because there are x's in both the base and the exponent, use log differentiation.

$$f(x) = x^{3x^2 - 5}$$
$$y = x^{3x^2 - 5}$$

Take the natural log of both sides.

$$\ln(y) = \ln[x^{3x^2 - 5}]$$

Use the log property: $\ln a^b = b \ln a$.

$$\ln y = (3x^2 - 5)(\ln x)$$

Differentiate both sides with respect to x, including dy/dx for the chain rule.

$$\frac{1}{y}\frac{dy}{dx} = (3x^2 - 5)\left(\frac{1}{x}\right) + (\ln x)(6x)$$

Solve for dy/dx.

$$\frac{dy}{dx} = y\left[3x - \frac{5}{x} + 6x\ln x\right]$$

Substitute for y.

$$= (x^{3x^2 - 5})\left[3x - \frac{5}{x} + 6x\ln x\right]$$

This answer is perfectly fine. However, if it is not one of the choices on a multiple-choice question, consider doing the following force factoring:

$$\frac{dy}{dx} = (x^{3x^2 - 5})\left(\frac{1}{x}\right)[3x^2 - 5 + 6x^2\ln x]$$

$$= (x^{3x^2 - 5})(x^{-1})[3x^2 - 5 + 6x^2\ln x]$$

$$\Rightarrow f'(x) = (x^{3x^2 - 6})[3x^2 - 5 + 6x^2\ln x]$$

Sample

Given $f(x) = x^{3x^2 - 5}$, find the equation of the line tangent to the curve at the point where $x = 1$.

From the previous example,

$$f'(x) = (x^{3x^2 - 6})[3x^2 - 5 + 6x^2\ln x]$$
$$\Rightarrow f'(1) = (1)(3 - 5 + 6 \cdot 0) = -2$$

which is the slope of the tangent line. And because $f(1) = 1$, the equation is

$$y - 1 = -2(x - 1)$$
$$y = -2x + 3$$

Parametric Derivatives (BC Only)

The parametric forms of the first and second derivatives are a direct result of the chain rule. The usual applications for derivatives, e.g., slope of a tangent line and concavity, use these formulas.

Parametric Form of the Derivative

If a smooth* curve is given parametrically by $x = f(t)$ and $y = g(t)$, then the derivative, dy/dx, is given by

$$\frac{dy}{dx} = \frac{\frac{dy}{dt}}{\frac{dx}{dt}}, \quad \frac{dx}{dt} \neq 0$$

Note: A curve is smooth if both *dx/dt* and *dy/dt* are continuous and not simultaneously 0. In practice, this means that the derivative of a parametrically defined curve does NOT exist at a sharp turn, known as a "cusp," where both *dx/dt* AND *dy/dt* are 0.

Parametric Form of the Second Derivative

To find the second derivative of a parametrically defined function, differentiate both sides of the first derivative equation with respect to x. However, since the first derivative is a function of the parameter t, it is necessary to include the chain rule:

$$\frac{dy}{dx} = \frac{\frac{dy}{dt}}{\frac{dx}{dt}} = D(t) \quad \text{some function of } t, \text{ call it } D(t)$$

Differentiating both sides with respect to x,

$$\frac{d^2 y}{dx^2} = D'(t) \cdot \frac{dt}{dx}$$

$$\frac{d^2 y}{dx^2} = \frac{D'(t)}{\frac{dx}{dt}} = \frac{\frac{d\left[\frac{dy}{dx}\right]}{dt}}{\frac{dx}{dt}}$$

Sample

For the curve below, find the slope of the tangent line at any point. Use it to determine if the graph has any horizontal tangents. Also determine where the graph is concave up and concave down.

$$x = 5 - t^2 \quad y = t^2 + 3t$$

A sketch of this graph is shown below.

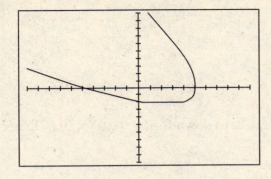

```
WINDOW
  Tmin =-10
  Tmax =10
  Tstep =1
  Xmin =-10
  Xmax =10
  Xscl =1
  Ymin=-10
  Ymax=10
  Yscl=1
```

For the first derivative,

$$\frac{dy}{dx} = \frac{\frac{dy}{dt}}{\frac{dx}{dt}} = \frac{2t+3}{-2t}$$

which is the slope of the tangent line at any point.

For a horizontal tangent, the derivative must be 0, so here the numerator needs to be 0 while the denominator is NOT 0.

$$2t + 3 = 0$$
$$2t = -3$$
$$t = -1.5$$

Thus, the graph has a horizontal tangent where $t = -1.5$, at the point (2.75, –2.25).

For the second derivative,

$$\frac{d^2 y}{dx^2} = \frac{\frac{d\left[\frac{2t+3}{-2t}\right]}{dt}}{\frac{dx}{dt}}$$

$$= \frac{\frac{(-2t)(2) - (2t+3)(-2)}{(-2t)^2}}{-2t}$$

$$= \frac{-4t + 4t + 6}{(-2t)^3}$$

$$= \frac{6}{-8t^3}$$

$$= \frac{-3}{4t^3}$$

For critical numbers,

$$\frac{d^2 y}{dx^2} = 0 \;\; \text{or} \;\; \frac{d^2 y}{dx^2} \;\; \text{D.N.E.}$$

never $\xleftarrow[\;\;\;\; 0 \;\;\;\;]{+ \;\; -} \dfrac{d^2 y}{dx^2}$

Thus, the graph is concave up for $t < 0$ and concave down for $t > 0$, so (5, 0) (where $t = 0$) is an inflection point.

Differentiation with Polar Curves (BC Only)

Differentiating polar equations typically requires finding one of two different expressions, $dr/d\theta$ or dy/dx. The first, $dr/d\theta$, gives the instantaneous rate of change of r with respect to θ. It might be necessary to find $dr/d\theta$ for a simple multiple-choice problem, or to find out the rate of change of the radius with respect to the angle as a particle moves along a polar curve. The second expression, dy/dx, is used to find the slope of a tangent line, and can be derived from the basic polar expressions.

Sample

> Find $dr/d\theta$ for $r = 3 + 2\sin(3\theta)$.

$r = 3 + 2\sin(3\theta)$

$\dfrac{dr}{d\theta} = 2\cos(3\theta) \cdot 3$

$\qquad = 6\cos(3\theta)$

Caution: The expression $dr/d\theta$ does NOT represent the slope of the line tangent to a polar curve.

Slope in Polar

The basic polar equations, $x = r\cos\theta$ and $y = r\sin\theta$, can each be differentiated with respect to θ. The quotient of these two expressions, $dy/d\theta$ and $dx/d\theta$, then yields the formula for dy/dx and the slope of a tangent line.

$$x = r\cos\theta \qquad\qquad\qquad y = r\sin\theta$$

$$\frac{dx}{d\theta} = r(-\sin\theta) + \cos\theta\left(\frac{dr}{d\theta}\right) \qquad \frac{dy}{d\theta} = r(\cos\theta) + \sin\theta\left(\frac{dr}{d\theta}\right)$$

$$\frac{dy}{dx} = \frac{\frac{dy}{d\theta}}{\frac{dx}{d\theta}} = \frac{r\cos\theta + \sin\theta\frac{dr}{d\theta}}{-r\sin\theta + \cos\theta\frac{dr}{d\theta}}$$

It may be easier to derive this formula as above than to try and memorize it.

Sample

Find the slope of the line tangent to $r = 2 - 2\cos\theta$ at the point where $\theta = \pi/4$.

$$\frac{dy}{dx} = \frac{r\cos\theta + \sin\theta\frac{dr}{d\theta}}{-r\sin\theta + \cos\theta\frac{dr}{d\theta}}$$

$$= \frac{(2 - 2\cos\theta)\cos\theta + \sin\theta(2\sin\theta)}{-(2 - 2\cos\theta)\sin\theta + \cos\theta(2\sin\theta)}$$

$$\left.\frac{dy}{dx}\right|_{\theta = \frac{\pi}{4}} = \frac{(2 - 2\cos\frac{\pi}{4})\cos\frac{\pi}{4} + 2(\sin\frac{\pi}{4})^2}{-(2 - 2\cos\frac{\pi}{4})\sin\frac{\pi}{4} + 2(\cos\frac{\pi}{4})(\sin\frac{\pi}{4})}$$

$$= \frac{(2 - 2\cdot\frac{\sqrt{2}}{2})(\frac{\sqrt{2}}{2}) + 2(\frac{\sqrt{2}}{2})^2}{-(2 - 2\cdot\frac{\sqrt{2}}{2})\frac{\sqrt{2}}{2} + 2(\frac{\sqrt{2}}{2})(\frac{\sqrt{2}}{2})}$$

$$= \frac{(2 - \sqrt{2})(\frac{\sqrt{2}}{2}) + 2(\frac{1}{2})}{-(2 - \sqrt{2})\frac{\sqrt{2}}{2} + 2(\frac{1}{2})}$$

$$= \frac{\sqrt{2} - 1 + 1}{-(\sqrt{2} - 1) + 1}$$

$$= \frac{\sqrt{2}}{2 - \sqrt{2}}$$

The slope formula can also be used to determine where a polar graph has a vertical or horizontal tangent line.

Sample

> Find the polar coordinate of all points where $r = 2 - 2\cos\theta$ has horizontal and vertical tangent lines.

From the example above, an expression for the slope at any point is given by

$$\frac{dy}{dx} = \frac{(2 - 2\cos\theta)\cos\theta + 2\sin^2\theta}{-(2 - 2\cos\theta)\sin\theta + 2\sin\theta\cos\theta}$$

To find horizontal tangents, the slope must be 0. This will occur where the numerator is equal to 0.

$$(2 - 2\cos\theta)\cos\theta + 2\sin^2\theta = 0$$

$$2\cos\theta - 2\cos^2\theta + 2(1 - \cos^2\theta) = 0$$

$$-4\cos^2\theta + 2\cos\theta + 2 = 0$$

$$2\cos^2\theta - \cos\theta - 1 = 0$$

$$(2\cos\theta + 1)(\cos\theta - 1) = 0$$

$$\cos\theta = -\frac{1}{2} \text{ or } \cos\theta = 1$$

$$\theta = \frac{2\pi}{3}, \frac{4\pi}{3} \qquad \theta = 0: \text{curve has a sharp turn, so no tangent line}$$

$$\therefore (3, \frac{2\pi}{3})(3, \frac{4\pi}{3})$$

The vertical tangents will occur where the denominator is 0 while the numerator is not.

$$-(2 - 2\cos\theta)\sin\theta + 2\sin\theta\cos\theta = 0$$

$$-2\sin\theta + 2\sin\theta\cos\theta + 2\sin\theta\cos\theta = 0$$

$$-2\sin\theta + 4\sin\theta\cos\theta = 0$$

$$2\sin\theta(-1 + 2\cos\theta) = 0$$

$$\sin\theta = 0 \qquad \cos\theta = \frac{1}{2}$$

$$\theta = k\pi \qquad \theta = \frac{\pi}{3}, \frac{5\pi}{3}$$

$$(4, \pi) \qquad (1, \frac{\pi}{3})(1, \frac{5\pi}{3})$$

Limits and Continuity of Vector-Valued Functions

To find the limit of a vector-valued function, simply find the limits of the real-valued functions that make up the **i** and **j** components. The definition of continuity is completely analogous to that for real-valued functions.

Limit and Continuity of a Vector-Valued Function

If $\mathbf{R}(t) = f(t)\,\mathbf{i} + g(t)\,\mathbf{j}$ is a vector-valued function, then

$$\lim_{t \to a} \mathbf{R}(t) = [\lim_{t \to a} f(t)]\,\mathbf{i} + [\lim_{t \to a} g(t)]\,\mathbf{j}.$$

$\mathbf{R}(t)$ is continuous at the point $t = a$ if $\lim_{t \to a} \mathbf{R}(t) = \mathbf{R}(a)$ [assuming the limit exists].

$\mathbf{R}(t)$ is continuous on an interval if it is continuous at every point in the interval.

Sample

For $\mathbf{R}(t) = \left(\dfrac{1}{t+2}\right)\mathbf{i} + (\ln t)\,\mathbf{j}$, find $\lim_{t \to 1} \mathbf{R}(t)$. For what values of t is $\mathbf{R}(t)$ continuous?

$$\lim_{t \to 1} \mathbf{R}(t) = \frac{1}{3}\,\mathbf{i} + 0\mathbf{j}$$

$$= \frac{1}{3}\,\mathbf{i}$$

$\dfrac{1}{t+2}$ is discontinuous only at $t = -2$

$\ln t$ is continuous on its domain, $t > 0$

$\therefore \mathbf{R}(t)$ is continuous on its domain, $t > 0$

Differentiation of Vector-Valued Functions (BC Only)

The limit definition for the derivative of a vector-valued function is virtually identical to the one for real-valued functions. This definition can be used to prove theorems similar to the familiar ones for finding derivatives analytically: To find the derivative of a vector-valued function, simply find the derivatives of the real-numbered functions that make up the x and y components.

Derivative of a Vector-Valued Function

If $\mathbf{R}(t) = f(t)\,\mathbf{i} + g(t)\,\mathbf{j}$ is a vector-valued function, then

by definition $\mathbf{R}'(t) = \lim_{\Delta t \to 0} \dfrac{\mathbf{R}(t + \Delta t) - \mathbf{R}(t)}{\Delta t}$

which implies that $\mathbf{R}'(t) = f'(t)\,\mathbf{i} + g'(t)\mathbf{j}$

Sample

For $S(t) = (t - t^3)i + (\tan 3t)j$, find $S'(0)$.

$S'(t) = (1 - 3t^2)i + (3\sec^2 3t)j$

$S'(0) = 1i + 3j$

Higher order derivatives of vector-valued functions are found in the same way: Simply find the higher order derivative of the real-valued x and y components. Higher order derivatives can be used to solve position/velocity/acceleration problems where the particle moves not along a line, but follows a curve (vector-valued function or parametric equation) in a plane.

Sample

A particle <u>moves</u> along a curve defined by the vector-valued function
$R(t) = (2\sqrt{3t + 1})i + (3t^2 - 10)j$, $t \geq 0$.

Sketch a graph of the path and sketch the velocity and acceleration vectors at the point $(4, -7)$.

The path of the particle is shown below, from using a calculator in parametric mode.

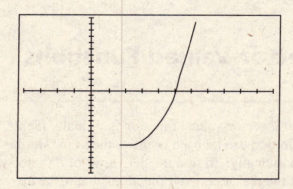

```
WINDOW
  Tmin =0
  Tmax =5
  Tstep =.1
  Xmin =-5
  Xmax =10
  Xscl =1
  Ymin=-20
  Ymax =10
  Yscl=1
```

The velocity function is found by differentiating the position.

$V(t) = R'(t) = (2 \cdot \frac{1}{2}(3t + 1)^{-1/2} \cdot 3)i + (6t)j$

$$= \frac{3}{\sqrt{3t + 1}}i + (6t)j$$

To find the velocity at a point, first find the t value that corresponds to the (x, y) point.

$x = 4 \Rightarrow 2\sqrt{3t + 1} = 4$ or $y = -7 \Rightarrow 3t^2 - 10 = -7$

$\qquad \sqrt{3t + 1} = 2 \qquad\qquad 3t^2 = 3$

$\qquad 3t + 1 = 4 \qquad\qquad t^2 = 1$

$\qquad\qquad t = 1 \qquad\qquad t = \pm 1$, but $t \geq 0$

Now, find $\mathbf{V}(1)$

$$V(1) = \frac{3}{\sqrt{3+1}}\mathbf{i} + 6 \cdot 1\mathbf{j}$$

$$= \frac{3}{2}\mathbf{i} + 6\mathbf{j}$$

So the velocity vector is $\frac{3}{2}\mathbf{i} + 6\mathbf{j}$

For the acceleration, find $\mathbf{V}'(t)$.

$$A(t) = V'(t) = \left[3 \cdot \tfrac{1}{2}(3t+1)^{-3/2} \cdot 3\right]\mathbf{i} + 6\mathbf{j} = \left(\frac{9}{2\sqrt{3t+1}}\right)\mathbf{i} + 6\mathbf{j}$$

And as with the velocity vector,

$$A(1) = \frac{9}{2\sqrt{3+1}}\mathbf{i} + 6\mathbf{j}$$

$$= \frac{9}{4}\mathbf{i} + 6\mathbf{j}$$

so the acceleration vector is $\frac{9}{4}\mathbf{i} + 6\mathbf{j}$

Both the velocity and acceleration vectors are shown in the second sketch of the particle's path, with the initial position of the vectors at the given point $(4, -7)$.

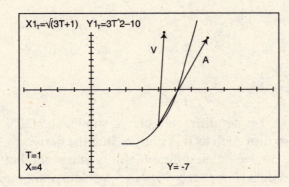

At the point $(4,-7)$, with $t=1$,

$\|v(1)\| = \sqrt{\left(\frac{3}{2}\right)^2 + 6^2}$

$\|v(1)\| \approx 6.185$

direction angle, θ_v,

is given by:

$\tan\theta_v = \frac{6}{\frac{3}{2}}$

$\theta_v = .422\pi$

$\|A(1)\| = \sqrt{\left(\frac{9}{4}\right)^2 + 6^2}$

$\|A(1)\| \approx 6.408$

direction angle, θ_A,

is given by:

$\tan\theta_A = \frac{6}{\frac{9}{4}}$

$\theta_A = .388\pi$

Differentiability and Continuity

The AP exam frequently includes questions that involve the relationship between differentiability and continuity.

Differentiability Implies Continuity

If $f(x)$ is differentiable at $x = c$, then $f(x)$ is continuous at $x = c$.

Translation: In order for the derivative to exist at some point, the function must be continuous at that point.

Caution: This theorem does not work the other way around. Just because a function is continuous at a point, it is not guaranteed to be differentiable at that point. See the following example.

Sample

> For the function $f(x) = x^{2/3}$, find $f'(0)$.

Apply the power rule.

$$f(x) = x^{2/3} \Rightarrow f'(x) = \frac{2}{3}x^{-1/3} = \frac{2}{3x^{1/3}} = \frac{2}{3\sqrt[3]{x}}$$

So $$f'(0) = \frac{2}{3\sqrt[3]{0}} = \frac{2}{0} \text{ which is undefined}$$

Therefore, the derivative does not exist at $x = 0$. Graphically, $y = x^{2/3}$ looks like this:

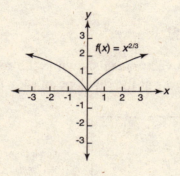

Figure 3.8

The function is obviously continuous at $x = 0$, but it is not differentiable, as shown above. Note that at $x = 0$ the graph has a "sharp turn." A sharp turn such as this implies that the derivative does not exist. Graphing is a quick and easy way to decide on differentiability at a point, but it is not sufficient justification on a free-response problem. For a free-response problem, either apply the differentiation rules as above, or use the definition of the derivative, as in the next example.

Sample

> Show that $f(x)$ is not differentiable at $x = 2$ when
>
> $$f(x) = \begin{cases} x^2 - 3 & \text{for } x \le 2 \\ \frac{1}{2}x & \text{for } x > 2 \end{cases}$$

It may help to begin with a sketch. If the function is discontinuous at $x = 2$, it cannot be differentiable at $x = 2$.

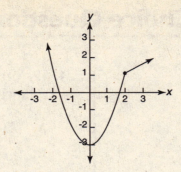

Figure 3.9

Because $f(x)$ is continuous at $x = 2$, find the derivative.

$$f(x) = \begin{cases} x^2 - 3 \text{ for } x \le 2 \\ \frac{1}{2}x \text{ for } x > 2 \end{cases} \Rightarrow f'(x) = \begin{cases} 2x \text{ for } x < 2 \\ \frac{1}{2} \text{ for } x > 2 \end{cases}$$

Now compare the derivative from the left, $f'(2^-)$, and the derivative from the right, $f'(2^+)$.

$$f'(2^-) = 2(2) = 4 \text{ and } f'(2^+) = \frac{1}{2}$$

Because $f'(2^-)$ and $f'(2^+)$ are not equal, $f'(2)$ does not exist; that is, $f(x)$ is not differentiable at $x = 2$.

Free-response problems may require the use of the definition of the derivative to justify that $f(x)$ is not differentiable at $x = 2$. Recall the definition of derivative at a point:

$$f'(c) = \lim_{x \to c} \frac{f(x) - f(c)}{x - c}$$

Use this definition and one-sided limits to show that the derivative from the left, $f'(2^-)$, and the derivative from the right, $f'(2^+)$, are not equal. From the left,

$$f'(2^-) = \lim_{x \to 2^-} \frac{f(x) - f(2)}{x - 2} = \lim_{x \to 2^-} \frac{(x^2 - 3) - 1}{x - 2}$$

$$= \lim_{x \to 2^-} \frac{x^2 - 4}{x - 2}$$

$$= \lim_{x \to 2^-} (x + 2) = 4$$

And from the right,

$$f'(2^+) = \lim_{x \to 2^+} \frac{f(x) - f(2)}{x - 2} = \lim_{x \to 2^+} \frac{(\frac{1}{2}x) - 1}{x - 2}$$

$$= \lim_{x \to 2^+} \frac{\frac{1}{2}(x - 2)}{x - 2} = \frac{1}{2}$$

Therefore, because $f'(2^-) \ne f'(2^+)$, the function is not differentiable at $x = 2$.

Sample Multiple-Choice Questions: Derivatives

1. If $y = \dfrac{x-3}{2-5x}$, then $\dfrac{dy}{dx} =$,

- **A.** $\dfrac{17-10x}{(2-5x)^2}$
- **B.** $\dfrac{13}{(2-5x)^2}$
- **C.** $\dfrac{x-3}{(2-5x)^2}$
- **D.** $\dfrac{17}{(2-5x)^2}$
- **E.** $\dfrac{-13}{(2-5x)^2}$

2. If $y = 2\sqrt{x} - \dfrac{1}{2\sqrt{x}}$, then the derivative of y with respect to x is given by

- **A.** $x + \dfrac{1}{x\sqrt{x}}$
- **B.** $\dfrac{1}{\sqrt{x}} + \dfrac{1}{x\sqrt{x}}$
- **C.** $\dfrac{4x-1}{4x\sqrt{x}}$
- **D.** $\dfrac{1}{\sqrt{x}} + \dfrac{1}{4x\sqrt{x}}$
- **E.** $\dfrac{4}{\sqrt{x}} + \dfrac{1}{x\sqrt{x}}$

3. The function $f(x) = \left| x^2 - 4 \right|$ is NOT differentiable at

- **A.** $x = 2$ only
- **B.** $x = -2$ only
- **C.** $x = 2$ or $x = -2$
- **D.** $x = 0$ only
- **E.** $x = 2$ or $x = -2$ or $x = 0$

4. If $f'(a)$ does NOT exist, which of the following MUST be true?

- **A.** $f(x)$ is discontinuous at $x = a$.
- **B.** $\lim\limits_{x \to a} f(x)$ does not exist.
- **C.** f has a vertical tangent at $x = a$.
- **D.** f has a "hole" for $x = a$.
- **E.** None of these is necessarily true.

5. For $y = \sqrt{3-2x}$, find $\dfrac{dy}{dx}$.

- **A.** $\dfrac{1}{2\sqrt{3-2x}}$
- **B.** $\dfrac{1}{\sqrt{3-2x}}$
- **C.** $\dfrac{2}{\sqrt{3-2x}}$
- **D.** $\dfrac{-1}{\sqrt{3-2x}}$
- **E.** $\dfrac{-2}{\sqrt{3-2x}}$

6. Given that j, k, and m are constants, and that $f(x) = m - 2kx$, find $f'(j)$.

- **A.** m
- **B.** $m - 2jk$
- **C.** $-2jk$
- **D.** $-2k$
- **E.** j

7. The slope of the curve $y = 6x^{1/2} + x$ at the origin is

- **A.** 4
- **B.** 3
- **C.** 1
- **D.** 0
- **E.** undefined

8. If $g(x) = \ln(x)$, which of the following is equal to $g'(x)$?

A. $\displaystyle\lim_{k \to 0} \frac{\ln(x+k)}{k}$

B. $\displaystyle\lim_{k \to 0} \frac{\frac{1}{x+k} - \frac{1}{x}}{k}$

C. $\displaystyle\lim_{k \to 0} \frac{\ln x - \ln k}{k}$

D. $\displaystyle\lim_{k \to 0} \frac{\ln(x+k) - \ln x}{k}$

E. $\displaystyle\lim_{k \to 0} \frac{\ln(x+k) - \ln x}{x-k}$

9. Let $f(x) = x^3$. Using the chain rule, determine an expression for $\dfrac{d}{dx}[f(f(g(x)))]$.

A. $3[g(x)]^2 g'(x)$

B. $3x^2 g'(x^3)$

C. $3[g(x)]^2$

D. $g'(x^3)$

E. none of these

10. If x and y are both differentiable functions of t, and $xy = 20$, find $x'(t)$ when $y'(t) = 10$ and $x = 2$.

A. -2

B. -1

C. 0

D. 3

E. 8

11. If $f(x) = \tan 5x$, then $f'(\pi/5)$ is

A. 5

B. 1

C. -1

D. -5

E. undefined

12. If $y = \sin^3(1 - 2x)$, then $\dfrac{dy}{dx} =$

A. $3\sin^2(1-2x)$

B. $-2\cos^3(1-2x)$

C. $-6\sin^2(1-2x)$

D. $-6\sin^2(1-2x)\cos(1-2x)$

E. $-6\cos^2(1-2x)$

13. If $f(x) = \sin x$ and $g(x) = \cos x$, then the set of all x for which $f'(x) = g'(x)$ is

A. $\dfrac{\pi}{4} + k\pi$

B. $\dfrac{\pi}{2} + k\pi$

C. $\dfrac{3\pi}{4} + k\pi$

D. $\dfrac{\pi}{2} + 2k\pi$

E. $\dfrac{3\pi}{2} + 2k\pi$

14. If $y = 3x^{50}$, then $\dfrac{d^{50}y}{dx^{50}} =$

A. 0

B. $150x^{49}$

C. $3(50!)$

D. $150!$

E. $3(500!)x$

15. If $y = \sqrt{x^2 + 16}$, then $\dfrac{d^2y}{dx^2} =$

A. $\dfrac{-1}{4(x^2+16)^{3/2}}$

B. $4(3x^2+16)$

C. $\dfrac{x}{(x^2+16)^{1/2}}$

D. $\dfrac{2x^2+16}{(x^2+16)^{3/2}}$

E. $\dfrac{16}{(x^2+16)^{3/2}}$

16. Given $f(x) = \log_3(3 - 2x), f'(1) =$

   A. $\dfrac{2}{\ln 3}$

   B. $\dfrac{-2}{\ln 3}$

   C. $\dfrac{1}{\ln 3}$

   D. $\ln 3$

   E. $-2 \ln 3$

17. If $y = \ln|\sec x - \tan x|$, then $y'' =$

   A. $-\sec x$

   B. $\sec x \tan x - \sec^2 x$

   C. $\tan x$

   D. $-\sec x \tan x$

   E. $\sec x + \tan x$

18. If $f(x) = x^3 \ln x$, then $\dfrac{df}{dx} =$

   A. $3x^2 \ln x + x^2$

   B. $(3x^2 + 1)(\ln x)$

   C. $x^2 \ln x + x^2$

   D. $3x^2 \ln x$

   E. $3x$

19. $\dfrac{d}{dx}(\ln e^{2x}) =$

   A. $\dfrac{1}{e^{2x}}$

   B. $\dfrac{2}{e^{2x}}$

   C. $2x$

   D. 1

   E. 2

20. If $f(x) = \ln(\ln x)$, then $f'(e)$ is

   A. e

   B. 1

   C. $1/e$

   D. 0

   E. undefined

21. If $y = x^{(x^3)}$, then $\dfrac{dy}{dx} =$

   A. $x^{(x^3 + 2)}(1 + 3\ln x)$

   B. $x^{(x^3 + 2)}$

   C. $4x^{(x^3 + 2)}$

   D. $x^3(1 + 3\ln x)$

   E. $(\ln x)x^{(x^3)}$

22. If $y = e^{-x^2}$, then $y''(0) =$

   A. 2

   B. $2/e$

   C. 0

   D. -2

   E. -4

23. If $f(x) \dfrac{1}{3} e^{3 - 2x}$, then $f'(x) =$

   A. $\dfrac{-2}{3} e^{3 - 2x}$

   B. $\dfrac{-1}{6} e^{3 - 2x}$

   C. $\dfrac{1}{12} e^{4 - 2x}$

   D. e^{-2x}

   E. $\dfrac{1}{3} e^{3 - 2x}$

24. Let $f(t) = \dfrac{e^t - e^{t/2}}{2}$. Find $f'(0)$.

A. 0

B. $\dfrac{3}{16}$

C. $\dfrac{1}{4}$

D. $\dfrac{3}{8}$

E. $\dfrac{3}{4}$

25. $\dfrac{d}{dx}(\arctan 2x) =$

A. $\dfrac{2}{1 + 4x^2}$

B. $\dfrac{1}{1 + 4x^2}$

C. $\dfrac{2}{4x^2 - 1}$

D. $\dfrac{1}{4x^2 - 1}$

E. $\dfrac{1}{1 + 2x^2}$

26. If $x > 0$, then $\dfrac{d}{dx}\left(\arcsin \dfrac{1}{x}\right) =$

A. $\dfrac{-1}{|x|\sqrt{x^2 - 1}}$

B. $\dfrac{-|x|}{\sqrt{x^2 - 1}}$

C. $\dfrac{|x|}{\sqrt{1 - x^2}}$

D. $\dfrac{-1}{x^2\sqrt{1 - x^2}}$

E. $\dfrac{1}{|x|\sqrt{x^2 - 1}}$

27. The equation of the tangent to the curve $2x^2 - y^4 = 1$ at the point $(1, 1)$ is

A. $y = -x$

B. $y = x$

C. $4y + 5x + 1 = 1$

D. $x - 2y + 3 = 0$

E. $x - 4y + 5 = 0$

28. If $\sin x = \ln y$ and $0 < x < \pi$, then $\dfrac{dy}{dx} =$

A. $e^{\sin x}\cos x$

B. $e^{-\sin x}\cos x$

C. $\dfrac{e^{\sin x}}{\cos x}$

D. $e^{\cos x}$

E. $e^{\sin x}$

29. If $xy^2 - 3x + 4y - 2 = 0$ and is a differentiable function of x, then $\dfrac{dy}{dx} =$

A. $\dfrac{-1 + y^2}{2xy}$

B. $\dfrac{3}{2y + 4}$

C. $\dfrac{3}{2xy + 4}$

D. $\dfrac{3 - y^2}{2xy + 4}$

E. $\dfrac{5 - y^2}{2xy + 4}$

30. If $\sin(xy) = y$, then $\dfrac{dy}{dx} =$

A. $\sec(xy)$

B. $y\cos(xy) - 1$

C. $\dfrac{1 - y\cos(xy)}{x\cos(xy)}$

D. $\dfrac{y\cos(xy)}{1 - x\cos(xy)}$

E. $\cos(xy)$

Answers to Multiple-Choice Questions

1. E. Use the quotient rule.

$$y = \frac{x-3}{2-5x} \Rightarrow \frac{dy}{dx} = \frac{(2-5x)(1)-(x-3)(-5)}{(2-5x)^2}$$

$$= \frac{2-5x+5x-15}{(2-5x)^2}$$

$$= \frac{-13}{(2-5x)^2}$$

2. D. Rewrite with fractional and negative exponents, and then differentiate term by term.

$$y = 2\sqrt{x} - \frac{1}{2\sqrt{x}} \Leftrightarrow y = 2x^{1/2} - \frac{1}{2}x^{-1/2}$$

$$\Rightarrow \frac{dy}{dx} = 2 \cdot \frac{1}{2}x^{-1/2} - \frac{1}{2} \cdot \left(\frac{-1}{2}\right)x^{-3/2}$$

$$= x^{-1/2} + \frac{1}{4}x^{-3/2}$$

$$= \frac{1}{\sqrt{x}} + \frac{1}{4x\sqrt{x}}$$

3. C. A quick sketch will show that $f(x)$ has sharp turns at both $x = 2$ and $x = -2$.

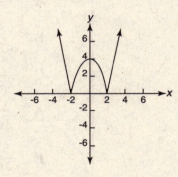

4. E. If the derivative at a point does not exist, the function *may* be discontinuous, but it does not *have* to be discontinuous, such as with $f(x) = x^{2/3}$. Thus you can eliminate choices A and D. If the derivative at a point does not exist, the limit *may* not exist, but it also *may* exist, as with $f(x) = x^{2/3}$ again. This eliminates choice B. A vertical tangent line at a point would mean that the derivative does not exist, but the derivative may be nonexistent in a variety of ways, so C is also eliminated. The conclusion is that none of A through D *must* be true, though they all *could* be true.

5. D. Rewrite with a fractional exponent and apply the power rule. Be careful with the chain rule.

$$y = \sqrt{3-2x} \Rightarrow y = (3-2x)^{1/2}$$

$$\frac{dy}{dx} = \frac{1}{2}(3-2x)^{-1/2}(-2) = \frac{-1}{\sqrt{3-2x}}$$

6. D. $f(x) = m - 2kx \Rightarrow f'(x) = -2k$

Thus $\qquad\qquad f'(j) = -2k$

If this type of problem bothers you, try substituting actual numbers for j, k, and m.

$$f(x) = m - 2kx$$

might be thought of as $f(x) = 5 - 2 \cdot 6x$

$$\Rightarrow f'(x) = -2 \cdot 6$$

which would be equivalent to $-2k$ since k was chosen as 6.

7. E. For slope of the curve, find the slope of the tangent at that point. That is, find $\left. \dfrac{dy}{dx} \right|_{x=0}$.

$$y = 6x^{1/2} + x \Rightarrow \frac{dy}{dx} 6 \cdot \frac{1}{2} x^{-1/2} + 1 = \frac{3}{\sqrt{x}} + 1$$

$\left. \dfrac{dy}{dx} \right|_{x=0} = \dfrac{3}{\sqrt{0}} + 1$ which is undefined

8. D. The answers are in the form of the limit definition of the derivative,

$$f'(x) = \lim_{\Delta x \to 0} \frac{f(x + \Delta x) - f(x)}{\Delta x}$$

but with an obvious notation change: $\Delta x = k$, and $f(x) = g(x)$.

$$\Rightarrow g'(x) = \lim_{k \to 0} \frac{g(x + k) - g(x)}{k}$$

$$\Rightarrow g'(x) = \lim_{k \to 0} \frac{\ln(x + k) - \ln x}{k}$$

9. A. By the chain rule,

$$\frac{d}{dx}[f(g(x))] = f'(g(x)) g'(x)$$

For this problem,

$$f(x) = x^3 \Rightarrow f'(x) = 3x^2$$

so $\qquad\qquad f'(g(x)) g'(x) = 3[g(x)]^2 g'(x)$

10. A. The question asks for $x'(t)$ or dx/dt. Realize that t is the independent variable in this problem.

$$xy = 20 \Rightarrow x \frac{20}{y} = -20y^{-1}$$

and now differentiate with respect to t

$$\Rightarrow \frac{dx}{dt} = 20(-1y^{-2})\frac{dy}{dt}$$

$$= \left(\frac{-20}{y^2}\right)\frac{dy}{dt}$$

We are also given $dy/dt = 10$, and $x = 2 \Rightarrow y = 10$. Thus

$$\left.\frac{dx}{dt}\right|_{x=2} = \frac{-20}{10^2}(10) = -2$$

11. A. $f(x) = \tan 5x \Rightarrow f'(x) = [\sec^2(5x)](5)$

$$\Rightarrow f'\left(\frac{\pi}{5}\right) = 5\left[\sec 5\left(\frac{\pi}{5}\right)\right]^2$$

$$= 5(\sec \pi)^2 = 5(-1)^2 = 5$$

12. D. $y = \sin^3(1 - 2x) \Leftrightarrow y = [\sin(1 - 2x)]^3$

$$\Rightarrow \frac{dy}{dx} = 3[\sin(1 - 2x)]^2[\cos(1 - 2x)](-2)$$

$$= -6\sin^2(1 - 2x)\cos(1 - 2x)$$

13. C.
$$\left. \begin{array}{l} f(x) = \sin x \Rightarrow f'(x) = \cos x \\ g(x) = \cos x \Rightarrow g'(x) = -\sin x \end{array} \right\}$$
$$\Rightarrow f'(x) = g'(x) \Leftrightarrow \cos x = -\sin x$$

Sine and cosine are exact opposites when

$$x = \frac{3\pi}{4} + 2k\pi \quad \text{or} \quad x = \frac{5\pi}{4} + 2k\pi$$

which is equivalent to

$$x = \frac{3\pi}{4} + k\pi$$

14. C. Actually finding 50 derivatives is impractical on a timed test. Find the first three or four derivatives, and see if a pattern develops.

$$y = 3x^{50} \Rightarrow \frac{dy}{dx} = 3 \cdot 50x^{49}$$

$$\Rightarrow \frac{d^2 y}{dx^2} = 3 \cdot 50 \cdot 49x^{48}$$

$$\Rightarrow \frac{d^3 y}{dx^3} = 3 \cdot 50 \cdot 49 \cdot 48x^{47}$$

$$\Rightarrow \frac{d^4 y}{dx^4} = 3 \cdot 50 \cdot 49 \cdot 48 \cdot 47x^{46}$$

etc.

$$\Rightarrow \frac{d^{49} y}{dx^{49}} = 3 \cdot 50 \cdot 49 \cdot 48 \cdot 47 \cdots 2x^{1}$$

$$\Rightarrow \frac{d^{50} y}{dx^{50}} = 3 \cdot 50 \cdot 49 \cdot 48 \cdot 47 \cdots 2 \cdot 1x^{0}$$

$$= 3(50!)$$

15. E. $y = \sqrt{x^2 + 16} \Rightarrow y = (x^2 + 16)^{1/2}$

$$\frac{dy}{dx} = \frac{1}{2}(x^2 + 16)^{-1/2}(2x)$$

$$= x(x^2 + 16)^{-1/2}$$

$$\Rightarrow \frac{d^2 y}{dx^2} = (x)\left[\frac{-1}{2}(x^2 + 16)^{-3/2}(2x)\right] + (x^2 + 16)^{-1/2}(1)$$

$$= -x^2(x^2 + 16)^{-3/2} + (x^2 + 16)^{-1/2}$$

$$= (x^2 + 16)^{-3/2}[-x^2 + (x^2 + 16)^{1}]$$

$$= \frac{16}{(x^2 + 16)^{3/2}}$$

16. B. Use the formula for derivatives of base-*a* logarithms.

$$\frac{d}{dx}(\log_a u) = \left(\frac{1}{\ln a}\right)\left(\frac{1}{u}\right)\left(\frac{du}{dx}\right)$$

$$f(x) = \log_3(3 - 2x) \Rightarrow f'(x) = \left(\frac{1}{\ln 3}\right)\left(\frac{1}{3 - 2x}\right)(-2)$$

$$= \left(\frac{-2}{\ln 3}\right)\left(\frac{1}{3 - 2x}\right)$$

$$\Rightarrow f'(1) = \left(\frac{-2}{\ln 3}\right)\left(\frac{1}{3 - 2}\right) = \frac{-2}{\ln 3}$$

17. D. Use the formula for the derivative of the natural log.

$$\frac{d}{dx}(\ln u) = \frac{1}{u}\frac{du}{dx}$$

$$y = \ln|\sec x - \tan x| \Rightarrow y' = \frac{1}{\sec x - \tan x}(\sec x \tan x - \sec^2 x)$$

$$= \frac{\sec x(\tan x - \sec x)}{\sec x - \tan x} = -\sec x$$

$$\Rightarrow y'' = -\sec x \tan x$$

18. A. Use the product rule for this problem.

$$f(x) = x^3 \ln x \Rightarrow \frac{df}{dx} = f'(x) = (x^3)\left(\frac{1}{x}\right) + (\ln x)(3x^2)$$

$$= x^2 + 3x^2 \ln x$$

19. E. Use the log property to simplify first.

$$\frac{d}{dx}(\ln e^{2x}) = \frac{d}{dx}(2x) = 2$$

20. C. Use the formula for the derivative of the natural log.

$$\frac{d}{dx}(\ln u) = \frac{1}{u}\frac{du}{dx} \text{ where } u = \ln x$$

$$f(x) = \ln(\ln x) \Rightarrow f'(x) = \left(\frac{1}{\ln x}\right)\left(\frac{1}{x}\right)$$

$$\Rightarrow f'(e) = \left(\frac{1}{\ln e}\right)\left(\frac{1}{e}\right) = \frac{1}{e}$$

21. A. Because the independent variable appears in both the base and the exponent, use log differentiation.

$$y = x^{(x^3)}$$

$$\ln(y) = \ln(x^{(x^3)})$$

$$\ln y = (x^3)(\ln x)$$

$$\Rightarrow \frac{1}{y}\frac{dy}{dx} = (x^3)\left(\frac{1}{x}\right) + (\ln x)(3x^2)$$

$$\frac{dy}{dx} = y(x^2 + 3x^2 \ln x)$$

$$= x^{(x^3)}(x^2 + 3x^2 \ln x)$$

$$= x^{(x^3)} x^2(1 + 3\ln x)$$

$$= x^{(x^3 + 2)}(1 + 3\ln x)$$

22. D. $y = e^{-x^2} \Rightarrow y' = (e^{-x^2})(-2x)$

$$\Rightarrow y'' = (e^{-x^2})(-2) + (-2x)[(e^{-x^2})(-2x)]$$
$$= -2e^{-x^2} + 4x^2 e^{-x^2}$$
$$= e^{-x^2}(-2 + 4x^2)$$
$$\Rightarrow y''(0) = e^0(-2 + 0) = (1)(-2) = -2$$

23. A. $f(x) = \frac{1}{3} e^{3-2x} \Rightarrow f'(x) = \frac{1}{3} e^{3-2x}(-2)$

$$= \frac{-2}{3} e^{3-2x}$$

24. D. $f(t) = \frac{e^t - e^{t/2}}{2} = \frac{1}{2}(e^t - e^{t/2})$

$$f'(t) = \frac{1}{2}\left(e^t - e^{t/2}\,\frac{1}{2}\right)$$

$$= \frac{1}{4}\left(2e^t - e^{t/2}\right)$$

$$f''(t) = \frac{1}{4}\left(2e^t - e^{t/2}\,\frac{1}{2}\right)$$

$$= \frac{1}{8}\left(4e^t - e^{t/2}\right)$$

$$f''(0) = \frac{1}{8}\left(4e^0 - e^0\right) = \frac{1}{8}(4 - 1) = \frac{3}{8}$$

25. A. Use the arctan rule, with $u = 2x$.

$$\frac{d}{dx}(\arctan u) = \frac{1}{1+u^2}\frac{du}{dx}$$

$$\frac{d}{dx}(\arctan 2x) = \frac{1}{1+(2x)^2}(2) = \frac{2}{1+4x^2}$$

26. A. Use the arcsin rule, with $u = 1/x$.

$$\frac{d}{dx}(\arcsin u) = \frac{1}{\sqrt{1-u^2}}\frac{du}{dx}$$

$$\frac{d}{dx}\left(\arcsin \frac{1}{x}\right) = \frac{1}{\sqrt{1-\left(\frac{1}{x}\right)^2}}\left(\frac{-1}{x^2}\right)$$

$$= \frac{1}{\sqrt{\dfrac{x^2-1}{x^2}}}\left(\frac{-1}{x^2}\right)$$

$$= \frac{|x|}{\sqrt{x^2-1}}\left(\frac{-1}{x^2}\right) = \frac{-1}{|x|\sqrt{x^2-1}}$$

27. B. Solving for y looks difficult, so use implicit differentiation.

$$2x^2 - y^4 = 1$$
$$\Rightarrow 4x - 4y^3 \frac{dy}{dx} = 0$$
$$\frac{dy}{dx} = \frac{-4x}{-4y^3} = \frac{x}{y^3}$$
$$\left.\frac{dy}{dx}\right|_{\substack{x=1 \\ y=1}} = \frac{1}{1} = 1 \Rightarrow m = 1$$

Thus the equation of the tangent is $y - 1 = 1(x - 1)$, or $y = x$.

28. A. Use implicit differentiation.

$$\sin x = \ln y$$
$$\cos x = \frac{1}{y}\frac{dy}{dx} \Rightarrow \frac{dy}{dx} = y \cos x$$

Because y does not appear in any of the answers, solve the original equation for y and then substitute.

$$\sin x = \ln y \Leftrightarrow y = e^{\sin x}$$
$$\frac{dy}{dx} = y \cos x = e^{\sin x} \cos x$$

Another approach:

$$\sin x = \ln y \Leftrightarrow y = e^{\sin x}$$
$$\frac{dy}{dx} = e^{\sin x} \cos x$$

29. D. Use implicit differentiation. The first term requires use of the product rule.

$$xy^2 - 3x + 4y - 2 = 0$$
$$\Rightarrow (x)\left(2y\frac{dy}{dx}\right) + (y^2)(1) - 3 + 4\frac{dy}{dx} - 0 = 0$$
$$\frac{dy}{dx}(2xy + 4) = 3 - y^2$$
$$\frac{dy}{dx} = \frac{3 - y^2}{2xy + 4}$$

30. D. Use implicit differentiation. The chain rule requires use of the product rule.

$$\sin(xy) = y$$

$$\Rightarrow \cos(xy)\left[x\frac{dy}{dx} + y(1)\right] = \frac{dy}{dx}$$

$$[\cos(xy)]x\frac{dy}{dx} + [\cos(xy)]y = \frac{dy}{dx}$$

$$[\cos(xy)]x\frac{dy}{dx} - \frac{dy}{dx} = -\cos(xy)y$$

$$\frac{dy}{dx}[x\cos(xy) - 1] = -y\cos(xy)$$

$$\frac{dy}{dx} = \frac{-y\cos(xy)}{x\cos(xy) - 1}$$

$$= \frac{y\cos(xy)}{1 - x\cos(xy)}$$

Sample Free-Response Question: Derivatives

1. Let f be the function given by $f(x) = \begin{cases} x^2 & \text{for } x \leq 1 \\ ax + b & \text{for } x > 1 \end{cases}$

A. Find an expression for a in terms of b such that $f(x)$ is continuous. Use the definition of continuity to justify your answer.

B. Find specific values of a and b such that $f(x)$ is differentiable. Use the definition of the derivative to justify your answer.

C. Use your results from parts A and B to sketch $f(x)$.

Answer to Free-Response Question

1. For part A, begin by stating the definition of continuity at a point.

A. $f(x)$ is continuous at $x = c$ iff $\begin{cases} f(c) \text{ exists} \\ \lim\limits_{x \to c} f(x) \text{ exists} \\ \lim\limits_{x \to c} f(x) = f(c) \end{cases}$

Here $f(x) = \begin{cases} x^2 & \text{for } x \leq 1 \\ ax + b & \text{for } x > 1 \end{cases} \Rightarrow \lim\limits_{x \to 1} f(x) = f(1)$; this will ensure continuity.

$$\left.\begin{array}{l} \lim_{x \to 1^+} f(x) = \lim_{x \to 1^+} (ax + b) = a + b \\[2mm] \lim_{x \to 1^-} f(x) = \lim_{x \to 1^-} (x^2) = 1 \\[2mm] f(1) = 1 \end{array}\right\} \Rightarrow \lim_{x \to 1} f(x)$$

$$= f(1) \Leftrightarrow a + b = 1 \text{ so } a = 1 - b$$

For part B, recall that a function must be continuous to be differentiable, so the relationship between a and b established in part A must still hold true. Now state the definition of the derivative, and use it to find a second relationship between a and b.

B. $f(x)$ is differentiable at $x = c$ iff

$$\lim_{x \to c^-} \frac{f(x) - f(c)}{x - c} = \lim_{x \to c^+} \frac{f(x) - f(c)}{x - c}$$

$$\left.\begin{array}{l} \lim_{x \to c^-} \frac{f(x) - f(c)}{x - c} = \lim_{x \to 1^-} \frac{x^2 f(1)}{x - 1} = \lim_{x \to 1^-} \frac{x^2 - 1}{x - 1} \\[3mm] = \lim_{x \to 1^-} \frac{(x + 1)(x - 1)}{x - 1} = \lim_{x \to 1^-} (x + 1) = 2 \\[3mm] \lim_{x \to c^+} \frac{f(x) - f(c)}{x - c} = \lim_{x \to 1^+} \frac{ax + b - f(1)}{x - 1} = \lim_{x \to 1^+} \frac{ax + b - (a + b)}{x - 1} \\[3mm] = \lim_{x \to 1^+} \frac{a(x - 1)}{x - 1} = \lim_{x \to 1^+} a = a \end{array}\right\}$$

$$\Rightarrow a = 2 \text{ for differentiability}$$

But a function must be continuous to be differentiable, so, from part A,

$a + b = 1$

Thus $a = 2$ and $b = -1$ guarantee differentiability.

For part C, sketch the function.

C. $f(x) = \begin{cases} x^2 & \text{for } x \leq 1 \\ 2x - 1 & \text{for } x > 1 \end{cases}$

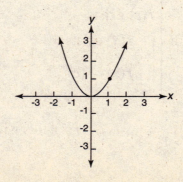

Applications of the derivative provide material for many of the free-response problems on the AP exam. These include finding tangent and normal lines, relating rates of change, optimizing applications, and sketching curves.

Tangent and Normal Lines

Finding the line that is **tangent** to a curve at a point is frequently the first application of the derivative that calculus students learn. Because the derivative can be considered as the instantaneous rate of change of the slope (rise over run), finding the derivative at a point gives the slope of the tangent. The line that is **normal** to a curve at a point is simply the line that is perpendicular to the tangent line, as shown in the following graph. Perpendicular lines have slopes that are negative reciprocals, so finding the slope of the normal line requires finding the negative reciprocal of the derivative.

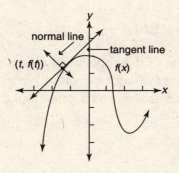

Figure 4.1

To find the equation of the tangent or normal line:

1. Find the slope of the line by first evaluating the derivative at the given point.

   a. For tangent lines, the slope (m_t) is just this derivative.

   b. For normal lines, the slope (m_n) is the negative reciprocal of the derivative.

2. Find the point of tangency by evaluating the function at the given point.

3. Apply the point/slope form to the results from the first two steps.

Sample

> Find the equation of the line that is tangent to the curve $f(x) = 3\cos 2x - \sin x$ at the point where $x = \frac{\pi}{7}$.

Find the slope of the tangent line by finding the derivative at $x = \frac{\pi}{7}$, that is, $f'\left(\frac{\pi}{7}\right)$.

$$f(x) = 3\cos 2x - \sin x \Rightarrow f'(x) = 3(-\sin 2x)(2) - \cos x$$

$$\Rightarrow f'\left(\frac{\pi}{7}\right) = -6\sin\frac{2\pi}{7} - \cos\frac{\pi}{7}$$

$$\approx -5.591957763 \approx -5.6, \text{ so } m_t = -5.6$$

$$f\left(\frac{\pi}{7}\right) = 3\cos\left(\frac{2\pi}{7}\right) - \sin\left(\frac{\pi}{7}\right) \approx 1.436525666$$

$$\approx 1.4$$

Therefore, $\left(\frac{\pi}{7}, 1.4\right)$ is the point of tangency.

Apply the point/slope form: $y - y_1 = m(x - x_1)$

$$y - 1.4 = -5.6\left(x - \frac{\pi}{7}\right)$$

If this answer does not appear as one of the choices on a multiple-choice problem, you may need to change its form by switching to fractions, simplifying, or solving for y. Always examine the format of the multiple-choice answers as a guide to the form to work toward.

Sample

> Find the equation of the line normal to the curve $g(x) = e^{2x-3}$ at the point where $x = 0$.

$$g(x) = e^{2x-3} \Rightarrow g'(x) = (e^{2x-3})(2)$$

$$\Rightarrow g'(0) = 2e^{-3} = \frac{2}{e^3} \Rightarrow m_t = \frac{2}{e^3}$$

But the problem asks for the normal line, which is perpendicular to the tangent line.

$$\Rightarrow m_n = \frac{-1}{m_t} = \frac{-1}{\frac{2}{e^3}} = -\frac{e^3}{2} = -\frac{1}{2}e^3$$

since $g(0) = e^{-3} = \frac{1}{e^3} \Rightarrow \left(0, \frac{1}{e^3}\right)$ is the point of tangency.

Apply the point/slope form: $y - y_1 = m(x - x_1)$

$$y - \frac{1}{e^3} = -\frac{1}{2} e^3 (x - 0)$$

$$y = -\frac{1}{2} e^3 x + \frac{1}{e^3}$$

Other forms might be found as multiple-choice answers because of the use of a calculator.

Sample

> Find the x and y coordinates of any points where the graph of
> $f(x) = \left(\frac{2}{3}\right) x^3 - \left(\frac{1}{2}\right) x^2 - 3x + 1$ has a horizontal tangent line.

For the tangent line to be horizontal, its slope must be 0; that is, $f'(x) = 0$.

$$f(x) = \frac{2}{3} x^3 - \frac{1}{2} x^2 - 3x + 1 \Rightarrow f'(x) = \frac{2}{3}(3x^2) - \frac{1}{2}(2x) - 3$$

$$f'(x) = 2x^2 - x - 3$$

$$f'(x) = 0 \Rightarrow 2x^2 - x - 3 = 0$$

$$(2x - 3)(x + 1) = 0$$

$x = \frac{3}{2}$ or $x = -1$

$f(\frac{3}{2}) = \frac{2}{3}(\frac{3}{2})^3 - \frac{1}{2}(\frac{3}{2})^2 - 3(\frac{3}{2}) + 1 = -\frac{19}{8}$

$\Rightarrow$ horizontal tangent at $(\frac{3}{2}, -\frac{19}{8})$

$f(-1) = \frac{2}{3}(-1)^3 - \frac{1}{2}(-1)^2 - 3(-1) + 1 = \frac{17}{6}$

$\Rightarrow$ horizontal tangent at $(-1, \frac{17}{6})$

Although it is not necessary for this problem, sketching the graph may help clarify the idea of finding horizontal tangents.

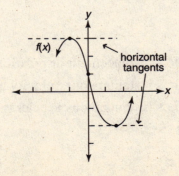

Figure 4.2

Sample

> Find the x-coordinates of any points where the graph of $y = \sqrt[3]{x}$ has a vertical tangent line.

For the tangent line at a point to be a vertical line, its slope must be nonexistent or undefined, and $f(x)$ must be continuous at the point. That is,

$$f'(x) = \frac{\text{constant}}{0} \text{ and } f(x) \text{ continuous}$$

$$f(x) = \sqrt[3]{x} = x^{\frac{1}{3}} \Rightarrow f'(x) = \frac{1}{3}x^{-\frac{2}{3}} = \frac{1}{3x^{\frac{2}{3}}}$$

$$\Rightarrow f'(0) = \frac{1}{0} \text{ and } y = \sqrt[3]{x} \text{ is continuous at } x = 0$$

Thus there is a vertical tangent at $x = 0$. Again, a sketch may help you visualize the vertical tangent, although it is not required.

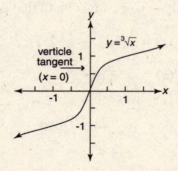

Figure 4.3

Position, Velocity, and Acceleration

Recall that the most general definition of the derivative is the instantaneous rate of change of one variable with respect to another. Applying this concept in the context of the movement of a particle along a fixed horizontal line results in a relationship among the particle's position, velocity, and acceleration (PVA) at any instant in time.

For this section,

$s(t)$ represents the particle's displacement or position at any time t.

$v(t)$ represents the particle's instantaneous velocity at any time t.

$a(t)$ represents the particle's instantaneous acceleration at any time t.

Theorem for PVA

$$\frac{d}{dt} s(t) = v(t) \qquad \frac{d^2}{dt^2} s(t) = a(t) \qquad \frac{d}{dt} v(t) = a(t)$$

Or, in prime notation,

$$s'(t) = v(t) \qquad s''(t) = a(t) \qquad v'(t) = a(t)$$

These relationships may look unfamiliar, but they are really just the calculus version of what happens when you drive a car. For example, if you travel for 3 hours and cover 180 miles, your *average* speed, or velocity, is given by

$$\frac{\text{change in position}}{\text{change in time}} = \frac{\Delta s}{\Delta t} = \frac{180}{3} = 60 \frac{\text{miles}}{\text{hour}}$$

Of course, your speed at any instant in time may be more or less than 60 mph; 60 is your *average* speed, or velocity. To find your instantaneous velocity, apply calculus to this relationship by considering the interval of time to be arbitrarily small ($\Delta t \to 0$):

$$v(t) = \lim_{\Delta t \to 0} \frac{\Delta s}{\Delta t} = \lim_{\Delta t \to 0} \frac{s(t + \Delta t) - s(t)}{\Delta t} = s'(t)$$

Acceleration is the instantaneous rate of change of velocity with respect to time, or

$$a(t) = \lim_{\Delta t \to 0} \frac{\Delta v}{\Delta t} = \lim_{\Delta t \to 0} \frac{v(t + \Delta t) - v(t)}{\Delta(t)} = v'(t)$$

On the AP test, for particle problems involving motion along a horizontal line, the positive direction is almost always to the right of the origin. The time interval is frequently limited to $t \geq 0$, but it is occasionally restricted further or even left as the set of real numbers; read the directions. The following translations of English to calculus may help with PVA problems:

English	Calculus
particle at rest	$v(t) = 0$
particle moving right	$v(t) > 0$
particle moving left	$v(t) < 0$
particle changes direction	$v(t)$ changes sign
total distance traveled from time t_1 to time t_2	$\left| s(t_1) - s(t_c) \right| + \left| s(t_c) - s(t_2) \right|$ where $t_c =$ time when particle changes direction

You should be able to indicate the proper units for the position, velocity, or acceleration if required to do so.

Function	Units	Examples / Abbreviations
$s(t)$	linear units	feet or meters: ft or m
$v(t)$	linear units per unit of time	feet per second: ft/s meters per second: m/s
$a(t)$	linear units per unit of time squared	feet per second squared: ft/s^2 centimeters per second squared: cm/s^2

Sample

A particle moves along a horizontal line such that its position at any time $t \geq 0$ is given by $s(t) = t^3 - 6t^2 + 9t + 1$, where s is measured in meters and t in seconds.

A. Find any time(s) when the particle is at rest.

B. Find any time(s) when the particle changes direction.

C. Find any intervals when the particle is moving left.

D. Find the total distance the particle travels in the first 2 seconds.

E. Find the velocity of the particle when the acceleration is 0.

Justify all answers in detail.

It may be helpful to begin by finding $v(t)$ and $a(t)$ so that they are handy when you need them.

$$s(t) = t^3 - 6t^2 + 9t + 1 \Rightarrow v(t) = 3t^2 - 12t + 9 \Rightarrow a(t) = 6t - 12$$
$$= 3(t^2 - 4t + 3)$$
$$= 3(t - 1)(t - 3)$$

(a) "At rest" $\Rightarrow v(t) = 0$

$$\Rightarrow v(t) = 0 \text{ when } t = 1 \text{ or } t = 3$$

(b) Changes direction" $\Rightarrow v(t)$ changes sign

The potential places where $v(t)$ changes sign are, of course, where $v(t) = 0$ — that is, where $t = 1$ and $t = 3$. However, you must still justify that $v(t)$ changes sign by using a number line or a chart. Whichever diagram you prefer, label it clearly as $v(t)$.

```
        pos      neg      pos
    ├─────────┼─────────┼─────────   v(t)
    0         1         3
```

t	$0 \leq t < 1$	$t = 1$	$1 < t < 3$	$t = 3$	$t > 3$
$v(t)$	pos	0	neg	0	pos

Thus the particle changes direction at $t = 1$ and $t = 3$.

(c) "Moving left" $\Rightarrow v(t) < 0$

From the number line or chart, $v(t) < 0$ when $1 < t < 3$.

(d) "Total distance $t = 0$ to $t = 2$" $\Rightarrow |s(0) - s(1)| + |s(1) - s(2)|$

$$= |1 - 5| + |5 - 3|$$
$$= 4 + 2 = 6\text{m}$$

(e) "Velocity when acceleration = 0" $a(t) = 0$

$$6t - 12 = 0$$
$$t = 2$$
$$v(2) = 3(2 - 1)(2 - 3) = -3\text{m/s}$$

Although it is not requested in this problem, a diagram showing the motion of the particle may help answer some PVA questions and may also serve as a way of checking your calculus. The motion is along a horizontal line, which should be labeled so as to include all "important" times and locations, such as when the particle is at rest, when it is changing direction, and so on.

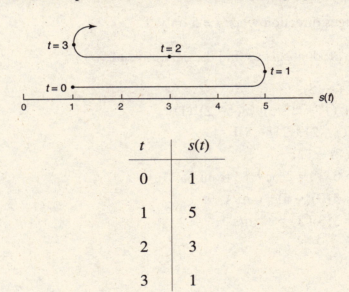

t	$s(t)$
0	1
1	5
2	3
3	1

The single axis here is labeled to correspond with the values in the table above. For other PVA problems, the axis may require a far different configuration. Complete the table of important values first, and then choose the appropriate system of labels. Even though the motion is along a single horizontal line, the path is described along three different horizontal lines in order to show the changes in direction. Note that the times are shown next to the changes. Trace the path of the particle from $t = 0$ to $t = 2$; now, examine again the work for part (d) above. The first absolute bars give the distance traveled as the particle moves *right* from $t = 0$ to $t = 1$. At $t = 1$, the particle changes direction. The second set of absolute-value bars gives the distance the particle moves *left* from $t = 1$ to $t = 2$.

Sample

A particle travels along a horizontal line such that at any time $t \geq 0$, its velocity is given by $v(t) = 3(t-2)^2(t-5)$ meters per second.

(a) At what times, if any, does the particle change direction?

(b) Find the acceleration of the particle at any times when it is at rest.

Justify all answers in detail.

(a) "Change direction" $\Rightarrow v(t)$ changes sign

First, find when $v(t) = 0$, and then find when it changes direction.

$$v(t) = 3(t-2)^2(t-5) = 0 \Rightarrow t = 2 \text{ or } t = 5$$

t	$0 < t < 2$	$t = 2$	$2 < t < 5$	$t = 5$	$t > 5$
$v(t)$	neg	0	neg	0	pos

Thus the particle changes direction when $t = 5$ only.

(b) Find $a(t)$ using the product rule to find the derivative of $v(t)$.

$$v(t) = 3(t-2)^2(t-5)$$
$$\Rightarrow a(t) = 3[(t-2)^2(1) + (t-5)(2)(t-2)^1(1)]$$
$$= 3(t-2)[(t-2) + 2(t-5)]$$
$$a(t) = 3(t-2)(3t-12)$$

"At rest" $\Rightarrow v(t) = 0 \Rightarrow t = 2$ or $t = 5$ from part (a)
$$a(2) = 3(0)(-6) = 0 \text{ m/s}^2$$
$$a(5) = 3(3)(3) = 27 \text{ m/s}^2$$

Related Rates

One typical kind of calculus problem that often appears on the AP exam involves finding the instantaneous rate of change of two variables that are related by a third variable. Here is an example:

Sample Problem

A paper cup in the shape of a cone has a 3-inch top diameter and is 5 inches high. Water is being poured into the cup at the rate of $\frac{1}{2}$ cubic inch (in^3) per second. How fast is the water rising when the water level is halfway up the cup?

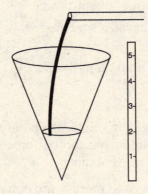

Figure 4.4

For related-rates problems, realize that even though a known rate may be constant, the rates related to it may *not* be constant. In this problem, for example, even though the water is pouring in at a constant rate of $\frac{1}{2}$ (in^3), the rate of change of the height of the water level in the cup is *not* constant. At the bottom of the cup there is very little volume to fill, so the level rises very quickly (from level 1 to level 2 in the left cone in Figure 4.5). Further up the cup, it takes a much longer time to change the water level the same amount, because there is more volume to fill (from level 3 to level 4 in the right cone in Figure 4.5).

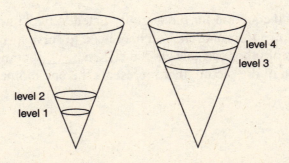

Figure 4.5

Most related-rates problems can be solved with the following five-step process:

1. **Sketch and define.**

   Most related-rates problems are "real life" situations that have one or more pictures accompanying them. Begin with a large sketch and label it to define variables. If it isn't obvious what variables will be needed, return to the sketch and label as you progress through the problem. Pick logical letters to represent the needed quantities; for example, use r for a radius instead of x.

2. **Symbolize.**

   One key to solving related-rates problems is to be able to symbolize both the given information and the unknown quantity you are seeking. Follow this format:

   "find ____"   usually a differential quantity like $\dfrac{dy}{dt}$

   "when ____"   a point in time, usually specified by noting when a variable reaches a certain value

   "given ____"   usually a differential quantity like $\dfrac{dv}{dt}$

3. **Write the equation.**

   a. Write an equation that will provide a relationship between the variables in the problem. Related-rates equations usually come from three sources: trigonometry, the Pythagorean theorem, and formulas (provided on AP exam).

   b. For some problems, you may have to modify the equation you wrote in step a. The equation must contain only the variables in the "find ____ when ____, given ____" in step 2 above. The method used to modify the equation depends on the type of problem: It may require algebra, geometry, or trig.

4. **Differentiate.**

   All rates are taken with respect to time (for example, feet *per second* or miles *per hour*), so differentiation is done with respect to time, symbolized with a lowercase t. Implicit differentiation is needed: Whenever a variable quantity is differentiated, the appropriate differential quantity must be inserted, such as *dv/dt*.

5. **Solve and substitute.**

   Solve the differentiated equation for the quantity listed in the "find ____" section, and then substitute the known information. You may need to solve a small side problem in order to discover values of other variables at the "when ____" point in time. It may help to sketch another version of the picture that represents the one moment in time in question.

Sample

Use the five-step process to solve the first sample problem: A paper cup in the shape of a cone has a 3-inch top diameter and is 5 inches high. Water is being poured into the cup at the rate of $\frac{1}{2}$ in^3 per second. How fast is the water rising when the water level is halfway up the cup?

1. Sketch and define.

Begin with a sketch. Label the top diameter and height. Show some arbitrary amount of water in the cup. Let r and h be the radius and height, respectively, of the filled portion of the cup.

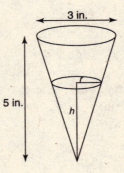

Figure 4.6

2. Symbolize.

"how fast water level is rising" $\Rightarrow$ find $\dfrac{dh}{dt}$

"halfway up the cup" $\Rightarrow$ when $h = 2.5$ in.

"poured into the cup at . . ." $\Rightarrow$ given $\dfrac{dv}{dt} = \dfrac{1}{2}$ in^3/s

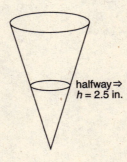

halfway $\Rightarrow$
$h = 2.5$ in.

Figure 4.7

3. Write the equation.

The equation must relate the volume (V) and the height (h) of a cone. On the AP exam, the equation will be given to you. It is

$$V = \frac{1}{3}\pi r^2 h$$

This equation has an "extra" variable: r. The "find ____ when ___, given ____" in step 2 has only v and h, so the given formula must be modified. Seek a relationship between r and either h or v.

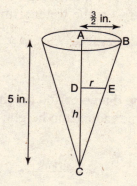

Figure 4.8

Examine triangles ABC and DEC in the picture. The two triangles are similar, which means that corresponding parts are in proportion:

$$\frac{AB}{AC} = \frac{DE}{DC} \Rightarrow \frac{\frac{3}{2}}{5} = \frac{r}{h} \Rightarrow r = \frac{3}{10}h$$

$$V = \frac{1}{3}\pi r^2 h \Rightarrow V\frac{1}{3}\pi\left(\frac{3h}{10}\right)^2 h$$

$$V = \frac{1}{3}\pi\frac{9h^2}{100}h$$

$$V = \frac{3\pi}{100}h^3$$

4. Differentiate both sides with respect to t.

$$V = \frac{3\pi}{100}h^3$$

$$\frac{dV}{dt} = \frac{3\pi}{100}3h^2\frac{dh}{dt}$$

$$\frac{dV}{dt} = \frac{9\pi}{100}h^2\frac{dh}{dt}$$

5. Solve for $\frac{dh}{dt}$ and substitute.

$$\frac{dh}{dt} = \frac{100}{9\pi h^2}\frac{dV}{dt}$$

$$\left.\frac{dh}{dt}\right|_{h=2.5} = \frac{100}{9\pi\left(\frac{5}{2}\right)^2}\left(\frac{1}{2}\right)$$

$$= \left(\frac{100}{9\pi}\right)\left(\frac{4}{25}\right)\left(\frac{1}{2}\right) = \frac{8}{9\pi}\text{ in./s}$$

Here are a few more hints to help you avoid some of the most common mistakes made when doing related-rates problems.

1. Be sure to substitute at the right time.

   Be careful that you do not substitute a numerical value for a variable until after you differentiate. In the previous problems, for example, in an effort to eliminate *r*, it is tempting (but *incorrect*) to replace *r* with 2.5, the value of *r* at the specified point in time. Because *r* changes during the problem, you cannot substitute a constant for *r* until after you differentiate. However, do use constants when appropriate. If a particular quantity does not change at all during the entire problem, then it should be represented by a constant and not a variable.

2. Differentiate with respect to time.

   A very common mistake with related-rates problems is applying implicit differentiation incorrectly — that is, forgetting to include $\frac{dy}{dt}$ when differentiating *y*, $\frac{dx}{dt}$ when differentiating *x*, $\frac{d\theta}{dt}$ when differentiating θ, and so on.

3. Include units.

   When a problem is finished, be sure to include the appropriate units for the answer. Rates should be done as measurement units per unit of time. For example,

for linear rates:	feet per second or meters per second
for area rates:	square feet per second or square meters per second
for volume rates:	cubic feet per second or cubic meters per second
for angular rates:	radians per second

4. "Rate of change" means derivative.

   In setting up related-rates problems, remember that an instantaneous rate of change is represented by the derivative. Any quantity that is described as changing per second (or minute or other unit of time), needs to be represented with a derivative like $\frac{dy}{dt}$.

5. "Decreasing" quantities should have negative rates.

   If a quantity is decreasing over the course of time, it is best to represent its rate of change with a negative number; for example, $\frac{dy}{dt} = -8$ ft/s.

6. The derivative of a constant is 0.

   Any time a constant is differentiated, the derivative should be 0. This comes up frequently in Pythagorean theorem problems.

Sample

For the previous sample problem on page 163, find the rate at which the exposed surface area of the water is changing when the water level is halfway up the cup.

1. Sketch and define.

   Let A = the exposed surface area.

   Figure 4.9

2. Symbolize.

   "rate of change of surface area" $\Rightarrow$ find $\dfrac{dA}{dt}$

   "halfway up the cup" $\Rightarrow$ when $h = 2.5$

   "poured into the cup at $\Rightarrow$ given $\dfrac{dV}{dt} = \dfrac{1}{2}$ in³/s

   and, from the previous problem, $\dfrac{dh}{dt} = \dfrac{8}{9\pi}$ in./s

3. Write the equation.

   The exposed surface area of the water is a circle, so use the formula for the area of a circle. (Very simple formulas such as this may not be provided on the AP exam.)

   $A = \pi r^2$

   Because of the "find _____ when _____, given _____" in step 2, the equation must be in terms of A, h, and/or V; r must be eliminated.

   $r = \dfrac{3}{10} h$ from the previous problem

   $\Rightarrow A = \pi \left(\dfrac{3h}{10}\right)^2 = \dfrac{9\pi}{100} h^2$

4. Differentiate both sides with respect to t.

   $\dfrac{dA}{dt} = \dfrac{9\pi}{100} (2h) \dfrac{dh}{dt}$

5. Solve and substitute.

   $\left.\dfrac{dA}{dt}\right|_{h = 2.5} = \dfrac{9\pi}{100} (5)\left(\dfrac{8}{9\pi}\right) = \dfrac{2}{5}$ in²/s

   The answer to the previous example was used to help solve this problem. A similar situation may arise on the free-response section of the AP exam. You may have to use, for example, the answer to part (b) to do part (c). If you cannot get an answer to part (b) and you need it to finish (c), make up a *reasonable* value for the missing answer, and use it to finish part (c). Explain on your test what you are doing, and show clearly where the made-up value enters. Do *not* write a paragraph about how you would finish the problem if you could; make something up and actually *do* the problem.

Sample

A 12-foot ladder leans against the side of a house. The base of the ladder is pushed toward the house at a rate of 2 feet per second. When the bottom of the ladder is 3 feet from the house, find

(a) how fast the top of the ladder is moving up the side of the house.

(b) how fast the area of the triangle created by the ladder, the side of the house, and the ground is changing.

(c) how fast the angle the ladder makes with the ground is changing.

(a)1. Sketch and define.

Label the triangle ABC. Let $x = BC$ and $y = AB$.

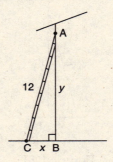

Figure 4.10

2. Symbolize.

"top of the ladder moving up . . ." $\Rightarrow$ find $\dfrac{dy}{dt}$

"bottom is 3 feet from house" $\Rightarrow$ when $x = 3$

"pushed toward the house . . ." $\Rightarrow$ given $\dfrac{dx}{dt} = -2$

3. Write the equation.

Triangle ABC is a right triangle throughout the problem, so the Pythagorean theorem can be applied.

$$x^2 + y^2 = 12^2$$

No variables need to be eliminated because the "find _____ when _____, given _____" has x and y only, as does the equation. Note that a variable was not used for the hypotenuse of the triangle. The hypotenuse is the ladder, and because the length of the ladder does not change throughout the entire problem, the constant value of 12 should be used in the equation.

4. Differentiate both sides with respect to t.

$$x^2 + y^2 = 12^2$$

$$2x\frac{dx}{dt} + 2y\frac{dy}{dt} = 0$$

5. Solve and substitute.

$$2y\frac{dy}{dt} = -2x\frac{dx}{dt}$$

$$\frac{dy}{dt} = \frac{-2x}{2y}\frac{dx}{dt}$$

$$\frac{dy}{dt} = \frac{-x}{y}\frac{dx}{dt}$$

You need to find a value of y that corresponds to the given value of x in order to substitute. Drawing a picture that represents the moment when $x = 3$ may help.

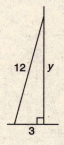

Figure 4.11

$$y^2 + 3^2 = 12^2 \Rightarrow y = \sqrt{135} = 3\sqrt{15}$$

$$\left.\frac{dy}{dt}\right|_{x=3} = \frac{-3}{3\sqrt{15}}(-2) = \frac{2}{\sqrt{15}} \approx 0.52 \text{ ft/s}$$

(b)1. Sketch and define. (See Figure 4.10.)

Let a = area of triangle ABC

2. Symbolize.

"area of triangle changing" $\Rightarrow$ find $\frac{da}{dt}$

"bottom is 3 feet from house" $\Rightarrow$ when $x = 3$

from the previous problem $y = 3\sqrt{15}$

"pushed toward the house $\Rightarrow$ given $\frac{dx}{dt} = -2$

from the previous problem $\frac{dy}{dt} = \frac{2}{\sqrt{15}}$

3. Write the equation.

The area of a triangle is given by

$$\text{area} = \frac{1}{2}(\text{base})(\text{height})$$

$$a = \frac{1}{2}xy$$

The equation can be differentiated now, because the "find _____ when _____, given _____" section has enough information in it.

4. Differentiate with respect to t. Use the product rule.

$$a = \frac{1}{2}xy$$

$$\frac{da}{dt} = \frac{1}{2}\left[x\frac{dy}{dt} + y\frac{dx}{dt}\right]$$

5. Solve and substitute.

$$\frac{da}{dt} = \frac{1}{2}\left[(3)\left(\frac{2}{\sqrt{15}}\right) + (3\sqrt{15})(-2)\right]\text{ft}^2/\text{s}$$

This answer is acceptable on the AP exam. Answers do not have to be simplified unless a decimal answer is requested, in which case you would, of course, use a calculator. But if you prefer a simpler form, use

$$\frac{da}{dt} = \frac{3}{\sqrt{15}} - 3\sqrt{15} = \frac{-42\sqrt{15}}{15}\text{ft}^2/\text{s}$$

(c) 1. Sketch and define.

Let θ = the angle the ladder makes with the ground.

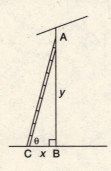

Figure 4.12

2. Symbolize.

"angle is changing" $\Rightarrow$ find $\dfrac{d\theta}{dt}$

"bottom is 3 feet from house" $\Rightarrow$ when $x = 3$

from the previous problem $\qquad y = 3\sqrt{15}$

"pushed toward the house . . ." $\Rightarrow$ given $\dfrac{dx}{dt} = -2$

from the previous problem $\dfrac{dy}{dt} = \dfrac{2}{\sqrt{15}}$

3. Write the equation.

   Trig is required for any problem that asks for the rate of change of an angle. Several different trig functions may work:

   $\sin\theta = \dfrac{y}{12}$ or $\cos\theta = \dfrac{x}{12}$ or even $\tan\theta = \dfrac{y}{x}$

   The cosine equation requires only information given at the beginning of the problem, and no intermediate results from previous parts, so use it.

4. Differentiate both sides with respect to t.

   $$\cos\theta = \dfrac{x}{12}$$

   $$-\sin\theta\,\dfrac{d\theta}{dt} = \dfrac{1}{12}\dfrac{dx}{dt}$$

5. Solve and substitute.

   $$\dfrac{d\theta}{dt} = \dfrac{1}{-\sin\theta}\dfrac{1}{12}\dfrac{dx}{dt}$$

   You need to find $\sin\theta$ before substituting. You can use a calculator, but just applying the trig ratios is probably easier:

   $$\dfrac{d\theta}{dt}\bigg|_{x=3}\left(\dfrac{-4}{\sqrt{15}}\right)\left(\dfrac{1}{12}\right)(-2) = \dfrac{2}{3\sqrt{15}}\ \text{rad/s}$$

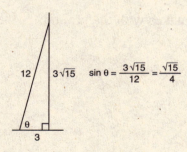

$$12 \quad\quad 3\sqrt{15} \quad \sin\theta = \dfrac{3\sqrt{15}}{12} = \dfrac{\sqrt{15}}{4}$$

$$\theta \qquad 3$$

Figure 4.13

Relative Extrema and the First Derivative Test

The derivative can play a key role in determining what the graph of a function looks like, because it can be used to determine where a function is increasing or decreasing.

Theorem on Increasing and Decreasing

If $f'(x) < 0$ for all x in some interval (a, b), then $f(x)$ is decreasing on (a, b).

If $f'(x) > 0$ for all x in some interval (a, b), then $f(x)$ is increasing on (a, b).

Examine the slopes of the following tangent lines. For $-4 < x < -\frac{1}{2}$, the slopes of the tangent lines l, m, and n are obviously positive, so $f'(x) > 0$, and the function is clearly increasing. For $-\frac{1}{2} < x < 4$, the slopes of the tangent lines p, q, and r are negative, so $f'(x) < 0$ and the function is decreasing.

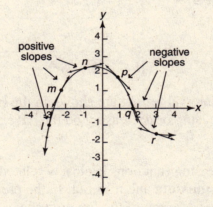

Figure 4.14

To determine where a function is increasing and decreasing, take these steps:

1. Find **critical numbers** — that is, where

    $f'(x) = 0$ or $f'(x)$ does not exist

2. Find the sign of $f'(x)$ in each of the intervals determined by the critical numbers.

3. Apply the foregoing theorem:

    $f'(x) > 0 \Rightarrow f(x)$ is increasing

    $f'(x) < 0 \Rightarrow f(x)$ is decreasing

Sample

Find all intervals where $f(x) = 4x^3 - 3x^2 - 18x + 6$ is increasing and all intervals where it is decreasing.

Find critical numbers and do interval testing.

$$f(x) = 4x^3 - 3x^2 - 18x + 6 \Rightarrow f'(x) = 12x^2 - 6x - 18$$
$$= 6(2x^2 - x - 3)$$
$$= 6(2x - 3)(x + 1)$$

critical numbers $\Rightarrow f'(x) = 0$ or $f'(x)$ does not exist

Therefore, $x = \frac{3}{2}$ and $x = -1$ are critical numbers.

Now find the sign of $f'(x)$ in the intervals determined by these critical numbers.

x	$x < -1$	$x = -1$	$-1 < x < \frac{3}{2}$	$x = \frac{3}{2}$	$x > \frac{3}{2}$
$f'(x)$	positive	0	negative	0	positive
$f(x)$	increasing		decreasing		increasing

Note that conclusions from the interval testing are shown in the last row, which is labeled $f(x)$. To justify that a function is increasing or decreasing on the AP exam, you must use this or a similar format.

The test for increasing and decreasing functions is closely related to the idea of **extreme values** of a function, also known as the **maxima** and **minima**. In the previous problem, $f(x)$ had two critical numbers, $x = -1$ and $x = \frac{3}{2}$. A graph of the function shows that these two points are the **relative maximum** and the **relative minimum** of $f(x)$, respectively.

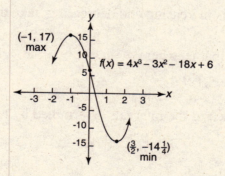

Figure 4.15

This relationship between extrema and the derivative can be summarized as follows:

First Derivative Test for Extrema

Given that $x = c$ is a critical number of the function $f(x)$:

> If $f'(x)$ changes sign from positive to negative at $x = c$, then $f(x)$ has a relative maximum at $x = c$.
>
> If $f'(x)$ changes sign from negative to positive at $x = c$, then $f(x)$ has a relative minimum at $x = c$.

A shorthand notation for this theorem is

$$f'(x): + \rightarrow - \text{ at } x = c \Rightarrow \text{rel max}$$
$$f'(x): - \rightarrow + \text{ at } x = c \Rightarrow \text{rel min}$$

Sample

> Find the relative extrema of $y = \sin x - 2\cos x$ in the interval $[0, 2\pi]$. Justify your answer by using the first derivative test.

Find critical numbers and do interval testing.

$$y = \sin x - 2\cos x \Rightarrow y' = \cos x + 2\sin x$$

critical numbers $\Rightarrow f'(x) = 0$ or $f'(x)$ does not exist

$$\cos x + 2\sin x = 0$$

$$2\sin x = -\cos x \text{ (assuming that } \cos x = 0 \text{ is not a solution)}$$

$$\tan x = -\frac{1}{2} \Rightarrow x \approx -0.46 + k\pi \text{ radians}$$

Thus in the interval $[0, 2\pi]$, $x \approx 2.68$ or $x \approx 5.82$.

Now do interval testing on y'.

x	$0 \le x < 2.68$	$x = 2.68$	$2.68 < x < 5.82$	$x = 5.82$	$5.82 < x \le 2\pi$
y'	positive	0	negative	0	positive
y	increasing	rel max	decreasing	rel min	increasing

Thus there is a relative maximum at $(2.68, 2.24)$ and a relative minimum at $(5.82, -2.24)$.

Sample

Find the relative extrema of $f(x) = 3x^{\frac{2}{3}} - x$, and sketch the function on the interval $[-1, 27]$.

Find critical numbers and do interval testing.

$$f(x) = 3x^{\frac{2}{3}} - x \Rightarrow f'(x) = 3\left(\frac{2}{3}x^{-\frac{1}{3}}\right) - 1$$

$$= \frac{2}{\sqrt[3]{x}} - 1 = \frac{2 - \sqrt[3]{x}}{\sqrt[3]{x}}$$

critical numbers $\Rightarrow f'(x) = 0$ or $f'(x)$ does not exist

Therefore, $x = 8$ and $x = 0$ are critical numbers.

x	$-1 \leq x < 0$	$x = 0$	$0 < x < 8$	$x = 8$	$8 < x \leq 27$
$f'(x)$	neg	D.N.E.	pos	0	neg
$f(x)$	decr	rel min sharp turn	incr	rel max	decr

Thus there is a relative minimum at (0, 0) and a relative maximum at (8, 4).

The relative minimum at $x = 0$ is indicated in the chart as a "sharp turn." Because the domain of $f(x)$ is all real numbers, but the derivative at $x = 0$ does not exist, there are two possibilities for the graph at $x = 0$: a vertical tangent or a sharp turn. Only the sharp turn is consistent with $x = 0$ also being the relative minimum.

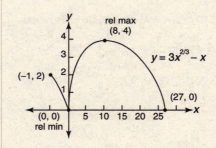

Figure 4.16

Caution: Do not assume that *all* critical numbers are some type of extremum. The derivative must *change sign* on either side of the critical number in order for the critical number to be an extremum. Always justify extrema by showing the sign change in the derivative.

Sample

> Find any relative extrema of $g(x) = 3x^4 - 8x^3 + 6x^2$.

Find the critical numbers and do interval testing.

$$g(x) = 3x^4 - 8x^3 + 6x^2 \Rightarrow g'(x) = 12x^3 - 24x^2 + 12x$$
$$= 12x(x^2 - 2x + 1)$$
$$= 12x(x - 1)^2$$

critical numbers $\Rightarrow f'(x) = 0$ or $f'(x)$ does not exist

Therefore, $x = 0$ and $x = 1$ are critical numbers.

x	$x < 0$	$x = 0$	$0 < x < 1$	$x = 1$	$x > 1$
$f'(x)$	neg	0	pos	0	pos
$f(x)$	decr	rel min	incr	no extremum	incr

The only extremum is a relative minimum at $(0, 0)$. A sketch of $g(x)$ follows.

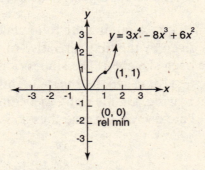

Figure 4.17

Concavity and the Second Derivative Test

A second way to use derivatives to help sketch curves is with the second derivative, because the second derivative can be used to find the **concavity** of a graph. Visually, concavity is easy to recognize. If a graph is "smiling" at you, it is concave up; if it is "frowning" at you, it is concave down.

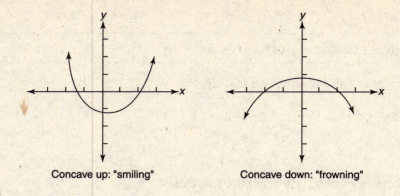

Concave up: "smiling"   Concave down: "frowning"

Figure 4.18

Not surprisingly, a more mathematical definition of concavity involves derivatives:

Definition of Concavity

A function $f(x)$ is concave up on an interval if $f'(x)$ is increasing on the interval.

A function $f(x)$ is concave down on an interval if $f'(x)$ is decreasing on the interval.

This definition can be demonstrated by examining the following graphs, while keeping in mind that the slope of a tangent line is given by the first derivative of the function. On the left, four tangent lines $l_1, l_2, l_3,$ and l_4, have been sketched. The slopes of the tangent lines $l_1, l_2, l_3,$ and l_4 are (approximately) $m_1 = -1, m_2 = -1/2, m_3 = 1,$ and $m_4 = 3$. This series of numbers is obviously increasing, so the derivative is increasing. On the right, the situation is reversed: the slopes $m_5 = 2, m_6 = 1, m_7 = 0,$ and $m_8 = -1$ are decreasing, and thus so is the derivative.

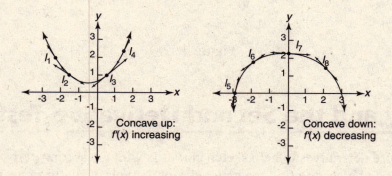

Concave up:
$f'(x)$ increasing

Concave down:
$f'(x)$ decreasing

Figure 4.19

The foregoing definition is just that: a *definition* of concavity. There is, however, an easier and more commonly used *test* for concavity.

Theorem: Test for Concavity

If $f''(x) > 0$ on an interval, then $f(x)$ is concave up on that interval.

If $f''(x) < 0$ on an interval, then $f(x)$ is concave down on that interval.

This test is derived by combining the definition of concavity with the test for increasing and decreasing functions in the previous section. Here is a shorthand notation that incorporates the definition and the test:

concave up $\Leftrightarrow f'(x)$ increasing $\Leftrightarrow f''(x)$ positive

concave down $\Leftrightarrow f'(x)$ decreasing $\Leftrightarrow f''(x)$ negative

To find the concavity of a function:

1. Find where $f''(x) = 0$ or $f''(x)$ does not exist (sometimes known as the second derivative critical numbers).

2. Find the sign of $f''(x)$ in each of the intervals determined by the numbers in the first step.

3. Apply the test-for-concavity theorem.

Sample

> Find all intervals where the graph of $y = 2x^3 - 6x^2$ is concave up.

Find the second derivative critical numbers and do interval testing.

$$y = 2x^3 - 6x^2 \Rightarrow y' = 6x^2 - 12x$$
$$\Rightarrow y'' = 12x - 12$$

$y'' = 0$ or y'' does not exist

$12x - 12 = 0$

$x = 1$

x	$x < 1$	$x = 1$	$x > 1$
y''	neg	0	pos
y	concave down		concave up

Thus the graph is concave up on $x > 1$.

Definition of Point of Inflection

If a function changes concavity at a point, that point is called a **point of inflection** (POI), provided that a tangent line exists at that point.

In the foregoing example, $(1, -4)$ is a point of inflection, and a sketch of $y = 2x^3 - 6x^2$ shows the change in concavity.

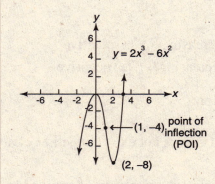

Figure 4.20

On the AP exam, free-response problems often deal with finding relative extrema and points of inflection, and then they require a sketch of the graph, along with justification of your solution. The next example is a typical free-response problem. Note that you are asked for several other pieces of information, as well as for the extrema and POI. When drawing the sketch at the end of the problem, take into account all of the information you have discovered, and be consistent.

Sample

Consider the function $f(x) = x^4 - 8x^2$

(a) Show that $f(x)$ is symmetric with respect to the y-axis.

(b) Find all the zeros of $f(x)$.

(c) Find the x- and y-coordinates of all relative extrema, and identify them as relative maxima or minima.

(d) Find the x- and y-coordinates of all points of inflection.

(e) Using the information from parts (a) through (d), sketch the graph of $f(x)$.

Justify all your answers.

(a) To justify symmetry with respect to the y-axis, show that $f(-x) = f(x)$

$$f(x) = x^4 - 8x^2 \Rightarrow f(-x) = (-x)^4 - 8(-x)^2$$
$$= x^4 - 8x^2$$
$$= f(x)$$

Thus $f(-x) = f(x)$, so $f(x)$ is symmetric with respect to the y-axis.

(b) For zeros, find where $f(x) = 0$.

$$f(x) = x^4 - 8x^2 = 0$$
$$x^2(x^2 - 8) = 0$$
$$x^2 = 0 \quad \text{or} \quad x^2 = 8$$
$$x = 0 \quad \text{or} \quad x = \pm 2\sqrt{2}$$

Thus the zeros are $(0, 0), (2\sqrt{2}, 0),$ and $(-2\sqrt{2}, 0)$.

(c) For extrema, find $f'(x)$ find the critical numbers, and do interval testing.

$$f(x) = x^4 - 8x^2 \Rightarrow f'(x) = 4x^3 - 16x$$
$$= 4x(x^2 - 4)$$

critical numbers: $f'(x) = 0$ or $f'(x)$ does not exist

Therefore, $x = 0$ and $x = \pm 2$ are critical numbers.

x	$x < -2$	$x = -2$	$-2 < x < 0$	$x = 0$	$0 < x < 2$	$x = 2$	$x > 2$
$f'(x)$	neg	0	pos	0	neg	0	pos
$f(x)$	decr	rel min	incr	rel max	decr	rel min	incr

Thus $(-2, -16)$ and $(2, -16)$ are relative minima and $(0, 0)$ is a relative maximum.

(d) For POI, find $f''(x)$ critical numbers and do interval testing.

$$f'(x) = 4x^3 - 16x \Rightarrow f''(x) = 12x^2 - 16$$
$$= 4(3x^2 - 4)$$

critical numbers: $f''(x) = 0$ or $f''(x)$ does not exist

$$3x^2 - 4 = 0$$

$$x = \pm \frac{2}{\sqrt{3}} = \pm \frac{2\sqrt{3}}{3}$$

x	$x < -\dfrac{2\sqrt{3}}{3}$	$x = -\dfrac{2\sqrt{3}}{3}$	$-\dfrac{2\sqrt{3}}{3} < x < \dfrac{2\sqrt{3}}{3}$	$x = \dfrac{2\sqrt{3}}{3}$	$x > \dfrac{2\sqrt{3}}{3}$
$f''(x)$	pos	0	neg	0	pos
$f(x)$	concave up	POI	concave down	POI	concave up

Therefore, $\left(-\dfrac{2\sqrt{3}}{3}, -\dfrac{80}{9} \right)$ and $\left(\dfrac{2\sqrt{3}}{3}, -\dfrac{80}{9} \right)$ are points of inflection.

(e)

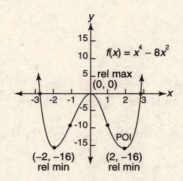

Figure 4.21

Some students prefer to find both derivatives and their critical numbers first and then put both types of critical numbers into a single chart to do the interval testing. This method is *not* recommended, however, because it can result in testing more intervals than are necessary. It also can lead to incorrect conclusions, such as a first derivative critical number turning into a point of inflection.

Second Derivative Test for Extrema

Concavity also provides a second method for justifying relative extrema.

Given that $f'(c) = 0$ and $f''(x)$ exists in an interval about $x = c$:

    If $f''(c) < 0$, then $x = c$ is a relative maximum.
    If $f''(c) > 0$, then $x = c$ is a relative minimum.
    If $f''(c) = 0$, the test fails, and you should use the first derivative test.

Caution: When applying this test, be sure you put the *first* derivative critical numbers into the *second* derivative.

This test may seem a bit backward: if the second derivative is *negative*, the result is a relative *maximum*. But if you picture a relative maximum, you will see that the function is clearly concave *down* around the maximum; hence $f''(x) < 0$. Similarly, for a relative minimum, the function is concave *up* around the minimum; hence $f''(x) > 0$.

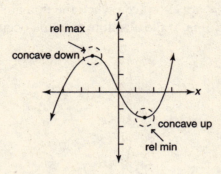

Figure 4.22

Sample

Use the second derivative test to find the extrema $f(x) = 3x^4 - 8x^3 + 6x^2$ (This is the same problem as the last one in the previous section, page 175).

$$f(x) = 3x^4 - 8x^3 + 6x^2 \Rightarrow f'(x) = 12x^3 - 24x^2 + 12x$$
$$= 12x(x^2 - 2x + 1)$$
$$= 12x(x - 1)^2$$
$$f'(x) = 0 \Rightarrow x = 0 \text{ or } x = 1$$

Now find the second derivative, and test the sign at $x = 0$ and $x = 1$.

$$f'(x) = 12x^3 - 24x^2 + 12x \Rightarrow f''(x) = 36x^2 - 48x + 12$$
$$= 12(3x^2 - 4x + 1)$$
$$f''(0) = 12 \Rightarrow f''(0) > 0 \Rightarrow \text{relative minimum at } (0, 0)$$
$$f''(1) = 0 \Rightarrow \text{test fails, use first derivative test (see page 173)}$$

Absolute Extrema and Optimization

A common application of the derivative involves finding the **absolute extrema** of a function. Absolute extrema are just what they sound like: the very largest or smallest values of a function. Absolute extrema can occur at the relative extrema of the function or at the endpoints of a given closed interval. This concept is summarized in the following theorem.

Extreme Value Theorem

If a function is continuous on a closed interval, then the function is guaranteed to have an absolute maximum and an absolute minimum in the interval. To *guarantee* the existence of absolute extrema, the interval *must* be closed. However, some functions may have absolute extrema even when the interval is open, or even when the domain is the set of real numbers. Study the following examples. Some of the absolute extrema occur at endpoints, and others occur at the relative extrema.

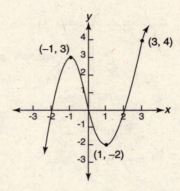

Figure 4.23

on [–2, 2]	absolute maximum at (–1, 3)
	absolute minimum at (1, –2)
on [–2, 0]	absolute maximum at (–1, 3)
	absolute minimum at (–2, 0) and (0, 0)
on [0, 3]	absolute maximum at (3, 4)
	absolute minimum at (1, –2)
on (0, ∞)	no absolute maximum
	absolute minimum at (1, –2)
on (–2, 1)	absolute maximum at (–1, 3)
	no absolute minimum

Sample

Find the absolute extrema of $f(x) = x^{\frac{2}{3}} - 1$ on each of the following intervals:

(a) [–1, 2]

(b) (–1, 2)

(c) [0, ∞)

(d) (0, ∞)

(e) the real numbers

Begin by finding the relative extrema, if any. A sketch may help.

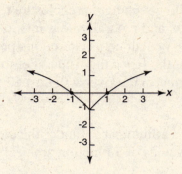

Figure 4.24

$$f(x) = x^{\frac{2}{3}} - 1 \Rightarrow f'(x) = \frac{2}{3} x^{-\frac{1}{3}} = \frac{2}{3 \sqrt[3]{x}}$$

critical numbers: $f'(x) = 0$ or $f'(x)$ does not exist
$x = 0$

x	$x < 0$	$x = 0$	$x > 0$
$f'(x)$	neg	D.N.E.	pos
$f(x)$	decr	rel min sharp turn	incr

Therefore, $f(x)$ has a relative minimum at $(0, -1)$.

(a) on $[-1, 2]$

x	-1	0	2
$f(x)$	0	-1	0.59

absolute minimum at $(0, -1)$
absolute maximum at approximately $(2, 0.59)$

(b) on $(-1, 2)$

no absolute maximum
absolute minimum at $(0, -1)$

(c) $[0, \infty)$

no absolute maximum
absolute minimum at $(0, -1)$

(d) on $(0, \infty)$

no absolute maximum
no absolute minimum

(e) on the real numbers

no absolute maximum
absolute minimum at $(0, -1)$

Word problems that apply the concept of extrema are characterized as optimization problems. Study the following example.

Sample Problem

An Australian rancher wants to build a rectangular enclosure to house his flock of emus. He has only $900 to spend on the fence, and naturally he wants to enclose the largest area possible for his money. He plans to build the pen along a river on his property, so he does not have to put a fence on that side. The side of the fence that is parallel to the river will cost $5 per foot to build, whereas the sides perpendicular to the river will cost $3 per foot to build. What dimensions should he choose?

This problem requires finding the maximum area, under the constraint of spending $900. The techniques of finding the extreme values of a function are useful here. To solve optimization problems:

1. Define variables to represent the quantities in the problem. A sketch may be needed.

2. Identify the quantity to optimize with a short phrase, such as "maximize area."

3. Write equation(s):

   (a) involving the quantity to be optimized.

   (b) involving any constraints, if needed.

4. Combine the two equations in step 3 to get an equation that expresses the quantity to be optimized in terms of a single independent variable. Find the domain of this independent variable.

5. Find the absolute extreme value required by the problem. If the domain is a closed interval, check the function values at the endpoints of the interval.

6. Answer the question.

Sample

Solve the foregoing sample problem.

Sketch the pen and river, and define the variables.

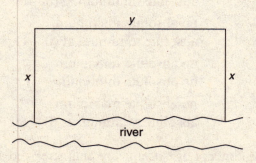

Figure 4.25

maximize area: A

$A = xy$

$3x + 3x + 5y = 900 \Rightarrow 6x + 5y = 900$

$$5y = 900 - 6x$$

$$y = \frac{900 - 6x}{5}$$

Substituting the constraint into the area equation yields

$$A = xy = x\left(\frac{900 - 6x}{5}\right)$$

$$A = \frac{1}{5}(900x - 6x^2) \quad \text{Domain: } x > 0$$

$$\frac{dA}{dx} = 900 - 12x$$

critical numbers: $\frac{dA}{dx} = 0$ or $\frac{dA}{dx}$ does not exist

$$x = \frac{900}{12} = 75$$

Justify the maximum.

x		$0 < x < 75$	$x = 75$	$x > 75$
$\frac{dA}{dx}$		pos	0	neg
A		incr	rel max	decr

$$x = 75 \Rightarrow y = \frac{900 - 6(75)}{5} = 90$$

Thus $x = 75$ yields the maximum value on the domain.

Therefore, the farmer should build his enclosure to measure 75 feet by 90 feet.

Sample

Find the point on the parabola $y = \frac{1}{2}x^2 - 2$ that is closest to the origin.

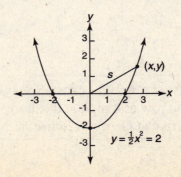

Figure 4.26

minimize distance: s

$$s = \sqrt{(x-0)^2 + (y-0)^2}$$

$$y = \frac{1}{2}x^2 - 2$$

Substituting the constraint into the distance formula yields

$$s = \sqrt{x^2 + \left(\frac{1}{2}x^2 - 2\right)^2}$$

The minimum value of s will occur when the radicand is a minimum, so let the radicand be represented by a single variable — say r.

$$r = x^2 + \left(\frac{1}{2}x^2 - 2\right)^2$$

$$r = x^2 + \frac{1}{4}x^4 - 2x^2 + 4$$

$$r = \frac{1}{4}x^4 - x^2 + 4 \qquad \text{Domain}: x \in \text{the real numbers}$$

$$\frac{dr}{dx} = x^3 - 2x$$

critical numbers: $\dfrac{dr}{dx} = 0$ or $\dfrac{dr}{dx}$ does not exist

$$x^3 - 2x = 0$$
$$x(x^2 - 2) = 0$$
$$x = 0 \text{ or } x = \pm\sqrt{2}$$

Justify the minimum.

x	$x < -\sqrt{2}$	$x = -\sqrt{2}$	$-\sqrt{2} < x < 0$	$x = 0$	$0 < x < \sqrt{2}$	$x = \sqrt{2}$	$x > \sqrt{2}$
$\dfrac{dr}{dx}$	neg	0	pos	0	neg	0	pos
r	decr	rel min	incr	rel max	decr	rel min	incr

Thus the points on the parabola that are closest to the origin are $(-\sqrt{2}, -1)$ and $(\sqrt{2}, -1)$.

If the problem had asked for the actual minimum distance, and not the points where the minimum occurred, the answer would have been the value of s (not r) that corresponds to $x = \sqrt{2}$.

Sample

Anna is in a rowboat 3 miles from a straight coast. She wants to go to George's house 2 miles down the coast. Anna can row at 4 mph and can jog at 6 mph. Where should she land on the coast in order to arrive at George's house in the shortest time possible?

Make a sketch and define the variables.

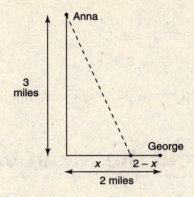

Figure 4.27

minimize: T where

$T =$ (time on water) + (time on land)

$T = t_w + t_l$

$r \cdot t = d \Rightarrow t = \dfrac{d}{r}$

Substituting the constraint into the time equation yields

$$T = \frac{d_w}{r_w} + \frac{d_l}{r_l}$$

$$T = \frac{\sqrt{x^2 + 9}}{4} + \frac{2 - x}{6} \qquad \text{Domain: } 0 \le x \le 2$$

$$T = \frac{1}{12} \left[3\left(x^2 + 9\right)^{\frac{1}{2}} + 4 - 2x \right]$$

$$\frac{dT}{dx} = \frac{1}{12} \left[\frac{3}{2}\left(x^2 + 9\right)^{-\frac{1}{2}}(2x - 2) \right]$$

$$= \frac{1}{12} \left[\frac{3x}{\sqrt{x^2 + 9}} - 2 \right]$$

$$= \frac{1}{12} \left[\frac{3x - 2\sqrt{x^2 + 9}}{\sqrt{x^2 + 9}} \right]$$

critical numbers: $\dfrac{dT}{dx} = 0$ or $\dfrac{dT}{dx}$ does not exist

$$3x = 2\sqrt{x^2 + 9}$$

$$9x^2 = 4x^2 + 36$$

$$x^2 = \frac{36}{5}$$

$$x = \pm \frac{6}{\sqrt{5}} \approx \pm 2.7$$

Because the only critical numbers are outside the domain, the extrema must occur at the endpoints.

x	0	2
T	$\frac{13}{12} \approx 1.083$	$\frac{\sqrt{13}}{4} \approx 0.901$

Therefore, Anna should row directly toward George's and not jog at all.

Rolle's Theorem and the Mean Value Theorem

Two theorems that are applied to many calculus proofs are Rolle's theorem and the mean value theorem. Although you will not be required to apply them to proofs on the AP exam, either (or both) might appear on multiple-choice questions or perhaps as one part of a free-response problem. These problems are some of the easiest applications of the derivative, *if* you have memorized the hypothesis and conclusion of the theorems. They are impossible if you haven't.

Rolle's Theorem

If $f(x)$ is continuous on $[a, b]$ and differentiable on (a, b), and if $f(a) = f(b)$, then there exists at least one number c in (a, b) such that $f'(c) = 0$.

Translation: As long as the function is continuous, with no sharp turns or vertical tangents, and as long as $f(a) = f(b)$, then there is at least one place where the graph has a horizontal tangent.

To satisfy the hypothesis of Rolle's theorem, you must show that all three conditions are satisfied: continuity, differentiability, and $f(a) = f(b)$. Frequently, the last condition is modified to $f(a) = f(b) = 0$ because this makes the condition easier to satisfy. On the AP exam, the interval may be specified, but be sure to show that the hypothesis is satisfied. Graphically, Rolle's theorem looks like this:

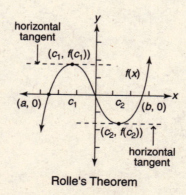

Rolle's Theorem

Figure 4.28

Sample

For the function $f(x) = 3x^2 - 2x$, show that the hypothesis of Rolle's theorem is satisfied on the interval $\left[0, \frac{2}{3}\right]$, and find the number guaranteed by Rolle's theorem.

Show that the three criteria are satisfied; then solve $f'(x) = 0$

1. All polynomial functions are everywhere continuous.

2. All polynomial functions are differentiable.

3. $f(0) = 3(0) - 2(0) = 0$

$f\left(\frac{2}{3}\right) = 3\left(\frac{2}{3}\right)^2 - 2\left(\frac{2}{3}\right) = 3\left(\frac{4}{9}\right) - \frac{4}{3} = 0$

Therefore, the hypothesis of Rolle's theorem is satisfied.

$$f(x) = 3x^2 - 2x \Rightarrow f'(x) = 6x - 2$$

Thus $\quad f'(x) = 0 \Rightarrow 6x - 2 = 0$

$$x = \frac{1}{3}$$

A sketch of the graph shows the horizontal tangent at $x = 1/3$.

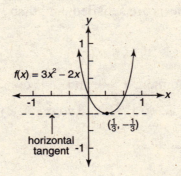

Figure 4.29

Mean Value Theorem

If $f(x)$ is continuous on $[a, b]$ and differentiable on (a, b), then there exists at least one number c in the interval such that

$$f'(c) = \frac{f(b) - f(a)}{b - a}$$

Translation: As long as the function is continuous, with no sharp turns or vertical tangents, there is at least one place where the graph has a tangent line that is parallel to the line through the endpoints.

Graphically, the mean value theorem looks like this:

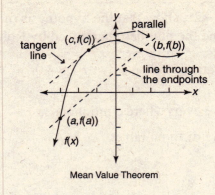

Mean Value Theorem

Figure 4.30

Sample

For the function $f(x) = \ln x$, show that the hypothesis of the mean value theorem is satisfied on the interval [1, 3], and find the number guaranteed by the conclusion of the mean value theorem to the nearest hundredth. Sketch a graph showing the tangent line at this point.

Show that both parts of the hypothesis are satisfied, and then solve the equation

$$f'(x) = \frac{f(b) - f(a)}{b - a}$$

1. $y = \ln x$ is continuous on its domain, $x > 0$, and so is continuous on [1, 3].

2. $f'(x) = \frac{1}{x} \Rightarrow f(x)$ is differentiable on $x > 0$ and so on (1, 3).

$$f'(x) = \frac{f(b) - f(a)}{b - a} \Rightarrow \frac{1}{x} = \frac{\ln 3 - \ln 1}{3 - 1}$$

$$\frac{1}{x} = \frac{\ln 3}{2}$$

$$x = \frac{2}{\ln 3} \approx 1.82$$

Sketch:

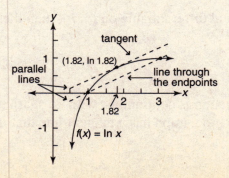

Figure 4.31

Differentials

One of the notations used to represent the derivative, dy/dx, is known as differential notation. The expression dy/dx should be thought of as a quotient of two separate quantities, dy and dx, each known as a **differential.** Individually, differentials are used for approximating values of variables and in solving differential equations.

In the following graph of $f(x)$, the tangent line at $(1, 1)$ is shown as line l. A point B has been chosen to the right of $(1, 1)$. Point C is on the tangent line directly above B, and point D is on the graph of $f(x)$ directly above B and C.

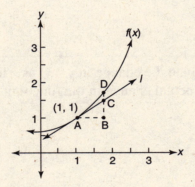

Figure 4.32

Considering the slope of tangent line l both as the ratio of vertical change to horizontal change and as the derivative,

$$m_l = \frac{BC}{AB} \text{ and } m_l = \frac{dy}{dx}$$

makes it possible to think of the individual differentials as

$$dx = AB \text{ and } dy = BC$$

Now, if AB is also considered as an increment in x that corresponds to an increment of BD in the function values of $f(x)$, then

$$\Delta x = AB \text{ and } \Delta y = BD$$

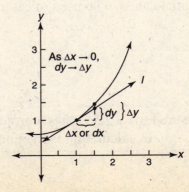

Figure 4.33

From Figures 4.32 and 4.33 it should be clear that BC and BD are approximately equal and that this approximation will be better for smaller values of AB. Thus

$BC \approx BD$ for "small" values of AB

$\Rightarrow dy \approx \Delta y$ for "small" Δx

And because $\dfrac{dy}{dx} = f'(x) \Rightarrow dy = f'(x)\, dx$

it is clear that $\qquad \Delta y \approx dy = f'(x)\, dx$

This last line is the form in which differentials are used for approximations.

Sample

> Use differentials to approximate the change in $y = x^3$ as x increases from 1 to 1.002, and compare your answer to the actual change in the function values over the same interval.

For this problem,

$f(x) = x^3 \Rightarrow f'(x) = 3x^2$

$\quad dx = \Delta x = 0.002$ and $x = 1$

$\quad \Delta y \approx dy = f'(x)\, dx$

$\Rightarrow \Delta y \approx 3\,(1)^2\,(0.002) = 0.006$

For the actual change in $f(x)$,

$f(1) = 1$ and $f(1.002) = (1.002)^3 = 1.006012008$

$\Rightarrow \Delta y = 1.006012008 - 1 = 0.006012008$

Thus the differential approximation is correct to three decimal places.

Without a calculator, using differentials to approximate a change in a function is generally easier than finding the actual change in the function. The differential employs the derivative, which is usually simpler than the original function and thus results in an easier and shorter calculation. Furthermore, the differential requires only one operation, whereas calculating the actual change in a function requires evaluating the function at two separate points and then finding the difference. The differential can also be used to estimate propagated error, as in the next example.

Sample

> The radius of a sphere is measured to be 2.5 inches, correct to within 0.01 inch. Approximate the error propagated in calculating the volume of the sphere.

Use dV to approximate ΔV.

$$V = \frac{4}{3}\pi r^3 \Rightarrow \frac{dv}{dr} = 4\pi r^2$$

$$\Delta V \approx dV = (4\pi r^2)(dr)$$

$$\Delta V \approx 4\pi(2.5)^2(\pm 0.01)$$

$$\Delta V \approx \pm 0.785\text{in}^3$$

L'Hôpital's Rule (BC Only)

Another method for finding limits uses derivatives. This method, known as L'Hôpital's rule, is useful when direct substitution results in the indeterminate form $\frac{0}{0}$ or $\frac{\infty}{\infty}$. Problems on the AB exam will not *require* the use of L'Hôpital's rule; however, it may be possible to use it as an alternative or backup method for some limit problems. The BC exam will require the use of L'Hôpital's rule in many types of problems. Be sure to remember both the hypothesis and the conclusion of L'Hôpital's rule.

Theorem: L'Hôpital's Rule

If $\lim\limits_{x\to} \dfrac{f(x)}{g(x)} = \dfrac{0}{0}$ or $\dfrac{\infty}{\infty}$, then $\lim\limits_{x\to} \dfrac{f(x)}{g(x)} = \lim\limits_{x\to} \dfrac{f'(x)}{g'(x)}$

Notation: For this theorem, $\lim\limits_{x\to}$ is used to represent $\lim\limits_{x\to c}, \lim\limits_{x\to c^+}, \lim\limits_{x\to c^-}, \lim\limits_{x\to \infty}, \lim\limits_{x\to -\infty}$, ∞/∞ is used to represent $\frac{+\infty}{+\infty}, \frac{-\infty}{+\infty}, \frac{+\infty}{-\infty}$, or $\frac{-\infty}{-\infty}$.

Caution: To apply L'Hôpital's rule, find the derivatives of the numerator and denominator individually; do *not* apply the quotient rule, even though it is a quotient.

Sample

> Find $\lim\limits_{x\to 0} \dfrac{\sin x}{x}$ by using L'Hôpital's rule.

Substituting 0 into the numerator and denominator directly yields

$$\frac{\sin 0}{0} = \frac{0}{0}$$

This is one of the indeterminate forms, so the hypothesis of L'Hôpital's rule is satisfied.

$$\lim_{x\to 0} \frac{\sin x}{x} = \lim_{x\to 0} \frac{\cos x}{1} = \frac{1}{1} = 1$$

This is one way to prove the special trig limits discussed previously. But L'Hôpital's rule can be used with any functions that yield the indeterminate form.

L'Hôpital's rule can sometimes be used as an alternative to other limit techniques.

Sample

> Find $\lim\limits_{x \to 2} \dfrac{x^2 - 4}{x - 2}$ by using L'Hôpital's rule.

Substituting 2 directly yields

$$\frac{2^2 - 4}{2 - 2} = \frac{0}{0}$$

so the hypothesis of L'Hôpital's rule is satisfied.

$$\lim_{x \to 2} \frac{x^2 - 4}{x - 2} = \lim_{x \to 2} \frac{2x}{1} = \frac{2(2)}{1} = 4$$

This limit can also be found with the previously discussed techniques.

$$\lim_{x \to 2} \frac{x^2 - 4}{x - 2} = \lim_{x \to 2} \frac{(x + 2)(x - 2)}{x - 2}$$
$$= \lim_{x \to 2} (x + 2) = 4$$

Both methods give the appropriate limit; use whichever technique you prefer.

Sample

> Find $\lim\limits_{x \to \infty} \dfrac{3 - 2x^2}{x^2 + 5x}$ by using L'Hôpital's rule.

Direct substitution yields the indeterminate form $\frac{\infty}{\infty}$, so the hypothesis of L'Hôpital's rule is satisfied.

$$\lim_{x \to \infty} \frac{3 - 2x^2}{x^2 + 5x} = \lim_{x \to \infty} \frac{-4x}{2x + 5}$$

At this point L'Hôpital's rule can be applied again, because direct substitution into the last limit still yields the indeterminate form ∞/∞.

$$\lim_{x \to \infty} \frac{3 - 2x^2}{x^2 + 5x} = \lim_{x \to \infty} \frac{-4x}{2x + 5} = \lim_{x \to \infty} \frac{-4}{2} = -2$$

This limit, too, could have been found with the previous techniques (see the section on limits at infinity).

Sample

> Find $\lim\limits_{x \to 0} \dfrac{e^{5x} - 1}{3x}$.

Substituting 0 directly yields

$$\frac{e^0 - 1}{3(0)} = \frac{1-1}{0} = \frac{0}{0}$$

so the hypothesis of L'Hôpital's rule is satisfied.

$$\lim_{x \to 0} \frac{e^{5x} - 1}{3x} = \lim_{x \to 0} \frac{e^{5x}(5) - 0}{3}$$

$$= \frac{e^0(5)}{3} = \frac{1(5)}{3} = \frac{5}{3}$$

The major hazard in applying L'Hôpital's rule is in *over*applying it — that is, applying it when the hypothesis is not satisfied.

Sample

> The following problem is done *incorrectly*. Find where L'Hôpital's rule is applied when it should not be applied.
>
> $$\lim_{x \to 0} \frac{e^{2x} - 1}{x^2} = \lim_{x \to 0} \frac{2e^{2x}}{2x}$$
>
> $$= \lim_{x \to 0} \frac{e^{2x}}{x}$$
>
> $$= \lim_{x \to 0} \frac{2e^{2x}}{1}$$
>
> $$= 2 \quad \text{an } incorrect \text{ solution}$$

L'Hôpital's rule is applied incorrectly in deriving line 3 from line 2. Direct substitution of 0 into e^{2x}/x yields $e^0/0 = 1/0$. Thus the hypothesis of L'Hôpital's rule is *not* satisfied. Occasionally, other indeterminate forms, such as $\infty - \infty$ or $0 \cdot \infty$, may arise from limits. Limits such as these may be solved with L'Hôpital's rule, but only after some algebraic manipulation that results in $0/0$ or ∞/∞.

Sample

> Find $\lim_{x \to 0} \left(\dfrac{1}{\sin x} - \dfrac{1}{x} \right)$.

Direct substitution into the argument yields $\infty - \infty$.

$$\lim_{x \to 0} \left(\frac{1}{\sin x} - \frac{1}{x} \right) = \lim_{x \to 0} \left(\frac{x - \sin x}{x \sin x} \right)$$

L'Hôpital's rule can now be applied to this last limit, because direct substitution yields

$$\frac{0 - \sin 0}{0 \sin 0} = \frac{0}{0}$$

$$\lim_{x \to 0}\left(\frac{1}{\sin x} - \frac{1}{x}\right) = \lim_{x \to 0}\left(\frac{x - \sin x}{x \sin x}\right)$$

$$= \lim_{x \to 0}\left(\frac{1 - \cos x}{x \cos x + \sin x}\right)$$

$$= \lim_{x \to 0}\left(\frac{\sin x}{-x \sin x + \cos x + \cos x}\right)$$

$$= \frac{0}{0 \sin 0 + \cos 0 + \cos 0}$$

$$= \frac{0}{2} = 0$$

Sample

Find $\lim\limits_{x \to \infty}(x)\left(\dfrac{1}{\ln x}\right)$.

Direct substitution yields $\infty \cdot 0$.

$$\lim_{x \to \infty}(x)\left(\frac{1}{\ln x}\right) = \lim_{x \to \infty}\left(\frac{x}{\ln x}\right)$$

The last limit yields ∞ / ∞, so L'Hôpital's rule can be applied.

$$\lim_{x \to \infty}(x)\left(\frac{1}{\ln x}\right) = \lim_{x \to \infty}\left(\frac{x}{\ln x}\right)$$

$$= \lim_{x \to \infty}\left(\frac{1}{1/x}\right)$$

$$= \lim_{x \to \infty} x$$

$$= \infty$$

This solution is correct, even though it is ∞. L'Hôpital's rule doesn't guarantee that the limit will exist.

Occasionally, a more involved applications of L'Hôpital's rule may be required. This occurs when powers such as 1^∞ or 0^0 arise from direct substitution. For these power applications of L'Hôpital's rule, it is necessary to take the natural log of both sides of the function in order to use the log property to move the exponential function into the base location.

Sample

Find $\lim\limits_{x \to 0^+} (\sin 2x)^x$.

let $y = (\sin 2x)^x$

$\ln y = \ln (\sin 2x)^x$

$\ln y = x \ln (\sin 2x)$

$\lim\limits_{x \to 0^+} (\ln y) = \lim\limits_{x \to 0^+} [x \ln (\sin 2x)]$

$$= \lim\limits_{x \to 0^+} \frac{\ln (\sin 2x)}{\dfrac{1}{x}} = \left(\frac{-\infty}{\infty}\right)$$

$$= \lim\limits_{x \to 0^+} \frac{\dfrac{2 \cos 2x}{\sin 2x}}{-\dfrac{1}{x^2}}$$

$$= \lim\limits_{x \to 0^+} \left(\frac{-2x^2 \cos 2x}{\sin 2x}\right)$$

$$= \lim\limits_{x \to 0^+} \frac{-2x^2}{\tan 2x} = \left(\frac{0}{0}\right)$$

$$= \lim\limits_{x \to 0^+} \frac{-4x}{2 \sec^2 2x}$$

so, $\lim\limits_{x \to 0^+} (\ln y) = 0$

The exponential function is continuous on its domain, so it is possible to apply a theorem about the limit of a composite function here. Translated, this gives "the limit of the log" as the same as the "log of the limit," and so the last line above now becomes

$\ln \left(\lim\limits_{x \to 0^+} y\right) = 0$

$\Rightarrow \lim\limits_{x \to 0^+} y = e^0 = 1$

L'Hôpital's rule is required for limits where direct substitution yields the following indeterminate forms.

Summary of Forms Requiring L'Hôpital's Rule

$\dfrac{0}{0}, \dfrac{+\infty}{+\infty}, 0 - (\pm\infty), \infty - \infty, 0^0, (\pm\infty)^0, 1^0$

Note that $0^{+\infty}$ is NOT an indeterminate form: $0^{+\infty} = 0$ and does NOT require L'Hôpital's rule.

Sample Multiple-Choice Questions: Applications of the Derivative

1. Find the x-coordinate of the absolute minimum of $f(x) = x^3 - x^2 - x + 1$ on the interval $[-2, 2]$.

   A. -2

   B. $-\dfrac{1}{3}$

   C. 0

   D. 1

   E. 2

2. The function $f(x) = x^3 - 2x^2$ is increasing on which of the following interval(s)?

   A. $x < 0$ only

   B. $x > \dfrac{4}{3}$ only

   C. $0 < x < \dfrac{4}{3}$

   D. $x < 0$ or $x > \dfrac{4}{3}$

   E. $x < 0$ or $x > \dfrac{3}{4}$

3. Given $f(x) = \dfrac{1}{5}x^5 - \dfrac{1}{24}x^4$ find where the relative extrema of $f'''(x)$ occur.

   A. $x = 0, \dfrac{1}{12}$

   B. $x = \dfrac{1}{8}$

   C. $x = \dfrac{1}{24}$

   D. $x = 0, \dfrac{1}{8}$

   E. $x = 0, \dfrac{1}{6}$

4. The position of a particle moving along a horizontal line at any time t is given by $s(t) = 3t^2 - 2t - 8$. For what value(s) of t is the particle not moving?

   A. $t = 2$ or $t = -\dfrac{4}{3}$

   B. $t = 3$ only

   C. $t = \dfrac{1}{3}$ only

   D. $t = 1$ or $t = 4$

   E. $t = 2$ only

5. A particle moves in a straight line such that its distance at time t from a fixed point on the line is given by $8t - 3t^2$ units. What is the total distance covered by the particle from $t = 1$ to $t = 2$?

   A. 1 unit

   B. $\dfrac{4}{3}$ units

   C. $\dfrac{5}{3}$ units

   D. 2 units

   E. 5 units

6. A particle moves along a horizontal path such that its position at any time t is given by $s(t) = (2t - 3)^3$. The number of times the particle changes direction is

   A. 0

   B. 1

   C. 2

   D. 3

   E. not determinable from the information given

7. A particle moves along a horizontal path such that its position at any time t is given by the equation $y = e^{-t} \sin t$. For what value(s) of t will the particle change direction?

A. $t = \dfrac{\pi}{2} + 2k\pi$

B. $t = \dfrac{\pi}{2} + 2k\pi$

C. $t = \dfrac{\pi}{4} + 2k\pi$ or $t = \dfrac{3\pi}{4} + 2k\pi$

D. $t = \dfrac{\pi}{4} + k\pi$

E. $t = \dfrac{3\pi}{4} + 2k\pi$

8. Find the number guaranteed by Rolle's theorem for the function $f(x) = x^3 - 3x^2$ on the interval $0 \le x \le 3$.

A. 1

B. $\sqrt{2}$

C. $\dfrac{3}{2}$

D. 2

E. 3

9. A sphere is increasing in volume at the rate of $3\pi\,\text{cm}^3/\text{s}$. At what rate is its radius changing when the radius is $\frac{1}{2}$cm? (The volume of a sphere is given by $V = \left(\dfrac{4}{3}\right)\pi r^3$.)

A. πcm/s

B. 3 cm/s

C. 2 cm/s

D. 1 cm/s

E. $\dfrac{1}{2}$cm/s

10. A balloon rises straight up at 10 ft/s. An observer is 40 ft away from the spot where the balloon left the ground. Find the rate of change (in radians per second) of the balloon's angle of elevation when the balloon is 30 ft off the ground.

A. $\dfrac{3}{20}$

B. $\dfrac{4}{25}$

C. $\dfrac{1}{5}$

D. $\dfrac{1}{3}$

E. $\dfrac{25}{64}$

11. A point moves along the curve $y = x^2 + 1$ such that its x-coordinate is increasing at the rate of 1.5 units per second. At what rate is the point's distance from the origin changing when the point is at $(1, 2)$?

A. $\dfrac{7\sqrt{5}}{10}$ units/s

B. $\sqrt{5}$ units/s

C. $\dfrac{3\sqrt{5}}{2}$ units/s

D. $3\sqrt{5}$ units/s

E. $\dfrac{15}{2}$ units/s

12. Find the equation of the line tangent to the curve $y = e^x \ln x$ at the point where $x = 1$.

A. $y = ex$

B. $y = e^x + 1$

C. $y = e(x - 1)$

D. $y = ex + 1$

E. $y = x - 1$

13. The function $f(x) = \sqrt[3]{4 - x^2}$ has a vertical tangent at

A. $x = 0$

B. $x = -2$ and $x = 2$

C. $x = 0$, $x = -2$, and $x = 2$

D. $x = -1$ and $x = 1$

E. none of these

14. The slope of the line normal to the curve $h(x) = 2 \cos 4x$ at $x = \dfrac{\pi}{12}$ is

A. $-4\sqrt{3}$

B. -4

C. $\dfrac{\sqrt{3}}{12}$

D. $\dfrac{1}{4}$

E. $4\sqrt{3}$

15. A farmer builds a fence to enclose a rectangular region along a river (no fence is needed along the river) and to divide the region into two areas by adding a fence perpendicular to the river. She has 600 ft of fencing and wants to enclose the largest possible area. How far from the river should she build that part of the fence that is parallel to the river?

A. $10\sqrt{6}$ ft

B. 75 ft

C. 100 ft

D. 150 ft

E. 200 ft

16. A particle travels along a horizontal path so that its position at any time $t\,(t \geq 0)$ is given by $s(t) = 3t^3 - e^{t-2}$. The number of times the particle changes direction is

A. 0

B. 1

C. 2

D. 3

E. none of these

17. Given the function $f(x) = e^{\frac{x}{2}}$ on the closed interval $[-1, 4]$, if c is the number guaranteed by the mean value theorem, then c (correct to three decimal places) is approximately

A. 0.998

B. 1.163

C. 1.996

D. 2.065

E. 2.325

*18. $\displaystyle \lim_{x \to 0} x \cdot \ln x =$

A. $-e$

B. 1

C. 0

D. -1

E. e

*BC topic only

*19. A particle moves in the xy-plane such that at time $t > 0$ its position vector is $\left(e^{t^2}, \ln(3 + t^2)\right)$. At $t = 1$, its velocity vector is

   A. $(e, \ln 4)$

   B. $(1, \frac{1}{2})$

   C. $(e + 2, 1)$

   D. $(2e, \frac{1}{2})$

   E. $(e + 2, e)$

*20. $\displaystyle\lim_{x \to 1^+} \left(\frac{2}{x^2 - 1} - \frac{x}{x - 1}\right) =$

   A. -3

   B. $-\frac{3}{2}$

   C. -1

   D. 0

   E. 1

*21. If $x = t^3 - 1$ and $y = t^2$, then $\dfrac{d^2 y}{dx^2} =$

   A. $\dfrac{-2}{3t^2}$

   B. $6t$

   C. $\dfrac{-2}{9t^4}$

   D. 2

   E. $\dfrac{2}{3t}$

*22. $\displaystyle\lim_{x \to \infty} e^{-\sqrt{x}} \cdot \sqrt{x} =$

   A. $-\infty$

   B. $-\dfrac{1}{e}$

   C. 0

   D. $\dfrac{1}{e}$

   E. ∞

*23. $\displaystyle\lim_{x \to \infty} (x - 1)^{\frac{1}{x}} =$

   A. $-e$

   B. -1

   C. 0

   D. 1

   E. e

*BC topic only

Answers to Multiple-Choice Questions

1. A. Find the relative extrema and compare them with the endpoints.

$$f(x) = x^3 - x^2 - x + 1 \Rightarrow f'(x) = 3x^2 - 2x - 1$$
$$= (3x + 1)(x - 1)$$

critical numbers: $f'(x) = 0$ or $f'(x)$ does not exist

$$\Rightarrow x = \frac{-1}{3} \text{ or } x = 1$$

Find the function values that correspond to the critical numbers, to $x = -2$, and to $x = 2$

x	$f(x)$
-2	9
$\frac{-1}{3}$	$\frac{32}{27}$
1	0
2	3

Thus the absolute minimum occurs where $x = -2$.

2. D. Find the critical numbers and do interval testing.

$$f(x) = x^3 - 2x^2 \Rightarrow f'(x) = 3x^2 - 4x$$
$$= x(3x - 4)$$

critical numbers: $f'(x) = 0$ or $f'(x)$ does not exist
$$x = 0 \text{ or } x = \frac{4}{3}$$

Thus $f(x)$ is increasing on $x < 0$ and on $x > \frac{4}{3}$.

3. C. The problem requires the relative extrema of the *third* derivative. To find these extrema, begin by finding the derivative of the third derivative, that is, $f^{iv}(x)$.

$$f(x) = \frac{1}{5}x^5 - \frac{1}{24}x^4 \Rightarrow f'(x) = x^4 - \frac{1}{6}x^3$$
$$f''(x) = 4x^3 - \frac{1}{2}x^2$$
$$f'''(x) = 12x^2 - x$$
$$f^{iv}(x) = 24x - 1$$

critical numbers: $f^{iv}(x) = 0$ or $f^{iv}(x)$ does not exist

$x = \dfrac{1}{24}$

Interval testing on $f^{iv}(x)$ shows that $x = \dfrac{1}{24}$ is a relative minimum.

4. C. "not moving" $\Rightarrow v(t) = 0$

$s(t) = 3t^2 - 2t - 8 \Rightarrow v(t) = 6t - 2$

$\qquad v(t) = 0 \Rightarrow t = \dfrac{1}{3}$

5. C. "total distance" $\Rightarrow$ check for sign change in $v(t)$ and apply $\left| s(1) - s(t_c) \right| + \left| s(t_c) - s(2) \right|$

$s(t) = 8t - 3t^2 \Rightarrow v(t) = 8 - 6t$

$\qquad v(t) = 0 \Rightarrow t = \dfrac{4}{3}$

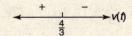

Because $v(t)$ changes sign $t = \dfrac{4}{3}$, the particle changes direction at $t = \dfrac{4}{3}$

$\left| s(1) - s(t_c) \right| + \left| s(t_c) - s(2) \right| = \left| s(1) - s\left(\dfrac{4}{3}\right) \right| + \left| s\left(\dfrac{4}{3}\right) - s(2) \right|$

$\qquad\qquad\qquad\qquad = \left| 5 - \dfrac{16}{3} \right| + \left| \dfrac{16}{3} - 4 \right|$

$\qquad\qquad\qquad\qquad = \dfrac{1}{3} + \dfrac{4}{3} = \dfrac{5}{3}$

6. A. "changes direction" $\Rightarrow v(t)$ changes sign

$s(t) = (2t - 3)^3 \Rightarrow v(t) = 3(2t - 3)^2 (2) = 6(2t - 3)^2$

$v(t)$ is positive for all values of t.

Thus the particle never changes direction.

7. D. "changes direction" $\Rightarrow v(t)$ changes sign

$s(t) = e^{-t} \sin t \Rightarrow v(t) = (e^{-t})(\cos t) + (\sin t)(-e^{-t})$

$\qquad\qquad\qquad\qquad = e^{-t}(\cos t - \sin t)$

$\cos t - \sin t = 0$ or $v(t) = 0 \Rightarrow e^{-t} = 0$

$\qquad \cos t = \sin t$

$\qquad\qquad t = \dfrac{\pi}{4} + k\pi$ and $v(t)$ changes sign at these values

8. D. Because $f(x)$ is continuous and differentiable on the interval, and because $f(0) = f(3)$, Rolle's theorem applies. Find where $f'(x) = 0$

$$f(x) = x^3 - 3x^2 \Rightarrow f'(x) = 3x^2 - 6x = 3x(x - 2)$$
$$f'(x) = 0 \Rightarrow x = 0 \text{ or } x = 2$$

Thus in the given interval, $x = 2$ is the number guaranteed by Rolle's theorem.

9. B. Find $\dfrac{dr}{dt}$ when $r = \dfrac{1}{2}$, given $\dfrac{dV}{dt} = 3\pi$ cm^3/s

$$V = \frac{4}{3}\pi r^3 \Rightarrow \frac{dV}{dt} = \frac{4\pi}{3} 3r^2 \frac{dr}{dt}$$
$$\frac{dr}{dt} = \frac{1}{4\pi r^2} \frac{dV}{dt}$$
$$\left.\frac{dr}{dt}\right|_{r = \frac{1}{2}} = \frac{1}{4\pi \left(\frac{1}{2}\right)^2}(3\pi) = 3 \text{ cm/s}$$

10. B. Find $\dfrac{d\theta}{dt}$ when $h = 30$ ft, given $\dfrac{dh}{dt} = 10$ ft/s

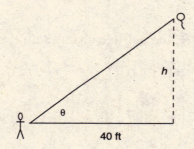

$$\tan\theta = \frac{h}{40} \Rightarrow h = 40\tan\theta$$
$$\frac{dh}{dt} = 40\sec^2\theta \frac{d\theta}{dt}$$
$$\frac{d\theta}{dt} = \frac{1}{40}\cos^2\theta \frac{dh}{dt}$$
$$\left.\frac{d\theta}{dt}\right|_{h = 30} = \frac{1}{40}\left(\frac{4}{5}\right)^2(10)$$
$$= \frac{4}{25} \text{ rad/s}$$

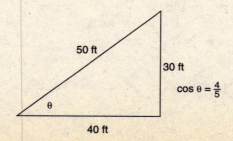

$\cos\theta = \dfrac{4}{5}$

11. C. Find ds/dt when $x = 1$ and $y = 2$, given $\dfrac{dx}{dt} = \dfrac{3}{2}$ units/s.

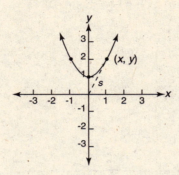

$$s = \sqrt{(x-0)^2 + (y-0)^2}$$

$$s^2 = x^2 + y^2$$

$$s^2 = x^2 + (x^2 + 1)^2$$

$$2s\frac{ds}{dt} = 2x\frac{dx}{dt} + 2(x^2 + 1)(2x)\frac{dx}{dt}$$

$$\frac{ds}{dt} = \frac{3x + 2x^3}{s}\frac{dx}{dt}$$

$$\left.\frac{ds}{dt}\right|_{x=1} = \frac{5}{\sqrt{5}}\left(\frac{3}{2}\right) = \frac{3\sqrt{5}}{2}$$

12. C. Find the slope of the tangent by finding $f'(1)$, find the point of tangency, and use the point/slope form.

$$y = e^x \ln x \Rightarrow \frac{dy}{dx} = (e^x)\left(\frac{1}{x}\right) + (\ln x)(e^x)$$

$$\left.\frac{dy}{dx}\right|_{x=1} = (e^1)(1) + (\ln 1)(e^1) = e + 0 = e,$$

$$\text{so } m_t = e$$

$x = 1 \quad \Rightarrow y = 0$, so the point of tangency is $(1, 0)$

$$y - 0 = e(x - 1) \Rightarrow y = e(x - 1)$$

13. B. $f(x) = \sqrt[3]{4 - x^2} \Rightarrow f(x) = \left(4 - x^2\right)^{\frac{1}{3}}$

$$f'(x) = \frac{1}{3}\left(4 - x^2\right)^{-\frac{2}{3}}(-2x)$$

$$= \frac{-2x}{3\left(4 - x^2\right)^{\frac{2}{3}}}$$

$f'(x)$ does not exist at $x = \pm 2$, and the tangent lines exist. Thus there is a vertical tangent at $x = 2$ and at $x = -2$.

14. C. The slope of a normal line is the negative reciprocal of the derivative.

$$h(x) = 2\cos 4x \Rightarrow h'(x) = 2(-\sin 4x)(4) = -8\sin 4x$$

$$h'\left(\frac{\pi}{12}\right) = -8\sin\left(\frac{\pi}{3}\right) = -8\left(\frac{\sqrt{3}}{2}\right) = -4\sqrt{3}$$

$$\Rightarrow m_t = -4\sqrt{3}, \text{ so } m_n = \frac{1}{4\sqrt{3}} = \frac{\sqrt{3}}{12}$$

15. C.

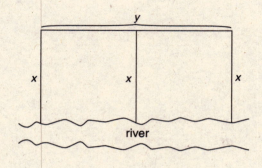

maximize area: $A = xy$

constraint: $600 = 3x + y \Rightarrow y = 600 - 3x$

$$\Rightarrow A = x(600 - 3x) = 600x - 3x^2$$

$$\frac{dA}{dx} = 600 - 6x$$

critical numbers: $\frac{dA}{dx} = 0$ or $\frac{dA}{dx}$ does not exist

$x = 100$

Justify the maximum.

x		$0 < x < 100$	100	$x > 100$
$\frac{dA}{dx}$		pos	0	neg
A		incr	rel max	decr

Therefore, the farmer should build the part of the fence that is parallel to the river 100 ft from the river.

16. C. To find when a particle changes direction, find any times when the velocity changes sign.

$$v(t) = 9t^2 - e^{t-2}$$

A calculator graph shows that $v(t)$ has one zero around $t = 8$, and at least one more around $t = 0$.

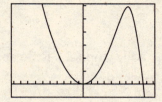

Since this scale was rather large, $(-10 \le x \le 10$ and $-20 \le y \le 300$, changing to a closer scale may give a better view to determine the zeros near $t = 0$. Using $-0.3 \le x \le 0.3$ and $-1 \le y \le 1$ clearly shows that $v(t)$ also changes sign near $x = -0.1$ and $x = 0.15$. Thus for $t > 0$, $v(t)$ changes sign twice, once at about $t = 0.15$ and again around $t = 8.5$.

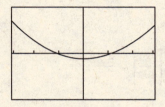

17. C. For the mean value theorem, $f'(x) = \dfrac{f(4) - f(-1)}{4 - (-1)}$

$$\frac{1}{2}e^{\frac{x}{2}} = \frac{e^2 - e^{-\frac{1}{2}}}{5}$$

$$e^{\frac{x}{2}} = \frac{2}{5}\left(e^2 - e^{-\frac{1}{2}}\right)$$

$$\frac{x}{2} = \ln\left(\frac{2}{5}\left(e^2 - e^{-\frac{1}{2}}\right)\right)$$

$$x = 2\ln\left(\frac{2}{5}\left(e^2 - e^{-\frac{1}{2}}\right)\right) \approx 1.996$$

18. C. $\displaystyle\lim_{x \to 0} x \cdot \ln x$ 　　　　form "$0 \cdot -\infty$" so cannot apply L'Hôpital's Rule

$$= \lim_{x \to 0} \frac{\ln x}{\frac{1}{x}}$$ 　　　　form "$\dfrac{-\infty}{\infty}$" so L'Hôpital's Rule is applicable

$$= \lim_{x \to 0} \frac{\frac{1}{x}}{-\frac{1}{x^2}}$$

$$= \lim_{x \to 0}(-x)$$

$$= 0$$

19. D. position vector is $\left(e^{t^2}, \ln(3 + t^2)\right)$

differentiating, velocity vector is $\left(e^{t^2} \cdot 2t, \dfrac{2t}{3 + t^2}\right)$

at $t = 1$, velocity vector is $\left(e^1 \cdot 2, \dfrac{2}{3 + 1}\right) = \left(2e, \dfrac{1}{2}\right)$

20. B. $\lim\limits_{x \to 1^+}\left(\dfrac{2}{x^2-1} - \dfrac{x}{x-1}\right)$ form $\infty - \infty$ so L'Hôpital's Rule cannot be used

$= \lim\limits_{x \to 1^+}\left(\dfrac{2 - x(x+1)}{x^2-1}\right)$

$= \lim\limits_{x \to 1^+}\left(\dfrac{-x^2 - x - 2}{x^2-1}\right)$ form $\dfrac{"0"}{0}$ so L'Hôpital's Rule applicable

$= \lim\limits_{x \to 1^+}\left(\dfrac{-2x-1}{2x}\right)$

$= \dfrac{-3}{2}$

21. C. $x = t^3 - 1 \qquad y = t^2$

$\dfrac{dx}{dy} = 3t^2 \qquad \dfrac{dy}{dt} = 2t$

Then $\dfrac{dy}{dx} = \dfrac{\frac{dy}{dt}}{\frac{dx}{dt}} = \dfrac{2t}{3t^2} = \dfrac{2}{3t} \Rightarrow \dfrac{d}{dt}\left[\dfrac{dy}{dx}\right] = \dfrac{-2}{3t^2}$

Next $\dfrac{d^2 y}{dx^2} = \dfrac{d}{dx}\left[\dfrac{dy}{dx}\right] = \dfrac{\frac{d}{dt}\left[\frac{dy}{dx}\right]}{\frac{dx}{dt}} = \dfrac{\frac{-2}{3t^2}}{3t^2} = \dfrac{-2}{9t^4}$

Or, by eliminating the parameter t, and then differentiating:

$x = t^3 - 1$

$x + 1 = t^3$

$(x+1)^{\frac{1}{3}} = t$

since $y = t^2$

$y = (x+1)^{\frac{2}{3}}$

$\dfrac{dy}{dx} = \dfrac{2}{3}(x+1)^{-\frac{1}{3}}$

$\dfrac{d^2 y}{dx^2} = \dfrac{-2}{9}(x+1)^{-\frac{1}{3}}$

$= \dfrac{-2}{9(x+1)^{\frac{4}{3}}}$

$= \dfrac{-2}{9t^4}$

22. C. $\lim\limits_{x \to \infty} e^{-x} \cdot \sqrt{x}$ form "$0 \cdot \infty$" so L'Hôpital's Rule is not applicable

$$= \lim\limits_{x \to \infty} \frac{\sqrt{x}}{e^x} \quad \text{form "}\frac{\infty}{\infty}\text{" so can apply L'Hôpital's Rule}$$

$$= \lim\limits_{x \to \infty} \frac{\dfrac{1}{2\sqrt{x}}}{e^x}$$

$$= \lim\limits_{x \to \infty} \frac{1}{2e^x \sqrt{x}}$$

$$= 0$$

23. D.

$\lim\limits_{x \to \infty} (x-1)^{\frac{1}{x}}$ since we have a variable base and a variable power, we proceed as follows

Let $y = \lim\limits_{x \to \infty} (x-1)^{\frac{1}{x}}$

$\ln y = \ln\left[\lim\limits_{x \to \infty} (x-1)^{\frac{1}{x}}\right]$

$\ln y = \lim\limits_{x \to \infty}\left[\ln(x-1)^{\frac{1}{x}}\right]$

$\ln y = \lim\limits_{x \to \infty}\left[\dfrac{1}{x}\ln(x-1)\right]$ form "$0 \cdot \infty$" so L'Hôpital's Rule is unusable here

$\ln y = \lim\limits_{x \to \infty}\left[\dfrac{\ln(x-1)}{x}\right]$ form "$\dfrac{\infty}{\infty}$" so can apply L'Hôpital's Rule

$\ln y = \lim\limits_{x \to \infty} \dfrac{\dfrac{1}{x-1}}{1}$

$\ln y = \lim\limits_{x \to \infty} \dfrac{1}{x-1}$

$\ln y = 0$

Therefore $y = e^0 = 1$

so $\lim\limits_{x \to \infty} (x-1)^{\frac{1}{x}} = 1$

Sample Free-Response Questions: Applications of the Derivative

1. The graph that follows is the graph of $f'(x)$ — that is, the derivative of $f(x)$. The function $f(x)$ has these properties:

   (i) $f(x)$ has domain $[-2, 5]$.

   (ii) $f(x)$ is everywhere differentiable on its domain.

   (iii) $f(-2) = 3$ and $f(5) = 1$.

   (iv) $f(x)$ has exactly four zeros on its domain.

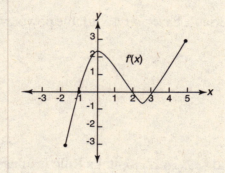

   (a) For what x-coordinate(s), if any, does $f(x)$ have relative extrema? Classify these extrema as maxima or minima. Justify your answer.

   (b) For what x-coordinate(s), if any, does $f(x)$ have a point of inflection? Justify your answer.

   (c) Sketch a possible graph of $f(x)$ that fits the information given.

2. Let $f(x)$ be a continuous function with domain $[-7, 0]$ such that
$$f'(x) = 1 - x\cos x + (\sin x)(e^x)$$

   (a) Find any values of x for which $f(x)$ has a relative minimum. Justify your answer.

   (b) Find any values of x for which $f(x)$ has a relative maximum. Justify your answer.

   (c) Find the x-coordinates of any points of inflection of the graph of $f(x)$. Justify your answer.

Answers to Free-Response Questions

1. The information given via the graph of $f'(x)$ is in an unfamiliar form. It may be helpful to begin by recasting the information into the more familiar chart form and then to fill in conclusions from this form.

(a) critical numbers: $f'(x) = 0$ or $f'(x)$ does not exist

$x = -1$ or $x = 2$ or $x = 3$

x	$-2 < x < -1$	$x = -1$	$-1 < x < 2$	$x = 2$	$2 < x < 3$	$x = 3$	$3 < x < 5$
$f'(x)$	neg	0	pos	0	neg	0	pos
$f(x)$	decr	rel min	incr	rel max	decr	rel min	incr

Therefore, $f(x)$ has a relative minimum at $x = -1$ and at $x = 3$ and a relative maximum at $x = 2$.

(b) To find any points of inflection, recall the definition of *concavity:*

$f(x)$ concave up $\Leftrightarrow f'(x)$ is increasing

$f(x)$ concave down $\Leftrightarrow f'(x)$ is decreasing

From the graph,

$f'(x)$ is increasing on $-2 < x < 0$ and $2.5 < x < 5$
and $f'(x)$ is decreasing on $0 < x < 2.5$ $\Bigg\} \Rightarrow$

x	$-2 < x < 0$	$x = 0$	$0 < x < 2.5$	$x = 2.5$	$2.5 < x < 5$
$f'(x)$	incr	rel max	decr	rel min	incr
$f(x)$	concave up	POI	concave down	POI	concave up

Therefore, $f(x)$ has points of inflection at $x = 0$ and $x = 2.5$.

(c) One possible graph of $f(x)$ is shown below.

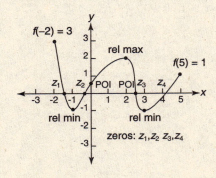

2. (a) and (b) The function $f(x)$ will have relative extrema at any points where $f'(x)$ changes sign. The graph of $f'(x)$ is shown below with a window of X[–7, 0] and Y[–3, 8].

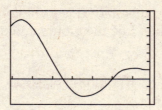

To the nearest hundredth, the zeros of $f'(x)$ are $x = -4.99$ and $x = -2.02$. Therefore, $f(x)$ has a relative maximum at $x = -4.49$, since $f'(x)$ changes from positive to negative at that point. Similarly, $f(x)$ has a relative minimum at $x = -2.02$, since $f'(x)$ changes from negative to positive.

(c) The function $f(x)$ has a point of inflection where a change in concavity occurs and the tangent line exists. By definition, a function $f(x)$ is concave up when its derivative $f'(x)$ is increasing, and $f(x)$ is concave down when $f'(x)$ is decreasing. From the graph of $f'(x)$ in part (a) $f'(x)$ has three relative extrema; that is, places where $f'(x)$ changes from increasing to decreasing or vice versa. The relative extrema of $f'(x)$ are at $x = -0.89$, $x = -3.42$, and $x = -6.44$ so these are the inflection points of $f(x)$.

An alternative approach might be to graph $f''(x)$ and observe that $f''(x)$ changes from positive to negative at $x = -0.89$, negative to positive at $x = -3.42$, and positive to negative at $x = -6.44$, thus confirming that $f(x)$ has inflection points at these coordinates.

The second major branch of calculus, integral calculus, is based on the concept of the antiderivative. As with derivatives, there are a number of antidifferentiation rules you should memorize, plus some general techniques that must be applied along with these rules. The definition of the antiderivative has recently been added to the AP outline, as have several methods for approximating the definite integrals.

Antiderivatives

Until now, the problems and applications in this book have all dealt with the concept of finding the derivative of a function — that is, differential calculus. From here on, the problems and applications will involve the opposite concept: finding the **antiderivative** of a function. Finding an antiderivative is just what it sounds like, as shown by the following definition.

Definition of an Antiderivative

Given a function $f(x)$ and its derivative $g(x)$ (that is, $g(x) = f'(x)$), then $f(x)$ is called an antiderivative of $g(x)$.

To see how this definition works, consider three functions, $f_1(x)$, $f_2(x)$, and $f_3(x)$, and their derivatives.

$$f_1(x) = x^2 - 2 \qquad f'_1(x) = 2x$$
$$f_2(x) = x^2 \qquad f'_2(x) = 2x$$
$$f_3(x) = x^2 + 24 \qquad f'_3(x) = 2x$$

By the foregoing definition, all the functions in the left column are antiderivatives of the function $g(x) = 2x$. Obviously, the three functions on the left are different, although they differ by only a constant. This difference is why the definition is phrased in terms of *an* antiderivative rather than *the* antiderivative.

Theorem on Antiderivatives

If $f(x)$ is an antiderivative of $g(x)$, then any function of the form $f(x) + C$, where C is any constant, is a member of the family of antiderivatives of $g(x)$. The expression $f(x) + C$ is called the general antiderivative of $g(x)$.

When asked to find the antiderivative of a function, you should typically leave the answer in the form $f(x) + C$, unless a given constraint makes it possible to find a specific value for C.

Notation

A special notation is used to indicate that an antiderivative is to be found:

$$\int g(x)\,dx = f(x) + C$$

With this notation, the initial example can be rewritten as

$$\int 2x\,dx = x^2 + C$$

Vocabulary

The operation of finding antiderivatives can be called antidifferentiation or integration. The antiderivative can also be called the indefinite integral. In the expression $\int f(x)\,dx$, $f(x)$ is known as the integrand, and dx is the differential that indicates that the variable of integration is x.

The operations of finding the derivative and the antiderivative are inverses; that is,

$$\frac{d}{dx}\left[\int f(x)\,dx\right] = f(x) \text{ and } \int f'(x)\,dx = f(x) + C$$

This relationship provides an entire set of rules for finding antiderivatives that are based on the previous rules for finding derivatives:

Constant Multiple Rule

$$\frac{d}{dx}(cf(x)) = c\frac{d}{dx}f(x) \Rightarrow \int cf(x)\,dx = c\int f(x)\,dx$$

Sum and Difference Rule

$$\frac{d}{dx}(f(x) \pm g(x)) = \frac{d}{dx}f(x) \pm \frac{d}{dx}g(x)$$

$$\Rightarrow \int [f(x) \pm g(x)]\,dx = \int f(x)\,dx \pm \int g(x)\,dx$$

Trig Rules

$$\frac{d}{dx}(\sin u) = \cos u \frac{du}{dx} \qquad \Rightarrow \int \cos u \; du = \sin u + C$$

$$\frac{d}{dx}(\cos u) = -\sin u \frac{du}{dx} \qquad \Rightarrow \int \sin u \; du = -\cos u + C$$

$$\frac{d}{dx}(\tan u) = \sec^2 u \frac{du}{dx} \qquad \Rightarrow \int \sec^2 u \; du = \tan u + C$$

$$\frac{d}{dx}(\sec u) = \sec u \tan u \frac{du}{dx} \qquad \Rightarrow \int \sec u \tan u \; du = \sec u + C$$

$$\frac{d}{dx}(\csc u) = -\csc u \cot u \frac{du}{dx} \qquad \Rightarrow \int \csc u \cot u \; du = -\csc u + C$$

$$\frac{d}{dx}(\cot u) = -\csc^2 u \frac{du}{dx} \qquad \Rightarrow \int \csc^2 u \; du = -\cot u + C$$

Power Rule

$$\frac{d}{dx}(u^n) = nu^{n-1}\frac{du}{dx} \Rightarrow \int u^n du = \frac{u^{n+1}}{n+1} + C \quad (n \neq -1)$$

Translation: To find the antiderivative of a power, increase the exponent by 1, and divide by this new exponent.

Sample

> Find $\int (3x^2 + 2x^4 - \frac{1}{2}x^3 - 7x + 1)\,dx$.

The antiderivative can be broken up into five separate antiderivatives, and each one done individually using the rules above.

$$\int (3x^2 + 2x^4 - \frac{1}{2}x^3 - 7x + 1)\,dx$$

$$= \int 3x^2\,dx + \int 2x^4\,dx - \int \frac{1}{2}x^3\,dx - \int 7x\,dx + \int 1\,dx$$

$$= 3\int x^2\,dx + 2\int x^4\,dx - \frac{1}{2}\int x^3\,dx - 7\int x\,dx + \int x^0\,dx$$

$$= 3\frac{x^3}{3} + 2\frac{x^5}{5} - \frac{1}{2}\frac{x^4}{4} - 7\frac{x^2}{2} + \frac{x^1}{1} + C$$

$$= x^3 + \frac{2}{5}x^5 - \frac{1}{8}x^4 - \frac{7}{2}x^2 + x + C$$

To save time, the intermediate steps are usually done mentally, and only the last one or two lines are written down.

Sample

> Find $\int (3\sqrt{x} + 5x^{-\frac{2}{3}})\,dx$.

Rewrite the radical with a fractional exponent and apply the antiderivative rules.

$$\int (3\sqrt{x} + 5x^{-\frac{2}{3}})\,dx = \int (3x^{\frac{1}{2}} + 5x^{-\frac{2}{3}})\,dx$$

$$= 3\frac{x^{\frac{3}{2}}}{\frac{3}{2}} + 5\frac{x^{\frac{1}{3}}}{\frac{1}{3}} + C$$

$$= 2x^{\frac{3}{2}} + 15x^{\frac{1}{3}} + C$$

Sample

> Find $\int \dfrac{5x^3 - \dfrac{1}{x}}{3\sqrt{x}}\,dx$.

Simplify first.

$$\int \frac{5x^3 - x^{-1}}{3\sqrt{x}}\,dx = \int \left(\frac{5}{3}x^{\frac{5}{2}} - \frac{1}{3}x^{-\frac{3}{2}}\right)dx$$

$$= \frac{5}{3}\frac{x^{\frac{7}{2}}}{\frac{7}{2}} - \frac{1}{3}\frac{x^{-\frac{1}{2}}}{\frac{-1}{2}} + C$$

$$= \frac{10}{21}x^{\frac{7}{2}} + \frac{2}{3}x^{-\frac{1}{2}} + C$$

This answer is fine. However, if it does not appear as a choice on a multiple-choice problem, you may need to factor. The goal is to factor in such a way that one term is a polynomial with integral coefficients. Begin by forcing the integral coefficients, and then factor out the lowest power of x.

$$= \frac{10}{21}x^{\frac{7}{2}} + \frac{2}{3}x^{-\frac{1}{2}} + C$$

$$= \frac{2}{21}\left(5x^{\frac{7}{2}} + 7x^{-\frac{1}{2}}\right) + C$$

$$= \frac{2}{21}x^{-\frac{1}{2}}\left(5x^4 + 7\right) + C$$

$$= \frac{2\left(5x^4 + 7\right)}{21\sqrt{x}} + C$$

Sample

> Given that $g'(t) = 1 + \sec t \tan t$ and that $g(\pi) = 2$, find $g(t)$.

$g(t)$ is the antiderivative of $g'(t)$.

$$g(t) = \int (1 + \sec t \tan t)\,dt$$

$$g(t) = t + \sec t + C$$

Now use the given boundary condition to find a specific value of C.

$$g(\pi) = \pi + \sec \pi + C = 2$$
$$\pi - 1 + C = 2$$
$$C = 3 - \pi$$

Thus $g(t) = t + \sec t + 3 - \pi$

The Chain Rule for Antiderivatives

As with derivatives, the chain rule for antiderivatives must be applied on the AP exam frequently. The antiderivative form is simply the derivative form backwards: The integrand takes the form of the end result of a derivative chain rule — that is, $f(h(x))h'(x)$. Once the integrand is in this form, find the antiderivative of f — that is, some function g such that $g'=f$.

Chain Rule for Antiderivatives

$\int f(h(x))h'(x)\,dx = g(h(x)) + C$ where g is an antiderivative of f, that is — where $g'(u) = f(u)$ or $\int f(u)\,du = g(u) + C$

The chain rule needs to be applied when the integrand is a composition of functions — that is, where there is an interior function present. For example,

$$\int \cos(3x)\,dx$$

has an integrand that is the composition of the cosine function and $y = 3x$:

$$f(x) = \cos x \text{ and } h(x) = 3x \Rightarrow f(h(x)) = \cos(3x)$$

In order to be able to find this antiderivative, it is necessary to force the integrand to look like the end result of a derivative chain rule, so that the "old" derivative rules can be applied in reverse.

$$\frac{d}{dx}[\sin(3x)] = \cos(3x)(3) \Rightarrow \int \cos(3x)(3)\,dx = \sin(3x) + C$$

But the problem asks only for $\int \cos(3x)\,dx$, and not for $\int \cos(3x)(3)\,dx$. An "extra" factor of 3 needs to be present as part of the integrand. Of course, simply putting in a factor of 3 would be incorrect, however helpful. The extra 3 *can* be introduced, however, if it is balanced by a canceling factor of 1/3.

$$\int \cos(3x)\,dx = \int \cos(3x)(3)(\tfrac{1}{3})\,dx$$

Now the factor of 1/3 can be factored out of the integrand.

$$\int \cos(3x)\,dx = \int \cos(3x)(3)(\tfrac{1}{3})\,dx$$

$$= \tfrac{1}{3}\int \cos(3x)(3)\,dx$$

$$= \tfrac{1}{3}\sin(3x) + C$$

Sample

Find $\int \sqrt{3x+5}\,dx$.

Rewrite the integrand with a rational exponent.

$$\int \sqrt{3x+5}\,dx = \int (3x+5)^{1/2}\,dx$$

The interior function in this case is $h(x) = 3x+5$, and $h'(x) = 3$. Introduce factors of 3 and 1/3.

$$\int \sqrt{3x+5}\,dx = \int (3x+5)^{1/2}\,dx$$

$$= \tfrac{1}{3}\int (3x+5)^{1/2}(3)\,dx$$

$$= \tfrac{1}{3}\frac{(3x+5)^{3/2}}{\tfrac{3}{2}} + C$$

$$= \tfrac{2}{9}(3x+5)^{3/2} + C$$

Sample

Find $\int (3x^2-5)^6 x\,dx$.

The interior function is $h(x) = 3x^2 - 5$, and $h'(x) = 6x$. The factor of x is already present in the integrand, so insert factors of 6 and 1/6.

$$\int (3x^2-5)^6 x\,dx = \tfrac{1}{6}\int (3x^2-5)^6 (6x)\,dx$$

$$= \tfrac{1}{6}\frac{(3x^2-5)^7}{7} + C$$

$$= \tfrac{1}{42}(3x^2-5)^7 + C$$

Sample

> Find $\int x \cos x^2 \, dx$.

In this problem the interior function is $h(x) = x^2$, and $h'(x) = 2x$. Thus the integrand must have a factor of $2x$ present. Because the x is already in the integrand, simply introduce a factor of 2 and a canceling factor of 1/2.

$$\int x \cos x^2 \, dx = \frac{1}{2} \int (\cos x^2)(2x) \, dx$$

$$= \frac{1}{2} \sin x^2 + C$$

Many students often wonder what happens to the derivative of the interior function; specifically, why doesn't it show up as part of the answer? In the foregoing problem, for example, what happens to the $2x$? The best answer to this question can be found by checking the integration by doing the derivative.

$$\frac{d}{dx}\left(\frac{1}{2}\sin x^2 + C\right) = \frac{1}{2}(\cos x^2)(2x) = x \cos x^2$$

which verifies the result of the integration $\int x \cos x^2 \, dx = (1/2)\sin x^2 + C$.

Caution: Never try to introduce variables as "extra" factors, even with the corresponding canceling factors. Only constants can be "fudged," not variables. For example,

$$\int \cos x^2 \, dx \neq \frac{1}{x} \int (\cos x^2)(x) \, dx$$

Introducing variable factors is *incorrect* and will result in totally *wrong* answers.

Sample

> Find $\int \cos^2 4x \sin 4x \, dx$.

The interior function in this case may not be so easy to find. Rewrite the first part of the integrand with parentheses.

$$\int \cos^2 4x \sin 4x \, dx = \int (\cos 4x)^2 \sin 4x \, dx$$

The interior function is $h(x) = \cos 4x$, and $h'(x) = -4 \sin 4x$. Introduce factors of -4 and $-1/4$.

$$\int (\cos 4x)^2 \sin 4x \, dx = \frac{-1}{4} \int (\cos 4x)^2 (-4 \sin 4x) \, dx$$

$$= \frac{-1}{4} \frac{(\cos 4x)^3}{3} + C$$

$$= \frac{-1}{12} \cos^3 4x + C$$

The rule used for the integration in this last problem was the power rule, in spite of all the trig. With complicated problems such as this one, a more formal method of applying the chain rule may be required. This formal technique is known as *u*-substitution. *U*-**substitution** is simply a change of variables, in which a complicated function is replaced by a single variable. It is generally the interior function that is replaced by u. However, *all* parts of the entire integrand must be expressed in terms of u also.

Sample

> Find $\int \cos^2 4x \sin 4x \, dx$ by u-substitution.

Rewriting yields

$$\int \cos^2 4x \sin 4x \, dx = \int (\cos 4x)^2 \sin 4x \, dx$$

Now, for u-substitution, let $u = \cos 4x$.

$$\Rightarrow \frac{du}{dx} = -4 \sin 4x$$

$$\Rightarrow du = -4 \sin 4x \, dx$$

$$\Rightarrow \sin 4x \, dx = \frac{du}{-4}$$

$$\int (\cos 4x)^2 \sin 4x \, dx = \int u^2 \left(\frac{du}{-4} \right)$$

$$= \frac{-1}{4} \int u^2 \, du$$

$$= \frac{-1}{4} \frac{u^3}{3} + C$$

$$= \frac{-1}{12} u^3 + C$$

$$= \frac{-1}{12} (\cos 4x)^3 + C$$

$$= \frac{-1}{12} \cos^3 4x + C$$

The answer must always appear in terms of the same independent variable as the original problem, which is why the u is replaced with $\cos 4x$ above. This form of the problem perhaps demonstrates more clearly that the integration rule being applied is the power rule.

For some antiderivatives, u-substitution is *required* to solve the problem.

Sample

> Find $\int \frac{x}{\sqrt{x+6}} \, dx$.

For this type of problem, different selections of u may be possible. In general, for antiderivatives with radical expressions in them, choosing u to equal either the radicand or the radical generally works.

$$u = \sqrt{x+6} \Rightarrow u^2 = x+6$$
$$x = u^2 - 6$$
$$\frac{dx}{du} = 2u$$
$$dx = 2u\,du$$

$$\int \frac{x}{\sqrt{x+6}}\,dx = \int \frac{u^2 - 6}{u} 2u\,du$$
$$= 2 \int (u^2 - 6)\,du$$
$$= 2\left(\frac{u^3}{3} - 6u\right) + C$$
$$= \frac{2}{3} u(u^2 - 18) + C$$
$$= \frac{2}{3}\sqrt{x+6}\,(x+6-18) + C$$
$$= \frac{2}{3}\sqrt{x+6}\,(x-12) + C$$

Exponential Antiderivatives

The rule for finding the antiderivative of the exponential function is just as simple as that for finding the derivative. Be sure to apply the chain rule when necessary.

Exponential Antiderivative

$$\int e^u\,du = e^u + C$$

Sample

Find $\int e^{9-2x}\,dx$.

The exponent is $u = 9 - 2x$, so $du = -2\,dx$. Introduce factors of -2 and $-1/2$.

$$\int e^{9-2x}\,dx = \frac{-1}{2} \int e^{9-2x}(-2)\,dx$$
$$= \frac{-1}{2} e^{9-2x} + C$$

Sample

Find $\int xe^{4-2x^2}\,dx$.

For this problem $u = 4 - 2x^2$, so $du = -4x\,dx$.

$$\int xe^{4-2x^2}\,dx = \frac{-1}{4}\int e^{4-2x^2}(-4x)\,dx$$

$$= \frac{-1}{4}e^{4-2x^2} + C$$

Sample

If $g'(t) = e^{\cos t}\sin t$ and $g(0) = 9$, find $g(\pi/2)$.

The antiderivative of the derivative will yield the general function, $g(t) + C$, and then substitute to find C.

$$\int e^{\cos t}\sin t\,dt = (-1)\int e^{\cos t}(-\sin t)\,dt \Rightarrow g(t) = -e^{\cos t} + C$$

$$g(0) = -e^{\cos 0} + C = 9$$

$$C = 9 + e$$

Thus
$$g(t) = -e^{\cos t} + 9 + e$$

$$\Rightarrow g\left(\frac{\pi}{2}\right) = -e^{\cos(\pi/2)} + 9 + e$$

$$= -e^{0} + 9 + e$$

$$= -1 + 9 + e = 8 + e$$

Antiderivatives that involve exponential functions with other bases can be integrated in either of two ways: by memorizing the rule or by rewriting the exponential as a function of e and applying the foregoing rule.

Antiderivative of Other Exponentials

$$\int a^x \, dx = \frac{1}{\ln a} a^x + C$$

Sample

Find $\int 2^{3-4x} \, dx$.

$$\int 2^{3-4x} \, dx = \frac{-1}{4} \int 2^{3-4x} (-4) \, dx$$

$$= \frac{-1}{4} \frac{1}{\ln 2} 2^{3-4x} + C$$

or

$$\int 2^{3-4x} \, dx = \int (e^{\ln 2})^{3-4x} \, dx$$

$$= \int e^{(\ln 2)(3-4x)} \, dx$$

$$= \frac{-1}{4 \ln 2} \int e^{(\ln 2)(3-4x)} (-4 \ln 2) \, dx$$

$$= \frac{-1}{4 \ln 2} e^{(\ln 2)(3-4x)} + C$$

$$= \frac{-1}{4 \ln 2} 2^{3-4x} + C$$

Antiderivatives and the Natural Log

In the power rule for the antiderivative, a restriction is placed on the exponent; it is that $n \neq -1$. Obviously, if the usual power rule were applied to an exponent of -1, the result would be an undefined expression.

$$\int x^{-1} \, dx = \frac{x^0}{0} \text{ which is undefined}$$

This "gap" in the power rule is filled by the natural log function. Previously, the derivative of the natural log function was given as

$$\frac{d}{dx} (\ln u) = \frac{1}{u} \frac{du}{dx}$$

The corresponding antiderivative formula follows.

Antiderivative Rule for the Natural Log

$$\int \frac{1}{u} \, du = \ln|u| + C$$

The absolute-value bars on the natural log guarantee that the expression is defined. When applying this rule, keep in mind that the numerator must be the derivative of the denominator. To help them remember this, some students prefer to write the rule in this form:

$$\int \frac{u'}{u} = \ln|u| + C$$

The actual proof of both the derivative and antiderivative formulas will be shown in the next chapter.

Sample

Find $\int \frac{5}{3x+2} \, dx$.

Factor out the 5, and then introduce factors of 3 and 1/3 to set up the chain rule.

$$\int \frac{5}{3x+2} \, dx = 5 \int \frac{1}{3x+2} \, dx$$

$$= \frac{5}{3} \int \frac{3}{3x+2} \, dx$$

$$= \frac{5}{3} \ln|3x+2| + C$$

Sample

Find $\int \frac{\cos 3x}{2 - \sin 3x} \, dx$.

The derivative of the denominator is $\frac{d}{dx}(2 - \sin 3x) = -3\cos 3x$.

$$\int \frac{\cos 3x}{2 - \sin 3x} \, dx = \frac{-1}{3} \int \frac{-3\cos 3x}{2 - \sin 3x} \, dx$$

$$= \frac{-1}{3} \ln|2 - \sin 3x| + C$$

Sample

> Find $\int \dfrac{e^{2x}}{e^{2x}+4}\,dx$.

This problem, though it is easy, can be deceptive. Remember (1) that when the numerator of an integrand is the derivative of the denominator, the result is a natural log, and (2) that the exponential function is its own derivative.

$$\int \frac{e^{2x}}{e^{2x}+4}\,dx = \frac{1}{2}\int \frac{2e^{2x}}{e^{2x}+4}\,dx$$

$$= \frac{1}{2}\ln(e^{2x}+4)+C$$

Sample

> Find $\int \dfrac{x^2-2}{x+1}\,dx$.

Because the degree of the numerator is higher than the degree of the denominator, begin by dividing

$$
\begin{array}{r}
x-1 \\
x+1\overline{)x^2 \quad\ -2} \\
\underline{x^2+x} \\
-x-2 \\
\underline{-x-1} \\
-1
\end{array}
$$

or use synthetic division.

$$
\begin{array}{r}
\underline{-1}\ \ \ 1 \quad 0 \quad -2 \\
-1 \quad 1 \\
\hline
1-1\ |\ -1
\end{array}
$$

$$\Rightarrow \int \frac{x^2-x}{x+1}\,dx = \int\left(x-1-\frac{1}{x+1}\right)dx$$

$$= \frac{x^2}{2}-x-\ln|x+1|+C$$

The antiderivative rule for the natural log can be applied to find four more trig antiderivatives.

$$\int \tan u\,du = \int \frac{\sin u}{\cos u}\,du$$

$$= -1\int \frac{-\sin u}{\cos u}\,du$$

$$= -\ln|\cos u|+C$$

Similarly,

$$\int \cot u \; du = \ln|\sin u| + C$$

$$\int \sec u \; du = \ln|\sec u + \tan u| + C$$

$$\int \csc u \; du = -\ln|\csc u + \cot u| + C = \ln|\csc u - \cot u| + C$$

Trig Integrals

Antiderivatives that involve the trig functions frequently require the use of one or more identities before they can be solved. The most commonly used identities are the Pythagorean identities, the power-reducing identities, and the product-sum identities (see pages 32–33 for a list of trig identities).

Sample

Find $\int \sin^3 x \cos^2 x \, dx$.

When one of the powers of sine or cosine is odd and the other even, the simplest method is to keep out one factor of the odd function and convert the rest with a Pythagorean identity.

$$\int \sin^3 x \cos^2 x \, dx = \int \sin^2 x \cos^2 x \sin x \; dx$$

$$= \int (1 - \cos^2 x)(\cos^2 x)(\sin x) \, dx$$

$$= \int (\cos^2 x - \cos^4 x)(\sin x) \, dx$$

$$= \int \cos^2 x \sin x \; dx - \int \cos^4 x \sin x \; dx$$

$$= -\int (\cos x)^2 (-\sin x) \, dx + \int (\cos x)^4 (-\sin x) \, dx$$

$$= \frac{-\cos^3 x}{3} + \frac{\cos^5 x}{5} + C$$

$$= \frac{-1}{15} \cos^3 x (5 - 3 \cos^2 x) + C$$

A few of these steps can be consolidated as desired. Either of the last two lines could be potential forms for answers on a multiple-choice question.

Sample

Find $\int \sin^2 3x \cos^2 3x \, dx$.

When both powers are even, use the power-reducing identities to change the integrand to odd powers of cosine.

$$\int \sin^2 3x \cos^2 3x \, dx = \int \left(\frac{1 - \cos 6x}{2} \right) \left(\frac{1 + \cos 6x}{2} \right) dx$$

$$= \frac{1}{4} \int (1 - \cos^2 6x) \, dx$$

$$= \frac{1}{4} \int \left[1 - \left(\frac{1 + \cos 12x}{2} \right) \right] dx$$

$$= \frac{1}{4} \cdot \frac{1}{2} \int [2 - (1 + \cos 12x)] \, dx$$

$$= \frac{1}{8} \int (1 - \cos 12x) \, dx$$

$$= \frac{1}{8} \int dx - \frac{1}{8} \int \cos 12x \, dx$$

$$= \frac{1}{8} \int dx - \frac{1}{8} \cdot \frac{1}{12} \int (\cos 12x)(12) \, dx$$

$$= \frac{1}{8} x - \frac{1}{96} \sin 12x + C$$

$$= \frac{1}{96} (12x - \sin 12x) + C$$

This type of problem would probably be one of the more difficult to appear on the AP exam.

Sample

Find $\int \tan^3 x \, dx$.

For problems involving tangents and/or secants, recall that

$$\frac{d}{dx}(\tan u) = \sec^2 u \frac{du}{dx} \text{ and } \frac{d}{dx}(\sec u) = \sec u \tan u \frac{du}{dx}$$

Trial and error may be necessary before you find the combination of identities that produces a solution.

$$\int \tan^3 x \, dx = \int (\tan x)(\tan^2 x) \, dx$$

$$= \int (\tan x)(\sec^2 x - 1) \, dx$$

$$= \int \tan x \sec^2 x \, dx - \int \tan x \, dx$$

$$= \frac{\tan^2 x}{2} + \ln|\cos x| + C$$

The first integrand above can actually be integrated another way:

$$\int \tan^3 x \, dx = \int \tan x \sec^2 x \, dx - \int \tan x \, dx$$

$$= \int (\sec x)(\sec x \tan x) \, dx - \int \tan x \, dx$$

$$= \frac{\sec^2 x}{2} + \ln|\cos x| + C$$

Although the two answers appear different, they really differ only in the value of their respective constants, as shown below:

$$\frac{\tan^2 x}{2} + \ln|\cos x| + C_1 = \frac{\sec^2 x - 1}{2} + \ln|\cos x| + C_1$$

$$= \frac{\sec^2 x}{2} + \ln|\cos x| + \left(C_1 - \frac{1}{2}\right)$$

$$= \frac{\sec^2 x}{2} + \ln|\cos x| + C_2$$

Sample

Find $\int \sin 5x \cos 3x \, dx$.

Use the product-sum identity:

$$\sin(mx)\cos(nx) = \frac{1}{2}[\sin(m-n)x + \sin(m+n)x]$$

$$\int \sin 5x \cos 3x \, dx = \frac{1}{2} \int (\sin 2x + \sin 8x) \, dx$$

$$= \frac{1}{2} \cdot \frac{1}{2} \int \sin 2x \, (2) \, dx + \frac{1}{2} \cdot \frac{1}{8} \int (\sin 8x)(8) \, dx$$

$$= \frac{-1}{4} \cos 2x - \frac{1}{16} \cos 8x + C$$

Antiderivatives of Inverse Trig Functions

The formulas for the antiderivatives of the inverse trig functions are just the reverse of the derivative formulas. Fortunately, you need to memorize only three formulas. These three, along with the techniques of completing the square, are sufficient for solving any problems that appear on the AP exam.

Inverse Trig Antiderivatives

$$\int \frac{1}{\sqrt{a^2 - u^2}}\, du = \arcsin \frac{u}{a} + C$$

$$\int \frac{1}{a^2 + u^2}\, du = \frac{1}{a} \arctan \frac{u}{a} + C$$

$$\int \frac{1}{u\sqrt{u^2 - a^2}}\, du = \frac{1}{a} \operatorname{arc\,sec} \frac{u}{a} + C$$

Sample

Find $\int \dfrac{1}{9 + 4t^2}\, dt$.

This integral is in the pattern for the inverse tangent, where $a = 3$ and $u = 2t$. Note that it is necessary to insert factors of 2 and 1/2 because $du = 2dt$.

$$\int \frac{1}{9 + 4t^2}\, dt = \int \frac{1}{(3)^2 + (2t)^2}\, dt$$

$$= \frac{1}{2} \int \frac{2}{(3)^2 + (2t)^2}\, dt$$

$$= \frac{1}{6} \arctan \frac{2t}{3} + C$$

Sample

Find $\int \dfrac{1}{\sqrt{-3x^2 + 6x - 2}}\, dx$.

At first glance, it does not seem that this problem will fit into any of the inverse trig forms. Completing the square on the radicand will make it look more familiar.

$$-3x^2 + 6x - 2 = -3(x^2 - 2x + \,?) - 2$$

$$= -3(x^2 - 2x + 1) - 2 + 3$$

$$= -3(x - 1)^2 + 1$$

$$= 1 - 3(x - 1)^2$$

$$= 3\left[\frac{1}{3} - (x - 1)^2\right]$$

$$\Rightarrow \int \frac{1}{\sqrt{-3x^2 + 6x - 2}}\, dx = \int \frac{1}{\sqrt{3\left[\frac{1}{3} - (x - 1)^2\right]}}\, dx$$

$$= \frac{1}{\sqrt{3}} \int \frac{1}{\sqrt{\frac{1}{3} - (x - 1)^2}}\, dx$$

229

This is now in the form for inverse sine, where $a = \sqrt{1/3}$ and $u = x - 1$.

$$= \frac{1}{\sqrt{3}} \arcsin \frac{x-1}{\sqrt{\frac{1}{3}}} + C$$

$$= \frac{1}{\sqrt{3}} \arcsin \left[\sqrt{3}(x-1) \right] + C$$

Sample

> Find $\displaystyle \int \frac{1}{\sqrt{e^{2x}-1}} \, dx$.

In the denominator, a perfect square is already present in the radicand, although it may not be easy to spot. Applying u-substitution may help.

Let $\quad u = e^x \Rightarrow x = \ln u$

$$\Rightarrow dx = \frac{1}{u} \, du$$

$$\int \frac{1}{\sqrt{e^{2x}-1}} \, dx = \int \frac{1}{\sqrt{u^2-1}} \left(\frac{1}{u} \, du \right)$$

$$= \int \frac{1}{u\sqrt{u^2-1}} \, du$$

$$= \operatorname{arc sec} u + C$$

$$= \operatorname{arc sec} e^x + C$$

Other algebraic techniques similar to the ones in the foregoing examples may be needed for inverse trig problems.

Sample

> Find $\displaystyle \int \frac{9x^3-5}{x^2+9} \, dx$.

If the degree of the numerator is greater than the degree of the denominator, divide first.

$$
\begin{array}{r}
9x \\
x^2+9 \overline{)\, 9x^3 - 5} \\
\underline{9x^3 + 81x } \\
-81x - 5
\end{array}
$$

$$\Rightarrow \int \frac{9x^3-5}{x^2+9} \, dx = \int \left(9x - \frac{81x+5}{x^2+9} \right) dx$$

Another algebraic maneuver is to change one fraction into a sum of two separate fractions.

$$\int \left(9x - \frac{81x+5}{x^2+9}\right) dx = \int \left(9x - \frac{81x}{x^2+9} - \frac{5}{x^2+9}\right) dx$$

$$= \int 9x\,dx - 81 \int \frac{x}{x^2+9}\,dx - 5 \int \frac{1}{x^2+9}\,dx$$

$$= \int 9x\,dx - \frac{81}{2} \int \frac{2x}{x^2+9}\,dx - 5 \int \frac{1}{x^2+9}\,dx$$

$$= \frac{9x^2}{2} - \frac{81}{2}\ln(x^2+9) - \frac{5}{3}\arctan\frac{x}{3} + C$$

Integration by Parts (BC Only)

Integration by parts is a method used to "reshuffle" parts of an integrand that is unsolvable into a new integrand that can be solved.

Theorem: Integration by Parts

$$\int u\,dv = uv - \int v\,du$$

The formula can be proved quickly by using the product rule:

$$\frac{d}{dx}(uv) = u\frac{dv}{dx} + v\frac{du}{dx}$$

$$d(uv) = u\,dv + v\,du$$

$$\int d(uv) = \int u\,dv + \int v\,du$$

$$uv = \int u\,dv + \int v\,du$$

$$\int u\,dv = uv - \int v\,du$$

This may seem like an unprofitable exchange, but if the parts are chosen correctly, the modified version on the right can truly be simpler to solve. Note that the u in the original integrand appears only as du in the second version and that the dv from the original shows up as v in the new version. This leads to some general rules for choosing the parts:

1. Let u equal the part that has the simpler derivative or that simplifies better through differentiation.

2. Let dv be the part that can be integrated more easily.

These are general rules only; trial and error may be the only way to find the solution to a particular antiderivative via integration by parts.

Sample

Find $\int x \cos x \, dx$ using integration by parts.

Because x has a very simple derivative, whereas $\cos x$ has a derivative that is just another trig function, choose

$$u = x \qquad\qquad dv = \cos x \, dx$$

$$du = dx \qquad\qquad \int dv = \int \cos x \, dx$$

$$v = \sin x$$

$$\int u \, dv = uv - \int v \, du$$

$$\int x \cos x \, dx = x \sin x - \int \sin x \, dx$$

$$= x \sin x + \cos x + C$$

Sample

Find $\int (1 - x) e^x \, dx$.

This problem requires integration by parts.

$$u = 1 - x \qquad\qquad dv = e^x \, dx$$

$$du = - dx \qquad\qquad \int dv = \int e^x (dx)$$

$$v = e^x$$

$$\int u \, dv = uv - \int v \, du$$

$$\Rightarrow \int (1 - x) e^x \, dx = (1 - x) e^x - \int e^x (- dx)$$

$$= (1 - x) e^x + \int e^x \, dx$$

$$= e^x - xe^x + e^x + C$$

$$= 2e^x - xe^x + C$$

$$= e^x (2 - x) + C$$

Occasionally, repetition of integration by parts may be needed.

Sample

Find $\int x^2 \cos x \, dx$.

$$u = x^2 \qquad\qquad dv = \cos x \, dx$$

$$du = 2x \, dx \qquad\qquad \int dv = \int \cos x \, dx$$

$$v = \sin x$$

$$\int x^2 \cos x \, dx = x^2 \sin x - \int \sin x \, 2x \, dx$$

$$= x^2 \sin x - 2 \int x \sin x \, dx$$

The second integral is still not solvable; use parts again.

$$u = x \qquad\qquad dv = \sin x \, dx$$

$$du = dx \qquad\qquad \int dv = \int \sin x \, dx$$

$$v = -\cos x$$

$$\int x^2 \cos x \, dx = x^2 \sin x - 2 \int x \sin x \, dx$$

$$= x^2 \sin x - 2 [x(-\cos x) - \int (-\cos x) \, dx]$$

$$= x^2 \sin x + 2x \cos x - 2 \int \cos x \, dx$$

$$= x^2 \sin x + 2x \cos x - 2 \sin x + C$$

You are already familiar with antiderivatives that yield the natural log function. Integration by parts now provides a method for finding the antiderivative of the natural log function, although there seems to be only one "part."

$$\int \ln x \, dx = ?$$

$$u = \ln x \qquad\qquad dv = dx$$

$$du = \frac{1}{x} \, dx \qquad\qquad \int dv = \int dx$$

$$v = x$$

$$\int \ln x \, dx = (\ln x)(x) - \int x \frac{1}{x} \, dx$$

$$= x \ln x - \int 1 \, dx$$

$$= x \ln x - x + C$$

It may be worthwhile to memorize this formula for the antiderivative on $\ln x$, because it does occur frequently on the AP exam. The method above can also be applied to finding the antiderivatives of the inverse trig functions.

$$\int \arctan x\, dx = ?$$

$$u = \arctan x \qquad\qquad dv = dx$$

$$du = \frac{1}{1+x^2}\, dx \qquad\qquad v = x$$

$$\int \arctan x\, dx = (\arctan x)(x) - \int x\, \frac{1}{1+x^2}\, dx$$

$$= x\arctan x - \frac{1}{2} \int \frac{2x}{1+x^2}\, dx$$

$$= x\arctan x - \frac{1}{2} \ln(1+x^2) + C$$

The formulas for the antiderivatives of the inverse trig functions are too complicated to be worth memorizing.

Integration by Partial Fractions (BC Only)

Some rational functions that are at first apparently not integrable can be broken down into two or more separate fractions using the method of partial fractions. These separate fractions can then be integrated individually. For example,

$$\int \frac{5}{x^2+x-6}\, dx$$

is not at first glance integrable.

However, from basic algebra, the two fractions below have a difference that is equal to the original integrand. The two separate fractions are easily integrated as natural logs.

$$\frac{1}{x-2} - \frac{1}{x+3} = \frac{x+3}{(x-2)(x+3)} - \frac{x-2}{(x+3)(x-2)}$$

$$= \frac{x+3-(x-2)}{x^2+x-6}$$

$$= \frac{5}{x^2+x-6}$$

and

$$\int \frac{1}{x-2}\, dx - \int \frac{1}{x+3}\, dx = \ln|x-2| - \ln|x+3| + C$$

The process of creating the decomposition follows basic algebra rules. Begin by factoring the denominator into linear factors. For each linear factor present in the denominator, write a fraction with the unknown numerator as a variable (A, B, etc.)

$$\frac{5}{x^2+x-6} = \frac{5}{(x+3)(x-2)}$$

$$\frac{5}{x^2+x-6} = \frac{A}{x+3} + \frac{B}{x-2}$$

Next, multiply both sides of the resulting equation above by the original denominator in its factored form, thus eliminating the fractions.

$$(x+3)(x-2)\left(\frac{5}{x^2+x-6}\right) = \left[\frac{A}{x+3} + \frac{B}{x-2}\right]^{(x+3)(x-2)}$$

$$5 = A(x-2) + B(x+3)$$

There are now two ways to proceed to determine the values of A and B: (1) choose useful values for x and solve by inspection, or (2) expand the expression on the left and equate coefficients.

Method 1: Choose $x = 2$, and then $x = -3$

$$x = 2 \Rightarrow 5 = A(0) + B(5) \qquad x = -3 \Rightarrow 5 = A(-5) + B(0)$$

$$5 = 5B \qquad\qquad\qquad 5 = -5A$$

$$1 = B \qquad\qquad\qquad -1 = A$$

Method 2: Expanding Yields

$$5 = Ax - 2A + Bx + 3B$$
$$5 = (A + B)x + (-2A + 3B)$$

Equating the coefficients on the x terms gives

$$A + B = 0$$

while equating the constants gives

$$-2A + 3B = 5$$

This system of equations can be solved:

$$A + B = 0 \Rightarrow A = -B$$
$$-2A + 3B = 5$$
$$-2(-B) + 3B = 5$$
$$5B = 5$$
$$B = 1$$
$$A = -1$$

Both methods now yield the equation below.

$$\frac{5}{x^2+x-6} = \frac{-1}{x+3} + \frac{1}{x-2}$$

$$\text{so,} \int \frac{5}{x^2+x-6}\,dx = \int \frac{-1}{x+3}\,dx + \int \frac{1}{x-2}\,dx$$

$$= -\ln|x+3| + \ln|x-2| + C$$

$$= \ln\left|\frac{x-2}{x+3}\right| + C$$

The last answer above uses log properties to combine the two terms.

Sample

Find $\int \dfrac{17x - 8}{2x^2 - 9x - 5}\,dx$ using partial fractions.

$$\frac{17x - 8}{2x^2 - 9x - 5} = \frac{17x - 8}{(2x + 1)(x - 5)} = \frac{A}{2x + 1} + \frac{B}{x - 5}$$

$$17x - 8 = A(x - 5) + B(2x + 1)$$

$$x = 5 \Rightarrow 77 = A(0) + B(11)$$

$$77 = 11B$$

$$7 = B$$

$$x = -\frac{1}{2} \Rightarrow -\frac{33}{2} = A\left(-\frac{11}{2}\right) + B(0)$$

$$3 = A$$

so, $\displaystyle\int \frac{17x - 8}{2x^2 - 9x - 5}\,dx = \int \left(\frac{3}{2x + 1} + \frac{7}{x - 5}\right)dx$

$$= 3\int \frac{1}{2x + 1}\,dx + 7\int \frac{1}{x - 5}\,dx$$

$$= 3 \cdot \frac{1}{2}\int \frac{2}{2x + 1}\,dx + 7\int \frac{1}{x - 5}\,dx$$

$$= \frac{3}{2}\ln|2x + 1| + 7\ln|x - 5| + C$$

Improper Integrals (BC Only)

In the definition of the definite integral

$$\int_{a}^{b} f(x)\,dx$$

it was assumed that the integrand $f(x)$ was continuous on a closed (finite) interval $[a, b]$. Some definite integrals that do not meet these conditions can still be evaluated by a limit process. These are known as improper integrals. Integrals are improper in several ways. First, the upper or lower bound of integration (or both) may not be a finite constant, but given as ∞ or $-\infty$. Secondly, the integrand may have an infinite discontinuity at either the upper or lower bound of integration, or have an infinite discontinuity *between* the bounds of integration. Examples of the two types are given below.

Examples of Improper Integrals

infinite limits $\qquad \int\limits_{1}^{\infty} 2^{-x}\, dx \qquad \int\limits_{-\infty}^{3} \frac{1}{(x-4)^2}\, dx \qquad \int\limits_{-\infty}^{\infty} e^{3-x}\, dx$

infinite discontinuities $\qquad \int\limits_{1}^{2} \frac{1}{(x-2)^3}\, dx \qquad \int\limits_{0}^{3} \ln x\, dx \qquad \int\limits_{0}^{2} \frac{1}{(x-1)^3}\, dx$

Applications of improper integrals include finding area and volume. The idea behind the first type of improper integrals can perhaps best be illustrated by considering the following area problem.

Sample

> Consider the area bounded by the curves below and shaded in the corresponding graph. Find an expression in terms of b to represent the area of the region. What happens to this area as the right-hand boundary is moved further right? That is, what happens to the area expression as $b \to \infty$?
>
> $y = \dfrac{1}{x^2}$, x-axis, $x = 1$, $x = b\,(b > 1)$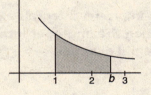

The area is given by

$$A = \int\limits_{1}^{b} \frac{1}{x^2}\, dx$$

$$= \int\limits_{1}^{b} x^{-2}\, dx$$

$$= -\frac{1}{x} \Big]_{1}^{b}$$

$$= -\frac{1}{b} - \left(-\frac{1}{1}\right)$$

$$A = -\frac{1}{b} + 1$$

So, as $b \to \infty$,

$$A = \lim_{b \to \infty} \left(-\frac{1}{b} + 1\right)$$

$$= 1$$

So, as the right hand boundary takes on larger and larger values, the area under the curve gets closer and closer to 1.

This leads to a general method for evaluating improper integrals with infinite bounds of integration.

237

Improper Integrals with Infinite Bounds of Integration

In general, converting to the limit expression requires replacing the infinite bound with a variable (usually a or b), and taking the limit as that variable increases or decreases without bound.

1. $\displaystyle\int_{a}^{\infty} f(x)\,dx = \lim_{b \to \infty} \int_{a}^{b} f(x)\,dx$

2. $\displaystyle\int_{-\infty}^{b} f(x)\,dx = \lim_{a \to -\infty} \int_{a}^{b} f(x)\,dx$

If both bounds are infinite, the integral is split into two pieces by choosing a value c (frequently taken as 0 or 1) and then applying both of the limits above

3. $\displaystyle\int_{-\infty}^{\infty} f(x)\,dx = \int_{-\infty}^{c} f(x)\,dx + \int_{c}^{\infty} f(x)\,dx$

$\displaystyle\qquad = \lim_{a \to -\infty} \int_{a}^{c} f(x)\,dx + \lim_{b \to \infty} \int_{c}^{b} f(x)\,dx$

> **Note:** Not all improper integrals exist, because the limits above do not always exist. If the limit exists, then the improper integral is said to converge. If the limit does not exist, the improper integral diverges.

Sample

> Evaluate the integral, if it converges.
>
> $\displaystyle\int_{2}^{\infty} xe^{-x}\,dx$

From the definition above,

$$\int_{2}^{\infty} xe^{-x}\,dx = \lim_{b \to \infty} \int_{2}^{b} xe^{-x}\,dx$$

The integration for this problem requires the use of parts. It may be easier to perform the integration by parts as a separate problem and then insert the resulting antiderivative into the limit form of the improper integral.

$$\int xe^{-x}\,dx = -xe^{-x} - \int -e^{x}\,dx \qquad u = x \qquad \int dv = \int e^{-x}\,dx$$

$$= -xe^{-x} - e^{-x} + C \qquad du = dx \qquad v = -e^{-x}$$

$$\text{so,} \int_{2}^{\infty} xe^{-x}\,dx = \lim_{b \to \infty} \int_{2}^{b} xe^{-x}\,dx$$

$$= \lim_{b \to \infty} [-xe^{-x} - e^{-x}]_{2}^{b}$$

$$= \lim_{b \to \infty} \left[(-be^{-b} - e^{-b}) - (-2e^{-2} - e^{-2}) \right]$$

$$= \lim_{b \to \infty} \left[-\frac{b}{e^{b}} - \frac{1}{e^{b}} + \frac{3}{e^{2}} \right]$$

$$= \lim_{b \to \infty} \frac{-b}{e^{b}} - \lim_{b \to \infty} \frac{1}{e^{b}} + \frac{3}{e^{2}}$$

Using L'Hôspital's rule on this first limit,

$$= \lim_{b \to \infty} \frac{-1}{e^{b}} - \lim_{b \to \infty} \frac{1}{e^{b}} + \frac{3}{e^{2}}$$

$$= 0 - 0 + \frac{3}{e^{2}}$$

$$= \frac{3}{e^{2}}$$

Sample

Find $\displaystyle \int_{-\infty}^{\infty} \frac{e^{x}}{1 + e^{2x}}\,dx$, if it converges.

$$\int_{-\infty}^{\infty} \frac{e^{x}}{1 + e^{2x}}\,dx = \int_{-\infty}^{0} \frac{e^{x}}{1 + e^{2x}}\,dx + \int_{0}^{\infty} \frac{e^{x}}{1 + e^{2x}}\,dx$$

$$= \lim_{a \to -\infty} \int_{a}^{0} \frac{e^{x}}{1 + e^{2x}}\,dx + \lim_{b \to \infty} \int_{0}^{b} \frac{e^{x}}{1 + e^{2x}}\,dx$$

$$= \lim_{a \to -\infty} \left[\tan^{-1} e^{x} \right]_{a}^{0} + \lim_{b \to \infty} \left[\tan^{-1} e^{x} \right]_{0}^{b}$$

$$= \lim_{a \to -\infty} \left[\tan^{-1} e^{0} - \tan^{-1} e^{a} \right] + \lim_{b \to \infty} \left[\tan^{-1} e^{b} - \tan^{-1} e^{0} \right]$$

$$= \lim_{a \to -\infty} \left[\frac{\pi}{4} - \tan^{-1} e^{a} \right] + \lim_{b \to \infty} \left[\tan^{-1} e^{b} - \frac{\pi}{4} \right]$$

$$= \left(\frac{\pi}{4} - 0 \right) + \left(\frac{\pi}{2} - \frac{\pi}{4} \right)$$

$$= \frac{\pi}{2}$$

Sample

> The unbounded region that is below $y = 1/x$, above the x axis and to the right of $x = 1$ is revolved around the x axis. Find the volume of the solid generated, if possible.

The region is shown in the figure to the right.

Using discs, an integral to represent the solid is given by

$$\pi \int_1^\infty \left(\frac{1}{x}\right)^2 dx$$

From the first example, we know that the definite integral has a value of 1, so the volume of the solid must be $\pi(1) = \pi$.

The second type of improper integral is sometimes more difficult to recognize, because there is no tell-tale ∞ anywhere in the problem. This type of improper integral has an infinite discontinuity at one or both of the bounds of integration, or at some point between the two bounds. It is still necessary to convert the integral to a limit expression to evaluate it.

Improper Integrals with Infinite Discontinuities

In general, to convert to the limit expression, replace the discontinuity with another variable, usually s or t, and take the one-sided limit as s or t approaches the constant where the discontinuity occurs.

1. infinite discontinuity at the right boundary where $x = b$

$$\int_a^b f(x)\,dx = \lim_{t \to b^-} \int_a^t f(x)\,dx$$

2. infinite discontinuity at the left boundary where $x = a$

$$\int_a^b f(x)\,dx = \lim_{s \to a^+} \int_s^b f(x)\,dx$$

3. infinite discontinuity between the boundaries where $x = c$, $a < c < b$

$$\int_a^b f(x)\,dx = \int_a^c f(x)\,dx + \int_c^b f(x)\,dx$$

$$= \lim_{t \to c^-} \int_a^t f(x)\,dx + \lim_{s \to c^+} \int_s^b f(x)\,dx$$

Note: As before, not all improper integrals exist, because the limits above do not always exist. If the limit exists, then the improper integral is said to converge. If the limit does not exist, the improper integral diverges.

Sample

> Find $\displaystyle\int_0^1 \frac{1}{\sqrt[3]{x}}\,dx$, if it converges.

The infinite discontinuity here is at the left boundary, $a = 0$.

$$\int_0^1 \frac{1}{\sqrt[3]{x}}\,dx = \lim_{s \to 0^-} \int_s^1 \frac{1}{\sqrt[3]{x}}\,dx$$

$$= \lim_{s \to 0^-} \int_0^1 x^{-\frac{1}{3}}\,dx$$

$$= \lim_{s \to 0^-} \left[\frac{3}{2} x^{\frac{2}{3}} \right]_s^1$$

$$= \lim_{s \to 0^-} \left[\frac{3}{2} - \frac{3}{2} s^{\frac{2}{3}} \right]$$

$$= \frac{3}{2} - 0$$

$$= \frac{3}{2}$$

Sample

> Find $\displaystyle\int_0^2 \frac{1}{(x-1)^{\frac{2}{3}}}\,dx$, if it converges.

Here, the infinite discontinuity is at $x = 1$, between the bounds of integration. Split the original integral into two pieces, from $x = 0$ to $x = 1$, and from $x = 1$ to $x = 2$, and then write limits for each of the two integrals.

$$\int_0^{2} \frac{1}{(x-1)^{2/3}}\, dx = \int_0^{1} \frac{1}{(x-1)^{2/3}}\, dx + \int_1^{2} \frac{1}{(x-1)^{2/3}}\, dx$$

$$= \lim_{t \to 1^-} \int_0^{t} \frac{1}{(x-1)^{2/3}}\, dx + \lim_{s \to 1^+} \int_s^{2} \frac{1}{(x-1)^{2/3}}\, dx$$

$$= \lim_{t \to 1^-} \int_0^{t} (x-1)^{-2/3}\, dx + \lim_{s \to 1^+} \int_s^{2} (x-1)^{-2/3}\, dx$$

$$= \lim_{t \to 1^-} \left[3(x-1)^{1/3}\right]_0^{t} + \lim_{s \to 1^+} \left[3(x-1)^{1/3}\right]_s^{2}$$

$$= \lim_{t \to 1^-} \left[3(t-1)^{1/3} - 3(-1)^{1/3}\right] + \lim_{s \to 1^+} \left[3(1)^{1/3} - 3(s-1)^{1/3}\right]$$

$$= 0 - 3(-1) + 3 - 3(0)$$

$$= 6$$

Occasionally, an improper integral may arise that is a combination of the two types given above.

Sample

> Find $\displaystyle\int_0^{\infty} \frac{1}{\sqrt{x}\,(x+1)}\, dx$, if it converges.

Obviously, the upper bound of integration is infinite. But, the lower bound of integration, $x = 0$, is an infinite discontinuity for the integrand. So, split the given integral into two parts, from $x = 0$ to $x = 1$, and from $x = 1$ to $x = \infty$. Also, for problems such as this, it may be useful to perform the rather complicated integration as a general antiderivative in a separate problem, and then insert the answer into the two limit expressions.

$$\int_0^{\infty} \frac{1}{\sqrt{x}\,(x+1)}\, dx = \int_0^{1} \frac{1}{\sqrt{x}\,(x+1)}\, dx + \int_1^{\infty} \frac{1}{\sqrt{x}\,(x+1)}\, dx$$

$$= \lim_{s \to 0^+} \int_s^{1} \frac{1}{\sqrt{x}\,(x+1)}\, dx + \lim_{b \to \infty} \int_1^{b} \frac{1}{\sqrt{x}\,(x+1)}\, dx$$

$$= \lim_{s \to 0^+} \left[2\tan^{-1}\sqrt{x}\right]_s^{1} + \lim_{b \to \infty} \left[2\tan^{-1}\sqrt{x}\right]_1^{b} \quad \text{** see interpretation below}$$

$$= \lim_{s \to 0^+} \left[2\tan^{-1}1 - 2\tan^{-1}\sqrt{s}\right] + \lim_{b \to \infty} \left[2\tan^{-1}\sqrt{b} - 2\tan^{-1}1\right]$$

$$= 2\left(\frac{\pi}{4}\right) - 2(0) + 2\left(\frac{\pi}{2}\right) - 2\left(\frac{\pi}{4}\right)$$

$$= \pi$$

$$** \int \frac{1}{\sqrt{x}\,(x+1)}\, dx = \int \frac{1}{u(u^2+1)}\, 2u\, du \qquad \text{where } u = \sqrt{x}$$

$$= 2\int \frac{1}{u^2+1}\, du \qquad\qquad x = u^2$$

$$= 2\tan^{-1}u + C \qquad\qquad dx = 2u\, du$$

$$= 2\tan^{-1}\sqrt{x} + C$$

Sample Multiple-Choice Questions: Antiderivatives

1. $\int \dfrac{x\,dx}{\sqrt{9-x^2}} =$

A. $\dfrac{-1}{2}\ln\sqrt{9-x^2}+C$

B. $\arcsin\dfrac{x}{3}+C$

C. $-\sqrt{9-x^2}+C$

D. $\dfrac{-1}{4}\sqrt{9-x^2}+C$

E. $2\sqrt{9-x^2}+C$

2. $\int \dfrac{-1}{\sqrt[3]{x}}dx =$

A. $\dfrac{3}{2}x^{2/3}+C$

B. $\dfrac{-3}{4}x^{4/3}+C$

C. $\dfrac{-2}{3}x^{3/2}+C$

D. $\dfrac{-3}{2}x^{2/3}+C$

E. $\dfrac{-2}{3}x^{2/3}+C$

3. $\int \dfrac{\sin\theta}{\sqrt{1-\cos\theta}}d\theta =$

A. $\arcsin(\cos\theta)+C$

B. $2\sqrt{1-\cos\theta}+C$

C. $\ln|1-\cos\theta|+C$

D. $-2\sqrt{1-\cos\theta}+C$

E. $\dfrac{1}{2}\sqrt{1-\cos\theta}+C$

4. $\int \dfrac{1}{(x+2)^2}dx =$

A. $\dfrac{-2}{(x+2)^3}+C$

B. $\dfrac{-1}{x+2}+C$

C. $\dfrac{1}{2(x+2)}+C$

D. $\dfrac{-1}{2(x+2)}+C$

E. $\dfrac{1}{x+2}+C$

5. $\int t(5+3t^2)^8\,dt =$

A. $\dfrac{2}{3}t(5+3t^2)^9+C$

B. $\dfrac{1}{6}(5+3t^2)^9+C$

C. $\dfrac{1}{9}(5+3t^2)^9+C$

D. $\dfrac{1}{54}(5+3t^2)^9+C$

E. $\dfrac{4}{3}(5+3t^2)^7+C$

6. $\int \sin^3 x\,dx =$

A. $\sin x - \sin x\cos^2 x + C$

B. $\cos x - \dfrac{1}{3}\cos^3 x + C$

C. $-\cos x + \dfrac{1}{3}\cos^3 x + C$

D. $-\cos x - \dfrac{1}{3}\cos^3 x + C$

E. $\dfrac{1}{4}\sin^4 x + C$

7. $\int \sin^2 3x \, dx =$

   A. $2 \sin 3x \cos 3x + C$

   B. $\frac{1}{2} + \frac{1}{2} \cos 6x + C$

   C. $\frac{1}{2} x - \frac{1}{12} \sin 6x + C$

   D. $\frac{1}{2} x + \frac{1}{12} \sin 6x + C$

   E. $\frac{1}{2} - \frac{1}{2} \cos 6x + C$

8. $\int (\cos^2 x - \sin^2 x) \, dx =$

   A. $\frac{1}{3} \cos^3 x - \frac{1}{2} \sin^3 x + C$

   B. $\frac{1}{2} \sin 2x + C$

   C. $\frac{-1}{2} \sin 2x + C$

   D. $\cos 2x + C$

   E. $2 \sin 2x + C$

9. $\int \cot 4x \, dx =$

   A. $\frac{1}{4} \ln |\sin 4x| + C$

   B. $\frac{1}{4} \ln |\cos 4x| + C$

   C. $\frac{-1}{4} \ln |\sin 4x| + C$

   D. $\frac{-1}{4} \ln |\cos 4x| + C$

   E. $\frac{1}{4} \ln |\tan 4x| + C$

10. $\int \csc x \cot x \, dx =$

   A. $\csc x + C$

   B. $-\csc x + C$

   C. $\frac{\csc^2 x}{2} + C$

   D. $\frac{\cot^2 x}{2} + C$

   E. $\frac{-\cot^2 x}{2} + C$

11. $\int \sin 5x \sin 2x \, dx =$

   A. $\frac{1}{42} (7 \sin 3x + 3 \sin 7x) + C$

   B. $\frac{-1}{21} (7 \cos 7x + 3 \cos 2x) + C$

   C. $\frac{-1}{42} (7 \cos 3x - 3 \cos 7x) + C$

   D. $\frac{-1}{42} (3 \cos 7x + 7 \cos 2x) + C$

   E. $\frac{1}{42} (7 \sin 3x - 3 \sin 7x) + C$

12. $\int \cos(2x + 3) \, dx =$

   A. $\frac{1}{2} \sin(2x + 3) + C$

   B. $\sin(2x + 3) + C$

   C. $-\sin(2x + 3) + C$

   D. $\frac{-1}{2} \sin(2x + 3) + C$

   E. $\frac{-1}{5} \sin(2x + 3) + C$

13. $\int \sec(1 - x) \tan(1 - x) \, dx =$

   A. $\cot(1 - x) + C$

   B. $-\cot(1 - x) + C$

   C. $\tan^2(1 - x) + C$

   D. $\sec^2(1 - x) + C$

   E. $-\sec(1 - x) + C$

14. $\int \dfrac{\cos x}{4 + 2\sin x}\, dx =$

    A. $\sqrt{4 + 2\sin x} + C$

    B. $\dfrac{-1}{2(4 + \sin x)} + C$

    C. $\ln\sqrt{4 + 2\sin x} + C$

    D. $2\ln|4 + 2\sin x| + C$

    E. $\dfrac{1}{4}\sin x - \dfrac{1}{2}\csc^2 x + C$

15. $\int \dfrac{x^2 + x - 1}{x^2 - x}\, dx =$

    A. $x + 2\ln|x^2 - x| + C$

    B. $\ln|x| + \ln|x - 1| + C$

    C. $1 + \ln|x^2 - x| + C$

    D. $x + \ln|x^2 - x| + C$

    E. $x - \ln|x| - \ln|x - 1| + C$

16. $\int x\sqrt{2x + 1}\, dx =$

    A. $\dfrac{1}{30}\sqrt{2x + 1}\,(3x - 1) + C$

    B. $\dfrac{2}{15}(\sqrt{2x + 1})^3 (3x - 1) + C$

    C. $\dfrac{1}{15}(\sqrt{2x + 1})^3 (3x - 1) + C$

    D. $\dfrac{1}{60}\sqrt{3x - 1}\,(2x + 1) + C$

    E. $\dfrac{1}{30}(2x + 1)^{3/2} + (3x - 1) + C$

17. $\int \dfrac{x}{\sqrt{2x - 1}}\, dx =$

    A. $\dfrac{1}{3}\sqrt{2x - 1}\,(x - 2) + C$

    B. $\dfrac{1}{3}\sqrt{2x - 1}\,(x - 1) + C$

    C. $\dfrac{1}{6}\sqrt{2x - 1}\,(x - 2) + C$

    D. $\dfrac{1}{3}\sqrt{2x - 1}\,(x + 1) + C$

    E. $\dfrac{1}{3}\sqrt{2x + 1}\,(x + 1) + C$

18. $\int 3^{2x}\, dx =$

    A. $\dfrac{\ln 3}{2} 3^{2x} + C$

    B. $\dfrac{1}{2\ln 3} 3^{2x} + C$

    C. $(2\ln 3) 3^{2x} + C$

    D. $\dfrac{2}{\ln 3} 3^{2x} + C$

    E. $\dfrac{1}{\ln 3} 3^{2x} + C$

19. $\int \dfrac{e^{3x} - e^{-x}}{e^{-x}}\, dx =$

    A. $\dfrac{1}{5}e^{5x} + x + C$

    B. $\dfrac{1}{4}e^{4x} - 1 + C$

    C. $\dfrac{1}{4}e^{4x} - x + C$

    D. $e^{4x} - x + C$

    E. $\dfrac{1}{2}e^{2x} - x + C$

20. $\int \dfrac{e^{-x} - e^{x}}{e^{x} + e^{-x}}\, dx =$

    A. $\ln|e^{2x} + 1| - x + C$

    B. $\ln|e^{x} + e^{-x}| + C$

    C. $\ln|e^{-x} - e^{x}| + C$

    D. $x + \ln|e^{2x} + 1| + C$

    E. $x - \ln|e^{2x} + 1| + C$

21. $\int \dfrac{6}{x(\ln x)^3}\, dx =$

   A. $\dfrac{-3}{2(\ln x)^4} + C$

   B. $\dfrac{-3}{(\ln x)^2} + C$

   C. $6\ln\left|(\ln x)^2\right| + C$

   D. $\dfrac{-18}{(\ln x)^4} + C$

   E. $\dfrac{3(\ln x)^4}{2} + C$

22. $\int \dfrac{(y-1)^2}{2y}\, dy =$

   A. $\dfrac{y^2}{4} - y + \dfrac{1}{2}\ln|y| + C$

   B. $y^2 - y + \ln|2y| + C$

   C. $y^2 - 4y + \dfrac{1}{2}\ln|2y| + C$

   D. $\dfrac{(y-1)^3}{3y^2} + C$

   E. $\dfrac{1}{2} - \dfrac{1}{2y^2} + C$

23. $\int \dfrac{e^x}{\sqrt{4 - e^{2x}}}\, dx =$

   A. $\arcsin \dfrac{e^x}{2} + C$

   B. $\dfrac{1}{2}\arcsin \dfrac{e^x}{2} + C$

   C. $\dfrac{-1}{2}\ln\left|4 - e^{2x}\right| + C$

   D. $-2\sqrt{4 - e^{2x}} + C$

   E. $-\sqrt{4 - e^{2x}} + C$

24. $\int \dfrac{x}{x^2 + 2x + 5}\, dx =$

   A. $\dfrac{1}{2}\ln\left|x^2 + 2x + 5\right| + C$

   B. $\dfrac{1}{2}\arctan\left(\dfrac{x+1}{2}\right) + C$

   C.
   $\dfrac{1}{2}\ln\left|x^2 + 2x + 5\right| - \dfrac{1}{2}\arctan\left(\dfrac{x+1}{2}\right) + C$

   D.
   $\dfrac{1}{2}\ln\left|x^2 + 2x + 5\right| - \dfrac{1}{2}\arctan(x+1) + C$

   E.
   $\dfrac{1}{2}\ln\left|x^2 + 2x + 5\right| - \arctan\left(\dfrac{x+1}{2}\right) + C$

25. $\int \dfrac{1}{16 + 9x^2}\, dx =$

   A. $\arctan\left(\dfrac{3x}{4}\right) + C$

   B. $\dfrac{1}{4}\arctan(3x) + C$

   C. $\dfrac{1}{4}\arctan\left(\dfrac{3x}{4}\right) + C$

   D. $\dfrac{1}{3}\arctan\left(\dfrac{3x}{4}\right) + C$

   E. $\dfrac{1}{12}\arctan\left(\dfrac{3x}{4}\right) + C$

26. $\int \dfrac{e^x}{8 + e^x}\, dx =$

   A. $\dfrac{\sqrt{2}}{4}\arctan\dfrac{\sqrt{2}\,e^x}{4} + C$

   B. $\dfrac{1}{2}\ln\left|8 + e^x\right| + C$

   C. $\dfrac{1}{8}\arctan\dfrac{e^x}{8} + C$

   D. $\dfrac{e^x}{8} - \dfrac{1}{e^x} + C$

   E. $\ln\left|8 + e^{2x}\right| + C$

27. A smooth curve $y = f(x)$ is such that $f'(x) = x^2$. The curve goes through the point $(-1,2)$. Find its equation.

A. $y = \dfrac{x^3}{3} + 7$

B. $x^3 - 3y + 7 = 0$

C. $y = x^3 + 3$

D. $y - 3x^3 - 5 = 0$

E. $y = \dfrac{x^3}{3} + 2$

28. $\displaystyle\int \frac{x^2 - 14x - 8}{x^3 - 4x}\, dx =$

A. $2\ln x - \ln|x^2 - 4| + C$

B. $\dfrac{1}{3}\ln|x^3 - 4x| + C$

C. $2\ln x + 3\ln|x + 2| - 4\ln|x - 2| + C$

D. $\ln x - 3\ln|x + 2| - 4\ln|x - 2| + C$

E. $\ln|x^3 - 4x| + C$

*29. $\displaystyle\int \frac{x + 16}{x^2 + 2x - 8}\, dx =$

A. $\ln|(x - 2)(x + 4)| + C$

B. $\ln\left|\dfrac{(x + 4)^2}{(x - 2)^3}\right| + C$

C. $\ln\left|\dfrac{(x - 2)^3}{(x + 4)^2}\right| + C$

D. $\dfrac{2}{3}\ln|(x - 2)(x + 4)| + C$

E. $\dfrac{1}{3}\ln\left|\dfrac{(x - 4)^{10}}{(x + 2)^7}\right| + C$

*30. $\displaystyle\int x \cdot e^x\, dx =$

A. $e^x + x \cdot e^x + C$

B. $x^2 \cdot e^x + C$

C. $-x \cdot e^x + e^x + C$

D. $x \cdot e^x - e^x + C$

E. $x \cdot e^x + e^x + C$

*31. $\displaystyle\int x^2 \cos x\, dx =$

A. $\dfrac{x^3}{3} \cdot \sin x + C$

B. $-2x \sin x + C$

C. $x^2 \cdot \sin x + 2x \cdot \cos x - 2\sin x + C$

D. $x^2 \cdot \sin x - 2x \cdot \cos x + 2\sin x + C$

E. $-x^2 \cdot \sin x + 2x \cdot \cos x + 2\sin x + C$

*32. $\displaystyle\int \frac{5x^2 - 10x - 8}{x^3 - 4x}\, dx =$

A. $\ln|x^2(x + 2)^4(x - 2)| + C$

B. $\ln\left|\dfrac{x^2(x - 2)}{(x + 2)^4}\right| + C$

C. $\ln\left|\dfrac{2x(x - 2)}{4(x + 2)}\right| + C$

D. $\ln\left|\dfrac{2x \cdot 4(x + 2)}{(x - 2)}\right| + C$

E. $\ln\left|\dfrac{x^2 \cdot (x + 2)^4}{(x - 2)}\right| + C$

*BC topic only

*33. $\displaystyle\int_1^e \ln x \; dx =$

   A. $e^2 - e + 1$

   B. $2e - 1$

   C. $e^2 + 1$

   D. 1

   E. 0

*34. When decomposing $\dfrac{5x - 12}{x^2 - 4x}$ by the method of partial fractions, one of the fractions obtained is:

   A. $\dfrac{2}{x - 4}$

   B. $\dfrac{-3}{x}$

   C. $\dfrac{-2}{x - 4}$

   D. $\dfrac{3}{x - 2}$

   E. $\dfrac{5}{x - 4}$

BC topic only

Answers to Multiple-Choice Questions

1. C. Rewrite with a negative fractional exponent and set up the chain rule.

$$\int \frac{xdx}{\sqrt{9-x^2}} = \int \left(9-x^2\right)^{-\frac{1}{2}} xdx$$

$$= \frac{-1}{2} \int \left(9-x^2\right)^{-\frac{1}{2}}(-2x)\,dx$$

$$= \frac{-1}{2} \frac{\left(9-x^2\right)^{\frac{1}{2}}}{\frac{1}{2}} + C$$

$$= -\sqrt{9-x^2} + C$$

2. D. Rewrite with a fractional exponent and use the power rule.

$$\int \frac{-1}{\sqrt[3]{x}}\,dx = -1\int x^{-\frac{1}{3}}\,dx$$

$$= -1\frac{x^{\frac{2}{3}}}{\frac{2}{3}} = C$$

$$= \frac{-3}{2} x^{\frac{2}{3}} + C$$

3. B. $\int \dfrac{\sin\theta}{\sqrt{1-\cos\theta}}\,d\theta = \int \left(1-\cos\theta\right)^{-\frac{1}{2}}(\sin\theta)\,d\theta$

$$= \frac{\left(1-\cos\theta\right)^{\frac{1}{2}}}{\frac{1}{2}} + C$$

$$= 2\sqrt{1-\cos\theta} + C$$

4. B. $\int \dfrac{1}{(x+2)^2}\,dx = \int (x+2)^{-2}\,dx$

$$= \frac{(x+2)^{-1}}{-1} + C$$

$$= \frac{-1}{x+2} + C$$

5. D. $\int t(5+3t^2)^8\,dt = \dfrac{1}{6}\int (5+3t^2)^8(6t)\,dt$

$$= \frac{1}{6} \frac{(5+3t^2)^9}{9} + C$$

$$= \frac{1}{54}(5+3t^2)^9 + C$$

6. C. $\displaystyle\int \sin^3 x\, dx = \int (\sin^2 x)(\sin x)\, dx$

$\displaystyle = \int (1 - \cos^2 x)(\sin x)\, dx$

$\displaystyle = \int (\sin x - \cos^2 x \sin x)\, dx$

$\displaystyle = \int \sin x\, dx + \int (\cos x)^2 (-\sin x)\, dx$

$\displaystyle = -\cos x + \frac{\cos^3 x}{3} + C$

7. C. $\displaystyle\int \sin^2 3x\, dx = \int \frac{1 - \cos 6x}{2}\, dx$

$\displaystyle = \frac{1}{2} \int (1 - \cos 6x)\, dx$

$\displaystyle = \frac{1}{2} \int 1\, dx - \frac{1}{2} \int \cos 6x\, dx$

$\displaystyle = \frac{1}{2} \int 1\, dx - \frac{1}{2} \cdot \frac{1}{6} \int (\cos 6x)(6)\, dx$

$\displaystyle = \frac{1}{2} x - \frac{1}{12} \sin 6x + C$

8. B. $\displaystyle\int (\cos^2 x - \sin^2 x)\, dx = \int \cos 2x\, dx$

$\displaystyle = \frac{1}{2} \int \cos 2x\,(2)\, dx$

$\displaystyle = \frac{1}{2} \sin 2x + C$

9. A. $\displaystyle\int \cot 4x\, dx = \frac{1}{4} \int \cot 4x\,(4)\, dx$

$\displaystyle = \frac{1}{4} \ln |\sin 4x| + C$

10. B. $\displaystyle\int \csc x \cot x\, dx = -\csc x + C$

11. E. $\displaystyle\int \sin 5x \sin 2x\, dx = \frac{1}{2}\int (\cos 3x - \cos 7x)\,dx$

$$= \frac{1}{2}\int \cos 3x\, dx - \frac{1}{2}\int \cos 7x\, dx$$

$$= \frac{1}{2}\cdot\frac{1}{3}\int \cos 3x\,(3)\,dx - \frac{1}{2}\cdot\frac{1}{7}\int \cos 7x\,(7)\,dx$$

$$= \frac{1}{6}\sin 3x - \frac{1}{14}\sin 7x + C$$

$$= \frac{1}{42}(7\sin 3x - 3\sin 7x) + C$$

12. A. $\displaystyle\int \cos(2x+3)\,dx = \frac{1}{2}\int \cos(2x+3)(2)\,dx$

$$= \frac{1}{2}\sin(2x+3) + C$$

13. E. $\displaystyle\int \sec(1-x)\tan(1-x)\,dx$

$$= (-1)\int \sec(1-x)\tan(1-x)(-1)\,dx$$

$$= -\sec(1-x) + C$$

14. C. $\displaystyle\int \frac{\cos x}{4 + 2\sin x}\,dx = \frac{1}{2}\int \frac{2\cos x}{4 + 2\sin x}\,dx$

$$= \frac{1}{2}\ln|4 + 2\sin x| + C$$

$$= \ln\sqrt{4 + 2\sin x} + C$$

15. D. Divide

$$x^2 - x\overline{\smash{\big)}\,x^3 + x - 1}$$

$$\dfrac{x^3 - x}{2x - 1}$$

$$\int \frac{x^2 + x - 1}{x^2 - x}\,dx = \int \left(1 + \frac{2x-1}{x^2-x}\right)dx = x + \ln|x^2 - x| + C$$

16. C. $u = \sqrt{2x+1} \Rightarrow u^2 = 2x + 1$

$x = \frac{1}{2}(u^2 - 1) \Rightarrow dx = u\,du$

So $\displaystyle\int x\sqrt{2x+1}\,dx = \int \frac{1}{2}(u^2-1)(u)(u\,du)$

$\displaystyle = \frac{1}{2}\int (u^4 - u^2)\,du$

$\displaystyle = \frac{1}{2}\left(\frac{u^5}{5} - \frac{u^3}{3}\right) + C$

$\displaystyle = \frac{1}{2}\cdot\frac{1}{15}(3u^5 - 5u^3) + C$

$\displaystyle = \frac{1}{30}u^3(3u^2 - 5) + C$

$\displaystyle = \frac{1}{30}(2x+1)^{3/2}\big[3(2x+1) - 5\big] + C$

$\displaystyle = \frac{1}{30}(2x+1)^{3/2}(6x-2) + C$

$\displaystyle = \frac{1}{15}(2x+1)^{3/2}(3x-1) + C$

17. D. $u = \sqrt{2x-1} \Rightarrow u^2 = 2x - 1$

$x = \frac{1}{2}(u^2 + 1) \Rightarrow dx = u\,du$

$\displaystyle\int \frac{x}{\sqrt{2x-1}}\,dx = \int \frac{\frac{1}{2}(u^2+1)}{u}\,u\,du$

$\displaystyle = \frac{1}{2}\int (u^2 + 1)\,du$

$\displaystyle = \frac{1}{2}\int \left(\frac{u^3}{3} + u\right) + C$

$\displaystyle = \frac{1}{2}\cdot\frac{1}{3}(u^3 + 3u) + C$

$\displaystyle = \frac{1}{6}u(u^2 + 3) + C$

$\displaystyle = \frac{1}{6}\sqrt{2x-1}(2x-1+3) + C$

$\displaystyle = \frac{1}{3}\sqrt{2x-1}(x+1) + C$

18. B. $\displaystyle\int 3^{2x}\,dx = \frac{1}{2}\int 3^{2x}(2)\,dx$

$$= \frac{1}{2}\frac{1}{\ln 3}3^{2x}+C$$

or

$$\int 3^{2x}\,dx = \int e^{(\ln 3)\,2x}\,dx$$

$$= \frac{1}{2\ln 3}\int e^{(\ln 3)\,2x}(2\ln 3)\,dx$$

$$= \frac{1}{2\ln 3}e^{(\ln 3)\,2x}+C$$

$$= \frac{1}{2\ln 3}3^{2x}+C$$

19. C. $\displaystyle\int\frac{e^{3x}-e^{-x}}{e^{-x}}\,dx = \int(e^{4x}-1)\,dx$

$$= \int e^{4x}\,dx - \int 1\,dx$$

$$= \frac{1}{4}\int e^{4x}(4)\,dx - \int 1\,dx$$

$$= \frac{1}{4}e^{4x}-x+C$$

20. E. $\displaystyle\int\frac{e^{-x}-e^{x}}{e^{x}+e^{-x}}\,dx = \int\frac{-(e^{x}-e^{-x})}{e^{x}+e^{-x}}\,dx$

$$= -\ln(e^{x}+e^{-x})+C$$

$$= -\ln\left(\frac{e^{2x}+1}{e^{x}}\right)+C$$

$$= \ln\left(\frac{e^{x}}{e^{2x}+1}\right)+C$$

$$= \ln(e^{x})-\ln(e^{2x}+1)+C$$

$$= x-\ln(e^{2x}+1)+C$$

Since $e^{2x}+1 > 0$ for all real numbers, no absolute value bars are required.

21. B. $\displaystyle\int\frac{6}{x(\ln x)^3}\,dx = 6\int(\ln x)^{-3}\left(\frac{1}{x}\right)dx$

$$= 6\frac{(\ln x)^{-2}}{-2}+C$$

$$= \frac{-3}{(\ln x)^2}+C$$

22. A. $\int \dfrac{(y-1)^2}{2y} dy = \dfrac{1}{2} \int \dfrac{y^2 - 2y + 1}{y} dy$

$$= \dfrac{1}{2} \int \left(y - 2 + \dfrac{1}{y} \right) dy$$

$$= \dfrac{1}{2} \left(\dfrac{y^2}{2} - 2y + \ln|y| \right) + C$$

$$= \dfrac{1}{4} y^2 - y + \dfrac{1}{2} \ln|y| + C$$

23. A. $\int \dfrac{e^x}{\sqrt{4 - e^{2x}}} dx = \int \dfrac{e^x}{\sqrt{(2)^2 - (e^x)^2}} dx = \arcsin \dfrac{e^x}{2} + C$

24. C. As written, the numerator is not quite the derivative of the denominator. By adding and subtracting 1 in the numerator, you can split the fraction into two parts, the first of which has the numerator as the derivative of the denominator.

$$\int \dfrac{x}{x^2 + 2x + 5} dx = \int \dfrac{x + 1 - 1}{x^2 + 2x + 5} dx$$

$$= \dfrac{1}{2} \int \dfrac{2x + 2}{x^2 + 2x + 5} dx - \int \dfrac{1}{(x+1)^2 + 4} dx$$

$$= \dfrac{1}{2} \ln|x^2 + 2x + 5| - \dfrac{1}{2} \arctan \left(\dfrac{x+1}{2} \right) + C$$

25. E. $\int \dfrac{1}{16 + 9x^2} dx = \int \dfrac{1}{(4)^2 + (3x)^2} dx$

$$= \dfrac{1}{3} \int \dfrac{3}{(4)^2 + (3x)^2} dx$$

$$= \dfrac{1}{3} \cdot \dfrac{1}{4} \arctan \dfrac{3x}{4} + C$$

$$= \dfrac{1}{12} \arctan \dfrac{3x}{4} + C$$

26. E. $\int \dfrac{e^x}{8 + e^x} dx = \ln|8 + e^x| + C$

27. B. $\int f'(x) dx = \int x^2 dx = \dfrac{x^3}{3} + C \Rightarrow f(x) = \dfrac{x^3}{3} + C$

$$f(-1) = 2 \Rightarrow \dfrac{(-1)^3}{3} + C = 2$$

$$C = 2 + \dfrac{1}{3} = \dfrac{7}{3}$$

Thus $\quad f(x) = \dfrac{x^3}{3} + \dfrac{7}{3} \Rightarrow y = \dfrac{x^3}{3} + \dfrac{7}{3}$

$$3y = x^3 + 7$$

$$x^3 - 3y + 7 = 0$$

28. C. $\dfrac{x^2-14x-8}{x^3-4x} = \dfrac{x^2-14x-8}{x(x+2)(x-2)} = \dfrac{A}{x} + \dfrac{B}{x+2} + \dfrac{C}{x-2}$

$x^2 - 14x - 8 = A(x+2)(x-2) + Bx(x-2) + Cx(x+2)$

$x = 0 \Rightarrow -8 = A(2)(-2) + B(0) + C(0)$

$\qquad -8 = -4A$

$\qquad 2 = A$

$x = -2 \Rightarrow 24 = A(0) + B(-2)(-4) + C(0)$

$\qquad 24 = 8B$

$\qquad 3 = B$

$x = 2 \Rightarrow -32 = A(0) + B(0) + C(2)(4)$

$\qquad -32 = 8C$

$\qquad -4 = C$

So, $\displaystyle\int \dfrac{x^2-14x-8}{x^3-4x}\, dx = \int \left(\dfrac{2}{x} + \dfrac{3}{x+2} - \dfrac{4}{x-2} \right) dx$

$\qquad = 2 \displaystyle\int \dfrac{1}{x}\, dx + 3 \int \dfrac{1}{x+2}\, dx - 4 \int \dfrac{1}{x-2}\, dx$

$\qquad = 2\ln x + 3\ln|x+2| - 4\ln|x-2| + C$

29. C. $\dfrac{x+16}{x^2+2x-18} = \dfrac{x+16}{(x+4)(x-2)} \qquad \dfrac{x+16}{(x+4)(x-2)} = \dfrac{A}{x+4} + \dfrac{B}{x-2}$

$x + 16 = A(x-2) + B(x+4)$

Letting $x = -4$: $12 = A(-6) + B(0)$

$\qquad 12 = -6A$

$\qquad -2 = A$

Letting $x = 2$: $18 = A(0) + B(6)$

$\qquad 18 = 6B$

$\qquad 3 = B$

Then $\displaystyle\int \dfrac{x+16}{x^2+2x-8}\, dx = \int \left(\dfrac{-2}{x+4} + \dfrac{3}{x-2} \right) dx$

$\qquad = -2 \displaystyle\int \dfrac{1}{x+4}\, dx + 3 \int \dfrac{1}{x-2}\, dx$

$\qquad = -2\ln|x+4| + 3\ln|x-2| + C$

$\qquad = \ln\left| \dfrac{(x-2)^3}{(x+4)^2} \right| + C$

30. D. $\quad \int x \cdot e^x \, dx \rightarrow$ Let $x = u$ and $dv = e^x \, dx$;

$\qquad = \int u \, dv \qquad$ then $dx = du$ and $v = e^x$

$\qquad = uv = \int v \, du$

$\qquad = x \cdot e^x - \int e^x \, dx$

$\qquad = x \cdot e^x - e^x + C$

31. C. $\quad \int x^2 \cos x \, dx$

Using a chart to simplify the process, differentiating down the left column and integrating down the right column

d		u	dv		i
i		x^2	$\cos x$		n
f		$2x$	$\sin x$		t
f					e
e		2	$-\cos x$		g
r		0	$-\sin x$		r
e					a
n					t
t					e

Starting with x^2, multiply diagonally down to the right and alternating signs, we get:

$x^2 \sin x - (2x \cdot - \cos x) + 2(-\sin x) + C$

$= x^2 \sin x + 2x \cos x - 2 \sin x + C$

Thus $\int x^2 \cos x \, dx = x^2 \sin x + 2x \cos x - 2 \sin x + C$

32. E. $\quad \dfrac{5x^2 - 10x - 8}{x^3 - 4x} = \dfrac{5x^2 - 10x - 8}{x(x^2 - 4)} = \dfrac{5x^2 - 10x - 8}{x(x+2)(x-2)}$

Then $\dfrac{5x^2 - 10x - 8}{x(x+2)(x-2)} = \dfrac{A}{x} + \dfrac{B}{x+2} + \dfrac{C}{x-2}$

$$5x^2 - 10x - 8 = A(x+2)(x-2) + Bx(x-2) + Cx(x+2)$$

If $\quad x = 0: -8 = A(-4)$

$$2 = A$$

If $x = -2: 32 = B(8)$

$$4 = B$$

If $x = 2: \quad -8 = C(8)$

$$-1 = C$$

Next $\displaystyle\int \frac{5x^2 - 10x - 8}{x^3 - 4x}\,dx = \int \left(\frac{2}{x} - \frac{1}{x-2} + \frac{4}{x+2}\right)dx$

$\displaystyle = 2\int \frac{1}{x}\,dx - \int \frac{1}{x-2}\,dx + 4\int \frac{1}{x+2}\,dx$

$\displaystyle = 2\ln|x| - \ln|x-2| + 4\ln|x+2| + C$

$\displaystyle = \ln\left|\frac{x^2 \cdot (x+2)^4}{(x-2)}\right| + C$

33. D. $\displaystyle\int_1^e x \cdot \ln x\,dx \qquad$ Let $u = \ln x$ and let $dv = dx$

$\displaystyle = \int_1^e u\,dv \qquad\qquad du = \frac{1}{x}\,dx \qquad v = x$

$\displaystyle = \left[uv - \int v\,du\right]_1^e$

$\displaystyle = \left[x \cdot \ln x - \int x \cdot \frac{1}{x}\,dx\right]_1^e$

$\displaystyle = \left[x \cdot \ln x - x\right]_1^e$

$= (e \cdot \ln e - e) - (1 \cdot \ln 1 - 1)$

$= e \cdot 1 - e - (0 - 1)$

$= e - e - 0 + 1$

$= 1$

34. A. $\dfrac{5x-12}{x^2-4x} = \dfrac{5x-12}{x(x-4)}$ Then $\dfrac{5x-12}{x(x-4)} = \dfrac{A}{x} + \dfrac{B}{x-4}$

$$5x - 12 = A(x-4) + Bx$$

Let $x = 0$ $\qquad \rightarrow -12 = A(-4)$

$\qquad\qquad 3 = A \rightarrow$ so one fraction is $\dfrac{3}{x}$

Let $x = 4$ $\qquad \rightarrow 8 = B(4)$

$\qquad\qquad 2 = B \rightarrow$ so one fraction is $\dfrac{2}{x-4}$

Applications of Antiderivatives and Definite Integrals

Some of the most interesting calculus problems are those that require the use of the definite integral. These include finding the area and volume of irregular geometric figures, differential equations, and exponential growth and decay. These types of problems regularly appear as free-response problems on the AP exam.

The Fundamental Theorem of Calculus

The indefinite integral or antiderivative also has applications as a **definite integral.** The relationship between the indefinite and the definite integral is formalized in the following theorem.

Fundamental Theorem of Calculus

If $f(x)$ is continuous on the interval $[a, b]$, then

$$\int_a^b f(x)\,dx = g(b) - g(a)$$

where $g'(x) = f(x)$ that is, g is the antiderivative of f.

The proof of the fundamental theorem is not on the AP exam. The actual definition of the definite integral is required for the AP exam. It will be covered in the next section, along with the most common graphical interpretation of a definite integral.

Sample

Find $\int_1^3 x^2\,dx$.

Find the antiderivative and substitute the bounds of integration.

$$\int_1^3 x^2\,dx = \left[\frac{x^3}{3}\right]_1^3$$

$$= \frac{1}{3}\left[3^3 - 1^3\right] = \frac{26}{3}$$

Notation

The expression $\int_a^b f(x)\,dx$ is read as "the definite integral of $f(x)$ from a to b." The function $f(x)$ is called the integrand, a is the lower bound of integration, and b is the upper bound of integration. After the antiderivative has been found, the bounds of integration are placed at the top and bottom of a large set of brackets and then substituted.

Sample

Find $\int_0^{\pi/4} \sec^2 x e^{\tan x}\,dx$.

$$\int_0^{\pi/4} \sec^2 x e^{\tan x}\,dx = \left[e^{\tan x}\right]_0^{\pi/4}$$
$$= e^{\tan \pi/4} - e^{\tan 0}$$
$$= e^1 - e^0$$
$$= e - 1$$

Sample

Find $\int_{-2}^3 x^2\left(x^3+7\right)^3 dx$.

$$\int_{-2}^3 x^2\left(x^3+7\right)^3 dx = \frac{1}{3}\int_{-2}^3 \left(x^3+7\right)^3\left(3x^2\right)dx$$
$$= \frac{1}{3}\left[\frac{\left(x^3+7\right)^4}{4}\right]_{-2}^3$$
$$= \frac{1}{3}\cdot\frac{1}{4}\left[\left(x^3+7\right)^4\right]_{-2}^3$$
$$= \frac{1}{12}\left[(27+7)^4-(-8+7)^4\right]$$
$$= \frac{1}{12}[1,336,336-1]$$
$$= 111,361.25$$

When using u-substitution with a definite integral, you must change the bounds of integration to their respective u-values, as well as the integrand and differential. Changing the bounds eliminates the necessity of changing the antiderivative back into terms of x. Leave everything in terms of u and simply substitute the new u-bounds.

Sample

Find $\int_{-1}^3 \frac{2x}{x-5}\,dx$.

$$u = x - 5 \Rightarrow x = u + 5$$
$$dx = du$$

x	u
3	−2
−1	−6

$$\int_{-1}^{3} \frac{2x}{x-5} \, dx = \int_{-6}^{-2} \frac{2(u+5)}{u} \, du$$
$$= 2 \int_{-6}^{-2} \left(1 + \frac{5}{u}\right) du$$
$$= 2 \left[u + 5 \ln|u|\right]_{-6}^{-2}$$
$$= 2 \left[(-2 + 5 \ln 2) - (-6 + 5 \ln 6)\right]$$
$$= 8 + 10 \ln 2 - 10 \ln 6$$
$$\approx -2.986$$

Definition of the Definite Integral

The definite integral is defined as the limit of a sum.

Definition of the Definite Integral

The most common interpretation of the limit of a sum is an application for finding the area bounded by one or more functions. While geometric formulas provide a method for finding the areas of rectangles and squares, calculus is required to find an area such as the one shaded below.

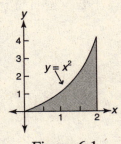

Figure 6.1

The area of this region can be *approximated* by using inscribed or circumscribed rectangles.

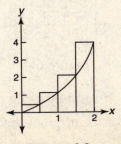

Figure 6.2

Better approximations can be obtained by using more rectangles, each with a smaller base.

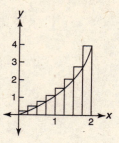

Figure 6.3

As the number of rectangles increases, the sum of the areas of the rectangles gets closer and closer to the actual area under the curve, although it is still an approximation. Finding the exact area would require an infinite number of rectangles. This corresponds to the calculus technique of taking the limit. The exact area is the limit of the sum of the areas of any set of rectangles, as the number of rectangles increases without bound:

$$\textit{Exact area} = \lim_{\#\text{rects} \to \infty} [\text{sum of areas of rects}]$$

More formally, if the base of the area is divided into n equal sub-intervals, and

n = number of subintervals and number of rectanles
c_i = any point in the ith rectangle
$f(c_i)$ = height of the ith rectangle
Δx_i = width of the ith rectangle

$$\Rightarrow f(c_i)\Delta x_i = \text{area of the } i\text{th rectangle}$$

then the *exact* area is given by

$$A = \lim_{n \to \infty} \sum_{i=1}^{n} f(c_i)\Delta x_i = \int_a^b f(x)\,dx$$

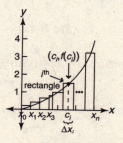

Figure 6.4

To actually find the value of a definite integral by using the definition is generally a lengthy and tedious process, as shown below for the original shaded area that is equal to $\int_0^2 x^2\,dx$.

width of each rectangle $= \dfrac{2}{n}$

using circumscribed rectangles

$$\Rightarrow \frac{2i}{n} = \text{right endpoint of } i\text{th rectangle.}$$

$$
\begin{aligned}
A &= \lim_{n \to \infty} \sum_{i=1}^{n} \left[f\!\left(\frac{2i}{n}\right)\!\left(\frac{2}{n}\right) \right] \\
&= \lim_{n \to \infty} \left[\sum_{i=1}^{n} \left(\frac{2i}{n}\right)^2 \left(\frac{2}{n}\right) \right] \\
&= \lim_{n \to \infty} \left[\sum_{i=1}^{n} \frac{8i^2}{n^3} \right] \\
&= \lim_{n \to \infty} \left[\frac{8}{n^3} \sum_{i=1}^{n} i^2 \right] \\
&= \lim_{n \to \infty} \left[\frac{8}{n^3} \cdot \frac{n(n+1)(2n+1)}{6} \right] \\
&= \lim_{n \to \infty} \left[\frac{16n^3 + 24n^2 + 8n}{6n^3} \right] \\
&= \frac{16}{6} = \frac{8}{3} = 2\frac{2}{3}
\end{aligned}
$$

This result is easily verified with the fundamental theorem.

$$\int_0^2 x^2 \, dx = \left[\frac{x^3}{3} \right]_0^2 = \frac{8}{3}$$

It is unlikely that you will be required to find the value of a definite integral by applying the definition. Such a problem would have to appear in the free-response section, and there are many, many better calculus problems to use for free-response questions. However, the definition could appear on the exam in a multiple-choice problem similar to the examples below.

Sample

Use a Riemann sum and five inscribed rectangles to approximate $\int_1^3 x^3 \, dx$, and check your approximation by using the fundamental theorem.

Sketch the graph of $y = x^3$, and show the five rectangles.

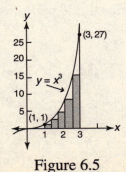

Figure 6.5

The base of each rectangle is 2/5 units because the distance from 1 to 3 is 2 and this interval is split into 5 subintervals. Because $f(x)$ is an increasing function, use the left endpoint of each interval to find the height of each of the inscribed rectangles.

$$A \approx \frac{2}{5}f(1) + \frac{2}{5}f(\tfrac{7}{5}) + \frac{2}{5}f(\tfrac{9}{5}) + \frac{2}{5}f(\tfrac{11}{5}) + \frac{2}{5}f(\tfrac{13}{5})$$

$$\approx \frac{2}{5}\left[1 + (\tfrac{7}{5})^3 + (\tfrac{9}{5})^3 + (\tfrac{11}{5})^3 + (\tfrac{13}{5})^3\right]$$

$$\approx 15.12$$

Thus the area is approximately 15.12 square units.

$$\int_1^3 x^3\, dx = \left[\frac{x^4}{4}\right]_1^3 = \frac{1}{4}\left[3^4 - 1^4\right] = 20$$

Therefore, the exact area is 20 square units.

Caution: Do *not* use the definite integral when asked for an approximation with a Riemann sum. As the example above shows, there may be a noticeable discrepancy between the two values.

Sample

> Use the definition to write a definite integral that is equivalent to
>
> $$\lim_{n \to \infty} \sum_{i=1}^{n} \left[4 - \left(-1 + \frac{3i}{n}\right)^2\right]\left(\frac{3}{n}\right)$$

The width of each subinterval is shown as $3/n$, which means that the total width of the interval must be 3 units. The value in the ith interval that is being plugged into the function is given by $-1 + 3i/n$, so the far left endpoint must be -1. The bounds of integration must be -1 and $2(-1 + 3 = 2)$. The function that gives the height of each rectangle follows the pattern $f(x) = 4 - x^2$.

$$\lim_{n \to \infty} \sum_{i=1}^{n} \left[4 - \left(-1 + \frac{3i}{n}\right)^2\right]\left(\frac{3}{n}\right) = \int_{-1}^{2}\left(4 - x^2\right)dx$$

Another method of approximating the definite integral is the **Trapezoidal rule.** It is very similar to the use of Riemann sums, except that instead of adding up the areas of rectangles, you add up the area of trapezoids. Although it is possible to find areas of individual trapezoids and then find the sum, the following generalized rule performs the same routine.

Theorem: Trapezoidal Rule

$$\int_a^b f(x) \approx \frac{b-a}{2n}\left[f(x_0) + 2f(x_1) + 2f(x_2) + \cdots + 2f(x_{n-1}) + f(x_n)\right]$$

where $f(x)$ is continuous on $[a, b]$, $x_0 = a$, and $x_n = b$.

The trapezoids that are being "circumscribed" above the curve appear as shown below. You can see that the amount of area that is not included is quite small. The trapezoidal rule generally gives very good approximations of a definite integral with a very few subintervals.

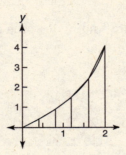

Figure 6.6

Trapezoidal rule problems that appear in Section 1B should, of course, be solved with a program on a graphing calculator.

Sample

Use the trapezoidal rule and five subintervals to approximate $\int_0^2 x^2\, dx$.

$$\int_a^b f(x) \approx \frac{b-a}{2n}\left[f(x_0) + 2f(x_1) + 2f(x_2) + \cdots + 2f(x_{n-1}) + f(x_n)\right]$$

$$\int_0^2 x^2\, dx \approx \frac{2-0}{2(5)}\left[f(0) + 2f\left(\frac{2}{5}\right) + 2f\left(\frac{4}{5}\right) + 2f\left(\frac{6}{5}\right) + 2f\left(\frac{8}{5}\right) + f(2)\right]$$

$$\approx \frac{1}{5}\left[0 + 2\left(\frac{4}{25}\right) + 2\left(\frac{16}{25}\right) + 2\left(\frac{36}{25}\right) + 2\left(\frac{64}{25}\right) + 4\right]$$

$$\approx \frac{68}{25}$$

Again, do *not* use the definite integral when asked for a trapezoidal rule approximation. In a multiple-choice question requesting the trapezoidal rule, one of the wrong answers will probably be the exact value of the definite integral.

The area interpretation of the definite integral can occasionally be used to find values for definite integrals that, on the surface, appear unintegrable.

Sample

Find $\int_{-4}^{4} \sqrt{16 - x^2}\, dx$.

Graphically, this problem translates into finding the area of a semicircle.

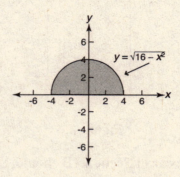

Figure 6.7

$$A = \frac{1}{2}\pi r^2 = \frac{1}{2}\pi\left(4^2\right) = 8\pi \Rightarrow \int_{-4}^{4}\sqrt{16-x^2}\,dx = 8\pi$$

Finding the antiderivative and evaluating the definite integral require the use of methods of integration that are not on the AP exam.

It should be noted that the area interpretation of the definite integral can be made only if $f(x)$ is nonnegative. If $f(x)$ is negative at any point between the bounds of integration, the area interpretation cannot be applied, although the definite integral may still exist.

Definite integrals can also be used to find the area *between* two curves, regardless of the type or location of the functions.

Theorem: Area Between Curves

If $f(x)$ and $g(x)$ are continuous on the interval $[a, b]$, and if $f(x) \geq g(x)$ in the interval, then the area between the curves bounded by $x =$ and $x = b$ is given by

$$A = \int_{a}^{b} \left[f(x) - g(x) \right] dx$$

or, in general, $\quad A = \int_{\text{left}}^{\text{right}} \left[\text{top} - \text{bottom} \right] dx$

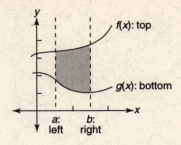

Figure 6.8

Similarly, if $h(y)$ *and* $k(y)$ are continuous between $y = a$ and $y = b$ and $h(y) \geq k(y)$, the area between the curves bounded by $y = a$ and $y = b$ is given by

$$A = \int_a^b \left[h(y) - k(y) \right] dy$$

or, in general, $A = \displaystyle\int_{\text{lower}}^{\text{upper}} \left[\text{right} - \text{left} \right] dy$

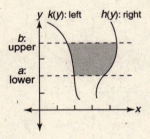

Figure 6.9

Sample

Find the area in the first quadrant bounded by $y = \sqrt[3]{x}$ and $y = x$.

First do a quick sketch, and find where the two curves intersect in order to determine which is on top, as well as the bounds of integration.

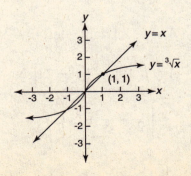

Figure 6.10

$$A = \int_{left}^{right} \left[top - bottom\right] dx$$

$$A = \int_0^1 \left[\sqrt[3]{x} - x\right] dx$$

$$= \left[\frac{x^{4/3}}{\frac{4}{3}} - \frac{x^2}{2}\right]_0^1$$

$$= \left[\frac{3}{4} \cdot 1^{4/3} - \frac{1}{2}\right] - [0] = \frac{1}{4} \text{ square units}$$

Sample

Find the area bounded by $x = y^2 - 2$ and $y = x$.

Again, sketch the two graphs. It may be necessary to find the points of intersection algebraically, rather than relying solely on the graph.

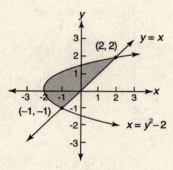

Figure 6.11

$$\left.\begin{array}{l} x = y^2 - 2 \\ y = x \end{array}\right\} \Rightarrow y^2 - 2 = y$$

$$y^2 - y - 2 = 0$$

$$(y - 2)(y + 1) = 0$$

$$y = 2 \text{ or } y = -1$$

$$A = \int_{lower}^{upper} \left[right - left\right] dy$$

$$A = \int_{-1}^2 \left[(y) - (y^2 - 2)\right] dy$$

$$= \left[\frac{y^2}{2} - \frac{y^3}{3} + 2y\right]_{-1}^2$$

$$= \left(2 - \frac{8}{3} + 4\right) - \left(\frac{1}{2} + \frac{1}{3} - 2\right)$$

$$= \frac{9}{2}$$

This problem could have been done in terms of x, although it would have required two separate definite integrals. This is because the top and bottom of the region are not consistently determined by the same curves. Between $x = -2$ and $x = -1$, the top and bottom curves are both determined by the parabola, whereas between $x = -1$ and $x = 2$, the top curve is the parabola and the bottom curve is the line. The choice of a y integration is the logical one, because the line is always to the right of the parabola between $y = -1$ and $y = 2$.

Properties of the Definite Integral

It is now possible, using the area interpretation of the definite integral, to explain several properties of the definite integral and the definition of **average value.** The area interpretation is simply a convenience here; these properties hold in all cases.

Four Properties of the Definite Integral

All of the following properties assume that $f(x)$ and/or $g(x)$ are integrable on the specified interval or at the specified point.

1. $\displaystyle\int_a^b f(x)\,dx + \int_b^c f(x)\,dx = \int_a^c f(x)\,dx$

   A geometric "proof" in terms of area is shown in the following diagram. This property is often used for integrating piece functions, such as absolute value.

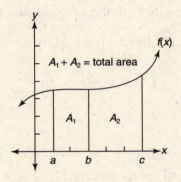

Figure 6.12

2. $f(x) \le g(x) \Rightarrow \displaystyle\int_a^b f(x)\,dx \le \int_a^b g(x)\,dx$

   Again, a simple area argument is the most convincing.

269

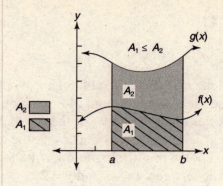

Figure 6.13

3. $\int_a^a f(x)\,dx = 0$

A "rectangle" with no width would naturally have no area.

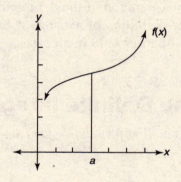

Figure 6.14

4. $\int_a^b f(x)\,dx = -\int_b^a f(x)$

This property can be proved easily with the fundamental theorem.

$$\int_a^b f(x)\,dx = g(b) - g(a) \text{ and } \int_b^a f(x) = g(a) - g(b)$$

$$\Rightarrow \int_a^b f(x)\,dx = -\int_b^a f(x)$$

Sample

Given that $h(x)$ is integrable and continuous on $[1, 3]$, $\int_1^3 h(x)\,dx = 2a$, and $\int_3^2 h(x)\,dx = b$, find the value for $\int_1^2 [3h(x) + 2]\,dx$.

By the additive property

$$\int_1^2 h(x)\,dx + \int_2^3 h(x)\,dx = \int_1^3 h(x)\,dx$$

$$\Rightarrow \int_1^2 h(x)\,dx = \int_1^3 h(x)\,dx - \int_2^3 h(x)\,dx$$

$$= \int_1^3 h(x)\,dx + \int_3^2 h(x)\,dx$$

Thus $\int_1^2 h(x)\,dx = 2a + b$

$$\int_1^2 \left[3h(x) + 2\right] dx = 3\int_1^2 h(x)\,dx + 2\int_1^2 dx$$

$$= 3(2a + b) + 2\left[x\right]_1^2$$

$$= 6a + 3b + 2(2 - 1)$$

$$= 6a + 3b + 2$$

Sample

Find $\int_{-2}^3 |x - 1|\,dx$.

The integrand can be written as a piece function.

$$|x - 1| = \begin{cases} x - 1 & \text{for } x \geq 1 \\ -x + 1 & \text{for } x < 1 \end{cases}$$

The definite integral can then be split into two pieces.

$$\int_{-2}^3 |x - 1|\,dx = \int_{-2}^1 (-x + 1)\,dx + \int_1^3 (x - 1)\,dx$$

$$= \left[\frac{-x^2}{2} + x\right]_{-2}^1 + \left[\frac{x^2}{2} - x\right]_1^3$$

$$= \left[\left(\frac{-1}{2} + 1\right) - (-2 - 2)\right] + \left[\left(\frac{9}{2} - 3\right) - \left(\frac{1}{2} - 1\right)\right]$$

$$= 6\frac{1}{2}$$

An easy way to check this solution is to graph the function and find the area geometrically.

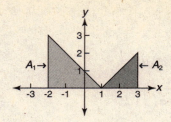

Figure 6.15

$$A = \frac{1}{2}(\text{base})(\text{height})$$

$$A_1 = \frac{1}{2}(3)(3) = \frac{9}{2} \qquad A_2 = \frac{1}{2}(2)(2) = 2$$

$$A_T = \frac{9}{2} + 2 = 6\frac{1}{2}$$

Property for Even and Odd Functions

Given that $f(x)$ is integrable on $[a, b]$,

1. $f(x)\,\text{even} \Rightarrow \displaystyle\int_{-a}^{a} f(x)\,dx = 2\int_{0}^{a} f(x)\,dx$

2. $f(x)\,\text{odd} \Rightarrow \displaystyle\int_{-a}^{a} f(x)\,dx = 0$

Both properties are easily "proved" using area arguments.

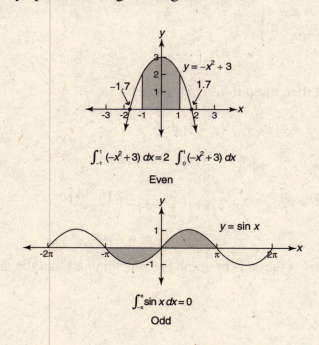

Figure 6.16

Although neither of these properties is listed on the AP outline, both can be useful time savers.

A variation on the definite integral can be created by replacing the upper bound of integration with a variable. This operation yields the antiderivative as a function of the upper bound.

Sample

> Find $\int_{2}^{x} \left(5t - 4t^2\right) dt$.

$$\int_{2}^{x} \left(5t - 4t^2\right) dt = \left[\frac{5}{2}t^2 - \frac{4}{3}t^3\right]_{2}^{x}$$
$$= \left(\frac{5}{2}x^2 - \frac{4}{3}x^3\right) - \left(\frac{5}{2}(4) - \frac{4}{3}(8)\right)$$
$$= \frac{5}{2}x^2 - \frac{4}{3}x^3 + \frac{2}{3}$$

Variable bounds of integration provide another property of definite integrals.

Variable Bounds Property

$$\frac{d}{dx}\left[\int_{a}^{x} f(t)\, dt\right] = f(x)$$

The theorem above can be demonstrated easily by using the previous example.

For $f(t) = 5t - 4t^2$,

$$\frac{d}{dx}\left[\int_{2}^{x} \left(5t - 4t^2\right) dt\right] = \frac{d}{dx}\left[\frac{5}{2}x^2 - \frac{4}{3}x^3 + \frac{2}{3}\right]$$
$$= 5x - 4x^2 = f(x)$$

Sample

> Find $\dfrac{d}{dx}\left[\int_{3}^{x} \sqrt{t^3 + 4t^2 - 1}\ dt\right]$.

Regardless of the value of the constant lower bound, simply substitute the upper-bound variable into the integrand. Finding the antiderivative is unnecessary.

$$\frac{d}{dx}\left[\int_{3}^{x} \sqrt{t^3 + 4t^2 - 1}\ dt\right] = \sqrt{x^3 + 4x^2 - 1}$$

Variable bounds of integration also provide the definition of the natural log function.

Definition of Natural Log

$$\ln x = \int_{1}^{x} \frac{1}{t}\, dt \ \ (\text{for } x > 0)$$

With this definition, and the previous property, the derivative of the natural log can now be proved.

$$\frac{d}{dx}\left[\ln|x|\right] = \frac{d}{dx}\left[\int_1^x \frac{1}{t}\, dt\right]$$
$$= \frac{1}{x}$$

And the derivative, of course, provides the antiderivative formula.

$$\int \frac{1}{x}\, dx = \ln|x| + C$$

Average-Value Property

Definition of Average Value

If $f(x)$ is continuous on $[a, b]$, then the average value of $f(x)$ on $[a, b]$ is given by

$$\frac{1}{b-a}\int_a^b f(x)\, dx$$

Sample

Find the average value of $y = 2x^3 - 3x$ on the interval $[2, 5]$.

$$\text{Average value} = \frac{1}{5-2}\int_2^5 \left(2x^3 - 3x\right) dx$$
$$= \frac{1}{3}\left[\frac{x^4}{2} + \frac{3x^2}{2}\right]_2^5$$
$$= \frac{1}{3}\cdot\frac{1}{2}\left[x^4 + 3x^2\right]_2^5$$
$$= \frac{1}{6}\left[\left(5^4 + 3\cdot 5^2\right) - \left(2^4 + 3\cdot 2^2\right)\right]$$
$$= 112$$

Average-value problems are very easy *if* you have memorized the definition.

Volume

In a method similar to that of finding area, definite integrals can also be used to find the volume of solids. For the AP exam, two different types of solids are used: solids of revolution, generated by revolving a figure around a vertical or horizontal line, and solids with known cross sections. For both types, it is important that you be able to visualize and/or sketch the solid. Study the following figures. The first eight are solids of revolution, generated by revolving the area A (bounded by the x-axis, $x = 2$, and $y = x^2$) around various lines. The last three figures show solids with known cross sections.

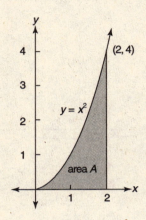

Figure 6.17

Vertical Axis of Revolution

1. Area A revolved around $x = 2$

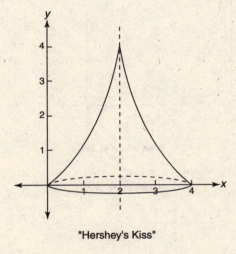

"Hershey's Kiss"

Figure 6.18

2. Area A revolved around $x = 0$ (y-axis)

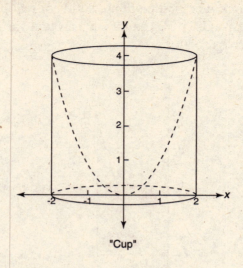

"Cup"

Figure 6.19

3. Area A revolved around $x = -1$

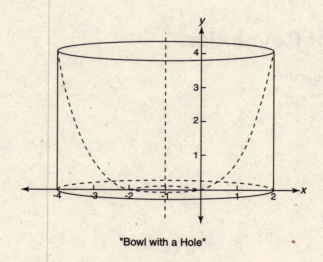

"Bowl with a Hole"

Figure 6.20

4. Area A revolved around $x = 3$

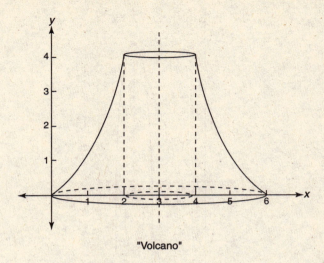

"Volcano"

Figure 6.21

Horizontal Axis of Revolution

5. Area A revolved around $y = 0$ (x-axis)

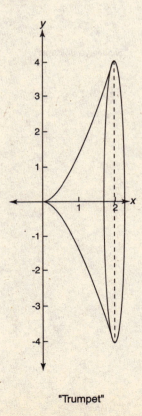

"Trumpet"

Figure 6.22

6. Area A revolved around $y = -1$

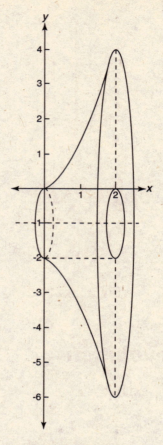

"Sideways Volcano"

Figure 6.23

7. Area A revolved around $y = 5.5$

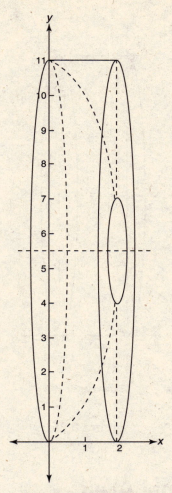

"Sideways Bowl with a Hole"

Figure 6.24

8. Area A revolved around $y = 4$

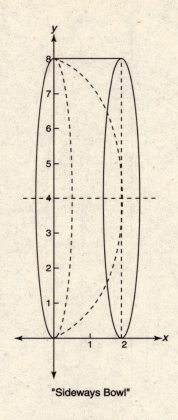

"Sideways Bowl"

Figure 6.25

Known Cross-Sectional Area

9. Circular base with square cross sections

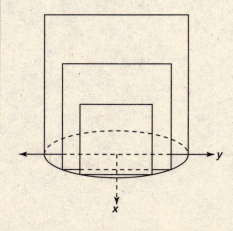

Figure 6.26

10. Circular base with isosceles triangle cross sections

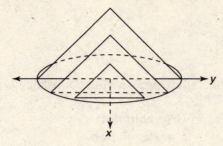

Figure 6.27

11. Triangular base with semicircular cross sections

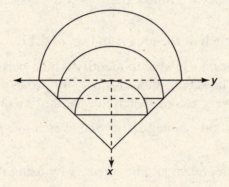

Figure 6.28

The volume of solids of revolution can be found by three different methods. The choice of method depends on the generating curve and the axis of revolution. For some solids, only one method may be possible, so knowing all three methods is essential.

Solids of Revolution

Disc Method

$$\pi \int_a^b (\text{radius})^2 \begin{cases} dx \text{ or} \\ dy \end{cases}$$

Washer Method

$$\pi \int_a^b \left(\frac{\text{outer}}{\text{radius}} \right)^2 - \left(\frac{\text{inner}}{\text{radius}} \right)^2 \begin{cases} dx \text{ or} \\ dy \end{cases}$$

Shell Method

$$2\pi \int_a^b \left(\begin{array}{c}\text{average} \\ \text{height}\end{array}\right)\left(\begin{array}{c}\text{average} \\ \text{radius}\end{array}\right)\left\{\begin{array}{l}dx \text{ or} \\ dy\end{array}\right.$$

The three integrals above are done as dx or as dy in accordance with the following chart.

	Horizontal Axis of Revolution	Vertical Axis of Revolution
Disc Method or Washer Method	dx	dy
Shell Method	dy	dx

To set up any of the integrands above, follow these steps.

1. Sketch the original area, such as the area A in Figure 6.17.

2. Sketch the solid of revolution. Be able to identify which parts of the figure are solid and which are empty space. The sketch should show any "holes" that pierce the solid. If you can visualize the solid, a very rough sketch may be sufficient.

3. Determine the proper method of integration, and sketch in a representative disc, washer, or shell.

4. Determine whether the integral should be dx or dy by using the foregoing chart.

5. Identify the needed parts of the integrand; then sketch and label (radius = r or inner radius = r, outer radius = R or height = h, radius = r). Express each of the needed parts in terms of x or y. If necessary, substitute from the original equation so that all parts are in terms of x or y only as determined in step 4.

6. Determine the bounds of integration by examining the extent of the original area along the x- or y-axis to correspond with the choice in step 4.

7. Set up the integral, following the pattern above. Don't forget the π or 2π.

8. Integrate and substitute.

Sample

Use the disc method to find the volume of the solid of revolution generated when area A is revolved around the line $x = 2$ ("Hershey's Kiss," Figure 6.18).

Follow the eight steps listed above.

1. Sketch area A.

2. Sketch the solid.

3. Sketch a representative disc (two are shown in Figure 6.29).

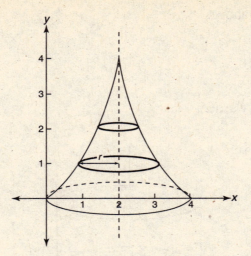

Figure 6.29

4. By discs with vertical axis of revolution $\Rightarrow dy$.

5. For discs, you need radius r. Label $r = 2 - x$. The integrand must be in terms of y.

$$y = x^2 \Rightarrow x = \sqrt{y} \Rightarrow r = 2 - \sqrt{y}$$

6. Along the y-axis, area A extends from $y = 0$ to $y = 4 \Rightarrow \displaystyle\int_0^4$.

7. $\pi \displaystyle\int_a^b (\text{radius})^2 \, dy \Rightarrow \pi \int_0^4 \left(2 - \sqrt{y}\right)^2 dy$

$$= \pi \int_0^4 \left(4 - 4\sqrt{y} + y\right) dy$$

$$= \pi \left[4y - \frac{4y^{3/2}}{\frac{3}{2}} + \frac{y^2}{2}\right]_0^4$$

8.

$$= \pi \left[\left(16 - \frac{8}{3} \cdot 4^{3/2} + \frac{1}{2}(16)\right) - (0)\right]$$

$$= \pi \left(16 - \frac{64}{3} + 8\right)$$

$$= \frac{8\pi}{3} \text{ units}^3$$

Sample

Use the washer method to find the volume of the solid of revolution generated when area A is revolved around the y-axis ("Cup," Figure 6.19).

Follow the eight steps listed above.

1. Sketch area A.

2. Sketch the solid.

3. Sketch a representative washer.

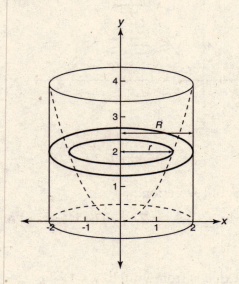

Figure 6.30

4. By washers with vertical axis of revolution $\Rightarrow dy$.

5. For washers, you need inner radius r and outer radius R.

$R = 2$ and $r = x$

The integrand must be in terms of y.

$y = x^2 \Rightarrow x = \sqrt{y} \Rightarrow r = \sqrt{y}$

6. Along the y-axis, area A extends from $y = 0$ to $y = 4 \Rightarrow \int_0^4$.

7. $\pi \int_a^b \left[\left(\dfrac{\text{outer}}{\text{radius}} \right)^2 - \left(\dfrac{\text{inner}}{\text{radius}} \right)^2 \right] dy \Rightarrow \pi \int_0^4 \left[2^2 - \left(\sqrt{y} \right)^2 \right] dy$

$$= \pi \int_0^4 (4 - y)\, dy$$

$$= \pi \left[4y - \frac{y^2}{2} \right]_0^4$$

$$= \pi \left[\left(16 - \frac{16}{2} \right) - 0 \right]$$

$$= 8\pi \text{ units}^3$$

8.

Sample

Use the shell method to find the volume of the solid of revolution generated when area A is revolved around the line $x = 3$ ("volcano").

Follow the eight steps listed above.

1. Sketch area A.
2. Sketch the solid.
3. Sketch a representative shell.

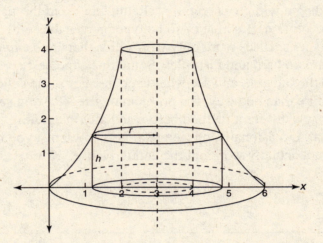

Figure 6.31

4. By shells with vertical axis of revolution $\Rightarrow dx$.

5. For shells, you need height h and radius r.

   $h = y$ and $r = 3 - x$

   The integrand must be in terms of x.

   $y = x^2 \Rightarrow h = x^2$

6. Along the x-axis, area A extends from $x = 0$ to $x = 2 \Rightarrow \int_0^2$.

7. $2\pi \displaystyle\int_a^b \left(\begin{array}{c}\text{average} \\ \text{height}\end{array}\right)\left(\begin{array}{c}\text{average} \\ \text{radius}\end{array}\right)dx \Rightarrow 2\pi \displaystyle\int_0^2 \left(x^2\right)(3-x)\,dx$

8.
$$= 2\pi \int_0^2 \left(3x^2 - x^3\right)dx$$
$$= 2\pi \left[x^3 - \frac{x^4}{4}\right]_0^2$$
$$= 2\pi \left[\left(8 - \frac{16}{4}\right) - 0\right]$$
$$= 8\pi \text{ units}^3$$

Many students have trouble choosing the correct method for finding the volume of a specific solid of revolution. To begin with, try mentally "slicing" the solid through the middle perpendicular to the axis of revolution. If a hole of some type pierces the solid either partially or completely, try washers or shells. Discs work only with solids that are *completely* solid. Other than this suggestion, there are no hard and fast rules. Sometimes, the best approach is simply to pick a method, try to set up the integral, and see what happens. For some solids, it may be possible to set up the integral more than one way. If a problem on the AP exam seems particularly difficult, you may want to try a different method before actually integrating; you may have overlooked an easier method. Occasionally, on free-response problems, you may be asked simply to set up the integral but not actually work out the antiderivative. *Be sure to follow the directions.*

Sample

Find the volume of the solid generated when the region bounded by $y = x^2$ and $y = 4x - x^2$ is revolved around:

(a) the x-axis

(b) the line $x = 3$

a) 1. Sketch the two parabolas.

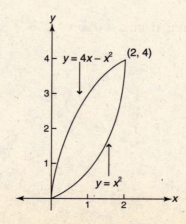

Figure 6.32

2. Sketch the solid.

3. Washer method: Sketch in a representative washer.

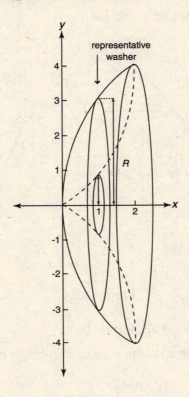

Figure 6.33

4. By washer with horizontal axis of revolution $\Rightarrow dx$.

5. For washers, you need the inner radius r and the outer radius R.

Inner radius r depends on the parabola that opens up; that is, $y = x^2 \Rightarrow r = x^2$.

Outer radius R depends on the parabola that opens down; that is, $y = 4x - x^2 \Rightarrow R = 4x - x^2$.

6. Along the x-axis, the original area extends from $x = 0$ to $x = 2 \Rightarrow \int_0^2$.

7. $\pi \int_a^b \left[\left(\begin{matrix} \text{outer} \\ \text{radius} \end{matrix} \right)^2 - \left(\begin{matrix} \text{inner} \\ \text{radius} \end{matrix} \right)^2 \right] dx$

8.
$$\Rightarrow \pi \int_0^2 \left[\left(4x - x^2 \right)^2 - \left(x^2 \right)^2 \right] dx$$
$$= \pi \int_0^2 \left[16x^2 - 8x^3 + x^4 - x^4 \right] dx$$
$$= \pi \int_0^2 \left(16x^2 - 8x^3 \right) dx$$
$$= \pi \left[\frac{16x^3}{3} - 2x^4 \right]_0^2$$
$$= \frac{32\pi}{3} \text{ units}^3$$

(b)1. See part (a) for parabolas.

   2. Sketch the solid.

   3. Shell method: sketch a representative shell.

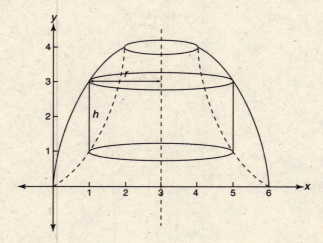

Figure 6.34

4. By shells with vertical axis of revolution $\Rightarrow dx$.

5. For shells, you need the average radius r and the average height h.

$$r = 3 - x \text{ and } h = y_1 - y_2 = \left(4x - x^2\right) - \left(x^2\right)$$

$$h = 4x - 2x^2$$

6. Along the x-axis, the original curve extends from $x = 0$ to $x = 2 \Rightarrow \int_0^2$.

7. $2\pi \int_a^b \left(\begin{array}{c}\text{average} \\ \text{radius}\end{array}\right)\left(\begin{array}{c}\text{average} \\ \text{height}\end{array}\right) dx$

8.
$$\Rightarrow 2\pi \int_0^2 (3-x)\left(4x-x^2\right) dx$$
$$= 2\pi \int_0^2 \left(12x - 7x^2 + x^3\right) dx$$
$$= 2\pi \left[6x^2 - \frac{7x^3}{3} + \frac{x^4}{4}\right]_0^2$$
$$= 2\pi \left[24 - \frac{56}{3} + 4\right]$$
$$= \frac{56\pi}{3} \text{ units}^3$$

Part (b) could also have been done with the washer method.

Solids with Known Cross Sections

If the area of a cross section is known, then the volume of a solid is given by

$$V = \int_a^b \left(\begin{array}{c} \text{area of cross} \\ \text{section} \end{array} \right) \left\{ \begin{array}{c} dx \text{ or} \\ dy \end{array} \right.$$

The integral is set up with respect to dx or dy on the basis of which axis the known cross sections are perpendicular to.

Rule: If the cross section is perpendicular to $\begin{cases} x\text{-axis} \Rightarrow dx \\ y\text{-axis} \Rightarrow dy \end{cases}$

To find the volume of a solid with a known cross section:

1. Sketch the base of the solid in the regular xy-coordinate plane.

2. Sketch or envision the solid. Usually, the x-axis is drawn coming "out of the paper" toward you to give the three-dimensional effect.

3. Determine whether the integral should be in terms of x or y by referring to the rule above.

4. Determine the bounds of integration by finding the extent of the base along the x- or y-axis to correspond to step 3.

5. Use geometry and the given equation(s) to find an expression for the area of the cross section.

6. Set up the integral according to the pattern above.

7. Integrate and substitute.

Sample

Find the volume of the solid whose base is the circle $x^2 + y^2 = 9$ and whose cross sections perpendicular to the x-axis are squares.

1. Sketch the base in the *xy*-plane.

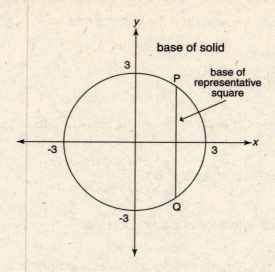

Figure 6.35

2. Sketch the solid.

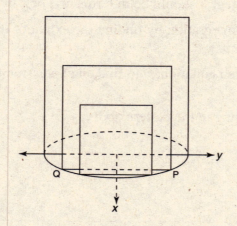

Figure 6.36

3. Cross sections $\perp$ to *x*-axis $\Rightarrow dx$.

4. Base extends from $x = -3$ to $x = 3 \Rightarrow \int_{-3}^{3}$ or, by applying symmetry, use $2\int_{0}^{3}$.

5. Square cross sections $\Rightarrow A = (\text{side})^2$.

One side of one representative square is shown as *PQ* in Figure 6.35.

$$PQ = 2y = 2\sqrt{9 - x^2}$$

6. $\int_a^b \left(\begin{array}{c} \text{area of cross} \\ \text{section} \end{array}\right) dx$

$\Rightarrow \int_{-3}^{3} \left[2\sqrt{9-x^2}\right]^2 dx$ or $2\int_0^3 \left[2\sqrt{9-x^2}\right]^2 dx$

7.

$= 2\int_0^3 4\left(9-x^2\right) dx$

$= 8\left[9x - \dfrac{x^3}{3}\right]_0^3$

$= 8\left[(27-9) - 0\right]$

$= 144 \text{ units}^3$

Sample

Find the volume of the solid of revolution whose base is bounded by the lines $f(x) = 1 - x$, $g(x) = x - 1$, *and* $x = 0$ and whose cross sections are semicircles perpendicular to the x-axis.

1. Sketch the base in the xy-plane.

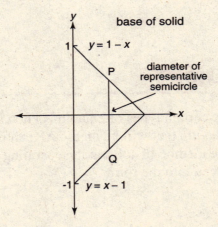

Figure 6.37

2. Sketch the solid.

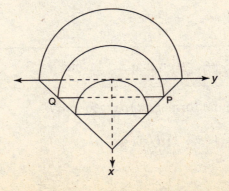

Figure 6.38

3. Cross sections $\perp$ to $x\text{-}axis \Rightarrow dx$.

4. Base extends from $x = 0$ to $x = 1$ along the x-axis.

5. Semicircular cross sections $\Rightarrow A = \frac{1}{2}\pi r^2$

   The *diameter* of one representative semicircle is labeled as PQ in Figure 6.37.

   $$PQ = (1-x) - (x-1) = 2 - 2x \Rightarrow d = 2 - 2x$$

   So $r = \dfrac{2-2x}{2} = 1 - x$

6. $\displaystyle\int_a^b \left(\begin{array}{c}\text{area of cross} \\ \text{section}\end{array}\right) dx$

7. $$\Rightarrow \frac{\pi}{2}\int_0^1 (1-x)^2\,dx = \frac{\pi}{2}\int_0^1 \left(1 - 2x + x^2\right) dx$$

   $$= \frac{\pi}{2}\left[x - x^2 + \frac{x^3}{3}\right]_0^1$$

   $$= \frac{\pi}{2}\left[1 - 1 + \frac{1}{3}\right]$$

   $$= \frac{\pi}{6}\ \text{units}^3$$

Differential Equations

Antiderivatives are used to solve certain types of equations known as **differential equations.** The only type of differential equation that will be on the AP exam is a separable differential equation, which is named for the method of solving it, separating the variables. These types of differential equations can be forced into the form

$$f(x)\,dx = g(y)\,dy$$

after which both sides are integrated. If a boundary condition is given, it is then substituted to find the value of the constant of integration. If not, the solution is left with "$+ C$" and is known as the general solution.

Sample

Find the solution of $y' = \dfrac{4x^3}{2y+1}$, given that $x = 1$ when $y = 2$.

First separate the variables into the form $f(x)\,dx = g(y)\,dy$.

$$y' = \frac{4x^3}{2y+1} \Rightarrow \frac{dy}{dx} = \frac{4x^3}{2y+1} \Rightarrow (2y+1)\,dy = \left(4x^3\right)dx$$

Then find the antiderivative of both sides.

$$\int (2y+1)\, dy = \int (4x^3)\, dx$$

$$\Rightarrow y^2 + y + C_1 = x^4 + C_2$$

By combining C_1 and C_2 into a single constant C, we get

$$y^2 + y - x^4 = C$$

Finally, substitute to find C.

$$(1,2) \Rightarrow 2^2 + 2 - 1^4 = C$$

$$\Rightarrow C = 5$$

Therefore, $y^2 + y - x^4 = 5$ is the solution to the equation.

Sample

Find the general solution of $\dfrac{dy}{dx}(5 - 3x^2) = 3xy$.

Rewrite the equation in the form $f(x)\, dx = g(y)\, dy$.

$$\frac{dy}{dx}(5 - 3x^2) = 3xy \Rightarrow dy(5 - 3x^2) = (3xy)\, dx$$

$$\Rightarrow \frac{1}{y}\, dy = \frac{3x}{5 - 3x^2}\, dx$$

Now find the antiderivative of both sides.

$$\int \frac{1}{y}\, dy = \int \frac{3x}{5 - 3x^2}\, dx$$

$$\int \frac{1}{y}\, dy = \frac{-1}{2} \int \frac{-6x}{5 - 3x^2}\, dx$$

$$\ln|y| + C_1 = \frac{-1}{2} \ln|5 - 3x^2| + C_2$$

$$\ln|y| = \ln (5 - 3x^2)^{-1/2} + C_3$$

If this form does not appear as one of the multiple-choice answers, you may need to solve the equation for y. Change from logarithmic form to exponential form $(\ln a = b \Rightarrow e^b = a)$.

$$e^{\ln (5 - 3x^2)^{-1/2} + C_3} = y$$

$$e^{\ln (5 - 3x^2)^{-1/2}} e^{C_3} = y$$

$$(5 - 3x^2)^{-1/2} C = y$$

$$\frac{C}{\sqrt{5 - 3x^2}} = y$$

Problems that involve exponential growth and decay often begin as separable differential equations. The differential equation may be given in the form

$$\frac{dy}{dt} = ky \text{ or } y' = ky$$

or the problem may contain the phrase "rate of change of y is proportional to y." In either case, you should follow the same general plan as outlined above: Separate the variables and find the antiderivative.

Sample

> The rate of change of a population of rabbits is proportional to the number of rabbits present at any given time. If 10 rabbits are present initially, and 195 rabbits are present in 6 months, how many rabbits will there be in 2 years?

Let y = number of rabbits at any time t. The phrase "rate of change . . . is proportional to the number . . . present" implies that

$$\frac{dy}{dt} = ky$$

Separate the variables.

$$\frac{1}{y}\,dy = k\,dt$$

And integrate.

$$\int \frac{1}{y}\,dy = \int k\,dt$$
$$\ln|y| = kt + C_1$$
$$e^{kt + C_1} = y$$
$$e^{kt} e^{C_1} = y$$
$$e^{kt} C = y$$
$$y = Ce^{kt}$$

Use the two boundary conditions given to find C and k. From "10 rabbits are present initially," you know that

$$t = 0 \Rightarrow y = 10$$

$$y = Ce^{kt} \Rightarrow 10 = Ce^{0}$$

Thus $C = 10$

So $y = 10e^{kt}$

From "195 rabbits are present in 6 months," you know that

$$t = 6 \Rightarrow y = 195$$

$$y = 10e^{kt} \Rightarrow 195 = 10e^{6k}$$

$$19.5 = e^{6k}$$

$$\ln(19.5) = 6k$$

$$k = \frac{\ln(19.5)}{6} \approx 0.4951$$

Thus the equation to describe the growth is $y = 10e^{0.4951t}$. To answer the question, simply plug in the given value for t and solve for y.

"2 years" $\qquad t = 24\,(\text{months}) \Rightarrow y = ?$

$$y = 10e^{0.4951t} \Rightarrow y = 10e^{(0.4951)(24)}$$

$$\approx 1,446,974 \text{ rabbits}$$

This rather extreme number assumes unlimited food, water, and space and ideal conditions, which, of course, won't be achieved, thank goodness.

Time-saving hint: If exponential growth or decay appears in a multiple-choice problem, you can immediately translate the phrase "rate of change of y is proportional to the amount of y present" into $y = Ce^{kt}$ without bothering to do the antiderivatives. Then solve for y. If exponential growth or decay appears in a free-response problem, however, be sure to include the work shown above by which you translate $y' = ky$ into $y = Ce^{kt}$.

Numerical Solutions to Differential Equations: Euler's Method

There are a variety of methods that can be used to approximate the coordinates of points on the graph of the solution to a differential equation of the form $\frac{dy}{dx} = f(x, y)$. This differential equation, $\frac{dy}{dx} = f(x, y)$, gives us a formula to compute the slope of the line tangent to the graph at any point on the graph of the solution. Given a point (x_0, y_0) on the graph of the solution, and given a specific x-coordinate of a point on the graph of the solution, we wish to find the y-coordinate of this point.

One way to find the desired y-coordinate is to use a tangent line approximation as we move from the given point (x_0, y_0) to the desired point $(x, ??)$.

Sample

> Let $y = g(x)$ be the solution to the differential equation $\frac{dy}{dx} = 2x$ with the initial condition of $g(1) = 1$. Find $g(1.5)$ using five equal increments, starting with $x = 1$ and ending with $x = 1.5$.

Our change in x, $\Delta x = \dfrac{1.5 - 1}{5} = \dfrac{0.5}{5} = 0.1$

Since $\frac{dy}{dx} = 2x$, $\frac{dy}{dx}$ at $(1, 1) = 2(1) = 2 =$ slope of the line tangent to the graph of $g(x)$ at $(1, 1)$. Therefore the point-slope form of equation at the tangent line at this point is:

$$y - 1 = 2(x - 1)$$
$$y - 1 = 2x - 2$$
$$y = 2x - 1$$

With increments of 0.1, the next point has an x-coordinate of $1 + \Delta x = 1 + 0.1 = 1.1$.

Using our previous equation, $y = 2x - 1$, we find the corresponding y-coordinate when $x - 1.1$:

$$y = 2x - 1$$
$$\text{when } x = 1.1 \rightarrow y = 2(1.1) - 1$$
$$= 2.2 - 1$$
$$y = 1.2$$

So our second point is $(1.1, 1.2)$.

Since $\frac{dy}{dx} = 2x$, $\frac{dy}{dx}$ at $(1.1, 1.2) = 2(1.1) = 2.2 =$ slope of the line tangent to graph of $g(x)$ at $(1.1, 1.2)$. The point-slope form of the equation of the tangent line at this point is:

$$y - 1.2 = 2.2(x - 1.1)$$
$$y - 1.2 = 2.2x - 2.42$$
$$y = 2.2x - 1.22$$

Our next point will have x-coordinate of $1.1 + \Delta x = 1.1 + 0.1 = 1.2$

$$\text{when } x = 1.2 \rightarrow y = 2.2(1.2) - 1.22$$
$$y = 2.64 - 1.22$$
$$y = 1.42$$

So the next point will be $(1.2, 1.42)$. We would continue this process until we arrived at the point with x-coordinate 1.5, also finding its corresponding y-coordinate.

As you can see, this is a very tedious process. A quicker way to find the desired y-coordinate is to use Euler's Method.

Euler's Method uses differentials (Δx, dy, etc.) to approximate the y-coordinate of the point having the desired x-coordinate. Again, we are given $\frac{dy}{dx} = f(x, y)$ and a point (x_0, y_0) on the graph of the solution to the differential equation.

Sample

First, for small value at Δx and dy:

$$\frac{dy}{dx}(\Delta x) \approx \Delta y \quad \text{(we reduce } \frac{1}{dx}(\Delta x) \approx 1$$

so that

$$dy \approx \Delta y$$

As in the previous example with $\frac{dy}{dx} = 2x$, $\Delta x = 0.1$, $x = 1$ when $y = 1$, we want to find y when $x = 1.5$. We complete the following chart:

x	y	$\frac{dy}{dx}(\Delta x) \approx \Delta y$	$x + \Delta x$	$y + \Delta y$
1	1	2(1)[0.1] = 0.2	1+0.1=1.1	1+0.2=1.2
1.1	1.2	2(1.1)[0.1] = .22	1.1+0.1=1.2	1.2+.22=1.42
1.2	1.42	2(1.2)[0.1] = .24	1.2+0.1=1.3	1.42+.24=1.66
1.3	1.66	2(1.3)[0.1] = .26	1.3+0.1=1.4	1.66+.26=1.92
1.4	1.92	2(1.4)[0.1] = .28	1.4+0.1=1.5	1.92+.28=2.2
1.5	2.2	——	——	——

Therefore, $y \approx 2.2$ when $x = 1.5$; so $g(1.5) \approx 2.2$

Just to check the accuracy of this approximation, we solve the given differential equation $\frac{dy}{dx} = 2x$ as follows:

$$\frac{dy}{dx} = 2x$$

$$dy = 2x\,dx$$

$$\int dy = \int 2x\,dx \quad \text{we "separated" the variables}$$

$$y = x^2 + C$$

since $g(1) = 1$
$$1 = 1^2 + C$$

$$0 = C$$

Therefore, $y = x^2$; in other words, $g(x) = x^2$.

When $x = 1.5 \rightarrow y = (1.5)^2$

$$y = 2.25$$

so $g(1.5) = 2.25$

Euler's Method gave us $g(1.5) \approx 2.2$.

Sample

Let $y = h(x)$ be the solution to the differential equation $\dfrac{dy}{dx} = x + y$ with the initial condition that $h(1) = 2$. What is the approximation for $h(2)$ using Euler's Method, starting at 1 with a step size of 0.5.

With $\dfrac{dy}{dx} = x + y$, original point $(1, 2)$ and $\Delta x = 0.5$, we seek y when $x = 2$.

x	y	$\dfrac{dy}{dx} (\Delta x) \approx \Delta y$	$x + \Delta x$	$y + \Delta y$
1	2	(1+2)(0.5) = 1.5	1+0.5=1.5	2+1.5=3.5
1.5	3.5	(1.5+3.5)(0.5) = 2.5	1.5+0.5=2.0	3.5+2.5=6.0
2.0	6.0	——	——	——

So, when $x = 2$, $y \approx 6$. Therefore, $h(2) \approx 6.0$.

Sample

Let $y = f(x)$ be the solution to the differential equation $\dfrac{dy}{dx} = y$ with the initial condition that $f(0) = 1$. Starting at $x = 0$, use 3 steps to approximate $f(0.6)$, using Euler's Method.

With $\dfrac{dy}{dx} = y$, original point $(0, 1)$ and $\Delta x = \dfrac{0.6 - 0}{3} = \dfrac{0.6}{3} = 0.2$, we complete the chart below.

x	y	$\dfrac{dy}{dx} (\Delta x) \approx \Delta y$	$x + \Delta x$	$y + \Delta y$
0	1	(1)(0.2) = 0.2	0+0.2=0.2	1+0.2=1.2
0.2	1.2	(1.2)(0.2) = .24	0.2+0.2=0.4	1.2+.24=1.44
0.4	1.44	(1.44)(0.2) = .288	0.4+0.2=0.6	1.44+.288=1.728
0.6	1.728	——	——	——

So the desired point has coordinates (0.6, 1.728); therefore $f(0.6) \approx 1.728$.

Next, just to check the accuracy of Euler's Method, we solve the differential equation

$$\frac{dy}{dx} = y$$

$$\frac{dy}{y} = dx$$

$$\int \frac{dy}{y} = \int dx$$

$$\ln y = x + C$$

$$y = e^{x+C}$$

$$y = k \cdot e^x$$

$$y = k \cdot e^x$$

with $f(0) = 1 \rightarrow 1 = k \cdot e^0$

$$1 = k$$

so $\qquad y = e^x$

with $\quad x = 0.6 \rightarrow y = e^{0.6}$

$$y \approx 1.822$$

Euler's Method as a Recursive Formula

The process used to complete the charts in the previous examples can be summarized in terms of the recursive formulas:

$$x_{n+1} = x_n + \Delta x \text{ and } y_{n+1} = y_n + \Delta x (f(x_n, y_n))$$

We start with (x_0, y_0), moving on to the points (x_1, y_1), (x_2, y_2), etc., until we arrive at the point having the desired x-coordinate. In the case of the previous example:

$$\frac{dy}{dx} = f(x, y) = y, \Delta x = 0.2, \text{ and } (x_0, y_0) = (0, 1)$$

Then $\quad x_1 = x_0 + \Delta x$

$$= 0 + 0.2$$

$$= 0.2$$

and $\quad y_1 = y_0 + \Delta x (f(x_0, y_0))$

$$= y_0 + \Delta x (y_0)$$

$$= 1 + (0.2)(1)$$

$$= 1 + 0.2$$

$$= 1.2$$

So $(x_1, y_1) = (0.2, 1.2)$

Then $x_2 = x_1 + \Delta x$

$\quad\quad = 0.2 + 0.2$

$\quad\quad = 0.4$

and $y_2 = y_1 + \Delta x (y_1)$

$\quad\quad = 1.2 + (0.2)(1.2)$

$\quad\quad = 1.2 + .24$

$\quad\quad = 1.44$

So $(x_2, y_2) = (0.4, 1.44)$

Then $x_3 = x_2 + \Delta x$

$\quad\quad = 0.4 + 0.2$

$\quad\quad = 0.6$

and $y_3 = y_2 + \Delta x (y_2)$

$\quad\quad = 1.44 + (0.2)(1.44)$

$\quad\quad = 1.44 + .288$

$\quad\quad = 1.728$

So $(x_3, y_3) = (0.6, 1.728)$ and thus $f(0.6) \approx 1.728$

The "chart" form is a quick alternative to the recursive process shown above.

Differential Equations and Slope Fields

Given a differential equation of the form $\dfrac{dy}{dx} = f(x, y)$ with solution $g(x, y)$, we can find the slope of the line tangent to the graph of g at any point (x, y). Since $g(x, y)$ is the antiderivative of $f(x, y)$, g actually represents a family of curves, each differing from the others by just a constant. For example, if $\dfrac{dy}{dx} = 2x$, then we have:

We have: $dy = 2x \, dx$

and $\displaystyle\int dy = \int 2x \, dx$

so that $\quad y = x^2 + C$

The family of solutions to $\frac{dy}{2x} = 2x$ consists of curves such as:

$y = x^2 - 2$

$y = x^2 - 1$

$y = x^2$

$y = x^2 + 1$

$y = x^2 + 2$, etc, etc...

To construct a **slope field,** at each point in the xy-plane, we draw a short segment whose slope is that of the line tangent to the graph of g at each point (x, y). We can view the general nature of the graph of the solution of the given differential equation, even though we may not be able to actually determine the solution's equation.

Sample

On the grid below, plot the slope field for the differential equation $\frac{dy}{dx} = \frac{xy}{2}$.

For each point with x or y coordinate equal 0, $\frac{dy}{dx} = 0$. So the segment drawn at each of these points should be horizontal. At other points (x, y), we compute the slope of the tangent segment using the formula $\frac{dy}{dx} = \frac{xy}{2}$; we then draw, at that point, a short segment having that slope. The result is a slope field for the given differential equation.

Point	(1, 1)	(1, 2)	(1, 3)	(1,4)	(2, 1)	(2, 2)	(2, 3)	(2, 4)	(3, 1)	(3, 2)	(3, 3)	(3, 4)	(4, 1)	(4, 2)	(4, 3)	(4, 4)
Slope	$\frac{1}{2}$	1	$\frac{3}{2}$	2	1	2	3	4	$\frac{3}{2}$	3	$\frac{9}{2}$	6	2	4	6	8

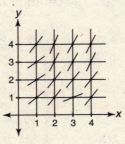

See below for calculator-produced slope field for $\frac{dy}{dx} = \frac{xy}{2}$.

If we use a program for the graphing calculator, we can quickly produce the graphs of many slope fields.

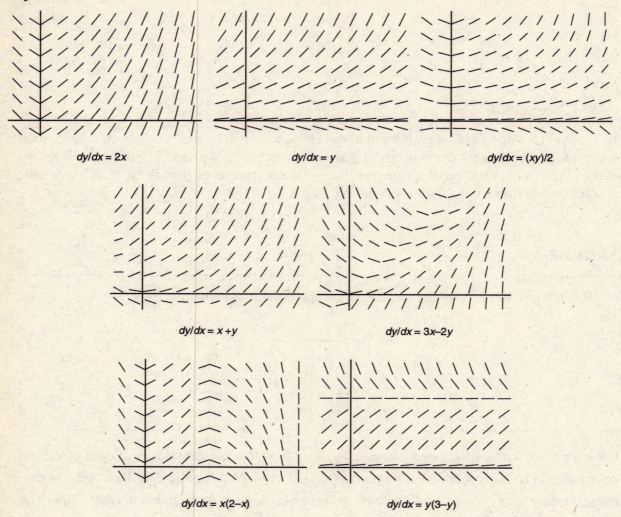

dy/dx = 2x   dy/dx = y   dy/dx = (xy)/2

dy/dx = x + y   dy/dx = 3x–2y

dy/dx = x(2–x)   dy/dx = y(3–y)

Sample

Which of the following could be a specific solution for the differential equation whose slope field is shown below?

A. $y = \ln x$

B. $y = \sin x$

C. $y = e^x$

D. $y = x^2$

E. $y = \cos x$

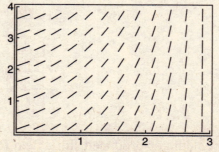

The correct answer is **C,** $y = e^x$. Since $\frac{d}{dx}(e^x) = e^x$, we would expect the slope of the line tangent to graph of e^x to increase without bound as x increases. The other choices — A, B, D, E — are shown below.

$y = x^2$ could be a specific solution for the differential equation whose slope field is shown at the right.

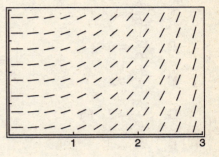

$y = \ln x$ could be a specific solution for the differential equation whose slope field is shown at the right.

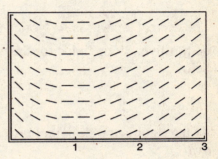

$y = \cos x$ could be a specific solution for the differential equation whose slope field is shown at the right.

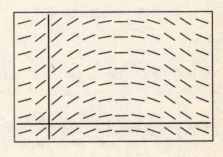

$y = \sin x$ could be a specific solution for the differential equation whose slope field is shown at the right.

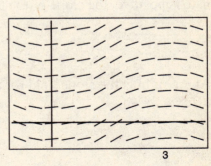

Sample

Shown below is a slope field for which of the following differential equations?

A. $\dfrac{dy}{dx} = x^2$

B. $\dfrac{dy}{dx} = y^3$

C. $\dfrac{dy}{dx} = x$

D. $\dfrac{dy}{dx} = 2x + y$

E. $\dfrac{dy}{dx} = xy$

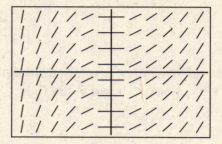

The correct answer is **A**. Notice that for $\dfrac{dy}{dx} = x^2$, all slopes at all non-zero coordinates should be positive. Slope fields for the other differential equations — B, C, D, and E — are shown below.

At the right is the slope field for the differential equation $dy/dx = y^3$

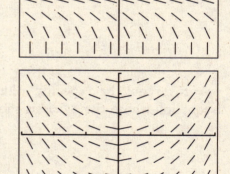

At the right is the slope field for the differential equation $dy/dx = x$

Note that when the x-coordinate is negative, the slope of the tangent at that point is negative. Similarly, when the x-coordinate is positive, the slope of the tangent is also positive.

At the right is the slope field for the differential equation $dy/dx = 2x + y$

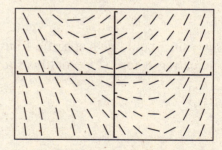

At the right is the slope field for the differential equation $dy/dx = xy$

Note that when x and y have the same sign $(-, -)$ or $(+, +)$, slope of the tangent is positive. And when x and y have different signs $(-, +)$ or $(+, -)$, slope of the tangent is negative.

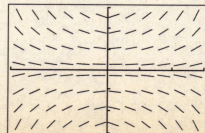

PVA with Antiderivatives

By using the antiderivative, you can now do position/velocity/acceleration problems in reverse — that is, starting with the acceleration or velocity function, and integrating to find position. The total relationship between the three functions is shown in the following expanded theorem.

Theorem for PVA

$s(t) = $ position function

$v(t) = $ velocity function

$a(t) = $ acceleration function

$$s(t) = \int v(t)\,dt = \int \left[\int a(t)\,dt \right] dt$$

$$s'(t) = v(t) = \int a(t)\,dt$$

$$s''(t) = v'(t) = a(t)$$

Sample

A particle moves along a horizontal path such that its velocity at any time $t(t > 0)$ is given by $v(t) = t/4 - 1/t$ meters per second. At $t = 1$, the particle is 3 units to the left of the origin.

(a) Find any time(s) when the particle changes direction.

(b) Find the total distance the particle travels from $t = 1$ to $t = 5$. Round to the nearest hundredth of a unit.

(c) Find the acceleration for any time(s) when the particle is at rest.

Justify all answers.

The problem provides the velocity. Because part (b) requires the position function, and part (c) the acceleration function, it may be expedient simply to find these functions immediately.

$$s(t) = \int v(t)\,dt \Rightarrow s(t) = \int \left(\frac{t}{4} - \frac{1}{t} \right) dt$$

$$s(t) = \frac{t^2}{8} - \ln|t| + C$$

"at $t = 1$ . . . 3 units to the left" $\Rightarrow s(1) = -3$

$$s(1) = \frac{1}{8} - \ln 1 + C = -3$$

$$\Rightarrow C = -3\frac{1}{8} = \frac{-25}{8}$$

Therefore $\quad s(t) = \dfrac{t^2}{8} - \ln t - \dfrac{25}{8}$

$$s(t) = \frac{1}{8}\left(t^2 - 8\ln t - 25\right) \ \textit{for } t > 0$$

$$a(t) = v'(t) \Rightarrow a(t) = \frac{d}{dt}\left(\frac{t}{4} - \frac{1}{t}\right)$$

$$a(t) = \frac{1}{4} + \frac{1}{t^2} = \frac{t^2 + 4}{4t^2}$$

(a) "changes direction" $\Rightarrow v(t)$ changes sign

$v(t) = \dfrac{t}{4} - \dfrac{1}{t} = \dfrac{t^2 - 4}{4t}$

$v(t) = 0 \Rightarrow t = -2, 2$ but $t > 0$

t	$0 < t < 2$	$t = 2$	$t > 2$
v(t)	neg	0	pos

Thus the particle changes direction at $t = 2$.

(b) "total distance . . . from $t = 1$ to $t = 5$" $\Rightarrow \left|s(1) - s(2)\right| + \left|s(2) - s(5)\right|$ due to change of direction at $t = 2$

t	$s(t) = \frac{1}{8}\left(t^2 - 8\ln t - 25\right)$
1	-3
2	$\dfrac{-21}{8} - \ln 2$
5	$-\ln 5$

$\left|s(1) - s(2)\right| + \left|s(2) - s(5)\right|$

$$= \left|-3 - \left(\frac{-21}{8} - \ln 2\right)\right| + \left|\left(\frac{-21}{8} - \ln 2\right) - (-\ln 5)\right|$$

$$= \left|\ln 2 - \frac{3}{8}\right| + \left|\ln 5 - \ln 2 - \frac{21}{8}\right|$$

$$= 0.31814718 + 1.708709268$$

$$= 2.026856448$$

$$\approx 2.03 \text{ meters}$$

(c) "acceleration when at rest" $\Rightarrow$ find $a(t)$ when $v(t) = 0$

from part (a): $v(t) = 0$ when $t = 2$

$$a(t) = \frac{t^2 + 4}{4t^2} \Rightarrow a(2) = \frac{4 + 4}{16} = \frac{1}{2} \ m/s^2$$

Sample

The acceleration of a particle moving along a horizontal line is given by
$a(t) = 2t + e^{2t}$ ft/s^2 for any time t ($t > 0$). At time $t = 1$, the particle is at the origin and its velocity is 6 ft/s. Find the position of the particle as a function of t.

$$v(t) = \int a(t)\,dt \Rightarrow v(t) = \int \left(2t + e^{2t}\right) dt$$

$$= \int 2t\,dt + \frac{1}{2} \int e^{2t}(2)\,dt$$

$$v(t) = t^2 + \frac{1}{2} e^{2t} + C$$

$v(1) = 6 \Rightarrow \qquad v(1) = 1^2 + \frac{1}{2} e^2 + C = 6$

$$C = 5 - \frac{1}{2} e^2$$

Thus $\quad v(t) = t^2 + \frac{1}{2} e^{2t} + 5 - \frac{1}{2} e^2$

$$s(t) = \int v(t)\,dt \Rightarrow s(t) = \int \left(t^2 + \frac{1}{2} e^{2t} + 5 - \frac{1}{2} e^2\right) dt$$

$$= \int t^2\,dt + \frac{1}{2} \int e^{2t}\,dt + \int \left(5 - \frac{1}{2} e^2\right) dt$$

$$= \int t^2\,dt + \frac{1}{2} \cdot \frac{1}{2} \int e^{2t}(2)\,dt + \int \left(5 - \frac{1}{2} e^2\right) dt$$

$$s(t) = \frac{t^3}{3} + \frac{1}{4} e^{2t} + \left(5 - \frac{1}{2} e^2\right) t + C$$

$s(1) = 0 \Rightarrow \qquad s(1) = \frac{1}{3} + \frac{1}{4} e^2 + 5 - \frac{1}{2} e^2 + C = 0$

$$\frac{16}{3} - \frac{1}{4} e^2 + C = 0$$

$$C = \frac{1}{4} e^2 - \frac{16}{3}$$

Thus $s(t) = \dfrac{t^3}{3} + \dfrac{1}{4} e^{2t} \left(5 - \dfrac{1}{2} e^2\right) t + \dfrac{1}{4} e^2 - \dfrac{16}{3}$

Exponential Decay and Newton's Law of Cooling

Another similar type of differential equation also results in exponential growth or decay. Here, the differential equation is of the form

$$\frac{dy}{dt} = k(y - A)$$

The problem may also contain the phrase "rate of change of y is directly proportional to the difference between y and a given constant A." A famous example of this type of problem is Newton's Law of Cooling, which states that the rate at which a body changes temperature is directly proportional to the difference between its temperature and the temperature of the surrounding medium.

Sample

> A cup of tea at a temperature of 200° is left to cool in a room at 72°. If the tea cools to 110° in 3 minutes, what will the temperature of the tea be after 5 minutes?

The differential equation is given by

$$\frac{dy}{dt} = k(y - 72)$$

separating the variables gives

$$\frac{1}{y - 72} \, dy = kdt$$

now integrate

$$\int \frac{1}{y - 72} \, dy = \int kdt$$

$$\ln|y - 72| = kt + C_1$$

$$e^{kt + C_1} = y - 72$$

$$e^{kt} \cdot e^{C_1} = y - 72$$

$$Ce^{kt} = y - 72$$

$$Ce^{kt} + 72 = y$$

Use the boundary conditions to find C and k. The initial temperature was 200°, so

$$t = 0 \Rightarrow y = 200$$

$$200 = Ce^{0} + 72$$

$$128 = C$$

thus, $C = 128$,

$$y = 128e^{kt} + 72$$

The temperature is given as 100° after 3 minutes, so

$t = 3 \Rightarrow y = 100$

$100 = 128e^{3k} + 72$

$28 = 128e^{3k}$

$\dfrac{28}{128} = e^{3k}$

$3k = \ln\left(\dfrac{28}{128}\right)$

$k = \dfrac{1}{3}\ln\left(\dfrac{28}{128}\right)$

≈ -0.5066

Thus, the equation to describe the growth is

$$y = 128e^{-0.5066t} + 72$$

To answer the question, plug in $t = 5$ and solve for y.

$$y = 128e^{-0.5066t} + 72$$

$$\approx 82.1654$$

So the temperature of the tea is approximately 83° after 5 minutes.

The graph is shown below.

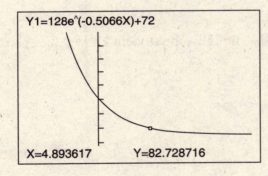
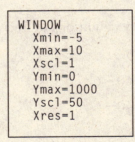

Bounded Growth

A third type of exponential growth is bounded growth. The general differential equation is

$$\frac{dy}{dt} = k(A - y)$$

Problems of this type would include the phrase "rate of change of y is proportional to the difference between a given constant A and y." Note the difference in the order of A and y between bounded growth the Newton's Law of Cooling example above. The type of graph that results here is sometimes called a learning curve.

Sample

> A student has 2 hours to study for a history exam and needs to memorize a set of 40 facts. The rate at which a person can memorize a set of facts is proportional to the number of facts remaining to be memorized. If the student initially knows nothing, and can memorize 10 facts in the first 15 minutes, how many facts will the student memorize in the 2 hours she has to study?

The differential equation is

$$\frac{dy}{dt} = k(40 - y)$$

Separating the variable gives

$$\frac{1}{40 - y} \, dy = k \, dt$$

now integrate

$$\int \frac{1}{40 - y} \, dy = \int k \, dt$$
$$-\ln(40 - y) = kt + C_1$$
$$\ln(40 - y) = -kt - C_1$$
$$40 - y = e^{-kt - C_1}$$
$$40 - y = e^{-kt} e^{-C_1}$$
$$40 - y = Ce^{-kt}$$
$$y = 40 - Ce^{-kt}$$

Use the boundary conditions to find C and k. Initially, the student knew 0 facts, so

$$t = 0 \Rightarrow y = 0$$
$$0 = 40 - Ce^\circ$$
$$0 = 40 - C$$

thus, $C = 40$

$$y = 40 - 40e^{-kt}$$

The student memorizes 10 facts in 15 minutes, so

$$t = 0.25 \Rightarrow y = 10$$

$$10 = 40 - 40e^{-k(0.25)}$$

$$-30 = -40e^{-k(0.25)}$$

$$\frac{-30}{-40} = e^{-k(0.25)}$$

$$\frac{3}{4} = e^{-0.25k}$$

$$\ln\left(\frac{3}{4}\right) = -0.25k$$

$$-4\ln\left(\frac{3}{4}\right) = k$$

$$-1.1507 \approx k$$

Thus, the equation to describe the growth is

$$y = 40 - 40e^{-1.1507t}$$

To answer the question, plug in $t = 2$ and solve for y.

$$y = 40 - 40e^{-1.1507(2)}$$

$$\approx 35.9954$$

So, she can memorize 36 facts in the 2 hours she has to study.

The graph of this model is shown below, demonstrating the typical bounded growth shape. Notice the graph is asymptotic to $y = 40$.

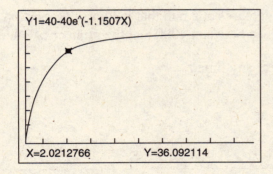

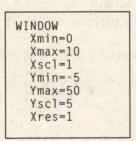

Logistic Growth (BC Only)

A special type of differential equation results in curves that show logistic growth. Just as with exponential or bounded growth, the key to solving these problems is to separate the variables and integrate (using partial fractions).

The general differential equation is given by

$$\frac{dy}{dt} = ky(A - y)$$

This equation may be given on the exam, or the problem may contain the phrase "rate of change of y is jointly proportional to y and the difference between a number A and y." Some typical examples and the resulting differential equations are given below.

Spread of a Rumor

In a school of 3,500 students, the rate at which a rumor spreads is jointly proportional to the number of people who have heard the rumor and the number of people who have NOT heard the rumor.

let y = the number of people who have heard the rumor at any time t
$$\frac{dy}{dt} = ky(3500 - y)$$

Spread of a Disease

In a community of 50,000, the rate of growth of a measles epidemic is jointly proportional to the number of people who have contracted the measles and the number of people who have not contracted the measles.

let y = the number of people who have the measles at any time t
$$\frac{dy}{dt} = ky(50,000 - y)$$

Population Growth

A population of rabbits in a certain area increases at a rate that is jointly proportional to the number of rabbits present, and the difference between 1000 and the number of rabbits present.

let y = the number of rabbits present at any time t
$$\frac{dy}{dt} = ky(1000 - y)$$

Sample

> For the rumor problem above, suppose 20 students hear the rumor initially, and that 200 have heard it after 2 hours. How many students will have heard the rumor after 5 hours?

From above, the differential equation is

$$\frac{dy}{dt} = ky(3500 - y)$$

Separating the variables gives

$$\frac{1}{y(3500 - y)}\, dy = k\, dt$$

Now integrate, using partial fractions

$$\int \frac{1}{y(3500-y)}\, dy = \int k\, dt$$

$$\left[\begin{array}{l} \dfrac{1}{y(3500-y)} = \dfrac{A}{y} + \dfrac{B}{3500-y} \\[2mm] 1 = A(3500-y) + By \\[2mm] \text{If } y = 0: \qquad \text{If } y = 3500: \\[2mm] 1 = A(3500) \qquad 1 = B(3500) \\[2mm] \dfrac{1}{3500} = A \qquad\quad \dfrac{1}{3500} = B \end{array}\right.$$

$$\int \frac{\frac{1}{3500}}{y} + \frac{\frac{1}{3500}}{3500-y}\, dy = \int k\, dt$$

$$\frac{1}{3500}\Big[\ln y - \ln(3500-y)\Big] = kt + C_1$$

$$-\ln y + \ln(3500-y) = -3500kt - 3500C_1$$

$$\ln\left(\frac{3500-y}{y}\right) = 3500kt + C_2$$

$$e^{-3500kt + C_2} = \frac{3500-y}{y}$$

$$e^{-3500kt}\, e^{C_2} = \frac{3500-y}{y}$$

$$Ce^{-3500kt} = \frac{3500}{y} - 1$$

$$Ce^{-3500kt} + 1 = \frac{3500}{y}$$

$$\frac{1}{Ce^{-3500kt}+1} = \frac{y}{3500}$$

Thus $\qquad y = \dfrac{3500}{Ce^{-3500kt}+1}$

Initially, 20 students heard the rumor, so

$$t = 0 \Rightarrow y = 20$$

$$20 = \frac{3500}{Ce^{0}+1}$$

$$C + 1 = \frac{3500}{20}$$

$$C + 1 = 175$$

So $C = 174$

After 2 hours, 200 students had heard the rumor, so

$$t = 2 \Rightarrow y = 200$$

$$200 = \frac{3500}{174e^{-3500k\,(2)} + 1}$$

$$174e^{-7000k} + 1 = \frac{3500}{200} = 17.5$$

$$174e^{-7000k} = 16.5$$

$$e^{-7000k} = \frac{16.5}{174}$$

$$-7000k = \ln\left(\frac{16.5}{174}\right) \approx -2.3557...$$

$$-3500k \approx -1.1778$$

Thus, the equation describing the growth is now

$$y = \frac{3500}{174e^{-1.1778t} + 1}$$

To answer the question, plug in $t = 5$ and solve for y.

$$y = \frac{3500}{174e^{-1.1778\,(5)} + 1}$$

$$\approx 2{,}361 \text{ students}$$

The graph below shows the typical shape of a logistic growth curve.

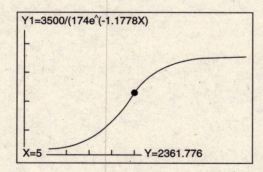

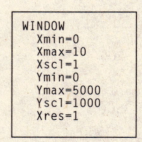

```
WINDOW
  Xmin=0
  Xmax=10
  Xscl=1
  Ymin=0
  Ymax=5000
  Yscl=1000
  Xres=1
```

Work (BC Only)

Scientists use the concept of **work** to determine how much energy is required to perform a task such as emptying a tank or compressing a spring. The amount of work done is found by multiplying the force by the displacement:

WORK = (force)(displacement)
        = FD

This simple definition applies only when the force is constant. When the force is NOT constant, calculus can be used to find the work done by using *FD* as the integrand in a definite integral. For motion along a straight line, the displacement *D* is represented by Δx. The bounds of the integral indicate the beginning and ending locations for the motion.

Work Along a Straight Line

$$W = \lim_{\|\Delta\| \to 0} \sum_{i=1}^{n} F(x) \Delta x$$

$$W = \int_{a}^{b} F(x) \, dx$$

Note on Units:

In the U.S system of measurement, work is typically expressed in foot-pounds (ft-lb) or foot-tons. In the CSG system, the work is expressed in dyne-centimeters (ergs) or newton-meters (joule).

Typical examples of work along a straight line that appear on the AP exam frequently include:

1. moving a particle along a straight line
2. compressing or stretching a spring (Hooke's law)
3. lifting a chain

Sample: Moving a Particle Along a Line

> A particle moves along the *x* axis so that the force required to move it when it is *x* feet from the origin is given by
>
> $F(x) = 5 + 3x^2$ lbs
>
> Find the amount of work done in moving the particle from $x = 3$ to $x = 7$.

The force is given by $F(x)$ and the distance is represented by Δx, which becomes Δx in the integral.

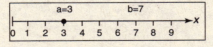

So, to find the work done:

$$W = \lim_{\|\Delta\| \to 0} \sum_{i=1}^{n} (5 + 3x^2) \Delta x$$

$$W = \int_{3}^{7} (5 + 3x^2) \, dx$$

$$= [5x + x^3]_{3}^{5}$$

$$= (25 + 125) - (15 + 27)$$

$$= 180 \, \text{ft-lbs}$$

Sample: Lifting a Chain

> A bucket weighing 10 pounds is filled with water weighing 15 pounds. The bucket is at the bottom of a 30 foot well, hanging from a chain that weighs 0.2 pounds per foot. How much work is done in lifting the bucket to the top of the well?

Here, the force function will be given by the total weight being lifted at any time. Taking the origin at the bottom of the well, the distance the bucket has traveled at any time is given by y feet.

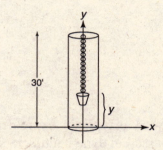

The force (total weight) is given by the weight of the bucket plus the weight of the water plus the weight of the chain. The total weight of the entire chain is $(30)(0.2) = 6$ lbs, but as the bucket is lifted the weight of the chain will decrease. Thus, the force (total weight) at any time is given by

$$F(y) = 10 + 15 + (6 - 0.2y)$$
$$= 31 - 0.2y$$

So, to find the work done, multiply this force by the distance, Δy, which becomes dy in the integral.

$$W = \lim_{\|\Delta\| \to 0} \sum_{i=1}^{n} (31 - 0.2y)\,\Delta y$$
$$= \int_{0}^{30} (31 - 0.2y)\,dy$$
$$= \left[31y - 0.1y^2\right]_{0}^{30}$$
$$= (930 - 90) - 0$$
$$= 840 \text{ ft-lbs.}$$

Sample

> Suppose in the example above, the bucket is leaking so that all the water has leaked out just as the bucket gets to the top of the well. How much work is done in lifting the leaky bucket to the top of the well?

The force function is similar to the one above, but the weight of water that has leaked out at any time needs to be subtracted. If the water has all leaked out just as the bucket gets to the top, it has lost 15 lbs in 30 feet, for a rate of 0.5 lbs/ft.

$$F(y) = 10 + (15 - 0.5y) + (6 - 0.2y)$$
$$= 31 - 0.7y$$

So, to find the work done, multiply this force by the distance, Δy, which becomes dy in the integral.

$$W = \lim_{\|\Delta\| \to 0} \sum_{i=1}^{n} (31 - 0.7y)\Delta y$$

$$= \int_0^{30} (31 - 0.7y)\,dy$$

$$= \left[31y - 0.35y^2\right]_0^{30}$$

$$= 930 - 315$$

$$= 615 \text{ ft-lbs.}$$

which is a lot of work just to get no water!

Sample: Springs and Hooke's Law

Suppose it takes 240 pounds of force to compress a spring 2 inches from its natural length of 12 inches. How much work is done in compressing it an additional 2 inches?

Hooke's Law states that the amount of force needed to stretch or compress a spring x units from its natural length is proportional to x:

$$F(x) = kx$$

where k is a constant that depends on the type of spring.

For this spring,

$$F(x) = kx$$
$$240 = k(2)$$
$$\Rightarrow k = 120$$

so, for this spring in general, $F(x) = 120x$

To find the work done, multiply this by Δx, which becomes dx in the integral.

The initial compression was 2 inches from its natural length ($x = 0$ to $x = 2$). An additional 2 inches would occur from $x = 2$ to $x = 4$. Thus, the work would be given by

$$W = \lim_{\|\Delta\| \to 0} \sum_{i=1}^{n} F(x)\Delta x$$

$$= \int_{2}^{4} 120x\,dx$$

$$= \left[60x^2 \right]_{2}^{4}$$

$$= 60 \cdot (16 - 4)$$

$$= 720 \text{ in-lbs.}$$

A more complicated form of work involves moving liquids in or out of tanks. Work is still found by multiplying force by displacement, however the force and distance expressions are somewhat different than in straight line motion. The force is calculated by multiplying the weight density of the liquid by the volume of a representative cross section of the tank, where the volume expression includes the Δy expression. So, the distance expression must appear in the integrand separate from the Δy entirely. The bounds of integration indicate the lowest and highest points of the liquid. (Note: weight density of water is 9810 N/m^3 or 62.5 lbs/ft^3.)

Liquid Work

$$W = \lim_{\|\Delta\| \to 0} \sum_{i=1}^{n} (\text{weight density})(\text{volume of crosssection})(\text{distance})$$

$$= \int_{a}^{b} (\text{weight density})(\text{volume of crosssection})(\text{distance})$$

Sample

A tank in the shape of a right circular cone is 4 feet tall and 2 feet in diameter at the top, and is half full of water. How much work is done in pumping the water to the top of the tank?

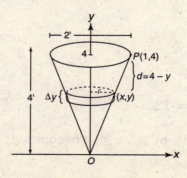

The tank is shown above, with the origin taken at the bottom of the tank.

The weight density is 62.5 lbs/ft^3.

A representative cross section of the tank is a cylinder, shown in the sketch, and so has a volume of

$$V = \pi r^2 h$$

where $h = \Delta y$.

The radius of the cross section is shown here as x, but needs to be expressed in terms of y to correspond to the $\Delta y = dy$ for the height. The equation of the line that is the right side of the cone (line $\overleftrightarrow{OP}$ in the diagram) will give a relationship between x and y. It has a slope of 4, and a y-intercept of 0, so its equation is $y = 4x$. Thus, the radius can be expressed as

$$r = x = \frac{1}{4}y$$

So the volume expression is now

$$V = \pi \left(\frac{1}{4}y\right)^2 (\Delta y)$$
$$= \frac{\pi}{16} y^2 \Delta y$$

The distance that the representative cross section must travel to get to the top of the tank is given by

$$d = 4 - y$$

The tank is half full of water, so the water starts where $y = 0$ and ends where $y = 2$.

The complete work formula now yields

$$W = \lim_{\|\Delta\| \to 0} \sum_{i=1}^{n} (\text{weight density})(\text{volume})(\text{distance})$$
$$= \lim_{\|\Delta\| \to 0} \sum_{i=1}^{n} (62.5)(\frac{\pi}{16} y^2 \Delta y)(4-y)$$
$$= 62.5 \cdot \frac{\pi}{16} \int_{0}^{2} y^2 (4-y)\, dy$$
$$\approx 81.81 \text{ ft-lbs (using a calculator)}$$

Variations on this type of problems occur by changing the height of the liquid, the location to which it is pumped, or type of liquid (and thus the weight density).

Sample

> In the example above, suppose the cone is completely full of oil weighing 50 lbs/ft³, and the oil is to be pumped to a spot 2 feet above the top of the cone. How much work is done?

$$W = \lim_{\|\Delta\| \to 0} \sum_{i=1}^{n} (\text{weight density})(\text{volume of cross section})(\text{distance})$$

$$= \lim_{\|\Delta\| \to 0} \sum_{i=1}^{n} (50)(\frac{\pi}{16} y^2 \Delta y)(6 - y)$$

$$= \frac{50\pi}{16} \int_{0}^{4} y^2 (6 - y) \, dy$$

$$\approx 628.32 \text{ ft-lbs}$$

Sample

> A trough is 15 feet long and its cross section is in the shape of an isosceles triangle 2 feet wide across the top and 3 feet tall. The trough is full of oil weighing 45 lbs/ft³. How much work is done in pumping the oil to the top of the tank?

A sketch of the tank is shown below, with the origin is taken at the bottom of the tank.

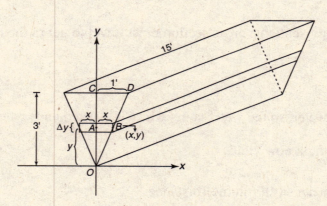

The weight density is given as 45 lbs/ft³.

A representative cross section of the tank is a rectangular solid, shown in the sketch, so it has a volume given by

$$V = l \, w \, h$$

The height is given by $h = \Delta y$ and the length is a constant, $l = 15$ feet.

The width of the cross section is shown here as $2x$, but needs to be expressed in terms of y to correspond to the $\Delta y = dy$ for the height. Using the similar triangles, ΔOAB and ΔOCD, the proportion below gives a relationship between x and y.

$$\frac{x}{y} = \frac{1}{3} \Rightarrow x = \frac{1}{3} y$$

$\Rightarrow 2x = \frac{2}{3} y$

So, the volume expression is now

$$V = (15)\left(\frac{2}{3}y\right)(\Delta y)$$
$$= 10y\Delta y$$

The distance that the representative cross section must travel to get to the top of the tank is given by

$$d = 3 - y$$

The tank is full of water, so the water begins at $y = 0$ and ends at $y = 3$

The complete work formula now yields

$$W = \lim_{\|\Delta\| \to 0} \sum_{i=1}^{n} (\text{weight density})(\text{volume of crosssection})(\text{distance})$$
$$= \lim_{\|\Delta\| \to 0} \sum_{i=1}^{n} (45)(10y\Delta y)(3-y)$$
$$450 \int_{0}^{3} y(3-y)\,dy$$
$$= 2025 \text{ ft-lbs}$$

Length of an Arc (BC Only)

The length along a curve is known as arc length, and can be found using a definite integral. The formula can be derived by: (1) subdividing the curve into n small approximately linear pieces, (2) using the distance formula to find the length of the line segments, (3) using this distance expression as the argument in a Riemann sum, and (4) finding the limit as the number of pieces increases without bound. This can be done with respect to either x or y, depending on the original curve.

Arc length problems on the BC exam frequently require the use of a calculator to evaluate the definite integral.

Length of an Arc

The arc length, L, along a smooth* curve $y = f(x)$ from x_1 to x_2 is given by

$$L = \int_{x_1}^{x_2} \sqrt{1 + \left(\frac{dy}{dx}\right)^2}\,dx = \int_{x_1}^{x_2} \sqrt{1 + \left[f'(x)\right]^2}\,dx$$

Similarly, the arc length, L, along a smooth* curve $x = g(y)$ from y_1 to y_2 is given by

$$L = \int_{y_1}^{y_2} \sqrt{1 + \left(\frac{dx}{dy}\right)^2}\,dy = \int_{y_1}^{y_2} \sqrt{1 + \left[g'(y)\right]^2}\,dy$$

*Note: A curve $f(x)$ is smooth if $f'(x)$ is continuous. In practice, this means that there are no sharp turns, known as "cusps" on the graph.

Sample

Find the arc length along $f(x) = 5e^{2x}$ from $x = 0$ to $x = 1$.

A graph is shown at right.

Find the derivative and use the formula.

$$f^1(x) = 5e^{2x}(2)$$
$$= 10e^{2x}$$
$$L = \int_0^1 \sqrt{1 + \left(10e^{2x}\right)^2}\, dx$$
$$= \int_0^1 \sqrt{1 + 100e^{4x}}\, dx$$
$$\approx 31.9669$$

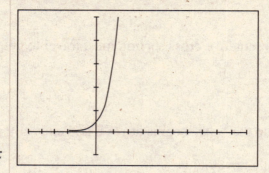

```
WINDOW
  Xmin =-5
  Xmax =10
  Xscl =1
  Ymin =-10
  Ymax =50
  Yscl =10
  Xres=1
```

Sample

Find the length of the arc in the previous example using the second method with respect to y.

Solve for x in terms of y, then differentiate and use the formula. The bounds of integration must also be in terms of y.

$$y = 5e^{2x}$$
$$\frac{y}{5} = e^{2x}$$
$$2x = \ln \frac{y}{5}$$
$$x = \frac{1}{2} \ln \frac{y}{5}$$
$$\frac{dx}{dy} = \frac{1}{2} \frac{\frac{1}{5}}{\frac{y}{5}}$$
$$= \frac{1}{2y}$$

$$x = 0 \Rightarrow y = 5e^0 = 5$$
$$x = 1 \Rightarrow y = 5e^2$$
$$L = \int_5^{5e^2} \sqrt{1 + \left(\frac{1}{2y}\right)^2}\, dy$$
$$= \int_5^{5e^2} \sqrt{1 + \frac{1}{4y^2}}\, dy$$
$$\approx 31.9669$$

Arc Length for Parametric Curves (BC Only)

On page 321, the method for finding the arc length, L, along a Cartesian curve from x_1 to x_2 was to evaluate the definite integral below:

$$L = \int_{x_1}^{x_2} \sqrt{1 + \left(\frac{dy}{dx}\right)^2}\, dx$$

This integration is obviously performed all in terms of x. For arc length in parametric form, the integration needs to be performed in terms of the parameter t. This is easily accomplished by rewriting the derivative dy/dx in its parametric form, $dy/dt\, /\, dx/dt$, and performing some simple algebra.

$$L = \int_{x_1}^{x_2} \sqrt{1 + \left(\frac{dy/dt}{dx/dt}\right)^2}\, dx$$

$$= \int_{x_1}^{x_2} \sqrt{\frac{(dx/dt)^2 + (dy/dt)^2}{(dx/dt)^2}}\, dx\left(\frac{dt}{dt}\right)$$

$$= \int_{t_1}^{t_2} \frac{\sqrt{(dx/dt)^2 + (dy/dt)^2}}{(dx/dt)^2}\left(\frac{dx}{dt}\right) dt$$

$$L = \int_{t_1}^{t_2} \sqrt{\left(\frac{dx}{dt}\right)^2 + \left(\frac{dy}{dt}\right)^2}\, dt$$

Arc Length in Parametric

For a smooth parametric curve given by $x = f(t)$ and $y = g(t)$, the arc length, L, from t_1 to t_2 is given by

$$L = \int_{t_1}^{t_2} \sqrt{\left(\frac{dx}{dt}\right)^2 + \left(\frac{dy}{dt}\right)^2}\, dt = \int_{t_1}^{t_2} \sqrt{\left[f'(t)\right]^2 + \left[g'(t)\right]^2}\, dt$$

Parametric arc length problems on the BC exam often require the use of a calculator to evaluate the definite integral.

Sample

> A particle moves along a parametric curve as defined below from $t = 0$ to $t = 3$. Find the distance the particle travels.

$x = 5 - t^2$ and $y = t^2 + 3t$

The path is indicated below on a graphing calculator screen.

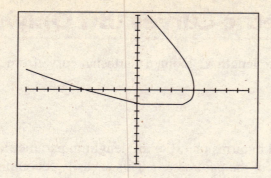

```
WINDOW
  Tmin =-10
  Tmax =10
  Tstep =1
  Xmin =-10
  Xmax =10
  Xscl =1
  Ymin=-10
  Ymax=10
  Yscl=1
```

Find the derivatives of the x and y equations, and plug them into the definite integral formula.

$$\frac{dx}{dt} = -2t \qquad \frac{dy}{dt} = 2t + 3$$

$$L = \int_0^3 \sqrt{(-2t)^2 + (2t+3)^2} \, dt$$

$$= \int_0^3 \sqrt{4t^2 + 4t^2 + 12t + 9} \, dt$$

$$= \int_0^3 \sqrt{8t^2 + 12t + 9} \, dt$$

$$\approx 153$$

Area and Arc Length for Polar Curves (BC Only)

Recall that to find the area of a region under a curve, the interval was subdivided into n pieces, and rectangles were inscribed under the curve. A Riemann sum was then set up, using the area of the ith rectangle in the argument. Taking the limit of this Riemann sum (as the width of each rectangle approached 0) resulted in a definite integral.

In a similar fashion, the polar region below has been subdivided into n sectors, each with an angle of $\Delta\theta$. To find the area, set up a Riemann sum, using the formula for the area of a sector of a circle from geometry $\left[A = \frac{1}{2} r^2 \theta \right]$. Then, take the limit of the sum (as the angle of each sector approaches 0) to get a definite integral.

Area in Polar

$$A = \lim_{\|\Delta\| \to 0} \sum_{i=1}^{n} \frac{1}{2} \left[f(\theta_i) \right]^2 \Delta\theta i$$

$$= \frac{1}{2} \int_\alpha^\beta \left[f(\theta) \right]^2 d\theta$$

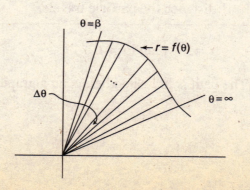

Sample

> Find the area enclosed by one petal of the rose curve $r = 4\cos(3\theta)$.

Begin by graphing the curve. At $\theta = 0$, the corresponding radius is $r = 4$.

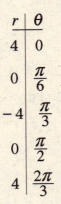

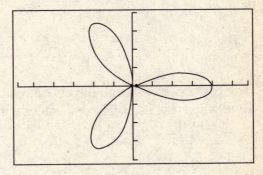

r	θ
4	0
0	$\dfrac{\pi}{6}$
-4	$\dfrac{\pi}{3}$
0	$\dfrac{\pi}{2}$
4	$\dfrac{2\pi}{3}$

In the chart above, notice that the first time the radius is 0 is when $\theta = \pi/6$. This follows logically from trig properties. The cosine function is first 0 when $\theta = \pi/2$.

For the function here, the argument of the cosine function is 3θ So, r will equal 0 when $3\theta = \dfrac{\pi}{2}$ which means $\theta = \pi/6$. This is useful in determining the bounds of integration. Since half of the first petal is swept out from $\theta = 0$ to $\theta = \pi/6$, the area of the entire first petal can be found by using these as bounds and multiplying by 2.

$$A = 2\left[\frac{1}{2}\int_0^{\frac{\pi}{6}}(4\cos 3\theta)\,d\theta\right]$$

$$= 16\int_0^{\frac{\pi}{6}}\cos^2 3\theta\,d\theta$$

$$\approx 4.189$$

Sample

> Find the area of the inner loop of the limacon $r = 2 - 4\sin\theta$.

Graph the curve.

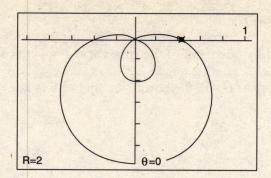

The curve goes through the pole any time that $r = 0$, the first time when $\theta = \pi/6$, and the next time when $\theta = 5\pi/6$. These r values can be found by solving $2 - 4\sin\theta = 0$.

$$2 - 4\sin\theta = 0$$

$$\sin\theta = \frac{1}{2}$$

$$\theta = \frac{\pi}{6} + 2k\pi \text{ or } \theta = \frac{5\pi}{6} + 2k\pi$$

So, the area inside the INNER loop can be found by the integral below.

$$A = \tfrac{1}{2} \int_{\frac{\pi}{6}}^{\frac{5\pi}{6}} (2 - 4\sin\theta)^2 \, d\theta$$

$$\approx 2.1741$$

Sample

Find the area of the region that is INSIDE $r = 1 + \cos\theta$ and OUTSIDE $r = 3\cos\theta$.

Begin by graphing both curves.

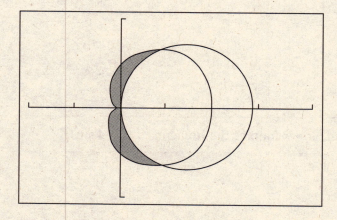

The area INSIDE the limacon and OUTSIDE the circle is shaded in the figure above.

To determine the bounds of integration, find the intersection of the two curves.

$$1 + \cos\theta = 3\cos\theta$$

$$1 = 2\cos\theta$$

$$\cos = \frac{1}{2}$$

$$\theta = \frac{\pi}{3} + 2k\pi, \frac{5\pi}{3} + 2k\pi$$

A closer view of quadrants 1 and 2, along with the line $\theta = \pi/3$ is shown below. The shaded region would be half of the area desired.

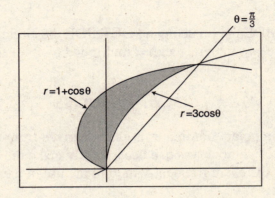

From the sketch above, it is clear that the next intersection point of the two curves will be at the pole, where $r = 0$.

for the limacon   for the circle

$$1 + \cos\theta = 0 \qquad\quad 3\cos\theta = 0$$

$$\cos\theta = -1 \qquad\qquad \cos\theta = 0$$

$$\theta = \pi + 2k\pi \qquad \theta = \frac{\pi}{2} + 2k\pi, \frac{3\pi}{2} + 2k\pi$$

Thus, the integrals below would give the areas shaded below in each case.

$$\frac{1}{2}\int_{\frac{\pi}{3}}^{\pi}(1 + \cos\theta)^2\, d\theta$$

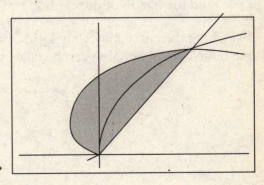

$$\frac{1}{2} \int_{\frac{\pi}{3}}^{\frac{\pi}{2}} (3\cos\theta)^2 \, d\theta$$

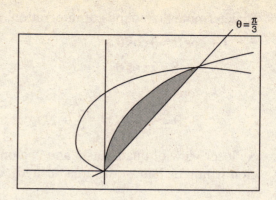

So, the area requested, INSIDE the limacon and OUTSIDE the circle, would be given by the DIFFERENCE between the two integrals above, multiplied by 2 for the third and fourth quadrants.

$$A = 2\left[\frac{1}{2}\int_{\frac{\pi}{3}}^{\pi}(1+\cos\theta)^2\,d\theta - \frac{1}{2}\int_{\frac{\pi}{3}}^{\frac{\pi}{2}}(3\cos)^2\,d\theta\right] \approx 0.7854$$

The formula for arclength in polar coordinates is easily derived from the one in parametric form. Using the symmetry of polar curves can occasionally make the problem simpler. Polar arc length problems on the BC exam frequently require the use of a calculator to evaluate the definite integral.

Arc Length in Polar

$$L = \int_{\alpha}^{\beta} \sqrt{\left(\frac{dr}{d\theta}\right)^2 + r^2} \, d\theta$$

Sample

Find the length of the cardiod $r = 2 - 2\cos\theta$.

Sketching the curve may be helpful in determining the bounds, or in applying symmetry. Here, the bounds of integration can be taken from $\theta = 0$ to $\theta = \pi$ and the integral multiplied by 2.

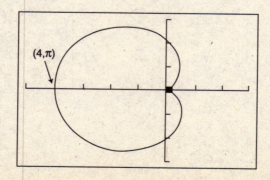

(4, π)

Find $dr/d\theta$ and apply the formula.

$$r = 2 - 2\cos\theta$$

$$\frac{dr}{d\theta} = 2\sin\theta$$

$$L = 2\left[\int_0^\pi \sqrt{(2 - 2\cos\theta)^2 + (\sin\theta)^2}\, d\theta\right]$$

$$= 2\int_0^\pi \sqrt{4 - 8\cos\theta + 4\cos^2\theta + 4\sin^2\theta}\, d\theta$$

$$= 2\int_0^\pi \sqrt{8 - 8\cos\theta}\, d\theta$$

$$= 16$$

Integration of Vector-Valued Functions (BC Only)

To find the integral of a vector-valued function, simply find the integrals of the real-numbered functions that make up the x and y components. That is, if $R(t) = f(t)\mathbf{i} + g(t)\mathbf{j}$ is a vector-valued function, then:

$$\int R(t)\, dt = \left[\int f(t)\, dt\right]\mathbf{i} + \left[\int g(t)\, dt\right]\mathbf{j} + C \ (C \text{ is a vector})$$

Sample

> If $R(t) = \left(6\sqrt{t}\right)\mathbf{i} + (\sin 2t)\,\mathbf{j}$ and if $V(0) = 2\mathbf{i} + 3\mathbf{j}$, find $V(t)$ where $V(t) = \int R(t)\, dt$.

$$R(t) = \left(6t^{\frac{1}{2}}\right)\mathbf{i} + (\sin 2t)\,\mathbf{j}$$

$$V(t) = \int R(t)\, dt = \left[\int\left(6t^{\frac{1}{2}}\right)dt\right]\mathbf{i} + \left[\int(\sin 2t)\, dt\right]\mathbf{j}$$

$$= \left[\frac{6t^{\frac{3}{2}}}{\frac{3}{2}}\right]\mathbf{i} + \left(-\frac{1}{2}\cos 2t\right)\mathbf{j} + c$$

So $V(t) = \left[4t^{\frac{3}{2}}\right]\mathbf{i} - \left(\frac{1}{2}\cos 2t\right)\mathbf{j} + c$

Since $V(o) = 2\mathbf{i} + 3\mathbf{j}$, we have:

$$V(o) = (4\cdot 0)\mathbf{i} - \left(\frac{1}{2}\cos 0\right)\mathbf{j} + c$$

$$= o\mathbf{i} - \frac{1}{2}\mathbf{j} + c$$

So $2\mathbf{i} + 3\mathbf{j} = o\mathbf{i} - \frac{1}{2}\mathbf{j} + c$

$$2\mathbf{i} + \frac{7}{2}\mathbf{j} = c$$

Therefore, $V(t) = \left[4t^{\frac{3}{2}}\right]\mathbf{i} - \left[\frac{1}{2}\cos 2t\right]\mathbf{j} + 2\mathbf{i} + \frac{7}{2}\mathbf{j}$

Or combining terms we have:

$$V(t) = \left[2 + 4t^{\frac{3}{2}}\right]\mathbf{i} - \left[\frac{1}{2}\cos 2t - \frac{7}{2}\right]\mathbf{j}$$

Sample Multiple-Choice Questions: Applications of Antiderivatives and Definite Integrals

1. $\int_{-2}^{3} |x - 1| \, dx =$

   A. $\frac{5}{2}$

   B. $\frac{7}{2}$

   C. $\frac{9}{2}$

   D. $\frac{11}{2}$

   E. $\frac{13}{2}$

2. Use a Riemann sum and four inscribed rectangles to approximate $\int_{0}^{4} x^2 + 1 \, dx$.

   A. 18

   B. 21

   C. 24

   D. 25

   E. 26

3. What is the average value of $y = 3t^3 - t^2$ over the interval $-1 \le t \le 2$?

   A. $\frac{11}{4}$

   B. $\frac{7}{2}$

   C. 8

   D. $\frac{33}{4}$

   E. 16

4. The area bounded by the curve $x = 3y - y^2$ and the line $x = -y$ is represented by

   A. $\int_{0}^{4} (2y - y^2) \, dy$

   B. $\int_{0}^{4} (4y - y^2) \, dy$

   C. $\int_{0}^{3} (3y - y^2) \, dy + \int_{0}^{4} y \, dy$

   D. $\int_{0}^{4} (y^2 - 4y) \, dy$

   E. $\int_{0}^{4} (2y - y^2)^2 \, dy$

5. $\int_{1}^{2} \frac{x^2 - 1}{x + 1} \, dx =$

   A. $\frac{1}{2}$

   B. 1

   C. $\ln 3$

   D. $\frac{5}{2}$

   E. 2

6. If $F(x) = \int_{1}^{x} \sqrt{t^2 + 3t} \, dt$, then $F'(x) =$

   A. $\frac{2}{3}\left[(x^2 + 3x)^{\frac{3}{2}} - 8\right]$

   B. $\sqrt{x^2 + 3x}$

   C. $\sqrt{x^2 + 3x} - 2$

   D. $\frac{1}{2}\frac{2x + 3}{\sqrt{x^2 + 3x}}$

   E. none of these

7. A bacteria culture is growing at a rate proportional to the number of bacteria present at any time t. Initially, there are 2000 bacteria present, and this population doubles in 3 hours. Which of the following equations describes this growth?

- **A.** $y = 2000e^{((\ln 2)/3)t}$
- **B.** $y = 2000e^{(\ln 2/3)t}$
- **C.** $y = 2000e^{(3\ln 1/2)t}$
- **D.** $y = 2000e^{(2\ln 3)t}$
- **E.** none of these

8. $\int_0^{1/2} \tan\frac{x}{2}\, dx \approx$

- **A.** -0.063
- **B.** 0.041
- **C.** 0.063
- **D.** 0.138
- **E.** 0.261

*9. Moving in the xy-plane at time $t > 0$, the velocity vector of a particle is $(3t^2, \frac{1}{t})$. Find its general position vector (in terms of t) for the particle if its position vector at $t = 2$ is $(9, \ln 2 + \ln e)$

- **A.** $(t^3 + 1, \ln t + 1)$
- **B.** $(9, 1 + \ln 4)$
- **C.** $(6t, -\frac{1}{t^2})$
- **D.** $(t^3 + e, \ln t + e)$
- **E.** $(t^3, \ln t)$

*10. The length of the arc described by the equation $y = \sqrt{x^3}$ from $x = 0$ to $x = \frac{4}{3}$ is

- **A.** $\frac{8}{27}$
- **B.** $\frac{12}{27}$
- **C.** $\frac{56}{27}$
- **D.** $\frac{64}{27}$
- **E.** $\frac{72}{27}$

*11. The length of the arc described by the parametric equations $x(t) = \frac{1}{2}t^4$ and $y(t) = \frac{3}{2}t^2$ where $0 \le t \le 3$ is given by

- **A.** $\int_0^3 \sqrt{2t^3 + 3t}\, dt$
- **B.** $\int_0^3 \sqrt{4t^6 + 9t^2}\, dt$
- **C.** $\int_0^3 \sqrt{\frac{t^8}{4} + \frac{9t^4}{4}}\, dt$
- **D.** $\int_0^3 \sqrt{4t^6 + 1}\, dt$
- **E.** $\int_0^3 \sqrt{1 + 9t^2}\, dt$

*12. Find the length of the arc of $y = \frac{1}{4}x^2 - \frac{1}{2}\ln x$ from $x = 1$ to $x = e$.

- **A.** $\frac{1}{4}(e^2 - 1)$
- **B.** $\frac{1}{4}(e^2 - 3)$
- **C.** $\frac{1}{4}(e^2 + 1)$
- **D.** $\frac{1}{4}(e^2 + 3)$
- **E.** $(e - 1)$

*13. The area of the region enclosed by the graph of the curve $r = 2\cos\theta$ is [calculator problem]

A. .333

B. 1.570

C. 3.141

D. 6.282

E. 12.566

*14. The area of the region enclosed by one petal of the graph of $r = 2\cos(3\theta)$ is [calculator problem]

A. .523

B. 1.047

C. 1.570

D. 3.141

E. 6.293

*15. The length of the entire curve $r = 1 - \sin\theta$ is [calculator problem]

A. $\frac{1}{2}$

B. 1

C. 2

D. 4

E. 8

*16. The length of the entire curve of $r = 3$ $(1 + \cos\theta)$ from $\theta = 0$ to $\theta = \frac{\pi}{2}$ is [calculator problem]

A. 1.570

B. 3.141

C. 6.282

D. 8.485

E. 16.970

*17. Let $y = p(x)$ be the solution to the differential equation $\frac{dy}{dx} = 3x - 2y$ with initial condition $p(0) = 1$. What is the approximation for $p(2)$, using Euler's Method, starting at 0 with step size 1?

A. 0

B. 1

C. 2

D. 3

E. 4

*18. Let $y = f(x)$ be the solution to the differential equation $\frac{dy}{dx} = 2x + y$ with initial condition $f(1) = 2$. Using Euler's Method, what is the approximation for $f(2.5)$, starting at 1 with step size of 0.5?

A. 2

B. 4

C. 13.25

D. 17.50

E. 21.75

*19. Determine whether the integral $\int_{1}^{3} \frac{dx}{\sqrt{x-1}}$ converges or diverges. If it converges, find the value to which it converges.

A. diverges

B. converges to 0

C. converges to 1

D. converges to e

E. converges to $2\sqrt{2}$

BC only

*20. Determine whether the integral

$$\int_{-\infty}^{0} \frac{e^x}{e^x+1}\,dx$$ converges or diverges. If it converges, find the value to which it converges.

   A. converges to 0

   B. converges to 1

   C. converges to ln 2

   D. converges to e

   E. diverges

*21. The integral $\displaystyle\int_{-\infty}^{\infty} \frac{e^x}{e^x+1}\,dx$

   A. diverges

   B. converges to 0

   C. converges to $\dfrac{1}{2}$

   D. converges to ln 2

   E. converges to e

* BC only

Answers to Multiple-Choice Questions

1. E. Because the integrand is never negative, the definite integral can be interpreted as the area bounded by the curve. Sketching the region shows two triangles, so the quickest method is to use geometry.

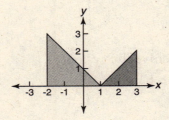

$$A = \tfrac{1}{2}(3)(3) + \tfrac{1}{2}(2)(2) = \tfrac{13}{2}$$

2. A. Sketch the area represented by the definite integral, and show the four inscribed rectangles. The base of each rectangle is one unit wide. The height of each rectangle is determined by the left-hand endpoint of the base, because the question asks for inscribed rectangles.

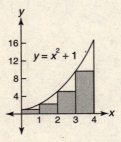

$$\int_{0}^{4} x^2 + 1\,dx \approx (1)f(0) + (1)f(1) + (1)f(2) + (1)f(3)$$

$$= 1[1 + 2 + 5 + 10]$$

$$= 18$$

3. A. average value $= \dfrac{1}{b-a}\displaystyle\int_a^b f(t)\,dt$

$$= \frac{1}{2-(-1)}\int_{-1}^2 \left(3t^3 - t^2\right)dt$$

$$= \frac{1}{3}\left[\frac{3t^4}{4} - \frac{t^3}{3}\right]_{-1}^2$$

$$= \frac{1}{3}\cdot\frac{1}{12}\left[9t^4 - 4t^3\right]_{-1}^2$$

$$= \frac{1}{36}\Big\{[144 - 32] - [9 - (-4)]\Big\}$$

$$= \frac{1}{36}(99) = \frac{11}{4}$$

4. B. Sketch the region as shown.

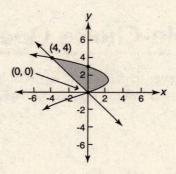

For the bounds of integration, solve the system:

$$\begin{cases} x = 3y - y^2 \\ x = -y \end{cases}$$

$$3y - y^2 = -y$$

$$y^2 - 4y = 0$$

$$y - 0 \text{ or } y = 4$$

So, using $\displaystyle\int_{\text{bottom}}^{\text{top}} \left(\text{right} - \text{left}\right)dy$

$$\Rightarrow \int_0^4 \left[\left(3y - y^2\right) - (-y)\right]dy = \int_0^4 \left(4y - y^2\right)dy$$

5. A. $\displaystyle\int_1^2 \frac{x^2 - 1}{x + 1}\,dx = \int_1^2 \frac{(x+1)(x-1)}{x+1}\,dx$

$$= \int_1^2 (x - 1)\,dx$$

$$= \left[\frac{x^2}{2} - x\right]_1^2$$

$$= (2 - 2) - \left(\frac{1}{2} - 1\right)$$

$$= \frac{1}{2}$$

6. B. Do not try to find the antiderivative. Simply substitute x in for the dummy variable t in the integrand.

7. A. The phrase "rate of change proportional to amount present" translates into

$$\frac{dy}{dt} = ky$$

Solving this differential equation yields

$$y = Ce^{kt}$$

"2000 present initially" $\Leftrightarrow y = 2000 \ when \ t = 0$

$$2000 = Ce^0 \Rightarrow C = 2000$$

Thus $y = 2000e^{kt}$

"doubles in 3 hours" $\qquad \Leftrightarrow y = 4000 \ when \ t = 3$

$$4000 = 2000e^{3k}$$

$$2 = e^{3k}$$

$$\ln 2 = 3k$$

$$k = \frac{\ln 2}{3}$$

Thus $y = 2000e^{((\ln 2)/3)t}$

If this form had not been present, an alternative form might have been

$$y = 2000\left(e^{\ln 2}\right)^{t/3} = 2000\left(2^{t/3}\right)$$

8. C. Find the value of the definite integral with your calculator.

```
Y1=tan (X/2)
fnInt(Y1,X,0,.5)
     .0631621025
■
```

9. A. velocity vector is $\left(3t^2, \frac{1}{t}\right)$

integrating, position vector is $\left(t^3 + C_1, \ln t + C_2\right)$

At $t = 2$, position vector is $\left(2^3 + C_1, \ln 2 + C_2\right) = (9, \ln 2 + \ln e)$

This means $2^3 + C_1 = 9$

$$8 + C_1 = 9$$

so $\quad C_1 = 1$

and $\ln 2 + C_2 = \ln 2 + \ln e$

$$C_2 = \ln e$$

so $\quad C_2 = 1$

Therefore, the general position vector is $\left(t^3 + 1, \ln 2 + 1\right)$

10. C. $y = \sqrt{x^3}$

$y = x^{\frac{3}{2}}$

$\dfrac{dy}{dx} = \dfrac{3}{2} x^{\frac{1}{2}}$

$L = \displaystyle\int_0^{\frac{4}{3}} \sqrt{1 + \left(\dfrac{dy}{dx}\right)^2}\, dx$

$= \displaystyle\int_0^{\frac{4}{3}} \sqrt{1 + \dfrac{9}{4} x}\, dx$

$= \dfrac{4}{9} \displaystyle\int_0^{\frac{4}{3}} \left(1 + \dfrac{9}{4} x\right)^{\frac{1}{2}} \cdot \dfrac{9}{4}\, dx$

$= \dfrac{4}{9} \left[\dfrac{\left(1 + \dfrac{9}{4} x\right)^{\frac{3}{2}}}{\dfrac{3}{2}} \right]_0^{\frac{4}{3}}$

$= \dfrac{8}{27} \left[\sqrt{\left(1 + \dfrac{9}{4} x\right)^3} \right]_0^{\frac{4}{3}}$

$= \dfrac{8}{27} \left[\sqrt{4^3} - 1 \right]$

$= \dfrac{8}{27} (8 - 1)$

$= \dfrac{56}{27}$

11. B. $x(t) = \dfrac{1}{2} t^4 \qquad y(t) = \dfrac{3}{2} t^2$

$\dfrac{dx}{dt} = 2t^3 \qquad\qquad \dfrac{dy}{dt} = 3t$

Then $L = \displaystyle\int_0^3 \sqrt{\left(\dfrac{dx}{dt}\right)^2 + \left(\dfrac{dy}{dt}\right)^2}\, dt$

$= \displaystyle\int_0^3 \sqrt{\left(2t^3\right)^2 + \left(3t\right)^2}\, dt$

$= \displaystyle\int_0^3 \sqrt{4t^6 + 9t^2}\, dt$

12. C.
$$y = \frac{1}{4}x^2 - \frac{1}{2}\ln x$$

$$\frac{dy}{dx} = \frac{1}{2}x - \frac{1}{2} \cdot \frac{1}{x}$$

$$\frac{dy}{dx} = \frac{1}{2}x - \frac{1}{2x}$$

$$\left(\frac{dy}{dx}\right)^2 = \frac{x^2}{4} - \frac{1}{2} + \frac{1}{4x^2}$$

$$1 + \left(\frac{dy}{dx}\right)^2 = 1 + \frac{x^2}{4} - \frac{1}{2} + \frac{1}{4x^2}$$

$$= \frac{x^2}{4} + \frac{1}{2} + \frac{1}{4x^2}$$

$$= \left(\frac{x}{2} + \frac{1}{2x}\right)^2$$

Then
$$L = \int_1^e \sqrt{1 + \left(\frac{dy}{dx}\right)^2}\, dx$$

$$= \int_1^e \sqrt{\left(\frac{x}{2} + \frac{1}{2x}\right)^2}\, dx$$

$$= \int_1^e \left(\frac{x}{2} + \frac{1}{2x}\right) dx$$

$$= \left[\frac{x^2}{4} + \frac{1}{2}\ln x\right]_1^e$$

$$= \left(\frac{e^2}{4} + \frac{1}{2}\ln e\right) - \left(\frac{1}{4} + \frac{1}{2}\ln 1\right)$$

$$= \frac{e^2}{4} + \frac{1}{2} - \frac{1}{4}$$

$$= \frac{e^2}{4} + \frac{1}{4} = \frac{1}{4}(e^2 + 1)$$

13. C. $r = 2\cos\theta = f(\theta)$

As seen in the chart below, the curve will be traced twice as θ ranges from 0 to 2π; so we will integrate from just 0 to π.

$$A = \frac{1}{2}\int_0^\pi [f(\theta)]^2\, d\theta$$

$$= \frac{1}{2}\int_0^\pi (2\cos\theta)^2\, d\theta$$

$$= \frac{1}{2}\int_0^\pi 4\cos^2\theta\, d\theta$$

$$A = 3.141\,(\pi \text{ exactly})$$

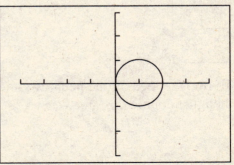

Graph of $r = 2\cos\theta$

θ	0	$\dfrac{\pi}{6}$	$\dfrac{\pi}{4}$	$\dfrac{\pi}{3}$	$\dfrac{\pi}{2}$	$\dfrac{4\pi}{3}$	$\dfrac{3\pi}{4}$	$\dfrac{5\pi}{6}$	π
r	2	$\sqrt{3}$	$\sqrt{2}$	1	0	-1	$-\sqrt{2}$	$-\sqrt{3}$	-2

Or if we write polar equation in rectangular form:

$r = 2\cos\theta$

$r \cdot r = r \cdot 2\cos\theta$

$r^2 = 2r\cos\theta$

$x^2 + y^2 = 2x$

$x^2 - 2x + y^2 = 0$

$(x^2 - 2x + 1) + y^2 = 0 + 1$

$(x - 1)^2 + y^2 = 1$

This is the equation of a circle with center (1, 0) and radius = 1. Then the area at this circle is

$A = \pi(1)^2$

$\quad = \pi(1)^2$

$A = \pi$

14. A. $r = 2\cos(3\theta)$

From the chart below, we note that $r = 0$ the first time when $\theta = \dfrac{\pi}{6}$. We can solve as follows:

θ	r
0	2
$\dfrac{\pi}{6}$	0
$\dfrac{\pi}{4}$	-2
$\dfrac{\pi}{3}$	0
$\dfrac{\pi}{2}$	2

$0 = 2\cos(3\theta)$

$0 = \cos(3\theta)$

$\dfrac{\pi}{2} = 3\theta$

so $\dfrac{\pi}{6} = \theta$

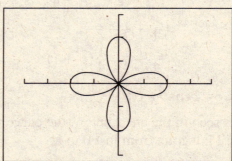

Graph of $r = 2\cos(3\theta)$

To find the area of one petal, we integrate from 0 to $\dfrac{\pi}{6}$ to get area at top half of petal — then just double this area.

$$A = 2 \cdot \left[\frac{1}{2} \int_0^{\frac{\pi}{6}} [f(\theta)]^2 \, d\theta \right]$$

$$= \int_0^{\frac{\pi}{6}} (2 \cos(3\theta))^2 \, d\theta$$

$$= \int_0^{\frac{\pi}{6}} 4 \cos^2(3\theta) \, d\theta$$

$$= \frac{\pi}{3} \approx .523$$

15. E. $r = 1 - \sin\theta = f(\theta)$

$$\frac{dr}{d\theta} = -\cos\theta = f'(\theta)$$

$$L = \int_0^{2\pi} \sqrt{[f'(\theta)]^2 + [f(\theta)]^2} \, d\theta$$

$$= \int_0^{2\pi} \sqrt{\left(\frac{dr}{d\theta}\right)^2 + r^2} \, d\theta$$

$$= \int_0^{2\pi} \sqrt{(-\cos\theta)^2 + (1 - \sin\theta)^2} \, d\theta$$

$$= \int_0^{2\pi} \sqrt{\cos^2\theta + 1 - 2\sin\theta + \sin^2\theta} \, d\theta$$

$$= \int_0^{2\pi} \sqrt{2 - 2\sin\theta} \, d\theta$$

$$= 8$$

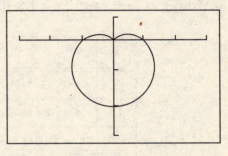

Graph of $r = 1 - \sin\theta$

16. D. $r = 3(1 + \cos\theta)$

$$= 3 + 3\cos\theta$$

$$\frac{dr}{d\theta} = -3\sin\theta$$

$$L = \int_0^{\frac{\pi}{2}} \sqrt{\left(\frac{dr}{d\theta}\right)^2 + r^2} \, d\theta$$

$$= \int_0^{\frac{\pi}{2}} \sqrt{(-3\sin\theta)^2 + (3 + 3\cos\theta)^2} \, d\theta$$

$$= \int_0^{\frac{\pi}{2}} \sqrt{9\sin^2\theta + 9 + 18\cos\theta + 9\cos^2\theta} \, d\theta$$

$$= \int_0^{\frac{\pi}{2}} \sqrt{18 + 18\sin\theta} \, d\theta$$

$$= 6\sqrt{2} \approx 8.485$$

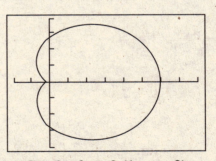

Graph of $r = 3(1 + \cos\theta)$

339

17. E. With $\dfrac{dy}{dx} = 3x - 2y$ and $\Delta x = 1$, the chart is completed:

x	y	$\dfrac{dy}{dx} (\Delta x) \approx \Delta y$	$x + \Delta x$	$y + \Delta y$
0	1	$(3 \cdot 0 - 2 \cdot 1)(1) = -2$	$0 + 1 = 1$	$1 + -2 = -1$
1	-1	$(3 \cdot 1 - 2 \cdot -1) = 5$	$1 + 1 = 2$	$-1 + 5 = 4$
2	4	——————	——————	——————

So when $x = 2$, $y \approx 4$; therefore $p(2) \approx 4$.

18. C. With $\dfrac{dy}{dx} = 2x + y$ and $\Delta x = 0.5$, the chart is completed:

x	y	$\dfrac{dy}{dx} (\Delta x) \approx \Delta y$	$x + \Delta x$	$y + \Delta y$
1	2	$(2 \cdot 1 + 2)(0.5) = 2.0$	$1 + 0.5 = 1.5$	$2 + 2 = 4$
1.5	4	$[2(1.5) + 4](0.5) = 3.5$	$1.5 + 0.5 = 2.0$	$4 + 3.5 = 7.5$
2.0	7.5	$[2(2) + 7.5](0.5) = 5.75$	$2.0 + 0.5 = 2.5$	$7.5 + 5.75 = 13.25$
2.5	13.25	——————	——————	——————

So when $x = 2.5$, $y \approx 13.25$; therefore $f(2.5) \approx 13.25$.

19. E. The integral $\displaystyle\int_1^3 \dfrac{dx}{\sqrt{x-1}}$ is improper since the function $f(x) = \dfrac{1}{\sqrt{1-x}}$ is discontinuous at $x = 1$, one of the limits of integration

$$\int_1^3 \frac{dx}{\sqrt{x-1}} = \lim_{C \to 1^+} \int_C^3 \frac{dx}{\sqrt{x-1}}$$

$$= \lim_{C \to 1^+} \int_1^3 (x-1)^{-1/2}\, dx$$

$$= \lim_{C \to 1^+} \left[\frac{(x-1)^{1/2}}{\frac{1}{2}} \right]_C^3$$

$$= \lim_{C \to 1^+} \left[2\sqrt{x-1} \right]_C^3$$

$$= \lim_{C \to 1^+} \left[2\sqrt{2} - 2\sqrt{C-1} \right]$$

$$= 2\sqrt{2} - 0$$

$$= 2\sqrt{2}$$

So the integral converges to $2\sqrt{2}$.

20. C. The improper integral $\displaystyle\int_{-\infty}^{0} \frac{e^x}{e^x+1}\,dx$ must be evaluated as a limit statement:

$$\int_{-\infty}^{0} \frac{e^x}{e^x+1}\,dx = \lim_{C \to -\infty} \int_{C}^{0} \frac{e^x}{e^x+1}\,dx$$

$$= \lim_{C \to -\infty} \left[\ln(e^x+1)\right]_{C}^{0}$$

$$= \lim_{C \to -\infty} \left[\ln(e^0+1) - \ln(e^C+1)\right]$$

$$= \ln 2 - \ln(e^{-\infty}+1)$$

$$= \ln 2 - \ln(0+1)$$

$$= \ln 2 - \ln 1$$

$$= \ln 2 - 0$$

$$= \ln 2$$

So the integral converges to ln 2.

21. A. The integral $\displaystyle\int_{-\infty}^{\infty} \frac{e^x}{e^x+1}\,dx$ is improper, having two infinite limits of integration. Choosing 0 as a convenient number within the interval $(-\infty, \infty)$, two improper integrals are formed.

$$\int_{-\infty}^{\infty} \frac{e^x}{e^x+1}\,dx = \int_{-\infty}^{0} \frac{e^x}{e^x+1}\,dx + \int_{0}^{\infty} \frac{e^x}{e^x+1}\,dx$$

$$= \lim_{C \to -\infty} \int_{C}^{0} \frac{e^x}{e^x+1}\,dx + \lim_{d \to \infty} \int_{0}^{d} \frac{e^x}{e^x+1}\,dx$$

$$= \lim_{C \to -\infty} \left[\ln(e^x+1)\right]_{C}^{0} + \lim_{d \to \infty} \left[\ln(e^x+1)\right]_{0}^{d}$$

$$= \lim_{C \to -\infty} \left[\ln 2 - \ln(e^C+1)\right] + \lim_{d \to \infty} \left[\ln(e^d+1) - \ln 2\right]$$

$$= \ln 2 - \ln 1 + \ln(e^{\infty}+1) - \ln 2$$

$$= \ln(e^{\infty} - 1)$$

$$= \infty$$

So the integral diverges.

Sample Free-Response Question: Applications of Antiderivatives and Definite Integrals

1. A water tank in the shape of a hemisphere has a radius of 4 feet. The water level is 1 foot below the top of the tank. How much work is done in pumping the water to a point 2 feet above the top of the tank?

Answer to Free-Response Question

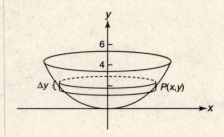

The tank is shown above, with the origin taken at the bottom of the tank.

The weight density of water is 62.5 lbs/ft^3.

A representative cross section is a cylinder, shown in the sketch, and so has a volume of

$$V = \pi r^2 h$$

where $h = \Delta y$.

The radius of the cross section is shown here as x, but needs to be expressed in terms of y to correspond to the $\Delta y = dy$ for the height. The point $P(x, y)$ is on the circle centered as (0, 4) with a radius of 4, so it has equation

$$(x - 0)^2 + (y - 4)^2 = 16$$

which gives a relationship between x and y

$$
\begin{aligned}
x^2 &= 16 - (y - 4)^2 \\
&= 16 - (y^2 - 8y + 16) \\
&= 8y - y^2
\end{aligned}
$$

So, the volume expression is now

$$V = \pi (8y - y^2) \Delta y$$

The distance the representative cross section must travel to get to a point 2 feet above the top of the tank is

$$d = 6 - y$$

The water level is 1 foot below the top of the tank, so the water begins as $y = 0$ and ends at $y = 3$.

The complete work formula is now

$$W = \lim_{\|\Delta\| \to 0} \sum_{i=1}^{n} (\text{weight density})(\text{volume of cross section})(\text{distance})$$

$$= \lim_{\|\Delta\| \to 0} \sum_{i=1}^{n} 62.5 [\pi (8y - y^2) \Delta y](6 - y)$$

$$= 62.5 \pi \int_0^3 (8y - y^2)(6 - y) \, dy \approx 21,647.54 \text{ ft-lbs}$$

Sequences, Infinite Series, and Polynomial Approximations (BC Only)

Infinite series ($\sum\limits_{n=1}^{\infty} a_n$) are used in calculus to approximate values of functions such as $f(x) = e^x$, $f(x) = \sin x$, and $f(x) = \ln x$ at a particular value of x by creating power series ($\sum\limits_{n=1}^{\infty} a_n (x-c)^n$) representations of these functions. The intervals in which these power series are close approximations to their respective functions can then be found by using some of the tests that will be used to determine the convergence or divergence of infinite series.

Sequences

A **sequence** $\{a_n\}$ is a function whose domain is the set of positive integers.

- The functional values $a_1, a_2, a_3, \ldots, a_n$ are called the **terms** of the sequence; the number a_n is called the **nth term** of the sequence.

- A sequence $\{a_n\}$ has the limit L if for each $\in\, > 0$, there exists a number $N > 0$ such that $|a_n - L| <\, \in$ whenever $n > N$; in this case we write $\lim\limits_{n \to \infty} a_n = L$. (**see note below**)

  a) If the sequence $\{a_n\}$ has a limit, we say that the sequence is **convergent** and a_n converges to that limit.

  b) If the sequence $\{a_n\}$ does not approach a specific limit, we say that the sequence is **divergent** and that the sequence diverges.

  ** This definition of the limit of a sequence $\{a_n\}$ is similar to that of the limit of a function $f(x)$ as x approaches ∞. In the statement "$\lim f(x) = L$", f is defined for all real numbers greater than some number N, while the statement "$\lim\limits_{n \to \infty} a_n = L$" is restricted to just positive integers $n > N$.

- A key theorem in calculus regarding limits at infinity states:

  i) If $\{a_n\}$ is a sequence and f is a function such that $f(n) = a_n$ for all positive integers n, AND

  ii) if $f(x)$ is defined for all real numbers $x \geq 1$, AND

  iii) if $\lim\limits_{x \to \infty} f(x)$ exists, then $\lim\limits_{n \to \infty} a_n$ exists and $\lim\limits_{n \to \infty} a_n = \lim\limits_{x \to \infty} f(x)$.

This theorem allows us to evaluate limits of sequences at infinity by using the results for evaluating limits of functions at infinity. In particular, L'Hôpital's Rule may be applied in these situations.

Sample

> Find the limit of the sequence $\left\{\dfrac{3n}{e^{5n}}\right\}$.

Let $f(x) = \dfrac{3x}{e^{5x}}$

then $\lim\limits_{x \to \infty} f(x) = \lim\limits_{x \to \infty}\left(\dfrac{3x}{e^{5x}}\right) = \lim\limits_{x \to \infty}\left(\dfrac{3}{5e^{5x}}\right) = 0$

(form $\dfrac{\infty}{\infty}$, so L'Hôpital's Rule can be applied)

therefore the sequence converges to 0.

Sample

> Show that the sequence $\left\{\dfrac{1 + 2n^3}{n^3}\right\}$ converges.

Let $f(x) = \left\{\dfrac{1 + 2x^3}{x^3}\right\}$

then $\lim\limits_{x \to \infty} f(x) = \lim\limits_{x \to \infty}\left(\dfrac{1 + 2x^3}{x^3}\right) = \lim\limits_{x \to \infty}\left(\dfrac{1 + 2x^3}{x^3}\cdot\dfrac{\frac{1}{x^3}}{\frac{1}{x^3}}\right) = \lim\limits_{x \to \infty}\left(\dfrac{\frac{1}{x^3} + 2}{1}\right) = \dfrac{2}{1} = 2$

therefore the limit of the sequence is 2 and the sequence converges.

OR

$\lim\limits_{x \to \infty} f(x) = \lim\limits_{x \to \infty}\left(\dfrac{1 + 2x^3}{x^3}\right) = \lim\limits_{x \to \infty}\left(\dfrac{6x^2}{3x^2}\right) = \lim\limits_{x \to \infty}\left(\dfrac{12x}{6x}\right) = \lim\limits_{x \to \infty}\left(\dfrac{12}{6}\right) = 2$

(form $\dfrac{\infty}{\infty}$ so L'Hôpital's Rule can be repeatedly applied)

Using Current Technology

A graphing calculator can be used to plot a sequence function in order to view its possible convergence or divergence. The calculator should be in parametric and dot mode. For the sequence above:

1. Let $x = t$ and let $y = \dfrac{1 + 2t^3}{t^3}$

2. Set the window as shown at the right

```
WINDOW
  Tmin=0
  Tmax=10
  Tstep=.1
  Xmin=-2
  Xmax=10
  Xscl=1
  Ymin=-2
  Ymax=10
  Yscl=1
```

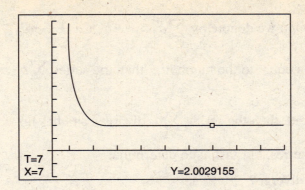

The coordinate of each point is represented by (x, y). In the case of our sequence function, the x-coordinate represents n, the term number, and the y-coordinate represents that term of the sequence. It appears that the nth term of the given sequence appears to approach 2. The 7th term of the sequence above is approximately equal to 2.0029155.

Sample

> If the first four terms of a sequence $\{a_n\}$ are $1, \dfrac{9}{7}, \dfrac{27}{11}, \dfrac{81}{15}$ find:
>
> a)   a formula for the nth term of the sequence
>
> b)   whether the sequence converges or diverges

a) rewriting the series $\qquad 1, \dfrac{9}{7}, \dfrac{27}{11}, \dfrac{81}{15} \cdots$

as $\dfrac{3^1}{3}, \dfrac{3^2}{7}, \dfrac{3^3}{11}, \dfrac{3^4}{15}, \cdots$

or as $\dfrac{3^1}{4(1)-1}, \dfrac{3^2}{4(2)-1}, \dfrac{3^3}{4(3)-1}, \dfrac{3^4}{4(4)-1}, \dots, \dfrac{3^n}{4n-1}$

therefore, the nth term is $a_n = \dfrac{3^n}{4n-1}$

b) Let $f(x) = \dfrac{3^x}{4x-1}$

$\lim\limits_{x \to \infty} f(x) = \lim\limits_{x \to \infty}\left(\dfrac{3^x}{4x-1}\right) = \lim\limits_{x \to \infty}\left[\dfrac{3^x(\ln 3)}{4}\right] = \infty$

(form $\dfrac{\infty}{\infty}$, so can apply L'Hôpital's Rule)

Since $\lim\limits_{x \to \infty} f(x) = \infty$, we can conclude that $\lim\limits_{n \to \infty} a_n = \infty$; so given sequence diverges.

Series

If $\{a_n\}$ is a sequence, then $S_n = a_1 + a_2 + a_3 + \dots + a_n$ is called the **nth partial sum,** $\{S_n\}$ is a **sequence of partial sums.** For example,

$S_1 = a_1, S_2 = a_1 + a_2, S_3 = a_1 + a_2 + a_3, S_n = a_1 + a_2 + a_3 + \dots + a_n.$

For the **infinite series** which we denote by $\sum_{n=1}^{\infty} a_n = a_1 + a_2 + a_3 + \ldots + a_n + \ldots$

- If $\lim_{n \to \infty} S_n$ exists and is equal to the number L, then the series $\sum_{n=1}^{\infty} a_n$ converges and L is the sum of the series.

- If $\lim_{n \to \infty} S_n$ is nonexistent, then the series $\sum_{n=1}^{\infty} a_n$ diverges and has no sum.

Given a specific infinite series, our task is to determine:

1. Does it converge or diverge?

2. If it does converge, what is the series' sum?

To this point we have used the definition of convergence to determine whether a given series converges or diverges, i.e., if it has a sum, it converges; otherwise it diverges. But the task of finding that sum is often quite difficult, if not impossible. So we turn our attention instead to the task of just determining whether or not a given series converges. We now discuss several tests that can be used specifically for this purpose.

Tests of Convergence or Divergence of an Infinite Series

Listed below is a summary of the most frequently used tests to determine the convergence or divergence of a given infinite series. Following each test are examples of how each test may be used.

1. nth Term Test

For the infinite series $\sum_{n=1}^{\infty} a_n$

i) if $\lim_{n \to \infty} a_n \neq 0$, then the series diverges

ii) BEWARE!! If $\lim_{n \to \infty} a_n = 0$, the series does not necessarily converge. The series may converge or diverge. (See #2 part C below.)

iii) if the series *does* converge, then $\lim_{n \to \infty} a_n = 0$.

Sample

Determine the convergence or divergence of $\sum_{n=1}^{\infty} 2^n$.

$\lim_{n \to \infty} 2^n = \infty$ Since $\lim_{n \to \infty} a_n \neq 0$, series *diverges*.

Sample

> Determine the convergence or divergence of $\displaystyle\sum_{n=1}^{\infty}\frac{2n!}{3n!-4}$.

$$\lim_{n \to \infty}\frac{2n!}{3n!-4}=\frac{2}{3}$$ Since $\displaystyle\lim_{n \to \infty}a_n \neq 0$, series *diverges*.

2. Specific Series Type

A) The **geometric series** $\displaystyle\sum_{n=1}^{\infty}a \cdot r^{n-1}\,(a \neq 0)$

   i) converges if $|r| < 1$ and has sum $\dfrac{a}{1-r}$

   ii) diverges if $|r| \geq 1$

Sample

> Determine the convergence or divergence of $\displaystyle\sum_{n=1}^{\infty}\frac{5}{3^n}$.

$\displaystyle\sum_{n=1}^{\infty}\frac{5}{3^n}=\sum_{n=1}^{\infty}5 \cdot \frac{1}{3^n}=\sum_{n=1}^{\infty}5 \cdot \frac{1}{3 \cdot 3^{n-1}}=\sum_{n=1}^{\infty}\frac{5}{3}\left(\frac{1}{3}\right)^{n-1}$. This is a geometric series with $a=\frac{5}{3}$ and $r=\frac{1}{3}$.
Since $|r| < 1$, series *converges*.

Note: Its sum is $\dfrac{a}{1-r}=\dfrac{\frac{5}{3}}{1-\frac{1}{3}}=\dfrac{5}{2}$

Sample

> Determine the convergence or divergence of $\displaystyle\sum_{n=1}^{\infty}\frac{6^n}{2 \cdot 5^n}$.

$\displaystyle\sum_{n=1}^{\infty}\frac{6^n}{2 \cdot 5^n}=\sum_{n=1}^{\infty}\frac{1}{2}\left(\frac{6}{5}\right)^n$. This is a geometric series with $a=\frac{1}{2}$ and $r=\frac{6}{5}$. Since $|r| > 1$, series *diverges*.

Sample

> Determine the convergence or divergence of $\displaystyle\sum_{n=1}^{\infty}3^{-n} \cdot 2^{n-1}$.

$\displaystyle\sum_{n=1}^{\infty}3^{-n} \cdot 2^{n-1}=\sum_{n=1}^{\infty}\frac{2^{n-1}}{3^n}=\sum_{n=1}^{\infty}\frac{1}{3}\left(\frac{2^{n-1}}{3^{n-1}}\right)=\sum_{n=1}^{\infty}\frac{1}{3}\left(\frac{2}{3}\right)^{n-1}$

This is a geometric series with $a=\frac{1}{3}$ and $r=\frac{2}{3}$. Since $|r| < 1$, series *converges*. Its sum is

$$\frac{a}{1-r}=\frac{\frac{1}{3}}{1-\frac{2}{3}}=1.$$

B) The **p-series** $\sum\limits_{n=1}^{\infty} \dfrac{1}{n^p}$

   i) converges if $p > 1$

   ii) diverges if $p \leq 1$

Sample

> Determine the convergence or divergence of $1 + \dfrac{1}{4} + \dfrac{1}{9} + \dfrac{1}{16} + \ldots + \dfrac{1}{n^2} + \ldots$

$$1 + \frac{1}{4} + \frac{1}{9} + \frac{1}{16} + \ldots + \frac{1}{n^2} + \ldots = \sum_{n=1}^{\infty} \frac{1}{n^2}$$

This is a p-series with $p = 2$. Since $p > 1$, series *converges*.

Sample

> Determine the convergence or divergence of $\sum\limits_{n=1}^{\infty} \dfrac{1}{\sqrt[5]{n^3}}$.

$$\sum_{n=1}^{\infty} \frac{1}{\sqrt[5]{n^3}} = \sum_{n=1}^{\infty} \frac{1}{n^{3/5}}$$

This is a p-series with $p = \dfrac{3}{5}$. Since $p < 1$, series *diverges*.

C) The **harmonic series** $\sum\limits_{n=1}^{\infty} \dfrac{1}{n}$ diverges (notice that this is just a p-series with $p = 1$)

Sample

> Determine the convergence or divergence of $\sum\limits_{n=1}^{\infty} \dfrac{5}{n}$.

$$\sum_{n=1}^{\infty} \frac{5}{n} = 5 \cdot \sum_{n=1}^{\infty} \frac{1}{n}$$

This series $\sum\limits_{n=1}^{\infty} \dfrac{1}{n}$ is a divergent p-series ($p \leq 1$), so $5 \cdot \sum\limits_{n=1}^{\infty} \dfrac{1}{n}$ also *diverges*.

D) The **alternating series** $\sum\limits_{n=1}^{\infty} (-1)^{n-1} a_n$ or $\sum\limits_{n=1}^{\infty} (-1)^n a_n$ converges if:

   i) $0 < a_{n+1} \leq a_n$, i.e., the series is non-increasing

     AND

   ii) $\lim\limits_{n \to \infty} a_n = 0$ (note that this condition by itself is *not* sufficient to determine convergence — see "BEWARE" in the nth term test above)

Sample

> Determine the convergence or divergence of $\displaystyle\sum_{n=1}^{\infty}\frac{(-1)^{n+1}}{3n}$.

$\displaystyle\sum_{n=1}^{\infty}\frac{(-1)^{n+1}}{3n}=\sum_{n=1}^{\infty}(-1)^{n+1}\cdot\frac{1}{3n}$ with $a_n=\frac{1}{3n}$ we must verify 2 conditions

1) $a_{n+1}<a_n$ $\qquad$ 2) $\displaystyle\lim_{n\to\infty}a_n=0$

$\dfrac{1}{3(n+1)}<\dfrac{1}{3n}$?? $\qquad$ $\displaystyle\lim_{n\to\infty}\frac{1}{3n}=0$ True

$\qquad\qquad 3n<3(n+1)$

$\qquad\qquad 3n<3n+3$

$\qquad\qquad\quad 0<3$ True

Therefore, series *converges* by alternating series test.

Sample

> Determine the convergence or divergence of $\displaystyle\sum_{n=1}^{\infty}\frac{n}{(-3)^{n-1}}$.

$\displaystyle\sum_{n=1}^{\infty}\frac{n}{(-3)^{n-1}}=\sum_{n=1}^{\infty}\left(-\frac{1}{3}\right)^{n-1}\cdot n=\sum_{n=1}^{\infty}(-1)^{n-1}\cdot\frac{n}{3^{n-1}}$

with $a_n=\dfrac{n}{3^{n-1}}$

1) $\quad$ Is $a_{n+1}<a_n$?

$\dfrac{n+1}{3^{(n+1)-1}}<\dfrac{n}{3^{n-1}}$

$\dfrac{n+1}{3^n}<\dfrac{3n}{3^{n-1}}$

$\left(3^{n-1}\right)(n+1)<3^n(n)$

$\dfrac{n+1}{n}<\dfrac{3n}{3^{n-1}}$

$\dfrac{n+1}{n}<3$

$n+1<3n$

$1<2n$

$\dfrac{1}{2}<n$

True for $n\geq 1$ (Remember n is a positive *integer*.)

2) Does $\lim\limits_{n \to \infty} a_n = 0$?

$\lim\limits_{n \to \infty} \dfrac{n}{3^{n-1}}$ form $\dfrac{\infty}{\infty}$ so use L'Hôpital's Rule

$= \lim\limits_{n \to \infty} \dfrac{1}{3^{n-1}(\ln 3)}$

$= 0$

Therefore given series *converges* by the alternating series test.

Sample

> Determine the convergence or divergence of $\sum\limits_{n=1}^{\infty} \dfrac{(-1)^n \cdot 3n}{\ln(4n)}$.

$\sum\limits_{n=1}^{\infty} \dfrac{(-1)^n \cdot 3n}{\ln(4n)} = \sum\limits_{n=1}^{\infty} (-1)^n \cdot \dfrac{3n}{\ln(4n)}$ with $a_n = \dfrac{3n}{\ln(4n)}$

1. Is $a_{n+1} < a_n$? This is difficult to determine, so let's instead try:

2. $\lim\limits_{n \to \infty} \dfrac{3n}{\ln(4n)} = \lim\limits_{n \to \infty} \dfrac{3}{\frac{4}{4n}} = \lim\limits_{n \to \infty} \dfrac{3}{\frac{1}{n}} = \lim\limits_{n \to \infty} 3n = \infty$

form $\dfrac{\infty}{\infty}$ so use L'Hôpital's Rule

Since $\lim\limits_{n \to \infty} a_n \neq 0$, series *diverges* by the nth term test.

Sample

> Determine the convergence or divergence of $\sum\limits_{n=1}^{\infty} (-1)^{n+1} \left(\dfrac{2n+3}{3n^2-4} \right)$.

1) To determine if $a_{n+1} < a_n$, we let $f(n) = a_n$ and try to show that $f(n)$ is a decreasing function by using the derivative of $f(n)$.

$f(n) = \dfrac{2n+3}{3n^2-4}$

$f'(n) = \dfrac{2(3n^2-4) - 6n(2n+3)}{(3n^2-4)^2}$

$= \dfrac{6n^2 - 8 - 12n^2 - 12n}{(3n^2-4)^2}$

$= \dfrac{-6n^2 - 12n - 8}{(3n^2-4)^2}$

$= \dfrac{-(6n^2 + 12n + 8)}{(3n^2-4)^2}$

Since $f'(n) < 0$, $f(n)$ is decreasing; thus $a_{n+1} < a_n$.

2) Show that $\lim\limits_{n \to \infty} a_n = 0$

$\lim\limits_{n \to \infty} \dfrac{2n+3}{3n^2-4}$ form $\dfrac{\infty}{\infty}$ so use L'Hôpital's Rule

$= \lim\limits_{n \to \infty} \dfrac{2}{6n}$

$= 0$

Therefore given series *converges* by the alternating series test.

Sample

> Another way to show that $a_{n+1} < a_n$ is to show that $0 < a_n - a_{n+1}$ or $a_n - a_{n+1} > 0$.

For example, using the series $\sum\limits_{n=1}^{\infty} \dfrac{n+5}{2n-1}$ With $a_n = \dfrac{n+5}{2n-1}$, show that

$$\dfrac{n+5}{2n-1} - \dfrac{(n+1)+5}{2(n+1)-1} = \dfrac{n+5}{2n-1} - \dfrac{n+6}{2n+1}$$

$$= \dfrac{(2n+1)(n+5) - (n+6)(2n-1)}{(2n-1)(2n+1)}$$

$$= \dfrac{2n^2 + 11n + 5 - (n^2 + 11n - 6)}{4n^2 - 1}$$

$$= \dfrac{n^2 + 15n + 11}{4n^2 - 1}$$

Since the numerator is positive, this fraction is greater than zero if

$$4n^2 - 1 > 0$$

$$4n^2 > 1$$

$$n^2 > \dfrac{1}{4}$$

$$n > \dfrac{1}{2}$$

Since n is a positive integer, this is true. Therefore $a_n - a_{n+1} > 0$ so $a_n > a_{n+1}$ or $a_{n+1} < a_n$.

3. Ratio Test

For the series $\sum\limits_{n=1}^{\infty} a_n$, find $\lim\limits_{n \to \infty} \left| \dfrac{a_{n+1}}{a_n} \right| = L$:

   i) if $L < 1$, then the series converges absolutely (*see below)

   ii) if $L > 1$ (or L is infinite), then the series diverges

   iii) if $L = 1$, the test is inconclusive — must try another test

[try this test if a_n contains factors such as $n!$ or x^n]

(The Ratio Test is used frequently on the AP Exam. It is particularly useful when we later discuss the interval of convergence of a power series.)

(*Note:* A series for which $\sum\limits_{n=1}^{\infty} |a_n|$ converges is called an **absolutely convergent** series. In addition, if the series is absolutely convergent, then it is also just convergent. However, if a series $\sum\limits_{n=1}^{\infty} a_n$ is convergent, but the series $\sum\limits_{n=1}^{\infty} |a_n|$ is divergent, then the series $\sum\limits_{n=1}^{\infty} a_n$ is called **conditionally convergent.** An example of this is the series $\sum\limits_{n=1}^{\infty} \dfrac{(-1)^{n+1}}{n}$, which is convergent by the alternating series test but the series $\sum\limits_{n=1}^{\infty} \left| \dfrac{(-1)^{n+1}}{n} \right| = \sum\limits_{n=1}^{\infty} \dfrac{1}{n}$ is a divergent harmonic series. So the series $\sum\limits_{n=1}^{\infty} \dfrac{(-1)^{n+1}}{n}$ is a conditionally convergent series.)

Sample

> Determine the convergence or divergence of $\sum\limits_{n=1}^{\infty} \dfrac{5^n}{n!}$.

With $a_n = \dfrac{5^n}{n!}$

$$\lim_{n \to \infty} \left| \frac{a_{n+1}}{a_n} \right| = \lim_{n \to \infty} \left| \frac{5^{n+1}}{(n+1)!} \cdot \frac{n!}{5^n} \right| = \lim_{n \to \infty} \left| \frac{5}{n+1} \right| = 0 = L$$

Since $L < 1$, given series *diverges* by the ratio test.

Sample

> Determine the convergence or divergence of $\sum\limits_{n=1}^{\infty} \dfrac{3^n}{n^3}$.

With $a_n = \dfrac{3^n}{n^3}$

$$\lim_{n \to \infty} \left| \frac{3^{n+1}}{(n+1)^3} \cdot \frac{n^3}{3^n} \right| = \lim_{n \to \infty} \left| 3 \cdot \frac{n^3}{(n+1)^3} \right| = 3 \cdot 1 = 3 = L$$

Since $L > 1$, given series *diverges* by the ratio test.

Sample

> Determine the convergence or divergence of $\sum\limits_{n=1}^{\infty} \dfrac{1}{n^4}$.

With $a_n = \dfrac{1}{n^4}$ we try the Ratio Test:

$$\lim_{n \to \infty} \left| \frac{a_{n+1}}{a_n} \right| = \lim_{n \to \infty} \left| \frac{1}{(n+1)^4} \cdot \frac{n^4}{1} \right| = \lim_{n \to \infty} \left| \frac{n^4}{(n+1)^4} \right| = 1 = L$$

With $L = 1$, Ratio Test is inconclusive. Note, however, that $\sum\limits_{n=1}^{\infty} \dfrac{1}{n^4}$ is just a p-series with $p = 4 > 1$, so given series *converges* absolutely.

4. Root Test

For the series $\sum\limits_{n=1}^{\infty} a_n$ find $\lim\limits_{n\to\infty} \sqrt[n]{|a_n|} = L$:

   i) if $L < 1$ then the series converges absolutely

   ii) if $L > 1$ (or L is infinite), then the series diverges

   iii) if $L = 1$, the test is inconclusive and another test may be used

The Root Test is used infrequently on the AP Exam.

Sample

> Determine the convergence or divergence of $\sum\limits_{n=1}^{\infty} \dfrac{e^{3n}}{n^n}$.

With $a_n = \dfrac{e^{3n}}{n^n}$

$$\lim_{n\to\infty} \sqrt[n]{|a_n|} = \lim_{n\to\infty} \sqrt[n]{\dfrac{e^{3n}}{n^n}} = \lim_{n\to\infty} \sqrt[n]{\left|\dfrac{e^{3n}}{n^n}\right|} = \lim_{n\to\infty} \left(\dfrac{e^{3n}}{n^n}\right)^{\frac{1}{n}}$$

Drop absolute value since all terms positive.

$$= \lim_{n\to\infty} \left(\dfrac{e^3}{n}\right) = 0 = L$$

Since $L < 1$, given series *converges* absolutely.

Sample

> Determine the convergence or divergence of $\sum\limits_{n=2}^{\infty} \dfrac{1}{(\ln n)^n}$.

$$\lim_{n\to\infty} \sqrt[n]{|a_n|} = \lim_{n\to\infty} \sqrt[n]{\left|\dfrac{1}{(\ln n)^n}\right|} = \lim_{n\to\infty} \sqrt[n]{\dfrac{1}{(\ln n)^n}} = \lim_{n\to\infty} \left(\dfrac{1}{(\ln n)^n}\right)^{\frac{1}{n}}$$

$$= \lim_{n\to\infty} \dfrac{1}{\ln n} = 0 = L$$

Since $L < 1$, given series *converges* absolutely.

Sample

> Determine the convergence or divergence of $\sum\limits_{n=1}^{\infty} \dfrac{(n+1)^n}{(2n+1)^n}$.

$$\lim_{n\to\infty} \sqrt[n]{\left|\dfrac{(n+1)^n}{(2n+1)^n}\right|} = \lim_{n\to\infty} \sqrt[n]{\dfrac{(n+1)^n}{(2n+1)^n}} = \lim_{n\to\infty} \left(\dfrac{n+1}{2n+1}\right) = 2 = L$$

Since $L > 1$, given series *diverges* by the Root Test.

5. Integral Test

For the series $\sum_{n=1}^{\infty} a_n$, where $a_n = f(n)$ and $f(n)$ is positive, continuous, and decreasing for $x \geq 1$:

  i) if the improper integral $\int_1^{\infty} f(x)\,dx$ exists, then the series $\sum_{n=1}^{\infty} a_n$ converges;

  ii) if the improper integral $\int_1^{\infty} f(x)\,dx = \infty$, then the series $\sum_{n=1}^{\infty} a_n$ diverges.

Sample

Determine the convergence or divergence of $\sum_{n=1}^{\infty} \dfrac{1}{3n+1}$.

Let $f(x) = \dfrac{1}{3x+1}$.   Note that $f(x)$ is positive, continuous, and decreasing for $x \geq 1$.

$$\int_1^{\infty} \frac{1}{3x+1}\,dx = \lim_{c \to \infty} \int_1^{c} \frac{1}{3x+1}\,dx = \lim_{c \to \infty} \frac{1}{3} \int_1^{c} \frac{3}{3x+1}\,dx = \lim_{c \to \infty} \frac{1}{3}\left[\ln|3x+1|\right]_1^{c}$$

$$= \frac{1}{3} \lim_{c \to \infty}\left[\ln|3x+1|\right]_1^{c} = \frac{1}{3} \lim_{c \to \infty}\left[\ln|3c+1| - \ln 4\right] = \infty$$

Therefore, given series *diverges* by the integral test.

Sample

Determine the convergence or divergence of $\sum_{n=1}^{\infty} \dfrac{2n+5}{(n^2+5n)^3}$.

Let $f(x) = \dfrac{2x+5}{(x^2+5x)^3}$ We note that $f(x)$ is positive, continuous, and decreasing for $x \geq 1$.

$$\int_1^{\infty} \frac{2x+5}{(x^2+5x)^3}\,dx = \lim_{c \to \infty} \int_1^{c} (x^2+5x)^{-3}\cdot(2x+5)\,dx = \lim_{c \to \infty}\left[\frac{(x^2+5x)^{-2}}{-2}\right]_1^{c}$$

$$= -\frac{1}{2}\lim_{c \to \infty}\left[\frac{1}{(x^2+5x)^2}\right]_1^{c} = -\frac{1}{2}\lim_{c \to \infty}\left[\frac{1}{(c^2+5c)^2} - \frac{1}{6}\right]$$

$$= \frac{1}{2}\left[0 - \frac{1}{6}\right]$$

$$= \frac{1}{12}$$

Since the improper integral exists, given series *converges* by the integral test.

Sample

Determine the convergence or divergence of $\sum_{n=1}^{\infty} n \cdot e^{-n}$.

Let $f(x) = x \cdot e^{-x} = \frac{x}{e^x}$; $f(x)$ is positive, continuous, and decreasing for $x \geq 1$. If asked to prove that $f(x)$ is decreasing, we proceed as follows:

$f(x) = x \cdot e^{-x}$

$f'(x) = 1(e^{-x}) + (e^{-x})(-1) \cdot x$

$\quad = e^{-x} - xe^{-x}$

$\quad = e^{-x}(1-x)$

$\quad = \frac{1-x}{e^x}$

If $x > 1$, $f'(x) < 0$, so $f(x)$ is decreasing.

Next, we evaluate $\int_{1}^{\infty} x \cdot e^{-x} \, dx$

$= \lim_{c \to \infty} \int_{1}^{c} x \cdot e^{-x} \, dx$.   Using integration by parts

$\qquad \int x \cdot e^{-x} \, dx \quad$ let $u = x$ and $dv = e^{-x} \, dx$

$\qquad = \int u \, dv \qquad dy = dx \quad v = (-1)e^{-x}$

$\qquad = uv - \int v \, du$

$\qquad = x(-e^{-x}) - \int (-1)e^{-x} \, dx$

$\qquad = -xe^{-x} - e^{-x} + c$

$\qquad = -e^{-x}(x+1) + c$

$\qquad = \frac{x+1}{-e^x} + c$

$= \lim_{c \to \infty} \left[\frac{x+1}{-e^x} \right]_{1}^{c}$

$= \lim_{c \to \infty} \left[\frac{c+1}{-e^c} + \frac{2}{e} \right]$

$= 0 + \frac{2}{e}$

$= \frac{2}{e}$

Since integral exists, given series *converges* by the integral test.

Sample

> Determine the convergence or divergence of $\sum\limits_{n=1}^{\infty}\dfrac{1}{n}$.

This is just a *divergent* harmonic series, or a divergent p-series with $p \leq 1$.

Let's try the Integral Test just to see what happens. Let $f(x) = \dfrac{1}{x}$. We note that for $x \geq 1$, $f(x)$ is positive, continuous, and decreasing.

Then $\displaystyle\int_1^{\infty} \dfrac{1}{x}\,dx = \lim_{c \to \infty} \int_1^c \dfrac{1}{x}\,dx = \lim_{c \to \infty}\Big[\ln|x|\Big]_1^c = \lim_{c \to \infty}\Big[\ln|c| - \ln 1\Big] = \infty$

Since the improper integral doesn't exist, given series *diverges*.

6. Comparison Test

Let $\sum\limits_{n=1}^{\infty} a_n$ and $\sum\limits_{n=1}^{\infty} b_n$ be a series or positive terms:

i) if $\sum\limits_{n=1}^{\infty} b_n$ is a known convergent series and $a_n \leq b_n$ for all positive n, then the series $\sum\limits_{n=1}^{\infty} a_n$ is convergent.

ii) if $\sum\limits_{n=1}^{\infty} b_n$ is a known divergent series and $a_n \geq b_n$ for all positive n, then the series $\sum\limits_{n=1}^{\infty} a_n$ is divergent.

Sample

> Determine the convergence or divergence of $\sum\limits_{n=1}^{\infty}\dfrac{5}{3+2^n}$.

Remember, we must compare this series to either a known convergent or a known divergent series.

Let $\sum\limits_{n=1}^{\infty} a_n = \sum\limits_{n=1}^{\infty}\dfrac{5}{3+2^n}$; consider the series $\sum\limits_{n=1}^{\infty} b_n = \sum\limits_{n=1}^{\infty}\dfrac{5}{2^n}$

1. $a_n = \dfrac{5}{3+2^n} < \dfrac{5}{2^n} = b_n$

2. $\sum\limits_{n=1}^{\infty} b_n = \sum\limits_{n=1}^{\infty}\dfrac{5}{2^n} = \sum\limits_{n=1}^{\infty} 5 \cdot \left(\dfrac{1}{2}\right)^n$ this is a convergent geometric series with $r = \dfrac{1}{2} < 1$. Since $a_n < b_n$ and $\sum\limits_{n=1}^{\infty} b_n$ converges, $\sum\limits_{n=1}^{\infty} a_n$ converges.

Sample

> Determine the convergence or divergence of $\sum_{n=1}^{\infty} \dfrac{1}{1+\sqrt{n}}$.

Consider the series $\sum_{n=1}^{\infty} \dfrac{1}{\sqrt{n}} = \sum_{n=1}^{\infty} \dfrac{1}{n^{\frac{1}{2}}}$, which is a divergent p-series with $p < 1$. Since

$a_n = \dfrac{1}{1+\sqrt{n}} < \dfrac{1}{\sqrt{n}} = b_n$, and $\sum_{n=1}^{\infty} b_n$ diverges, we know nothing about $\sum_{n=1}^{\infty} a_n$.

So, let's try again:

Consider the series $\sum_{n=1}^{\infty} \dfrac{1}{n}$, which is the divergent harmonic series. Then, $a_n = \dfrac{1}{1+\sqrt{n}} > \dfrac{1}{n} = b_n$;

since $\sum_{n=1}^{\infty} b_n$ diverges, $\sum_{n=1}^{\infty} a_n$ *diverges*.

Sample

> Determine the convergence or divergence of $\sum_{n=1}^{\infty} \dfrac{3^n}{5+7}$.

Consider the series $\sum_{n=1}^{\infty} \left(\dfrac{3}{5}\right)^n$, which is a convergent geometric series $r = \dfrac{3}{5} > 1$. Then

$a_n = \dfrac{3n}{5^n+7} < \dfrac{3^n}{5^n} = b_n$. Since $\sum_{n=1}^{\infty} b_n$ is convergent, $\sum_{n=1}^{\infty}$ is *convergent*.

Sample

> Determine the convergence or divergence of $\sum_{n=1}^{\infty} e^{-n^3}$.

First, $\sum_{n=1}^{\infty} e^{-n^3} = \sum_{n=1}^{\infty} \dfrac{1}{e^{n^3}}$. Compare this to the series $\sum_{n=1}^{\infty} \dfrac{1}{e^n} = \sum_{n=1}^{\infty} \left(\dfrac{1}{e}\right)^n$, which is a convergent

geometric series with $r = \dfrac{1}{e} < 1$. We see that $a_n = \dfrac{1}{e^{n^3}} < \dfrac{1}{e^n} = b_n$; therefore $\sum_{n=1}^{\infty} a_n$ converges by the

comparison test.

7. Limit Comparison Test

Let $\sum_{n=1}^{\infty} a_n$ and $\sum_{n=1}^{\infty} b_n$ be series of positive terms.

Find $\lim_{n \to \infty} \dfrac{a_n}{b_n} = L$:

 i) if $L > 0$, then the series $\sum_{n=1}^{\infty} a_n$ and $\sum_{n=1}^{\infty} b_n$ either both converge or both diverge.

 ii) if $L = 0$ and if $\sum_{n=1}^{\infty} b_n$ converges, then $\sum_{n=1}^{\infty} a_n$ converges.

 iii) if $L = \infty$ and if $\sum_{n=1}^{\infty} b_n$ converges, then $\sum_{n=1}^{\infty} a_n$ converges.

357

Sample

> Determine the convergence or divergence of $\displaystyle\sum_{n=1}^{\infty} \frac{1}{4n^2 - 5n + 3}$.

Choose the series $\displaystyle\sum_{n=1}^{\infty} \frac{1}{n^2}$, which is a convergent p-series ($p = 2 > 1$) with

$$a_n = \frac{1}{4n^2 - 5n + 3} \text{ and } b_n = \frac{1}{n^2}, \lim_{n \to \infty}\left(\frac{a_n}{b_n}\right) = \lim_{n \to \infty}\left(\frac{1}{4n^2 - 5n + 3} \cdot \frac{n^2}{1}\right) = \lim_{n \to \infty}\left(\frac{n^2}{4n^2 - 5n + 3}\right) = \frac{1}{4} > 0$$

So given series *converges* by the limit comparison test.

Sample

> Determine the convergence or divergence of $\displaystyle\sum_{n=1}^{\infty} \frac{n^2 + 3}{2n^5 + 4n^2 + 1}$.

Choose the series $\displaystyle\sum_{n=1}^{\infty} \frac{1}{n^3}$, which is a convergent p-series ($p = 3 > 1$). With

$$a_n = \frac{n^2 + 3}{2n^5 + 4n^2 + 1} \text{ and } b_n = \frac{1}{n^3}, \lim_{n \to \infty}\left(\frac{a_n}{b_n}\right) = \lim_{n \to \infty}\left(\frac{n^2 + 3}{2n^5 + 4n^2 + 1} \cdot \frac{n^3}{1}\right) = \lim_{n \to \infty}\left(\frac{n^5 + 3n^3}{2n^5 + 4n^2 + 1}\right) = \frac{1}{2} > 0$$

Since $\displaystyle\lim_{n \to \infty}\left(\frac{a_n}{b_n}\right) > 0$ and $\displaystyle\sum_{n=1}^{\infty} b_n$ converges, $\displaystyle\sum_{n=1}^{\infty} a_n$ *converges*.

Note: When choosing the second series to compare with the given series, find the ratio of the highest power of the variable in the numerator to the highest power of the variable in the denominator.

For the series $\displaystyle\sum_{n=1}^{\infty} \frac{n^2}{2n^5} \to \frac{n^2}{2n^5} = \frac{1}{2n^3} \to$ use series $\displaystyle\sum_{n=1}^{\infty} \frac{1}{n^3}$.

For the series $\displaystyle\sum_{n=1}^{\infty} \frac{3\sqrt{n}}{\sqrt{n^3 + 1}} \to \frac{3\sqrt{n}}{\sqrt{n^3}} = \frac{3n^{1/2}}{n^{3/2}} = \frac{3}{n} \to$ use series $\displaystyle\sum_{n=1}^{\infty} \frac{1}{n}$.

For the series $\displaystyle\sum_{n=1}^{\infty} \frac{5n^2}{\sqrt{n^5 + 3n^2 - 7}} \to \frac{5n^2}{\sqrt{n^5}} = \frac{5n^2}{n^{5/2}} = \frac{5}{n^{1/2}} \to$ use series $\displaystyle\sum_{n=1}^{\infty} \frac{1}{n^{1/2}}$.

For the series $\displaystyle\sum_{n=1}^{\infty} \frac{7}{3n\sqrt{n^2 + 3}} \to \frac{7}{3n\sqrt{n^2}} = \frac{7}{3n \cdot n} = \frac{7}{3n^2} \to$ use the series $\displaystyle\sum_{n=1}^{\infty} \frac{1}{n^2}$.

Sample

> Determine the convergence or divergence of $\displaystyle\sum_{n=1}^{\infty} \frac{n^3}{5n^4 + 1}$.

$\dfrac{n^3}{5n^4} = \dfrac{1}{5n}$ so use the series $\displaystyle\sum_{n=1}^{\infty} \frac{1}{n}$, which is the divergent harmonic series; with $a_n = \dfrac{n^3}{5n^4 + 1}$ and

$b_n = \dfrac{1}{n}$ we have $\displaystyle\lim_{n \to \infty}\left(\frac{a_n}{b_n}\right) = \lim_{n \to \infty}\left(\frac{n^3}{5n^4 + 1} \cdot \frac{n}{1}\right) = \lim_{n \to \infty}\left(\frac{n^4}{5n^4 + 1}\right) = \frac{1}{5} > 0$. Therefore, given series

diverges by the limit comparison test.

Note: If $\lim\limits_{n \to \infty}\left(\dfrac{a_n}{b_n}\right) > 0$, then the series $\sum\limits_{n=1}^{\infty} a_n$ and $\sum\limits_{n=1}^{\infty} b_n$ either converge or diverge *together*. If $\lim\limits_{n \to \infty}\left(\dfrac{a_n}{b_n}\right) = 0$ and one series converges, then the other series converges. But, if $\lim\limits_{n \to \infty}\left(\dfrac{a_n}{b_n}\right) = 0$ and one series diverges, we know *nothing* about the other series.

Other Useful Information Regarding Infinite Series

If c, A, and B are real numbers such that $\sum\limits_{n=1}^{\infty} a_n = A$ and $\sum\limits_{n=1}^{\infty} b_n = B$ and $S_N = \sum\limits_{n=1}^{N} a_n$, then:

i) $\sum\limits_{n=1}^{\infty} c \cdot a_n = c \cdot \sum\limits_{n=1}^{\infty} a_n = c \cdot A$, which implies that a constant times a convergent series yields another convergent series.

ii) $\sum\limits_{n=1}^{\infty} (a_n \pm b_n) = \sum\limits_{n=1}^{\infty} a_n \pm \sum\limits_{n=1}^{\infty} b_n = A \pm B$, which implies that the sum or difference of 2 convergent series yields another convergent series.

iii) $\sum\limits_{n=N+1}^{\infty} a_n = \sum\limits_{n=1}^{\infty} a_n - \sum\limits_{n=1}^{N} a_n = A - S_N$. This implies that if the first N terms of a series are dropped, the convergence or divergence of the series will not be affected.

iv) if the series $\sum\limits_{n=1}^{\infty} a_n$ is convergent and the series $\sum\limits_{n=1}^{\infty} b_n$ is divergent, then the series $\sum\limits_{n=1}^{\infty} (a_n + b_n)$ is divergent.

Summary of Tests for Convergence or Divergence of Infinite Series

Test	Series	Necessary Conditions	Conclusion
nth term	$\sum\limits_{n=1}^{\infty} a_n$	$\lim\limits_{n \to \infty} a_n \neq 0$	diverges
Geometric Series	$\sum\limits_{n=1}^{\infty} a_n$	$\lvert r \rvert < 1$	converges
		$\lvert r \rvert \geq 1$	diverges
p-Series	$\sum\limits_{n=1}^{\infty} 1/p^n$	$p > 1$	converges
		$p \leq 1$	diverges
Harmonic Series	$\sum\limits_{n=1}^{\infty} 1/n$		diverges
Alternating Series	$\sum\limits_{n=1}^{\infty} (-1)^{n-1} a_n$	$0 < a_{n+1} \leq a_n$ and $\lim\limits_{n \to \infty} a_n = 0$	converges

Test	Series	Necessary Conditions	Conclusion
Ratio	$\sum_{n=1}^{\infty} a_n$	$\lim_{n \to \infty} \left| \frac{a_{n+1}}{a_n} \right| < 1$	converges
		$\lim_{n \to \infty} \left| \frac{a_{n+1}}{a_n} \right| > 1$	diverges
		$\lim_{n \to \infty} \left| \frac{a_{n+1}}{a_n} \right| = 1$	inconclusive
Root	$\sum_{n=1}^{\infty} a_n$	$\lim_{n \to \infty} \sqrt[n]{|a_n|} < 1$	converges
		$\lim_{n \to \infty} \sqrt[n]{|a_n|} > 1$	diverges
		$\lim_{n \to \infty} \sqrt[n]{|a_n|} = 1$	inconclusive
Integral	$\sum_{n=1}^{\infty} a_n$	$a_n = f(n)$ and f is cont., pos., and inc.:	
		$\int_{1}^{\infty} f(x)\,dx$ exists	$\sum_{n=1}^{\infty} a_n$ converges
		$\int_{1}^{\infty} f(x)\,dx$ does not exist	$\sum_{n=1}^{\infty} a_n$ diverges
Comparison	$\sum_{n=1}^{\infty} a_n$	$0 < a_n \leq b_n$ and $\sum_{n=1}^{\infty} b_n$ conv.	$\sum_{n=1}^{\infty} a_n$ converges
		$a_n \geq b_n > 0$ and $\sum_{n=1}^{\infty} b_n$ div.	$\sum_{n=1}^{\infty} a_n$ diverges
Limit Comparison	$\sum_{n=1}^{\infty} a_n$	$\lim_{n \to \infty} \frac{a_n}{b_n} = L > 0$ and $\sum_{n=1}^{\infty} b_n$ conv.	$\sum_{n=1}^{\infty} a_n$ converges
		$\lim_{n \to \infty} \frac{a_n}{b_n} = L > 0$ and $\sum_{n=1}^{\infty} b_n$ div.	$\sum_{n=1}^{\infty} a_n$ diverges

Alternating Series Error Bound

If the sum of a convergent alternating series is approximated by using the sum of the first N terms of the series, an error is introduced. A theorem in calculus states that the absolute value of this error is less than the value of the $N + 1$st term. In other words, if the sum of the series is S and we approximate the series' sum by S_N (sum of the first N terms), then the error R_N is given by:

$$|S - S_N| = |R_N| \leq a_{N+1}$$

Sample

Approximate the sum of the following series by its first 5 terms

$$\sum_{n=1}^{\infty}(-1)^{n}\left(\frac{1}{n^{2}}\right)=-1+\frac{1}{4}-\frac{1}{9}+\frac{1}{16}-\frac{1}{25}+\frac{1}{36}-\frac{1}{49}+\dots$$

The sum of the first 5 terms is: $-1+\frac{1}{4}-\frac{1}{9}+\frac{1}{16}-\frac{1}{25}\approx-.838611$

The given series is convergent by the Alternating Series Test since
$a_{n+1}=\frac{1}{(n+1)^{2}}\leq\frac{1}{n^{2}}=a_{n}$ and $\lim_{n\to\infty}a_{n}=0$

The error bound is given by: $\left|S-S_{5}\right|=\left|R_{5}\right|\leq a_{6}=\frac{1}{36}\approx.027778$

So the actual sum lies between $S_{5}-.027778$ and $S_{5}+.027778$; therefore the sum, S, of the series lies in the interval

$-.838611-.027778\leq S\leq-.838611+.027778$

$-.866389\leq S\leq-.810833$

Sample

Find the sum of the infinite series $\sum_{n=1}^{\infty}\frac{(-1)^{n+1}}{n!}$ accurate to 3 decimal places.

$$\sum_{n=1}^{\infty}\frac{(-1)^{n+1}}{n!}=\frac{1}{1}-\frac{1}{2!}+\frac{1}{3!}-\frac{1}{4!}+\frac{1}{5!}-\frac{1}{6!}+\dots$$

Accuracy to 4 decimal places means we want $\left|\text{error}\right|<.0005$. In other words, we want to find which term of the series will be less than .0005. We want:

$\frac{1}{n!}<.0005$

$\frac{1}{.0005}<n!$

$2000<n!$

By trial and error, this is true when $n=7$ ($7!=5040$, but 6! is only 720). So we will approximate the sum of the series by using the first 6 terms:

$S_{6}=1-\frac{1}{2!}+\frac{1}{3!}-\frac{1}{4!}+\frac{1}{5!}-\frac{1}{6!}\approx.631944=.632$ accurate to 3 decimal places.

(**Note:** The given series is convergent since $a_{n+1}=\frac{1}{(n+1)!}\leq\frac{1}{n!}=a_{n}$ and $\lim_{n\to\infty}a_{n}=\lim_{n\to\infty}\frac{1}{n!}=0$).

Radius and Interval of Convergence of Power Series

The infinite series discussed so far, $\sum_{n=1}^{\infty} a_n$ have involved sums of constant terms where $a_n = f(n)$ for some function f. We now investigate infinite series whose terms are constant multiples of $x - c$, with c being a specific number.

A **power series centered at c** is a series of the form

$$\sum_{n=1}^{\infty} a_n \cdot (x-c)^n = a_0 \cdot (x-c)^0 + a_1 \cdot (x-c)^1 + a_2 \cdot (x-c)^2 + a_3 \cdot (x-c)^3 + \ldots + a_n \cdot (x-c)^n + \ldots$$

$$= a_0 + a_1 \cdot (x-c) + a_2 \cdot (x-c)^2 + a_3 \cdot (x-c)^3 + \ldots + a_n \cdot (x-c)^n + \ldots$$

For each value of the variable x, the power series represents a series of numbers whose convergence or divergence can be determined using the tests previously discussed.

- For any power series $\sum_{n=1}^{\infty} a_n \cdot (x-c)^n$, exactly one of the following conditions is true:

  i) the series is only convergent when $x = c$

  ii) the series is absolutely convergent for all x

  OR

  iii) there exists some positive number R for which the series converges absolutely for x such that $|x-c| < R$ and diverges for all x such that $|x-c| > R$.

- The number R is called the **radius of convergence** of the power series:

  i) if the series is only convergent at $x = c$, then the radius of convergence is $R = 0$

  ii) if the series is convergent for all x, the radius of convergence is infinity.

- The set of all number x for which the series is convergent is called the **interval of convergence** of the power series. As we shall soon see, a power series may converge at both endpoints, at just one endpoint, or at both endpoints of the interval of convergence. The interval of convergence may be in one of the following forms:

  $[c-R, c+R]$ or $(c-R, c+R)$ or $(c-R, c+R]$ or $[c-R, c+R)$

Sample

Find the radius of convergence for the power series $\sum_{n=0}^{\infty} x^n$.

With $a_n = x^n$, using the Ratio Test, we have:

$$\lim_{n \to \infty} \left| \frac{a_{n+1}}{a_n} \right| = \lim_{n \to \infty} \left| \frac{x^{n+1}}{x^n} \right| = \lim_{n \to \infty} |x| = |x|$$

If the limit above is less than 1, then the series converges absolutely. We solve $|x| < 1$ to get $-1 < x < 1$.

Next, check for convergence at the endpoints:

1. When $x = 1$, series is $\sum_{n=0}^{\infty} (1)^n = 1 + 1 + 1 + \ldots$ which diverges

2. When $x = -1$, series is $\sum_{n=0}^{\infty} (-1)^n = 1 + -1 + 1 + -1 + \ldots$ which diverges

After excluding both endpoints, the interval of convergence is $(-1, 1)$; radius of convergence is 1.

Sample

Find the interval of convergence for the series $\sum_{n=0}^{\infty} \frac{x^n}{n}$.

With $a_n = \frac{x^n}{n}$, using Ratio Test again:

$$\lim_{n \to \infty} \left| \frac{a_{n+1}}{a_n} \right| = \lim_{n \to \infty} \left| \frac{x^{n+1}}{n+1} \cdot \frac{n}{x^n} \right| = \lim_{n \to \infty} \left| \frac{n}{n+1} \cdot x \right| = 1 \cdot |x| = |x|$$

When this limit is less than 1, series converges: $|x| < 1 \Rightarrow -1 < x < 1$. Check for convergence at endpoints:

1. When $x = 1$, series is $\sum_{n=0}^{\infty} \frac{(1)^n}{n} = \sum_{n=0}^{\infty} \frac{1}{n}$, which is the divergent harmonic series.

2. When $x = -1$, series is $\sum_{n=0}^{\infty} \frac{(-1)^n}{n}$, which converges by alternating series test.

So we exclude $x = 1$, but include $x = -1$. Therefore interval of convergence is $-1 \le x < 1$ or $[-1, 1)$.

Sample

Find the interval of convergence for the series $\sum_{n=0}^{\infty} \frac{x^n}{n!}$.

Using Ratio Test,

$$\lim_{n \to \infty} \left| \frac{a_{n+1}}{a_n} \right| = \lim_{n \to \infty} \left| \frac{x^{n+1}}{(n+1)!} \cdot \frac{n!}{x^n} \right| = \lim_{n \to \infty} \left| \frac{x}{n+1} \right| = 0$$

Since this limit is < 1 for any value of x, this series converges for every real number x, interval of convergence is $(-\infty, \infty)$.

Sample

Find the interval of convergence for the series $\displaystyle\sum_{n=0}^{\infty} \frac{n(x-1)^n}{2^n}$.

$$\lim_{n \to \infty}\left|\frac{a_{n+1}}{a_n}\right| = \lim_{n \to \infty}\left|\frac{(n+1)(x-1)^{n+1}}{2^{n+1}} \cdot \frac{2^n}{n(x-1)^n}\right| = \lim_{n \to \infty}\left|\frac{(n+1)(x-1)}{2n}\right|$$

$$= \lim_{n \to \infty}\left|\frac{n+1}{n} \cdot \frac{x-1}{2}\right| = \lim_{n \to \infty}\left|\frac{n+1}{n}\right| \cdot \left|\frac{x-1}{2}\right| = 1 \cdot \left|\frac{x-1}{2}\right|$$

Series converges when:

$$\left|\frac{x-1}{2}\right| < 1$$

$$|x-1| < 2$$

$$-2 < x - 1 < 2$$

$$-1 < x < 3$$

Check endpoints of interval:

1. when $x = -1$, series is $\displaystyle\sum_{n=0}^{\infty} \frac{n(-2)^n}{2^n} = \sum_{n=0}^{\infty} n \cdot (-1)^n$, which diverges; so exclude $x = -1$.

2. when $x = 3$, series is $\displaystyle\sum_{n=0}^{\infty} \frac{n(2)^n}{2^n} = \sum_{n=0}^{\infty} n$, which also diverges; so exclude $x = 3$

Interval of convergence is therefore $-1 < x < 3$ or $(-1, 3)$.

Sample

Find the interval of convergence for the series $\displaystyle\sum_{n=0}^{\infty} n! x^n$.

$$\lim_{n \to \infty}\left|\frac{a_{n+1}}{a_n}\right| = \lim_{n \to \infty}\left|\frac{(n+1)! x^{n+1}}{n! x^n}\right| = \lim_{n \to \infty}|(n+1)x| = \begin{cases} 0 \text{ if } x = 0 \\ \infty \text{ if } x \neq 0 \end{cases}$$

This series converges only when $x = 0$.

Sample Multiple-Choice Questions:
Sequences and Infinite Series

1. The sequence $\left\{\dfrac{3n^2}{5-2n^2}\right\}$ converges to what number?

    A. $\dfrac{3}{5}$

    B. $\dfrac{3}{2}$

    C. $-\dfrac{3}{5}$

    D. $-\dfrac{3}{2}$

    E. 0

2. The sum of the infinite geometric series $\dfrac{2}{5}+\dfrac{6}{20}+\dfrac{18}{80}+\dfrac{54}{320}+\dots$ is

    A. $\dfrac{8}{15}$

    B. $\dfrac{2}{3}$

    C. $\dfrac{3}{4}$

    D. $\dfrac{5}{4}$

    E. $\dfrac{8}{5}$

3. Which of the following sequences converges?

    I. $\left\{\dfrac{n}{1-2n}\right\}$

    II. $\left\{\dfrac{1n(n)}{n^2}\right\}$

    III. $\left\{\dfrac{n^2}{2^n-1}\right\}$

    A. I only

    B. II only

    C. I and II only

    D. II and III only

    E. I, II, and III

4. What are the values of x for which the series $\displaystyle\sum_{n=0}^{\infty}\dfrac{x^{3n+1}}{(3n+1)!}$ converges?

    A. converges for all x

    B. $|x|<3$

    C. only at $x=0$

    D. $|x|<1$

    E. series diverges for all x

5. Which of the following series converge?

    I. $\displaystyle\sum_{n=1}^{\infty}\dfrac{3}{n}$

    II. $\displaystyle\sum_{n=1}^{\infty}\dfrac{n+1}{n+4}$

    III. $\displaystyle\sum_{n=1}^{\infty}\dfrac{-2}{(-5)^n}$

    A. I only

    B. I and II only

    C. I and III only

    D. II only

    E. III only

6. The radius of convergence for the series $\displaystyle\sum_{n=1}^{\infty}\dfrac{(x-3)^{2n}}{4^n}$ is

    A. $\dfrac{1}{2}$

    B. $\dfrac{3}{4}$

    C. 1

    D. 2

    E. 3

7. The sequence $\left\{ \dfrac{1n(2n)}{n^2} \right\}$ converges to what number?

A. e

B. 2

C. 1

D. $\dfrac{1}{2}$

E. 0

8. The interval of convergence of the series $\displaystyle\sum_{n=0}^{\infty} \dfrac{(x+2)^n}{3^n}$ is

A. $-1 < x < 1$

B. $-3 < x < 1$

C. $-5 \le x < 1$

D. $-5 < x \le 1$

E. $-5 < x < 1$

9. Which of the following series have the same radius of convergence?

I. $\displaystyle\sum_{n=0}^{\infty} \dfrac{x^n}{n^2 + 2}$

II. $\displaystyle\sum_{n=0}^{\infty} \dfrac{x^{3n+1}}{(3n+1)!}$

III. $\displaystyle\sum_{n=0}^{\infty} \dfrac{(-1)^{n+1}(x-2)^n}{n}$

A. I and II only

B. I and III only

C. II and III only

D. I, II, and III

E. none have the same radius of convergences

10. Which of the following sequences diverge?

I. $\left\{ \dfrac{2n^3 + 5n}{3n^2 - 7n} \right\}$

II. $\left\{ \dfrac{n \cdot 1n\ n}{e^n} \right\}$

III. $\left\{ \dfrac{e^n}{1n(n^2)} \right\}$

A. I only

B. II only

C. I and II only

D. I and III only

E. I, II, and III

For extra practice, determine whether each series converges or diverges.

11. $\displaystyle\sum_{n=1}^{\infty} \dfrac{5n - 2}{n \cdot 3^n}$

12. $\displaystyle\sum_{n=1}^{\infty} \dfrac{2n}{3n^2 + 1}$

13. $\displaystyle\sum_{n=1}^{\infty} \dfrac{5^n}{3n^2 + 1}$

14. $\displaystyle\sum_{n=1}^{\infty} \dfrac{1}{n(1n\ n)^2}$

15. $\displaystyle\sum_{n=1}^{\infty} \dfrac{\sin(n)}{3^n}$

16. $\displaystyle\sum_{n=1}^{\infty} \dfrac{n \cdot 3^n}{n!}$

Answers to Multiple-Choice Questions

1. D.

$$\left\{\frac{3n^2}{5-2n^2}\right\} \text{ Let } f(x) = \frac{3x^2}{5-2x^2}$$

$$\lim_{x \to \infty} f(x) = \lim_{x \to \infty} \frac{3x^2}{5-2x^2} \text{ "} \quad \infty/-\infty\text{" form — so we can apply L'Hôpital's Rule}$$

$$= \lim_{x \to \infty} \frac{6x}{-4x}$$

$$= \lim_{x \to \infty} \frac{-6}{4}$$

$$= \frac{-3}{2}$$

2. E. $\frac{2}{5} + \frac{6}{20} + \frac{18}{80} + \frac{54}{420} + \dots$ is a geometric series with $a_1 = \frac{2}{5}$ and $r = \frac{3}{4}$; its sum is

$$\frac{a_1}{1-r} = \frac{\frac{2}{5}}{1-\frac{3}{4}} = \frac{\frac{2}{5}}{\frac{1}{4}} = \frac{8}{5}.$$

3. E.

I. $\left\{\frac{n}{1-2n}\right\}$ with $f(x) = \frac{x}{1-2x}$

$$\lim_{x \to \infty} f(x) = \lim_{x \to \infty} \frac{x}{1-2x} \text{ form} \qquad \text{"}\infty/-\infty\text{" form — so we can apply}$$

$$\text{L'Hôpital's Rule}$$

$$= \lim_{x \to \infty} \frac{1}{-2}$$

$$= \frac{-1}{2} \text{ converges}$$

II. $\left\{\frac{\ln(n)}{n^2}\right\}$ with $f(x) = \frac{\ln x}{x^2}$

$$\lim_{x \to \infty} f(x) = \lim_{x \to \infty} \frac{\ln x}{x^2} \quad \text{form } \frac{\infty}{\infty}, \text{ so L'Hôpital's Rule can be applied}$$

$$= \lim_{x \to \infty} \frac{\frac{1}{x}}{2x}$$

$$= \lim_{x \to \infty} \frac{1}{2x^2}$$

$$= 0 \text{ converges}$$

III. $\left\{\dfrac{n^2}{2^n-1}\right\}$ with $f(x) = \dfrac{x^2}{2^x-1}$

$$\lim_{x \to \infty} f(x) = \lim_{x \to \infty} \frac{x^2}{2^x-1} \quad \text{form } \frac{\infty}{\infty} \to \text{use L'Hôpital's Rule}$$

$$= \lim_{x \to \infty} \frac{2x}{2^x(1n\,2)} \quad \text{form } \frac{\infty}{\infty} \to \text{use L'Hôpital's Rule}$$

$$= \lim_{x \to \infty} \frac{2}{2^x(1n\,2)^2}$$

$$= 0 \quad \text{converges}$$

All three sequences converge.

4. A. $\displaystyle\sum_{n=0}^{\infty} \dfrac{x^{3n+1}}{(3n+1)!}$

$$\lim_{n \to \infty} \left| \frac{a_{n+1}}{a_n} \right| = \lim_{n \to \infty} \left| \frac{x^{3(n+1)+1}}{(3(n+1)+1)!} \cdot \frac{(3n+1)!}{x^{3n+1}} \right|$$

$$= \lim_{n \to \infty} \left| \frac{x^{3n+4}}{(3n+4)!} \cdot \frac{(3n+1)!}{x^{3n+1}} \right|$$

$$= \lim_{n \to \infty} \left| \frac{x^3}{(3n+4)(3n+3)(3n+2)} \right|$$

$$= 0$$

Since $\displaystyle\lim_{n \to \infty} \left| \dfrac{a_{n+1}}{a_n} \right| = 0 < 1$, series converges for all x.

5. E.

I. $\displaystyle\sum_{n=1}^{\infty} \dfrac{3}{n}$

$$= 3 \cdot \sum_{n=1}^{\infty} \frac{1}{n}$$

divergent harmonic series

II. $\displaystyle\sum_{n=1}^{\infty} \dfrac{n+1}{n+4}$

$$\lim_{n \to \infty} a_n$$

$$= \lim_{n \to \infty} \frac{n+1}{n+4}$$

$$= 1 \neq 0$$

so diverges by nth term test

III. $\displaystyle\sum_{n=1}^{\infty} \frac{-2}{(-5)^n}$

$\displaystyle= \sum_{n=1}^{\infty} \frac{-2}{(-5)(-5)^{n-1}}$

$\displaystyle= \sum_{n=1}^{\infty} \frac{2}{5} \cdot \left(-\frac{1}{5}\right)^{n-1}$

convergent geometric series with $r = \frac{1}{5} (|r| < 1)$

6. D. $\displaystyle\sum_{n=1}^{\infty} \frac{(x-3)^{2n}}{4^n}$

$\displaystyle\lim_{n \to \infty} \left| \frac{a_{n+1}}{a_n} \right| = \lim_{n \to \infty} \left| \frac{(x-3)^{2(n+1)}}{4^{n+1}} \cdot \frac{4^n}{(x-3)^{2n}} \right|$

$\displaystyle= \lim_{n \to \infty} \left| \frac{(x-3)^{2n+2}}{4^{n+1}} \cdot \frac{4^n}{(x-3)^{2n}} \right|$

$\displaystyle= \lim_{n \to \infty} \left| \frac{(x-3)^2}{4} \right| = \left| \frac{(x-3)^2}{4} \right|$

The given series converges if $\left| \dfrac{(x-3)^2}{4} \right| < 1$

$\quad (x-3)^2 < 4$

$-2 < x - 3 < 2$

$\quad 1 < x < 5$

So the radius of convergence is 2.

7. E. $\left\{ \dfrac{\ln(2n)}{n^2} \right\}$ with $f(x) = \dfrac{\ln(2x)}{x^2}$

$\displaystyle\lim_{x \to \infty} f(x) = \lim_{x \to \infty} \frac{\ln(2x)}{x^2} \qquad \frac{\infty}{\infty}$ form — use L'Hôpital's Rule

$\displaystyle= \lim_{x \to \infty} \frac{\frac{2}{2x}}{2x}$

$\displaystyle= \lim_{x \to \infty} \frac{1}{2x^2}$

$= 0$

8. E. $\displaystyle\sum_{n=0}^{\infty}\frac{(x+2)^n}{3^n}$

$$\lim_{n\to\infty}\left|\frac{a_{n+1}}{a_n}\right| = \lim_{n\to\infty}\left|\frac{(x+2)^{n+1}}{3^{n+1}}\cdot\frac{3^n}{(x+2)^n}\right|$$

$$= \lim_{n\to\infty}\left|\frac{x+2}{3}\right|$$

$$= \left|\frac{x+2}{3}\right|$$

Series converges when $\left|\dfrac{x+2}{3}\right| < 1$

$$\left|\frac{x+2}{3}\right| < 1$$

$$|x+2| < 3$$

$$-3 < x+2 < 3$$

$$-5 < x < 1$$

Check endpoints for convergence:

  i. when $x = -5 \Rightarrow \displaystyle\sum_{n=0}^{\infty}\frac{(-5+2)^n}{3^n} = \sum_{n=0}^{\infty}\frac{(-3)^n}{3^n} = \sum_{n=0}^{\infty}(-1)^n$ diverges

     so exclude $x = -5$

  ii. when $x = 1 \Rightarrow \displaystyle\sum_{n=0}^{\infty}\frac{(1+2)^n}{3^n} = \sum_{n=0}^{\infty}\frac{3^n}{3^n} = \sum_{n=0}^{\infty}(1)^n$ diverges

     so exclude $x = 1$

Therefore interval of convergence is $-5 < x < 1$.

9. B.

  I. $\displaystyle\sum_{n=0}^{\infty}\frac{x^n}{n^2+2}$

$$\lim_{n\to\infty}\left|\frac{a_{n+1}}{a_n}\right| = \lim_{n\to\infty}\left|\frac{x^{n+1}}{(n+1)^2+2}\cdot\frac{n^2+2}{x^n}\right|$$

$$= \lim_{n\to\infty}\left|\frac{x\cdot(n^2+2)}{n^2+2n+3}\right|$$

$$= \lim_{n\to\infty}|x|\cdot\left|\frac{n^2+2}{n^2+2n+3}\right|$$

$$= |x|\cdot 1$$

$$= |x|$$

Series converges if $|x| < 1$

$-1 < x < 1$ radius at convergence is 1

II. $\displaystyle\sum_{n=0}^{\infty} \frac{x^{3n+1}}{(3n+1)!}$

$$\lim_{n \to \infty} \left| \frac{a_{n+1}}{a_n} \right| = \lim_{n \to \infty} \left| \frac{x^{3(n+1)+1}}{(3^{(n+1)}+1)!} \cdot \frac{(3n+1)!}{x^{3n+1}} \right|$$

$$= \lim_{n \to \infty} \left| \frac{x^{3n+4}}{(3n+4)!} \cdot \frac{(3n+1)!}{x^{3n+4}} \right|$$

$$= \lim_{n \to \infty} \left| \frac{x^3}{(3n+4)(3n+3)(3n+2)} \right|$$

$$= 0 < 1$$

So series converges everywhere; infinite radius of convergence.

III. $\displaystyle\sum_{n=1}^{\infty} \frac{(-1)^{n+1}(x-2)}{n}$

$$\lim_{n \to \infty} \left| \frac{a_{n+1}}{a_n} \right| = \lim_{n \to \infty} \left| \frac{(x-2)^{n+1}}{n+1} \cdot \frac{n}{(x-2)^n} \right|$$

$$= \lim_{n \to \infty} \left| (x-2) \cdot \frac{n}{n+1} \right|$$

$$= |x-2| \cdot 1$$

$$= |x-2|$$

Series converges if $|x-2| < 1$

$-1 < x - 2 < 1$

$1 < x < 3$ radius of convergence is 1

Therefore, I and III have the same radius of convergence.

10. D.

I. $\left\{ \dfrac{2n^3 + 5n^2 - 7}{3n^2 - 4n} \right\}$

with $f(x) = \dfrac{2x^3 - 5x - 7}{3x^2 - 4x}$

$$\lim_{x \to \infty} f(x) = \lim_{x \to \infty} \frac{2x^3 - 5x - 7}{3x^2 - 4x}$$

$$= \lim_{x \to \infty} \frac{6x^2 - 5}{6x - 4} \quad **$$

$$= \lim_{x \to \infty} \frac{12x}{6}$$

$$= \infty$$

diverges

371

II. $\left\{\dfrac{n \cdot \ln n}{e^n}\right\}$

with $f(x) = \dfrac{x \cdot \ln x}{e^x}$

$$\lim_{x \to \infty} f(x) = \lim_{x \to \infty} \frac{x \cdot \ln x}{e^x}$$

$$= \lim_{x \to \infty} \frac{(\ln x + 1)}{e^x} **$$

$$= \lim_{x \to \infty} \frac{\dfrac{1}{x}}{e^x}$$

$$= \lim_{x \to \infty} \frac{1}{x \cdot e^x}$$

$$= 0 \text{ converges}$$

III. $\left\{\dfrac{e^n}{\ln(n^2)}\right\}$

with $f(x) = \dfrac{e^x}{\ln(x^2)}$

$$\lim_{x \to \infty} f(x) = \lim_{x \to \infty} \frac{e^x}{\ln(x^2)}$$

$$= \lim_{x \to \infty} \frac{e^x}{\dfrac{2x}{x^2}} **$$

$$= \lim_{x \to \infty} \frac{e^x}{\dfrac{1}{x}}$$

$$= \lim_{x \to \infty} x \cdot e^x = \infty$$

diverges

**Note use of L'Hôpital's Rule in all three limits above.

Therefore, I and III diverge.

11. converges

$\displaystyle\sum_{n=1}^{\infty} \frac{5n-2}{n \cdot 3^n}$ simplify $\dfrac{5n}{n^{3n}} = \dfrac{5}{3^n}$ use series $\displaystyle\sum_{n=1}^{\infty} \frac{1}{3n} = \sum_{n=1}^{\infty} 1 \cdot \left(\frac{1}{3}\right)^n$, which is a convergent geometric series $|r| < 1$.

With $a_n = \dfrac{5n-2}{n \cdot 3^n}$ and $b_n = \dfrac{1}{3^n}$, find $\displaystyle\lim_{n \to \infty} \frac{a_n}{b_n} = \lim_{n \to \infty}\left[\frac{5n-2}{n \cdot 3^n} \cdot \frac{3^n}{1}\right] = \lim_{n \to \infty}\left[\frac{5n-2}{n}\right] = 5$. Since $\displaystyle\lim_{n \to \infty} \frac{a_n}{b_n} = 5 > 0$ and $\displaystyle\sum_{n=1}^{\infty} b_n$ is convergent, the series $\displaystyle\sum_{n=1}^{\infty} a_n$ is convergent by the limit comparison test.

12. diverges

$$\sum_{n=1}^{\infty} \frac{2n}{3n^2+1} \quad \text{simplify } \frac{2n}{3n^2} = \frac{2}{3n} \quad \text{use series } \sum_{n=1}^{\infty} \frac{1}{n}, \text{ which is a divergent harmonic series}$$

With $a_n = \dfrac{2n}{3n^2+1}$ and $b_n = \dfrac{1}{n}$ find $\displaystyle\lim_{n \to \infty} \frac{a_n}{b_n} = \lim_{n \to \infty}\left[\frac{2n}{3n^2+1} \cdot \frac{n}{1}\right] = \lim_{n \to \infty}\left[\frac{2n^2}{3n^2+1}\right] = \frac{2}{3} > 0.$ Since

$\displaystyle\sum_{n=1}^{\infty} b_n$ is divergent, the series $\displaystyle\sum_{n=1}^{\infty} a_n$ diverges by the limit comparison test.

13. diverges

$$\sum_{n=1}^{\infty} \frac{5^n}{3n^2+1}$$

$$\lim_{n \to \infty} a_n = \lim_{n \to \infty}\left(\frac{5^n}{3n^2+1}\right) = \lim_{n \to \infty}\left(\frac{5^n \cdot \ln 5}{6n}\right) = \lim_{n \to \infty}\left(\frac{5^n \cdot (\ln 5)^2}{6}\right) = \infty$$

$\dfrac{\infty}{\infty}$ form form — use L'Hôpital's Rule

Since $\displaystyle\lim_{n \to \infty} a_n \neq 0$, series diverges by the nth term test.

14. converges

$$\sum_{n=1}^{\infty} \frac{1}{n(\ln n)^2}$$

Letting $f(x) = \dfrac{1}{x(\ln x)^2}$; note that $f(x)$ is continuous, positive, and increasing for $x \geq 2$

$$\begin{aligned}
\text{Then } \int_2^{\infty} f(x)\,dx &= \int_2^{\infty} \frac{1}{x(\ln x)^2}\,dx \\
&= \lim_{c \to \infty} \int_2^c \frac{1}{x(\ln x)^2}\,dx \\
&= \lim_{c \to \infty} \int_2^c (\ln x)^{-2} \cdot \frac{1}{x}\,dx \\
&= \lim_{c \to \infty} \left[\frac{(\ln x)^{-1}}{-1}\right]_2^c \\
&= \lim_{c \to \infty} \left[\frac{-1}{\ln x}\right]_2^c \\
&= \lim_{c \to \infty} \left[\frac{-1}{\ln c} + \frac{1}{\ln 2}\right] \\
&= \frac{1}{\ln 2}
\end{aligned}$$

So series converges by the integral test.

15. converges

$$\sum_{n=1}^{\infty} \frac{\sin(n)}{3^n}$$

Since $-1 \le \sin(n) \le 1$

$$a_n = \frac{\sin(n)}{3^n} \le \frac{1}{3^n} = \left(\frac{1}{3}\right)^n = b_n$$

Since the series $\sum_{n=1}^{\infty} b_n$ is a convergent geometric series ($|r| < 1$) and $a_n \le b_n$, the series $\sum_{n=1}^{\infty} a_n$ converges by the comparison test.

16. converges

$$\sum_{n=1}^{\infty} \frac{n \cdot 3^n}{n!} \qquad \lim_{n \to \infty} \left| \frac{a_{n+1}}{a_n} \right| = \lim_{n \to \infty} \frac{(n+1) \cdot 3^{n+1}}{(n+1)!} \cdot \frac{n!}{n \cdot 3^n}$$

$$= \lim_{n \to \infty} \left| \frac{3^{n+1}}{n!} \cdot \frac{n!}{n \cdot 3n} \right|$$

$$= \lim_{n \to \infty} \left| \frac{3}{n} \right| = 0 < 1$$

Since $\lim_{n \to \infty} \left| \frac{a_{n+1}}{a_n} \right| < 1$, series converges.

Sample Free-Response Question: Sequences and Series

1. For the infinite series $\sum_{n=1}^{\infty} \frac{n}{n^4 + 1}$:

a) show that it converges by using the integral test

b) show that it converges by using the comparison test

Answer to Free-Response Question

1. a) $\displaystyle\sum_{n=1}^{\infty}\frac{n}{n^4+1}$ Let $f(x)=\dfrac{x}{x^4+1}$

$f(x)$ is continuous, positive, and decreasing for $x \geq 1$; so the integral test can be applied.

$$\int_1^{\infty} f(x)\,dx$$

$$= \lim_{c \to \infty}\int_1^c \frac{x}{x^4+1}\,dx$$

$$= \lim_{c \to \infty}\int_1^c \frac{x}{(x^2)^2+1}\,dx$$

$$= \lim_{c \to \infty}\left[\frac{1}{2}\int_1^c \frac{2x}{(x^2)^2+1}\,dx\right]$$

$$= \frac{1}{2}\lim_{c \to \infty}\left[\arctan(x^2)\right]_1^c$$

$$= \frac{1}{2}\lim_{c \to \infty}\left[\arctan(c^2)-\arctan(1)\right]$$

$$= \frac{1}{2}\left(\frac{\pi}{2}-\frac{\pi}{4}\right)$$

$$= \frac{1}{2}\left(\frac{\pi}{4}\right)$$

$$= \frac{\pi}{8}$$

So series converges by the integral test.

b) $\displaystyle\sum_{n=1}^{\infty}\frac{n}{n^4+1}$ Simplify $\dfrac{n}{n^4}=\dfrac{1}{n^3}$

Compare given series to $\displaystyle\sum_{n=1}^{\infty}\frac{1}{n^3}$, which is convergent p-series ($p = 3 > 1$). Then we need

to show that $a_n=\dfrac{n}{n^4+1}\leq\dfrac{1}{n^3}=b_n$

$$\frac{n}{n^4+1}\leq\frac{1}{n^3}$$

$$n(n^3)\leq n^4+1$$

$$n^4 \leq n^4+1$$

so $a_n \leq b_n$

Since $a_n \leq b_n$ and the series $\displaystyle\sum_{n=1}^{\infty}b_n$ converges, the series $\displaystyle\sum_{n=1}^{\infty}a_n$ converges by the comparison test.

Polynomial Approximations of Functions (Taylor and Maclaurin Polynomials)

If a function f has derivatives through order n, the nth degree Taylor polynomial for f at c is given by:

$$P_n(x) = f(c) + f'(c) \cdot (x-c) + \frac{f''(c) \cdot (x-c)^2}{2!} + \frac{f'''(c) \cdot (x-c)^3}{3!} + \ldots + \frac{f^{(4)}(c) \cdot (x-c)^4}{n!}$$

If the $c = 0$, then the nth degree polynomial

$$P_n(x) = f(0) + f'(0) \cdot x + \frac{f''(0) \cdot x^2}{2!} + \frac{f'''(0) \cdot x^3}{3!} + \ldots + \frac{f^{(n)}(0) \cdot x^n}{n!}$$

is called the **nth degree Maclaurin polynomial for f.**

Sample

Find the nth degree Maclaurin polynomial for $f(x) = e^x$.

$$f(x) = e^x \qquad f(0) = e^0 = 1$$
$$f'(x) = e^x \qquad f'(0) = e^0 = 1$$
$$\vdots$$
$$f^{(n)}(x) = e^x \qquad f^{(n)}(0) = e^0 = 1$$

$$P_n(x) = f(0) + f'(0) \cdot x + \frac{f''(0) \cdot x^2}{2!} + \frac{f'''(0) \cdot x^3}{3!} + \ldots + \frac{f^{(n)}(0) \cdot x^n}{n!}$$

$$= 1 + 1 \cdot x + \frac{1 \cdot x^2}{2!} + \frac{1 \cdot x^3}{3!} + \ldots + \frac{1 \cdot x^n}{n!}$$

$$P_n(x) = 1 + x + \frac{x^2}{2!} + \frac{x^3}{3!} + \ldots + \frac{x^n}{n!}$$

Sample

Find the first 4 Maclaurin polynomials for $f(x) = e^x$.

From previous example:

$$P_0(x) = 1$$
$$P_1(x) = 1 + x$$
$$P_2(x) = 1 + x + \frac{x^2}{2!} = 1 + x + \frac{x^2}{2}$$
$$P_3(x) = 1 + x + \frac{x^2}{2!} + \frac{x^3}{3!} = 1 + x + \frac{x^2}{2} + \frac{x^3}{6}$$

From the examples above, a power series for $f(x) = e^x$ could be written as

$$\sum_{n=0}^{\infty} \frac{f^{(n)}(0) \cdot x^n}{n!} = \sum_{n=0}^{\infty} \frac{(1) \cdot x^n}{n!} = \sum_{n=0}^{\infty} \frac{x^n}{n!}$$

The series $\displaystyle\sum_{n=0}^{\infty} \frac{x^n}{n!}$ has as an interval of convergence $(-\infty, \infty)$.

To show this $\displaystyle\lim_{n \to \infty} \left| \frac{a_{n+1}}{a_n} \right| = \lim_{n \to \infty} \left| \frac{x^{n+1}}{(n+1)!} \cdot \frac{n!}{x^n} \right| = \lim_{n \to \infty} \left| \frac{x}{n+1} \right| = 0$

Since this limit <1, series converges by the Ratio Test. Thus the Maclaurin series e^x converges to e^x for all values of x.

Shown below are graphs of $f(x) = e^x$ and the first, second, and third degree Maclaurin polynomials for e^x:

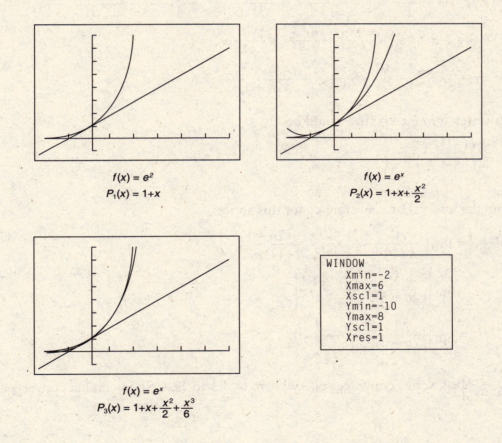

$f(x) = e^2$
$P_1(x) = 1+x$

$f(x) = e^x$
$P_2(x) = 1+x+\dfrac{x^2}{2}$

$f(x) = e^x$
$P_3(x) = 1+x+\dfrac{x^2}{2}+\dfrac{x^3}{6}$

```
WINDOW
  Xmin=-2
  Xmax=6
  Xscl=1
  Ymin=-10
  Ymax=8
  Yscl=1
  Xres=1
```

Notice that as n increases (from $n=1$ to $n=3$) the graph of the nth degree Maclaurin polynomial $P_n(x)$ becomes a closer approximation for the graph of $f(x) = e^x$. For

$f(x) = e^x$ and $P_3(x) = 1 + x + \dfrac{x^2}{2} + \dfrac{x^3}{6}$ note that $f(.9) = e^{.9} \approx 2.4596$ and

$P_3(.9) = 1 + (.9) + \dfrac{(.9)^2}{2} + \dfrac{(.9)^3}{6} \approx 2.4265$. If we were to use $P_n(x)$ for a larger value of n, the

value for $f(.9)$ and $P_n(.9)$ would be even closer together.

Sample

Find the nth degree Maclaurin polynomial for $\sin x$.

$$f(x) = \sin x \rightarrow f(0) = \sin(0) = 0$$

$$f'(x) = \cos x \rightarrow f'(0) = \cos(0) = 1$$

$$f''(x) = -\sin x \rightarrow f''(0) = -\sin(0) = 0$$

$$f'''(x) = -\cos x \rightarrow f'''(0) = -\cos(0) = -1$$

$$f^{(4)}(x) = \sin x \rightarrow f^{(4)}(0) = \sin(0) = 0$$

$$f^{(5)}(x) = \cos x \rightarrow f^{(5)}(0) = \cos(0) = 1$$

Then $P_n(x) = f(0) + \dfrac{f'(0) \cdot x}{1} + \dfrac{f''(0) \cdot x^2}{2!} + \dfrac{f'''(0) \cdot x^3}{3!} + \dfrac{f^{(4)}(0) \cdot x^4}{4!} + \dfrac{f^{(5)}(0) \cdot x^5}{5!} + \ldots$

$$P_n(x) = 0 + 1 \cdot x + \frac{0 \cdot x^2}{2!} - \frac{1 \cdot x^3}{3!} + \frac{0 \cdot x^4}{4!} + \frac{1 \cdot x^5}{5!} + \ldots$$

$$= x - \frac{x^3}{3!} + \frac{x^5}{5!} - \frac{x^7}{7!} + \frac{x^9}{9!} + \ldots + \frac{(-1)^n x^{2n+1}}{(2n+1)!}$$

So a power series for $f(x) = \sin x$ could be

$$\sin x = \sum_{n=0}^{\infty} \frac{(-1)^n x^{2n+1}}{(2n+1)!}$$

Determining the interval of convergence for this series:

$$\lim_{n \to \infty} \left| \frac{a_{n+1}}{a_n} \right| = \lim_{n \to \infty} \left| \frac{(-1)^{n+1} x^{2(n+1)+1}}{(2(n+1)+1)!} \cdot \frac{(2n+1)!}{(-1)^n x^{2n+1}} \right|$$

$$= \lim_{n \to \infty} \left| \frac{x^{2n+3}}{(2n+3)!} \cdot \frac{(2n+1)!}{x^{2n+1}} \right|$$

$$= \lim_{n \to \infty} \left| \frac{x^2}{(2n+3)(2n+2)} \right| = 0$$

Since $\lim_{n \to \infty} \left| \dfrac{a_{n+1}}{a_n} \right| < 1$, series converges everywhere by Ratio Test. So interval at convergence is $(-\infty, \infty)$.

Differentiation and Integration of Power Series

If f is a function defined by a power series, i.e.,

$$f(x) = \sum_{n=0}^{\infty} a_n (x-c)^n = a_0 + a_1(x-c) + a_2(x-c)^2 + a_3(x-c)^3 + \ldots$$

and has radius of convergence $R > 0$ on the interval $(c - R, c + R)$, then:

1. f is continuous, differentiable, and integrable
2. the derivative of f is $f'(x) = a_1 + 2a_2(x-c) + 3a_3(x-c)^2 + \ldots = \sum\limits_{n=1}^{\infty} n\, a_n(x-c)^{n-1}$
3. the integral of f is
$$\int f(x)\,dx = a_0(x-c) + a_1\frac{(x-c)^2}{2} + a_2\frac{(x-c)^3}{3} + \ldots + C_1 = \sum\limits_{n=0}^{\infty} \frac{a_n(x-c)^{n+1}}{n+c} + C_1$$
4. R is the radius of convergence for the series that results from differentiating or integrating the original power series. As in all power series, checking convergence at the endpoints of $(c-R, c+R)$ may result in an interval of convergence that differs from that of the original power series.

Sample

Find a Maclaurin series for $\cos x$.

Using the Maclaurin series for $\sin x$, we can differentiate to find the Maclaurin series for $\cos x$.

$$\sin x = x - \frac{x^3}{3!} + \frac{x^5}{5!} - \frac{x^7}{7!} + \ldots = \sum\limits_{n=0}^{\infty} \frac{(-1)^n x^{2n+1}}{(2n+1)!}$$

$$\cos x = 1 - 3\cdot\frac{x^3}{3!} + 5\cdot\frac{x^5}{5!} - 7\cdot\frac{x^6}{7!} + \ldots = \sum\limits_{n=0}^{\infty} \frac{(-1)^n \cdot (2n+1) x^{2n}}{(2n+1)!}$$

$$= 1 - \frac{x^2}{2!} + \frac{x^4}{4!} - \frac{x^6}{6!} + \ldots = \sum\limits_{n=0}^{\infty} \frac{(-1)^n x^{2n}}{(2n)!}$$

The interval of convergence will also be $(-\infty, \infty)$

Sample

Find the nth degree Taylor polynomial centered at 1 for the function $f(x) = \frac{1}{x}$.

$$f(x) = \frac{1}{x} \to f(1) = 1$$

$$f'(x) = \frac{-1}{x^2} \to f'(1) = -1$$

$$f''(x) = \frac{2}{x^3} \to f''(1) = 2$$

$$f'''(x) = \frac{-6}{x^4} \to f'''(1) = -6$$

$$f^{(4)}(x) = \frac{24}{x^5} \to f^{(4)}(1) = 24$$

Then, the nth degree Taylor polynomial is:

$$P_n(x) = f(1) + \frac{f'(1)(x-1)}{1} + \frac{f''(1)(x-1)^2}{2!} + \frac{f'''(1)(x-1)^3}{3!}$$

$$+ \frac{f^{(4)}(1)(x-1)^4}{4!} + \dots + \frac{f^{(n)}(1)(x-1)^n}{n!}$$

$$= 1 + -1(x-1) + \frac{2(x-1)^2}{2} + \frac{-6(x-1)^3}{6} + \frac{24(x-1)^4}{24} + \dots + \frac{(-1)^n n!(x-1)^n}{n!}$$

$$P_n(x) = 1 - (x-1) + (x-1)^2 - (x-1)^3 + (x-1)^4 + \dots + (-1)^n (x-1)^n$$

Sample

Find the interval of convergence for the power series for $f(x) = \frac{1}{x}$ derived in previous example.

$$\frac{1}{x} = P_n(x) = \sum_{n=0}^{\infty} (-1)^n (x-1)^n$$

With $a_n = (-1)^n (x-1)^n$

$$\lim_{n \to \infty} \left| \frac{a_{n+1}}{a_n} \right| = \lim_{n \to \infty} \left| \frac{(-1)^{n+1}(x-1)^{n+1}}{(-1)^n (x-1)^n} \right| = \lim_{n \to \infty} |x-1|$$

If this limit < 1, the series will converge. Therefore,

$$|x-1| < 1$$

$$-1 < x-1 < 1$$

$$0 < x < 2$$

Check for convergence at the endpoints:

1. if $x = 0$, series is $\sum_{n=0}^{\infty} (-1)^n (-1)^n = \sum_{n=0}^{\infty} (1)^n = \sum_{n=0}^{\infty} 1$

   this series diverges; so exclude $x = 0$.

2. if $x = 2$ series is $\sum_{n=0}^{\infty} (-1)^n (1)^n = \sum_{n=0}^{\infty} (-1)^n$ this series

   diverges; so exclude $x = 2$. therefore the interval at convergence is (0, 2).

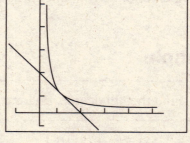

$f(x) = \frac{1}{x}$

$P_1(x) = 1 - (x-1)$

Sample

Write the first, second, third, and fourth degree Taylor polynomials for $f(x) = \frac{1}{x}$ centered at 1.

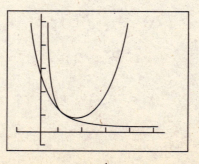

$f(x) = \frac{1}{x}$

$P_2(x) = 1 - (x-1) + (x-1)^2$

From the results of the work in previous examples,

$$P_1(x) = 1 - (x - 1)$$

$$P_2(x) = 1 - (x - 1) + (x - 1)^2$$

$$P_3(x) = 1 - (x - 1) + (x - 1)^2 + (x - 1)^3$$

and

$$P_4(x) = 1 - (x - 1) + (x - 1)^2 + (x - 1)^3 + (x - 1)^4$$

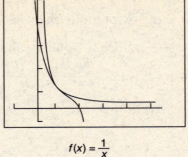

$$f(x) = \frac{1}{x}$$

$$P_3(x) = 1 - (x-1) + (x-1)^2 - (x-1)^3$$

The graphs at $f(x) = \frac{1}{x}$ and $P_1(x)$ through $P_4(x)$ are shown at the right and on the previous page.

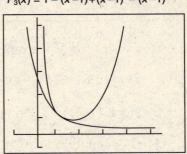

$$f(x) = \frac{1}{x}$$

$$P_4(x) = 1 - (x-1) + (x-1)^2 - (x-1)^3 + (x-1)^4$$

Note that as n increases from 1 to 4, the graph of $P_n(x)$ becomes a better and better approximation to the graph of $f(x) = \frac{1}{x}$ within the interval at convergence, $0 < x < 2$.

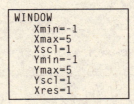

```
WINDOW
  Xmin=-1
  Xmax=5
  Xscl=1
  Ymin=-1
  Ymax=5
  Yscl=1
  Xres=1
```

Sample

Find the power series for $f(x) = \ln x$.

Since $\int \frac{1}{x}\, dx = \ln x + C$ (for $x \geq 1$) we can integrate the power series for $\frac{1}{x}$ to obtain the power series for $\ln x$. The Taylor series for $\frac{1}{x}$ centered at 1 was found to be:

$$\frac{1}{x} = 1 - (x - 1) + (x - 1)^2 - (x - 1)^3 + (x - 1)^4 + \ldots + (-1)^n (x - 1)^n$$

Integrating term by term, we obtain the series:

$$\ln x = (x - 1) - \frac{(x - 1)^2}{2} + \frac{(x - 1)^3}{3} + \frac{(x - 1)^4}{4} + \frac{(x - 1)^5}{5} + \ldots + \frac{(-1)^n (x - 1)^{n + 1}}{n + 1} + \ldots$$

Note that since we want powers of $(x-1)$, the first term should be $x-1$, since its derivative would be 1, the first term in the power series for $\frac{1}{x}$. Also, we can write the "last" term as $\frac{(-1)^{n-1}(x-1)^n}{n}$ since it would be the term before the last one integrated. Therefore, a power series for $\ln x$ is: $\ln x = \sum_{n=1}^{\infty} \frac{(-1)^{n-1}(x-1)^n}{n}$.

Sample

Find the power series for $f(x) = \dfrac{1}{1+x}$.

Using the power series for $\frac{1}{x}$, we replace each x with $1+x$ to obtain the desired series:

$$\frac{1}{x} = 1 - (x-1) + (x-1)^2 - (x-1)^3 + (x-1)^4 + \ldots + (-1)^n (x-1)^n + \ldots$$

$$\frac{1}{1+x} = 1 - ((x+1)-1) + ((x+1)-1)^2 - ((x+1)-1)^3 + ((x+1)-1)^4 + \ldots$$

$$+ (-1)^n ((x+1)-1)^n + \ldots$$

$$= 1 - x + x^2 - x^3 + x^4 + \ldots + (-1)^n x^n + \ldots$$

Sample

Find the power series for $f(x) = \dfrac{1}{(1+x)^2}$.

Since $\frac{d}{dx}\left(\frac{1}{1+x}\right) = \frac{d}{dx}\left((1+x)^{-1}\right) = -1(1+x^2)^{-2} = \frac{-1}{(1+x)^2}$, we can differentiate the power series for $\frac{1}{1+x}$ to obtain a power series for $\frac{1}{(1+x)^2}$.

$$\frac{1}{1+x} = 1 - x + x^2 - x^3 + x^4 + \ldots + (-1)^n x^n + \ldots$$

differentiating all terms yields:

$$\frac{-1}{(1+x)^2} = -1 + 2x - 3x^2 + 4x^3 + \ldots + (-1)^n n x^{n-1} + \ldots$$

multiplying both sides of equation by -1, we get

$$\frac{1}{(1+x)^2} = 1 - 2x + 3x^2 - 4x^3 + \ldots (-1)^{n+1} n x^{n-1} + \ldots$$

Therefore: $\dfrac{1}{(1+x)^2} = \sum_{n=1}^{\infty} (-1)^{n+1} n x^{n+1}$

Sample

Find the power series for $f(x) = \cos(x^2)$.

Using the power series for $\cos x$, we replace each x with x^2.

$$\cos x = 1 - \frac{x^2}{2!} + \frac{x^4}{4!} - \frac{x^6}{6!} + \frac{x^8}{8!} + \dots + \sum_{n=0}^{\infty} \frac{(-1)^n x^{2n}}{(2n)!} + \dots$$

$$\cos(x^2) = 1 - \frac{(x^2)^2}{2!} + \frac{(x^2)^4}{4!} - \frac{(x^2)^6}{6!} + \frac{(x^2)^8}{8!} + \dots + \sum_{n=0}^{\infty} \frac{(-1)^n (x^2)^{2n}}{(2n)!} + \dots$$

$$= 1 - \frac{x^4}{2!} + \frac{x^8}{4!} - \frac{x^{12}}{6!} + \frac{x^{16}}{8!} + \dots + \sum_{n=0}^{\infty} \frac{(-1)^n x^{4n}}{(2n)!} + \dots$$

Therefore, $\cos(x^2) = \sum_{n=0}^{\infty} \frac{(-1)^n x^{4n}}{(2n)!}$

Sample

Find the power series for $f(x) = \dfrac{\sin x}{x}$.

$$\sin x = x - \frac{x^3}{3!} + \frac{x^5}{5!} - \frac{x^7}{7!} + \frac{x^9}{9!} + \dots + \sum_{n=0}^{\infty} \frac{(-1)^n x^{2n+1}}{(2n+1)!} + \dots$$

multiplying each term of the above equation by $\frac{1}{x}$, we obtain:

$$\frac{1}{x}(\sin x) = \frac{1}{x}(x - \frac{x^3}{3!} + \frac{x^5}{5!} - \frac{x^7}{7!} + \frac{x^9}{9!} + \dots + \sum_{n=0}^{\infty} \frac{(-1)^n x^{2n+1}}{(2n+1)!} + \dots)$$

$$\frac{\sin x}{x} = 1 - \frac{x^2}{3!} + \frac{x^4}{5!} - \frac{x^6}{6!} + \frac{x^8}{9!} + \dots + \sum_{n=0}^{\infty} \frac{(-1)^n x^{2n}}{(2n+1)!} + \dots$$

Therefore, a power series for $\dfrac{\sin x}{x}$ is: $\dfrac{\sin x}{x} = \sum_{n=0}^{\infty} \frac{(-1)^n x^{2n}}{(2n+1)!}$

Sample

For the power series defined by $f(x) = \sum_{n=1}^{\infty} \frac{(x-2)^n}{n}$, find the interval of convergence for

a) $f(x)$

b) $f'(x)$

c) $\displaystyle\int f(x)\,dx$

a) $f(x) = \displaystyle\sum_{n=1}^{\infty} \frac{(x-2)^n}{n}$

$$\lim_{n \to \infty} \left| \frac{a_{n+1}}{a_n} \right| = \lim_{n \to \infty} \left| \frac{(x-2)^{n+1}}{n+1} \cdot \frac{n}{(x-2)^n} \right| = \lim_{n \to \infty} \left| (x-2) \cdot \frac{n}{n+1} \right| = |x-2| \cdot 1 = |x-2|$$

Series converges when $|x-2| < 1 \Rightarrow -1 < x < 1 \Rightarrow 1 < x < 3$

At endpoints:

i) $x = 1$ series $\displaystyle\sum_{n=1}^{\infty} \frac{(-1)^n}{n}$ converges by alternating series test, so include $x = 1$.

ii) $x = 3$ series $\displaystyle\sum_{n=1}^{\infty} \frac{(1)^n}{n} = \sum_{n=1}^{\infty} \frac{1}{n}$ divergent harmonic series, so exclude $x = 3$. Therefore, interval of convergence is $[1, 3)$ for $f(x)$.

b) $f'(x) = \displaystyle\sum_{n=1}^{\infty} \frac{n(x-2)^{n-1}}{n}$

$$\lim_{n \to \infty} \left| \frac{a_{n+1}}{a_n} \right| = \lim_{n \to \infty} \left| \frac{(n+1)(x-2)^n}{(n+1)} \cdot \frac{n}{n(x-2)^{n-1}} \right| = \lim_{n \to \infty} \left| (x-2) \cdot \frac{n}{n+1} \right| = |x-2| \cdot 1 = |x-2|$$

Series converges when $|x-2| < 1 \Rightarrow 1 < x < 3$

Check endpoints:

i) $x = 1$ series is $\displaystyle\sum_{n=1}^{\infty} \frac{n(-1)^{n-1}}{n} = \sum_{n=1}^{\infty} (-1)^{n-1}$ diverges so exclude $x = 1$.

ii) $x = 3$ series is $\displaystyle\sum_{n=1}^{\infty} \frac{n(1)^{n-1}}{n} = \sum_{n=1}^{\infty} (1)^{n-1}$ diverges so exclude $x = 1$.

Therefore, interval of convergence is $(1, 3)$ for $f'(x)$.

c) $\displaystyle\int f(x)\,dx = \sum_{n=1}^{\infty} \frac{(x-2)^{n+1}}{n(n+1)}$

$$\lim_{n \to \infty} \left| \frac{a_{n+1}}{a_n} \right| = \lim_{n \to \infty} \left| \frac{(x-2)^{n+2}}{(n+1)(n+2)} \cdot \frac{n(n+1)}{(x-2)^{n+1}} \right| = \lim_{n \to \infty} \left| (x-2) \cdot \frac{n}{n+2} \right| = |x-2| \cdot 1 = |x-2|$$

Series converges when $|x-2| < 1 \Rightarrow 1 < x < 3$

Check for convergence at endpoints:

i) $x = 1$ series is $\displaystyle\sum_{n=1}^{\infty} \frac{(-1)^{n+1}}{n(n+1)}$ converges by alternating series test so include $x = 1$.

ii) $x = 3$ series is $\displaystyle\sum_{n=1}^{\infty} \frac{(1)^{n+1}}{n(n+1)} = \sum_{n=1}^{\infty} \frac{1}{n^2 + n}$ converges when compared to convergent p-series $\displaystyle\sum_{n=1}^{\infty} \frac{1}{n^2}$ so include $x = 3$.

Therefore interval of convergence is $[1, 3]$ for $\displaystyle\int f(x)\,dx$.

Lagrange Form of the Remainder of a Taylor Polynomial

If an nth degree Taylor polynomial, $P_n(x)$, is used to approximate a functional value $f(x)$, there is some error resulting from the approximation. If we call this error the **remainder** $R_n(x)$, then it follows that $f(x) = P_n(x) + R_n(x)$; in other words, the actual functional value $f(x)$ is equal to the sum of the approximate value $P_n(x)$ and the remainder $R_n(x)$. Since $f(x) = P_n(x) + R_n(x)$, then $R_n(x) = f(x) - P_n(x)$. The absolute value of the remainder $R_n(x)$ is called the **error** resulting from the approximation, i.e., error $= |R_n(x)|$. Because $R_n(x)$ is the difference between $f(x)$ and $P_n(x)$, it follows that $P_n(x)$ will approach $f(x)$ as n approaches infinity only when $R_n(x)$ approaches 0 as n approaches infinity. Taylor's Theorem stated below gives us a method of determining the error resulting from our approximation.

Taylor's Theorem

Let f be a function that is differentiable through order $n + 1$ on the closed interval $[a, b]$ containing the number c. Then for each x in the interval $[a, b]$, there exists a number z between x and c such that:

$$f(x) = f(c) + f'(c) \cdot (x - c) + \frac{f''(c) \cdot (x - c)^2}{2!} + \frac{f'''(c) \cdot (x - c)^3}{3!} + \ldots + \frac{f^{(n)}(c) \cdot (x - c)^n}{n!} + R_n(x),$$

where $R_n(x) = \dfrac{f^{(n+1)}(z) \cdot (x - c)^{n+1}}{(n+1)!}$.

The number $R_n(x)$ is called the **Lagrange form of the remainder.**

Sample

> a) Use the fifth degree Maclaurin polynomial to approximate $\sin(0.4)$.
>
> b) Determine the accuracy of the approximation.

a) For $\sin x = x - \dfrac{x^3}{3!} + \dfrac{x^5}{5!} - \dfrac{x^7}{7!} + \ldots + (-1)^{n-1} \dfrac{x^{2n-1}}{(2n-1)!} + \ldots$

The fifth degree Maclaurin polynomial is

$$P_5(x) = x - \frac{x^3}{3!} + \frac{x^5}{5!} = x - \frac{x^3}{6} + \frac{x^5}{120}$$

Therefore $f(0.4) \approx P_5(0.4) = (0.4) - \dfrac{(0.4)^3}{3!} + \dfrac{(0.4)^5}{5!} = .378752$

b) Using the Legrange form of the remainder, $R_5(0.4) = \dfrac{f^{(6)}(z)(0.4)^6}{6!}$ where z is between 0 and 0.4. Since $f^{(6)}(x) = -\sin x$ for $f(x) = \sin x$ and since $|-\sin(z)| < 1$, we have:

$|R_5(0.4)| = \left| \dfrac{(-\sin(z))(0.4)^6}{6!} \right| < .000006 < .00001$. Thus when $P_5(0.4)$ is used to approximate $\sin(0.4)$, the value obtained is accurate to five decimal places, so we should adjust our approximation in part a) and write it as .37875.

Sample

> a) Determine the degree of the Maclaurin polynomial that should be used to approximate $\sqrt[3]{e}$ to four decimal places.
>
> b) Use this Maclaurin polynomial to estimate $\sqrt[3]{e}$ to four decimal places.

With $f(x) = e^x$, the nth degree Maclaurin polynomial is given by $P_n(x) = 1 + x + \dfrac{x^2}{2!} + \dfrac{x^3}{3!} + \ldots + \dfrac{x^n}{n!}$.

The Lagrange form of the remainder with $x = \dfrac{1}{3} \left(\sqrt[3]{e} = e^{1/3} \right)$ is: $R_n\left(\dfrac{1}{3}\right) = \dfrac{f^{(n+1)}(z)\left(\dfrac{1}{3}\right)^{n+1}}{(n+1)!}$ where

$0 < z < \dfrac{1}{3}$.

Since $f^{(n)}(x) = e^x$ for all derivatives of $f(x) = e^x$, we have

$\left| R_n\left(\dfrac{1}{3}\right) \right| < \dfrac{e^{1/3}}{(n+1)!} \left(\dfrac{1}{3}\right)^{n+1}$

$\left| R_n\left(\dfrac{1}{3}\right) \right| < \dfrac{e^{1/3}}{(n+1)! \, 3^{n+1}}$

but since $e < 27$, $e^{1/3} < 3$ and we have:

$\left| R_n\left(\dfrac{1}{3}\right) \right| < \dfrac{3}{(n+1)! \, 3^{n+1}}$

$\left| R_n\left(\dfrac{1}{3}\right) \right| < \dfrac{3}{(n+1)! \, 3^n}$

We are seeking $\sqrt[3]{e}$ with four decimal accuracy, so we need $\left| R_n\left(\frac{1}{3}\right) \right|$ to be less than 0.00005.

Thus $\left| R_n\left(\frac{1}{3}\right) \right| < .00005$ when $\frac{1}{(n+1)!\,3^n} < .00005$

By trial and error, this is true when $n = 5$. Since $\frac{1}{(5+1)!\,3^5} = \frac{1}{174960} \approx .000006$

Because .000006 is less than .00005, we use $P_5\left(\frac{1}{3}\right)$ as an approximate value of $\sqrt[3]{e}$ accurate to 4 decimal places.

b) Then $P_5(x) = 1 + x + \frac{x^2}{2!} + \frac{x^3}{3!} + \frac{x^4}{4!} + \frac{x^5}{x!}$ and

$$P_5\left(\frac{1}{3}\right) = 1 + \left(\frac{1}{3}\right) + \frac{\left(\frac{1}{3}\right)^2}{2!} + \frac{\left(\frac{1}{3}\right)^3}{3!} + \frac{\left(\frac{1}{3}\right)^4}{4!} + \frac{\left(\frac{1}{3}\right)^5}{5!} = \frac{5087}{3645} \approx 1.39561$$

So, $\sqrt[3]{e} \approx 1.3956$ accurate to 4 decimal places.

Power Series for Some Common Functions

Function	Power Series	Interval of Convergence
$1/x$	$= \sum_{n=0}^{\infty} (-1)^n (x-1)^n = 1 - (x-1) + (x-1)^2 - (x-1)^3 + (x-1)^4 + \ldots$	$(0, 2)$
$\dfrac{1}{(1+x)}$	$= \sum_{n=0}^{\infty} (-1)^n x^n = 1 - x + x^2 - x^3 + x^4 - x^5 \ldots$	$(-1, 1)$
$\ln x$	$= \sum_{n=0}^{\infty} \dfrac{(-1)^n (x-1)^{n+1}}{n+1} = (x-1) - \dfrac{(x-1)^2}{2} + \dfrac{(x-1)^3}{3} - \dfrac{(x-1)^4}{4} + \ldots$	$(0, 2]$
e^x	$= \sum_{n=0}^{\infty} \dfrac{x^n}{n!} = 1 + x + \dfrac{x^2}{2!} + \dfrac{x^3}{3!} + \dfrac{x^4}{4!} + \dfrac{x^5}{5!} + \ldots$	$(-\infty, \infty)$
$\sin x$	$= \sum_{n=0}^{\infty} \dfrac{(-1)^n x^{2n+1}}{(2n+1)!} = x - \dfrac{x^3}{3!} + \dfrac{x^5}{5!} - \dfrac{x^7}{7!} + \dfrac{x^9}{9!} + \ldots$	$(-\infty, \infty)$
$\cos x$	$= \sum_{n=0}^{\infty} \dfrac{(-1)^n x^{2n}}{(2n)!} = 1 - \dfrac{x^2}{2!} + \dfrac{x^4}{4!} - \dfrac{x^6}{6!} + \dfrac{x^8}{8!} + \ldots$	$(-\infty, \infty)$
$\arctan x$	$= \sum_{n=0}^{\infty} \dfrac{(-1)^n x^{2n+1}}{2n+1} = x - \dfrac{x^3}{3} + \dfrac{x^5}{5} - \dfrac{x^7}{7} + \dfrac{x^9}{9} + \ldots$	$[-1, 1]$

Sample Multiple-Choice Questions: Polynomial Approximations of Functions (Taylor and Maclaurin Polynomials)

1. The nth-degree Taylor polynomial for $f(x) = e^x$, centered at 1 is

A. $e + ex + \dfrac{ex^2}{2} + \dfrac{ex^3}{6} + ... + \dfrac{ex^n}{n!}$

B. $e - ex - \dfrac{ex^2}{2} - \dfrac{ex^3}{6} + ...$
$+ \dfrac{(-1)^{n+1}ex^n}{n!}$

C. $e + e(x-1) + \dfrac{e}{2}^{(x-1)^2} - \dfrac{e}{3}^{(x-1)^3} + ...$
$+ \dfrac{e}{n}^{(x-1)^n}$

D. $e + e(x-1) + \dfrac{e}{2}^{(x-1)^2} + \dfrac{e}{6}^{(x-1)^3} + ...$
$+ \dfrac{e}{n!}^{(x-1)^n}$

E. $1 + (x-1) + \dfrac{(x-1)^2}{2} + \dfrac{(x-1)^3}{6} + ...$
$+ \dfrac{(x-1)^n}{n!}$

2. Use the fourth-degree Maclaurin polynomial for $\cos x$ to approximate $\cos(0.1)$

A. .997

B. .995

C. .993

D. .257

E. .0001

3. A power series for $\sin(x^2)$ could be

A. $1 - \dfrac{x^4}{2!} + \dfrac{x^8}{4!} - \dfrac{x^{12}}{6!} + \dfrac{x^{16}}{8!} + ...$

B. $x^2 - \dfrac{x^6}{3} + \dfrac{x^{10}}{5} - \dfrac{x^{14}}{7} + \dfrac{x^{18}}{9} + ...$

C. $x^2 - \dfrac{x^6}{3!} + \dfrac{x^{10}}{5!} - \dfrac{x^{14}}{7!} + \dfrac{x^{18}}{9!} + ...$

D. $x^2 + \dfrac{x^6}{3!} + \dfrac{x^{10}}{5!} + \dfrac{x^{14}}{7!} + \dfrac{x^{18}}{9!} + ...$

E. $1 + x^2 + \dfrac{x^4}{2!} + \dfrac{x^6}{3!} + \dfrac{x^8}{4!} + ...$

4. A power series for $f(x) = \dfrac{1}{x}$ is
$\dfrac{1}{x} = 1 - (x-1) + (x-1)^2 - (x-1)^3 + ...$
$+ (-1)^n(x-1)^n = \sum_{n=0}^{\infty}(-1)^n (x-1)^n.$
Find a power series for $\dfrac{1}{1+x}$.

A. $\sum_{n=0}^{\infty}(-1)^{n+1}(x-1)^{n+1}$

B. $\sum_{n=0}^{\infty}(-1)^n(x)^{n+1}$

C. $\sum_{n=0}^{\infty}(-1)^{n+1}x^n$

D. $\sum_{n=0}^{\infty}(-1)^n(x-1)^{n+1}$

E. $\sum_{n=0}^{\infty}(-1)^n x^n$

5. A power series or $f(x) = \dfrac{1}{1+x^2}$ is

A. $1 - x^2 + x^4 - x^6 + x^8 + ...$

B. $1 + x^2 + x^4 + x^6 + x^8 + ...$

C. $1 + x^2 + \dfrac{x^4}{2!} + \dfrac{x^6}{3!} + \dfrac{x^8}{4!} + ...$

D. $1 - \dfrac{x^4}{2!} + \dfrac{x^8}{4!} + \dfrac{x^{12}}{6!} + \dfrac{x^{16}}{8!} ...$

E. $1 - (x^2 - 1) + (x^2 - 1)^2 - (x^2 - 1)^3$
$+ (x^2 - 1)^4 + ...$

6. The third-degree Taylor polynomial about 1 of e^{x^2} is

A. $e + 2e(x-1) + 3e(x-1)^2$
$+ \dfrac{10e(x-1)^3}{3}$

B. $e + e(x-1) + \dfrac{e(x-1)^2}{2} + \dfrac{e(x-1)^3}{6}$

C. $e(x-1) - \dfrac{e(x-1)^2}{3} + \dfrac{e(x-1)^3}{3}$

D. $1 + e(x-1) + 2e(x-1)^2$
$+ 3e(x-1)^3$

E. $e + e(x-1) + \dfrac{e(x-1)^2}{2} + \dfrac{e(x-1)^3}{3}$

7. The graph at the function represented by the Maclaurin series
$1 + x + \dfrac{x^2}{2!} + \dfrac{x^3}{3!} + \dots + \dfrac{x^n}{n!} + \dots$ intersects the graph of $y = x^2 - 1$ at the point with x-coordinate [calculator problem]

A. −4.74

B. −3.183

C. −1.293

D. −1.148

E. −.703

8. When the fourth-degree Maclaurin polynomial for e^x is used to approximate e, the value is

A. $2 + \dfrac{1}{2} - \dfrac{1}{6} + \dfrac{1}{12}$

B. $2 + \dfrac{1}{2} + \dfrac{1}{3} + \dfrac{1}{4}$

C. $2 + \dfrac{1}{2} + \dfrac{1}{6} + \dfrac{1}{12}$

D. $2 - \dfrac{1}{2} + \dfrac{1}{6} - \dfrac{1}{12}$

E. $2 - \dfrac{1}{2} + \dfrac{1}{3} - \dfrac{1}{4}$

9. Find the third-degree Taylor polynomial for $f(x) = \ln(5 - x)$, centered at 4.

A. $(x-4) - \dfrac{(x-4)^2}{2} + \dfrac{(x-4)^3}{3}$

B. $(x-4) + \dfrac{(x-4)^2}{2} + \dfrac{(x-4)^3}{3}$

C. $-(x-4) + \dfrac{(x-4)^2}{2} - \dfrac{(x-4)^3}{3}$

D. $-(x-4) - (x-4)^2 - (x-4)^3$

E. $-(x-4) - \dfrac{(x-4)^2}{2} - \dfrac{(x-4)^3}{3}$

10. The Maclaurin series for $\cos x$ is
$1 - \dfrac{x^2}{2!} + \dfrac{x^4}{4!} - \dfrac{x^6}{6!} + \dfrac{x^8}{8!} + \dots$ If g is a function such that $g(x) = \displaystyle\int \cos(x^2)\,dx$, then the coefficient of the x^9 in the Maclaurin series for $g(x)$ is

A. $\dfrac{-1}{9 \cdot 8!}$

B. $\dfrac{-1}{9 \cdot 4!}$

C. 0

D. $\dfrac{1}{9 \cdot 4!}$

E. $\dfrac{1}{9 \cdot 8!}$

Answers to Multiple-Choice Questions

1. D. $f(x) = e^x$ $f(1) = e$

$f'(x) = e^x$ $f'(1) = e$

$f''(x) = e^x$ $f''(1) = e$

$\vdots$ $\vdots$

$f^{(n)}(x) = e^x$ $f^{(n)}(1) = e^x$

Then $P_n(x) = f(1) + f'(1)(x-1) + \dfrac{f''(1)(x-1)^2}{2!} + \dfrac{f'''(1)(x-1)^3}{3!} + \ldots + \dfrac{f^n(1)(x-1)^n}{n!}$
centered at 1

$$= e + e(x-1) - \frac{e(x-1)^2}{2!} + \frac{e(x-1)^3}{3!} + \ldots + \frac{e(x-1)^n}{n!}$$

$$= e + e(x-1) - \frac{e(x-1)^2}{2} + \frac{e(x-1)^3}{6} + \ldots + \frac{e(x-1)^n}{n!}$$

2. B. $f(x) = \cos x$ $f(0) = 0$

$f'(x) = \sin x$ $f'(0) = 0$

$f''(x) = -\cos x$ $f''(0) = -1$

$f'''(x) = \sin x$ $f'''(0) = 0$

$f^{(4)}(x) = \cos x$ $f^{(4)}(0) = 1$

Then $P_4(x) = f(0) + f'(0)x + \dfrac{f''(0)x^2}{2!} + \dfrac{f'''(0)x^3}{3!} + \dfrac{f^{(4)}(0)x^4}{4!}$
centered at 0

$$= 1 + 0 \cdot x + \frac{(-1) \cdot x^2}{2} + \frac{0 \cdot x^3}{6} + \frac{1 \cdot x^4}{24}$$

$$= 1 - \frac{x^2}{2} + \frac{x^4}{24} \qquad \text{** see note below}$$

so $P_4(x) = 1 - \dfrac{x^2}{2} + \dfrac{x^4}{24}$

Then $P_4(0.1) = 1 - \dfrac{(0.1)^2}{2} + \dfrac{(0.1)^4}{24} \approx .995$

**We could have memorized the Maclaurin power series for
$\cos x = 1 - \dfrac{x^2}{2!} + \dfrac{x^4}{4!} - \dfrac{x^6}{6!} + \dfrac{x^8}{8!} + \ldots$ and used the first three terms.

3. C. Using $\sin x = x - \dfrac{x^3}{3!} + \dfrac{x^5}{5!} - \dfrac{x^7}{7!} + \dfrac{x^9}{9!} + \ldots$ and replacing each x with x^2, we obtain the series:

$$\sin(x^2) = x^2 - \frac{(x^2)^3}{3!} + \frac{(x^2)^5}{5!} - \frac{(x^2)^7}{7!} + \frac{(x^2)^9}{9!} + \ldots$$

$$= x^2 - \frac{x^6}{3!} + \frac{x^{10}}{5!} - \frac{x^{14}}{7!} + \frac{x^{18}}{9!} + \ldots$$

4. E. $\dfrac{1}{x} = 1 - (x-1) + (x-1)^2 - (x-1)^3 + \ldots + (-1)^n (x-1)^n = \displaystyle\sum_{n=0}^{\infty} (-1)^n (x-1)^n$

substituting $x+1$ for each x, we obtain:

$$\frac{1}{x+1} = 1 - ((x+1)-1) + ((x+1)-1)^2 - ((x+1)-1)^3 + \ldots$$

$$+ (-1)^n ((x+1)-1)^n = \sum_{n=0}^{\infty} (-1)^n ((x+1)-1)^n$$

so that

$$\frac{1}{x+1} = 1 - x + x + x^2 - x^3 + \ldots + (-1)^n (x^n) = \sum_{n=0}^{\infty} (-1)^n (x^n)$$

5. A. Since $\dfrac{d}{dx}(\arctan x) = \dfrac{1}{1+x^2}$, we can use the power series for arc tan x, differentiate each term, and obtain a power series for $\dfrac{1}{1+x^2}$

$$\arctan x = x - \frac{x^3}{3} + \frac{x^5}{5} - \frac{x^7}{7} + \frac{x^9}{9} + \ldots$$

$$\frac{d}{dx}(\arctan x) = 1 - \frac{3x^2}{3} + \frac{5x^4}{5} - \frac{7x^6}{7} + \frac{9x^8}{9} + \ldots = \frac{1}{1+x^2}$$

Therefore $\dfrac{1}{1+x^2} = 1 - x^2 + x^4 - x^6 + x^8 + \ldots$

Or ... Using the power series for $\dfrac{1}{1+x}$ and replacing each x with x^2:

$$\frac{1}{1+x} = 1 - x + x^2 - x^3 + x^4 + \ldots$$

$$\frac{1}{1+x^2} = 1 - x^2 + x^4 - x^5 + x^8 + \ldots$$

6. A. $\quad f(x) = e^{x^2} \ldots \qquad\qquad f(1) = e$

$\quad f'(x) = e^{x^2} \cdot 2x \ldots \qquad\quad f'(1) = e \cdot 2 = 2e$

$\quad f''(x) = (e^{x^2} \cdot 2x)\, 2x + 2 \cdot e^{x^2}$

$\qquad\quad = 4x^2 \cdot e^{x^2} + 2e^{x^2} \ldots \quad f''(1) = 4e + 2e = 6e$

$\quad f'''(x) = 8x \cdot e^{x^2} + (e^{x^2} \cdot 2x)\, 4x^2 + 2e^{x^2} + 2x$

$\qquad\quad = 8xe^{x^2} + 8x^3 e^{x^2} + 4xe^{x^2}$

$\qquad\quad = 12xe^{x^2} + 8x^3 e^{x^2} \ldots \quad f'''(1) = 12e + 8e = 20e$

$$\text{Then } P_3(x) \text{ centered at 1} \quad = f(1) + f'(1)(x-1) + \frac{f''(1)(x-1)^2}{2!} + \frac{f'''(1)(x-1)^3}{3!}$$

$$= e + 2e(x-1) + \frac{6e(x-1)^2}{2} + \frac{20e(x-1)^3}{6}$$

$$P_3(x) = e + 2e(x-1) + 3e(x-1)^2 + \frac{10e(x-1)^3}{3}$$

7. D. The Maclaurin series $1 + x + \frac{x^2}{2!} + \frac{x^3}{3!} + \dots + \frac{x^n}{n!} + \dots$ is a power series for e^x. Using a calculator, we solve the equation $e^x = x^2 - 1$ and obtain $x = -1.148$.

8. C. The fourth-degree Maclaurin polynomial for e^x is: $1 + x + \frac{x^2}{2!} + \frac{x^3}{3!} + \frac{x^4}{4!}$

$$e^1 = 1 + 1 + \frac{1}{2!} + \frac{1}{3!} + \frac{1}{4!}$$

Then
$$= 2 + \frac{1}{2} + \frac{1}{6} + \frac{1}{24}$$

9. E.
$$f(x) = 1n(5-x)\dots \qquad\qquad f(4) = |n1 = 0$$

$$f'(x) = \frac{-1}{5-x} = -1(5-x)^{-1}\dots \qquad f'(4) = \frac{-1}{1} = -1$$

$$f''(x) = 1(5-x)^{-2} \cdot -1$$

$$= -1(5-x)^{-2} = \frac{-1}{(5-x)^2}\dots \qquad f''(4) = \frac{-1}{1} = -1$$

$$f'''(x) = 2(5-x)^{-3} \cdot -1 = \frac{-2}{(5-x)^3}\dots \quad f'''(4) = \frac{-2}{1} = -2$$

$$\text{Then } P_3(x) \text{ centered at 4} \quad = f(4) + f'(4)(x-4) + \frac{f''(4)(x-4)^2}{2!} + \frac{f'''(4)(x-4)^3}{3!}$$

$$= 0 - 1(x-4) + \frac{(-1)(x-4)^2}{2} + \frac{(-2)(x-4)^3}{6}$$

$$= -(x-4) - \frac{(x-4)^2}{2} - \frac{(x-4)^3}{3}$$

10. D. The Maclaurin series for $\cos x$ is:

$$\cos x = 1 - \frac{x^2}{2!} + \frac{x^4}{4!} - \frac{x^6}{6!} + \frac{x^8}{8!} + \dots$$

Replacing each x with x^2, we obtain the Maclaurin series for

$$\cos(x^2) = 1 - \frac{x^4}{2!} + \frac{x^8}{4!} - \frac{x^{12}}{6!} + \frac{x^{16}}{8!} + \dots$$

Then integrating the Maclaurin series for $\cos(x^2)$, term by term, we get the Maclaurin series for $g(x)$:

$$g(x) = x - \frac{x^5}{5 \cdot 2!} + \frac{x^9}{9 \cdot 4!} - \frac{x^{13}}{13 \cdot 6!} + \frac{x^{17}}{17 \cdot 8!} + \dots$$

Therefore, the coefficient of x^9 is $\frac{1}{9 \cdot 4!}$

Sample Free-Response Question: Polynomial Approximation of Functions (Taylor and Maclaurin Polynomials)

1. Suppose $P(x) = -3 + 5(x-2) - 7(x-2)^2 + 6(x-2)^3$ is the third-degree Taylor polynomial for the function g about 2. Assume that g is differentiable for all orders for all real numbers.

a) Find $g(2)$

b) Find $g''2$

c) Write the fourth-degree Taylor polynomial for h, given that $h(x) = \int_2^x g(t)\,dt$ about 2

d) Write the second-degree Taylor polynomial for g' about 2

e) Use the result of part d to estimate $g'(2.1)$

Answer to Free-Response Question

a) $g(x) = -3 + 5(x-2) - 7(x-2)^2 + 5(x-2)^3$

$g(2) = -3 + 5(2-2) - 7(2-2)^2 + 6(2-2)^3$

$g(2) = -3 + 0 - 0 + 0$

$g(2) = -3$

b) $g(x) = -3 + 5(x-2) - 7(x-2)^2 + 6(x-2)^3$

$g'(x) = 5 - 14(x-2) + 18(x-2)^2$

$g''(x) = -14 + 36(x-2)$

$g''(2) = -14 + 36(0-0)$

$g''(2) = -14$

c) $h(x) = \int_2^x g(t)\,dt$

$= \int_2^x \left[-3 + 5(t-2) - 7(t-2)^2 + 6(t-2)^3 \right] dt$

$= \left[-3(t-2) + \frac{5(t-2)^2}{2} - \frac{7(t-2)^3}{3} + \frac{6(t-2)^4}{4} \right]_2^x$

$= -3(x-2) + \frac{5(x-2)^2}{2} - \frac{7(x-2)^3}{3} + \frac{3(x-2)^4}{4} - 0$

$-3(x-2) + \frac{5(x-2)^2}{2} - \frac{7(x-2)^3}{3} + \frac{3(x-2)^4}{4}$

d) $g(x) = -3 + 5(x-2) - 7(x-2)^2 + 6(x-2)^3$

$g'(x) = 5 - 14(x-2) + 18(x-2)^2$

e) from part d,

$g'(x) = 5 - 14(x-2) + 18(x-2)^2$

$g'(2.1) \approx 5 - 14(2.1-2) + 18(2.1-2)^2$

$= 5 - 14(0.1) + 18(0.1)^2$

$= 5 - 1.4 + 0.18$

$= 3.78$

PART III

AP CALCULUS AB AND BC PRACTICE TESTS

Answer Sheet for Practice Test 1 — AB

(Remove This Sheet and Use It to Mark Your Answers)

Section IA
Multiple-Choice Questions

1. Ⓐ Ⓑ Ⓒ Ⓓ Ⓔ
2. Ⓐ Ⓑ Ⓒ Ⓓ Ⓔ
3. Ⓐ Ⓑ Ⓒ Ⓓ Ⓔ
4. Ⓐ Ⓑ Ⓒ Ⓓ Ⓔ
5. Ⓐ Ⓑ Ⓒ Ⓓ Ⓔ
6. Ⓐ Ⓑ Ⓒ Ⓓ Ⓔ
7. Ⓐ Ⓑ Ⓒ Ⓓ Ⓔ
8. Ⓐ Ⓑ Ⓒ Ⓓ Ⓔ
9. Ⓐ Ⓑ Ⓒ Ⓓ Ⓔ
10. Ⓐ Ⓑ Ⓒ Ⓓ Ⓔ
11. Ⓐ Ⓑ Ⓒ Ⓓ Ⓔ
12. Ⓐ Ⓑ Ⓒ Ⓓ Ⓔ
13. Ⓐ Ⓑ Ⓒ Ⓓ Ⓔ
14. Ⓐ Ⓑ Ⓒ Ⓓ Ⓔ
15. Ⓐ Ⓑ Ⓒ Ⓓ Ⓔ
16. Ⓐ Ⓑ Ⓒ Ⓓ Ⓔ
17. Ⓐ Ⓑ Ⓒ Ⓓ Ⓔ
18. Ⓐ Ⓑ Ⓒ Ⓓ Ⓔ
19. Ⓐ Ⓑ Ⓒ Ⓓ Ⓔ
20. Ⓐ Ⓑ Ⓒ Ⓓ Ⓔ
21. Ⓐ Ⓑ Ⓒ Ⓓ Ⓔ
22. Ⓐ Ⓑ Ⓒ Ⓓ Ⓔ
23. Ⓐ Ⓑ Ⓒ Ⓓ Ⓔ
24. Ⓐ Ⓑ Ⓒ Ⓓ Ⓔ
25. Ⓐ Ⓑ Ⓒ Ⓓ Ⓔ
26. Ⓐ Ⓑ Ⓒ Ⓓ Ⓔ
27. Ⓐ Ⓑ Ⓒ Ⓓ Ⓔ
28. Ⓐ Ⓑ Ⓒ Ⓓ Ⓔ

Section IB
Multiple-Choice Questions

1. Ⓐ Ⓑ Ⓒ Ⓓ Ⓔ
2. Ⓐ Ⓑ Ⓒ Ⓓ Ⓔ
3. Ⓐ Ⓑ Ⓒ Ⓓ Ⓔ
4. Ⓐ Ⓑ Ⓒ Ⓓ Ⓔ
5. Ⓐ Ⓑ Ⓒ Ⓓ Ⓔ
6. Ⓐ Ⓑ Ⓒ Ⓓ Ⓔ
7. Ⓐ Ⓑ Ⓒ Ⓓ Ⓔ
8. Ⓐ Ⓑ Ⓒ Ⓓ Ⓔ
9. Ⓐ Ⓑ Ⓒ Ⓓ Ⓔ
10. Ⓐ Ⓑ Ⓒ Ⓓ Ⓔ
11. Ⓐ Ⓑ Ⓒ Ⓓ Ⓔ
12. Ⓐ Ⓑ Ⓒ Ⓓ Ⓔ
13. Ⓐ Ⓑ Ⓒ Ⓓ Ⓔ
14. Ⓐ Ⓑ Ⓒ Ⓓ Ⓔ
15. Ⓐ Ⓑ Ⓒ Ⓓ Ⓔ
16. Ⓐ Ⓑ Ⓒ Ⓓ Ⓔ
17. Ⓐ Ⓑ Ⓒ Ⓓ Ⓔ

Taking and Grading the Practice Exams

To use these practice exams most effectively, it is recommended that you simulate actual testing conditions as nearly as possible. You will need a quiet area where you will not be disturbed for about three and a half hours, several number two pencils, and some scratch paper. (On the actual exam, scratch paper is not allowed; the exam booklet has large amounts of blank space for you to work in.) For these practice exams, try to keep your work on your scratch paper organized so that you can look back to learn from your mistake. In between sections on the exam, take a fifteen-minute break. The exam is given at 8:00 A.M., so try taking at least one of the two tests some Saturday morning two or three weeks prior to the actual exam.

When grading the free-response questions, follow the suggested grading rubrics. Note: The AP readers will look at your work for consistency and follow through. If you miss an early part of a problem, don't assume that you have missed all the subsequent points. For example, suppose part (a) of a question requires you to find the first derivative of a given function, and part (b) requires the second derivative. If you answer part (a) incorrectly, you may still get all of the points on part (b) *if* you differentiate your part (a) answer correctly. If you aren't sure you did, give a fellow student or your AP teacher your part (a) answer to differentiate for you.

CUT HERE

Section I: Multiple-Choice Questions

Section IA

Time: 55 Minutes

28 Questions

Directions: The 28 questions that follow in Section IA of the exam should be solved using the space available for scratchwork. Select the best of the given choices and fill in the corresponding oval on the answer sheet. Material written in the test booklet will not be graded or awarded credit. Fifty-five minutes are allowed for Section IA. *No calculator of any type may be used in this section of the test.*

Notes: *(1) For this test, ln x denotes the natural logarithm of* x *(that is, logarithm of the base* e*).* *(2) The domain of all functions is assumed to be the set of real numbers* x *for which* f(x) *is a real number, unless a different domain is specified.*

1. $\ln(x+3) \geq 0$ if and only if

   A. $-3 < x < -2$

   B. $x > -2$

   C. $x \geq -2$

   D. $x > 4$

   E. $x \geq 4$

2. Which of the following is NOT symmetric with respect to the *y*-axis?

   I. $y = 2\cos x$

   II. $y = (x+2)^2$

   III. $y = \ln|x|$

   A. I only

   B. II only

   C. III only

   D. I and II only

   E. I and III only

GO ON TO THE NEXT PAGE

3. $\sin 2\theta =$

A. $\cos^2\theta - \sin^2\theta$

B. $2\sin\theta$

C. $\sin^2\theta$

D. $2\sin\theta\cos\theta$

E. $\frac{1}{2}(1 - \cos 2\theta)$

4. What is $\lim\limits_{b \to -\infty}\left(\dfrac{\sqrt{b^2+5}}{4-3b}\right)$?

A. $\dfrac{-5}{3}$

B. $\dfrac{-1}{3}$

C. $\dfrac{1}{3}$

D. 1

E. $\dfrac{5}{4}$

5. What is $\lim\limits_{x \to 2+}\left(\dfrac{3}{x-2} + x\right)$?

A. $+\infty$

B. 2

C. 0

D. $-\infty$

E. none of these

6. What is $\lim\limits_{t \to 1}\left(\dfrac{\cos(t-1)-1}{t-1}\right)$?

A. 0

B. 1

C. 2

D. 3

E. The limit does not exist.

7. What is $\lim\limits_{x \to 3^+}\left(\dfrac{5x}{5-x}\right)$?

A. $+\infty$

B. 15

C. $\dfrac{15}{2}$

D. 0

E. $-\infty$

8. $\lim\limits_{x \to 0}\left(\dfrac{x}{\sin 2x}\right) =$

A. -1

B. 0

C. $\dfrac{1}{2}$

D. 1

E. 2

9. Find a value for b such that $f(x)$ will be continuous, given that

$$f(x)\begin{cases} \dfrac{x^2-x}{x-1} & \text{for } x \neq 1 \\[2mm] b & \text{for } x = 1 \end{cases}$$

A. $b = 0$

B. $b = 1$

C. $b = 2$

D. $f(x)$ is continuous for any value of b.

E. $f(x)$ is not continuous for any value of b.

Use the following graph of f(x) for problems 10–12.

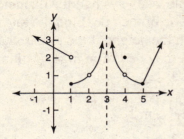

10. $f(x)$ is discontinuous for

   A. $x = 1, 3$ only

   B. $x = 1, 2, 4$ only

   C. $x = 2, 3, 4$ only

   D. $x = 1, 2, 3, 4$ only

   E. $x = 1, 2, 3, 4, 5$

11. $\lim\limits_{x \to a} f(x)$ does not exist for which of the following values of a?

   A. $a = 1, 3$ only

   B. $a = 1, 2, 4$ only

   C. $a = 2, 3, 4$ only

   D. $a = 1, 2, 3, 4$ only

   E. $a = 1, 2, 3, 4, 5$

12. $f(x)$ is NOT differentiable at

   A. $x = 1, 3$ only

   B. $x = 1, 2, 4$ only

   C. $x = 2, 3, 4$ only

   D. $x = 1, 2, 3, 4$ only

   E. $x = 1, 2, 3, 4, 5$

13. If $y = \dfrac{3}{4 + x^2}$ then $\dfrac{dy}{dx} =$

   A. $\dfrac{-6x}{\left(4 + x^2\right)^2}$

   B. $\dfrac{3x}{\left(4 + x^2\right)^2}$

   C. $\dfrac{6x}{\left(4 + x^2\right)^2}$

   D. $\dfrac{-3}{\left(4 + x^2\right)^2}$

   E. $\dfrac{3}{2x}$

14. Given that $y = x^{2x}$, find $\dfrac{dy}{dx}$.

   A. $x^{2x}\left[2 + 2\ln x\right]$

   B. $(2x)\left(x^{2x - 1}\right)$

   C. $(\ln x)\left(x^{2x}\right)$

   D. $2 + 2\ln x$

   E. $2x^{2x - 1}$

15. A particle moves along a horizontal path so its velocity at any time $t\,(t > 0)$ is given by $v(t) = t\ln t$ *ft/s*. Its acceleration is given by

   A. $a(t) = \dfrac{1}{t}$ ft/s^2

   B. $a(t) = 1 + \ln t$ ft/s^2

   C. $a(t) = t + \ln t$ ft/s^2

   D. $a(t) = \dfrac{\ln t}{t}$ ft/s^2

   E. $a(t) = \dfrac{t^2}{2}$ ft/s^2

GO ON TO THE NEXT PAGE

16. If $V = \frac{4}{3}\pi r^3$, what is $\left.\frac{dV}{dr}\right|_{r=3}$?

   A. 4π

   B. 12π

   C. 24π

   D. 36π

   E. 42π

17. The graph of $y = 3xe^{2x}$ has a relative extremum at

   A. $x = 0$ only

   B. $x = 0$ and $x = \frac{-1}{2}$

   C. $x = \frac{-1}{2}$ only

   D. $x = -2$ only

   E. The graph has no relative extrema.

18. Find the equation of the line that is normal to the curve $y = 3\tan\frac{x}{2}$ at the point where $x = \frac{\pi}{2}$.

   A. $2x + 12y = \pi + 36$

   B. $2x + 6y = 18 + \pi$

   C. $-6x + 2y = 3\pi - 6$

   D. $-2x + 6y = 18 + \pi$

   E. $6x - 2y = 3\pi - 6$

19. Find the area of the largest rectangle that has two vertices on the x-axis and two vertices on the curve $y = 9 - x^2$.

   A. $\sqrt{3}$

   B. $4\sqrt{3}$

   C. $12\sqrt{3}$

   D. $16\sqrt{3}$

   E. $24\sqrt{3}$

20. Sand is falling into a conical pile at the rate of $10\ \text{m}^3/\text{s}$ such that the height of the pile is always half the diameter of the base of the pile. Find the rate at which the height of the pile is changing when the pile is 5 m high. (Volume of a cone: $V = \frac{1}{3}\pi r^2 h$)

   A. $\frac{1}{25\pi}$ m/s

   B. $\frac{2}{5\pi}$ m/s

   C. $\frac{4}{5\pi}$ m/s

   D. $\frac{8}{5\pi}$ m/s

   E. 250π m/s

21. The antiderivative of $\frac{3}{x^2}$ is

   A. $\frac{3}{x} + C$

   B. $\frac{-6}{x^3} + C$

   C. $\frac{-3}{x} + C$

   D. $\frac{1}{x^3} + C$

   E. $\frac{-3}{x^2} + C$

22. $\int_0^\pi \cos\frac{x}{2} = dx$

   A. -2

   B. -1

   C. $-\frac{1}{2}$

   D. $\frac{1}{2}$

   E. 2

23. $\int 3^{2x}\,dx =$

A. $\dfrac{\ln 3}{2}3^{2x}+C$

B. $\dfrac{1}{2\ln 3}3^{2x}+C$

C. $(2\ln 3)3^{2x}+C$

D. $\dfrac{2}{\ln 3}3^{2x}+C$

E. $\dfrac{1}{\ln 3}3^{2x}+C$

24. $\int_0^{1/2}\dfrac{2x}{\sqrt{1-x^2}}\,dx =$

A. $1-\dfrac{\sqrt{3}}{2}$

B. $\dfrac{1}{2}\ln\dfrac{3}{4}$

C. $\sqrt{3}-2$

D. $\dfrac{\pi}{6}-1$

E. $2-\sqrt{3}$

25. $\int\dfrac{5}{\sqrt{9-4x^2}}\,dx =$

A. $\dfrac{-5}{2}\ln\left|9-4x^2\right|+C$

B. $\dfrac{-5}{8}\ln\left|9-4x^2\right|+C$

C. $\dfrac{-5}{4}\sqrt{9-4x^2}+C$

D. $\dfrac{-5}{2}\sqrt{9-4x^2}+C$

E. $\dfrac{5}{2}\arcsin\dfrac{2x}{3}+C$

26. $\int_1^{e^3}\dfrac{\ln x}{x}\,dx =$

A. 1

B. 4

C. $\dfrac{9}{2}$

D. $2e^3-1$

E. e^3-2

27. The area of the region bounded by the curve $y=e^{2x}$, the x-axis, the y-axis, and the line $x=2$ is

A. $\dfrac{e^4}{2}-e$ square units

B. $\dfrac{e^4}{1}-1$ square units

C. $\dfrac{e^4}{2}-\dfrac{1}{2}$ square units

D. $2e^4-e$ square units

E. $2e^4-2$ square units

28. The average value of $y=e^{3x}$ over the interval from $x=0$ to $x=4$ is

A. $\dfrac{e^{12}-1}{12}$

B. $\dfrac{e^{12}-1}{4}$

C. $\dfrac{e^{12}}{12}$

D. $\dfrac{e^{12}}{4}$

E. $e^{12}-1$

IF YOU FINISH BEFORE TIME IS CALLED, CHECK YOUR WORK ON THIS SECTION ONLY. DO NOT WORK ON ANY OTHER SECTION IN THE TEST.

STOP

Section IB

Time: 50 Minutes

17 Questions

Directions: The 17 questions that follow in Section IB of the exam should be solved using the space available for scratchwork. Select the best of the given choices and fill in the corresponding oval on the answer sheet. Material written in the test booklet will not be graded or awarded credit. Fifty minutes are allowed for Section IB. *A graphing calculator is required for this section of the test.*

Notes: *(1) If the exact numerical value does not appear as one of the five choices, choose the best approximation. (2) For this test, ln x denotes the natural logarithm function (that is, logarithm to the base e). (3) The domain of all functions is assumed to be the set of real numbers x for which f(x) is a real number, unless a different domain is specified.*

1. If $f(x) = |x|$, then $f'(2)$ is

   A. -2

   B. -1

   C. 1

   D. 2

   E.   nonexistent

2. If $y = 2e^6$, then $y' =$

   A. $\dfrac{2e^7}{7}$

   B. $12e^5$

   C. $2e^6$

   D. 2

   E. 0

3. The absolute maximum of $f(x) = 2x - \sin^{-1} x$ on its domain is approximately

   A.   0.523

   B.   0.571

   C.   0.685

   D.   0.866

   E.   0.923

4. Which of the following is equivalent to $\dfrac{d(\sin\theta)}{d\theta}\bigg|_{\theta = \pi/3}$?

   A. $\displaystyle\lim_{\theta \to \pi/3} \dfrac{\sin\theta - \frac{1}{2}}{\theta - \frac{\pi}{3}}$

   B. $\displaystyle\lim_{\theta \to \pi/3} \dfrac{\sin\theta - \frac{\sqrt{3}}{2}}{\theta - \frac{\pi}{3}}$

   C. $\displaystyle\lim_{\theta \to 0} \dfrac{\sin\theta - \frac{\sqrt{3}}{2}}{\theta - \frac{\pi}{3}}$

   D. $\displaystyle\lim_{h \to 0} \dfrac{\sin(\theta + h) - \sin\theta}{h}$

   E. $\displaystyle\lim_{h \to 0} \dfrac{\cos(\theta + h) - \cos\theta}{h}$

5. The function $g(x) = (\cos x)(e^x) - \frac{3}{2}$ has two real zeros between 0 and 2. If $(a, 0)$ and $(b, 0)$ represent these two zeros, then $a + b$ is approximately

   A.   2.17

   B.   2.00

   C.   1.55

   D.   0.99

   E.   0.45

6. Find the number guaranteed by the mean value theorem for the function $f(x) = e^{(1/2)x}$ on the interval [0, 2].

A. 1.083

B. 0.709

C. 0.614

D. –0.304

E. The mean value theorem cannot be applied on [0, 2].

7. Let A be the region completely bounded by $y = \ln x + 2$ and $y = 2x$. Correct to three decimal places, the area of A is approximately

A. 0.053

B. 0.162

C. 0.203

D. 1.216

E. 2.358

8. Which of the following is equivalent to
$$\lim_{n \to \infty} \sum_{i=1}^{n} \left[\left(1 + \frac{2i}{n}\right)^2 + 1\right]\left(\frac{2}{n}\right)?$$

A. $\int_2^4 (x^2 + 1)\,dx$

B. $\int_1^3 x^2\,dx$

C. $\int_1^2 (x^2 + 1)\,dx$

D. $\int_1^3 (x^2 - 1)\,dx$

E. $\int_1^3 (x^2 + 1)\,dx$

9. $\dfrac{d}{dz}\left[\int_0^z \left(e^{4x^2}\right)dx\right] =$

A. $e^{4x^2} + C$

B. $\dfrac{e^{4x^2}}{8x} + C$

C. $e^{4z^2} - 1$

D. e^{4z^2}

E. $\dfrac{e^{4z^2}}{8z} + C$

10. Approximate the slope of the line tangent to the graph of $f(x) = 4x \ln x$ at the point where $x = 2.1$.

A. 4.93

B. 5.07

C. 6.23

D. 6.97

E. 7.27

11. If $\dfrac{dy}{dt} = \pi y$, which of the following could represent y?

A. $\dfrac{1}{\pi}e^t$

B. $\pi e^{x/t}$

C. $e^{\pi t} + \pi$

D. πe^t

E. $\pi e^{\pi t}$

12. If $f(x) = \dfrac{x^3}{\sqrt[3]{x}}$, then $f'(x) =$

A. $\dfrac{8}{3} x \sqrt[3]{x^2}$

B. $\dfrac{3}{11} x \sqrt[3]{x^2}$

C. $\dfrac{8}{3} x^2 \sqrt[3]{x^2}$

D. $3x^3$

E. $\dfrac{10}{3} x \sqrt[3]{x^2}$

GO ON TO THE NEXT PAGE

13. Let A be the area bounded by one arch of the sine curve. Which of the following represents the volume of the solid generated when A is revolved around the x-axis?

   A. $2\pi \int_0^\pi x \sin x \, dx$

   B. $\pi \int_0^\pi \sin^2 x \, dx$

   C. $\pi \int_0^\pi x \sin x \, dx$

   D. $\pi \int_0^{2\pi} \sin^2 x \, dx$

   E. $2\pi \int_0^1 \arcsin y \, dy$

14. $\displaystyle \lim_{h \to 0} \frac{\sin(1+h) - \sin 1}{h}$ is approximately

   A.   0

   B.   0.54

   C.   0.63

   D.   0.89

   E.   none of these

15. The fundamental period of $y = \sin 3x + \cos 2x$ is

   A. π

   B. $\dfrac{2\pi}{3}$

   C. $\dfrac{4\pi}{3}$

   D. $\dfrac{5\pi}{3}$

   E. 2π

16. Approximate the value of $\displaystyle \int_1^3 \ln x \, dx$ using 4 circumscribed rectangles.

   A.   1.007

   B.   1.296

   C.   1.557

   D.   2.015

   E.   3.114

17. $\displaystyle \int \sin x \cos^2 x \, dx =$

   A. $-\dfrac{2}{3} \cos^3 x + C$

   B. $-\dfrac{1}{2} \sin^2 x + C$

   C. $\dfrac{1}{2} \sin^2 x + C$

   D. $\dfrac{1}{3} \cos^3 x + C$

   E. $-\dfrac{1}{3} \cos^3 x + C$

IF YOU FINISH BEFORE TIME IS CALLED, CHECK YOUR WORK ON THIS SECTION ONLY. DO NOT WORK ON ANY OTHER SECTION IN THE TEST.

STOP

Section II: Free-Response Questions

Section IIA

Time: 45 Minutes

3 Questions

Directions: For the three problems that follow in Section IIA, show all your work. Your grade will be determined on the correctness of your method, as well as the accuracy of your final answers. Some questions in this section may require the use of a graphing calculator. If you choose to give decimal approximations, your answer should be correct to three decimal places, unless a particular question specifies otherwise. During Section IIB, you will be allowed to return to Section IIA to continue your work on questions 1–3, but you will NOT be allowed the use of a calculator.

Notes: *(1) For this test, ln* x *denotes the natural logarithm function (that is, logarithm to the base* e*). (2) The domain of all functions is assumed to be the set of real numbers* x *for which* f(x) *is a real number, unless a different domain is specified.*

1. Let area A be the region bounded by $y = 2^x - 1$, $y = -2x + 3$, and the y-axis.

   (a) Find an exact value for the area of region A.

   (b) Set up, but do NOT integrate, an integral expression in terms of a single variable for the volume of the solid generated when A is revolved around the x-axis.

   (c) Set up an integral expression in terms of a single variable for the volume of the solid generated when A is revolved around the y-axis. Find an approximation for this volume correct to the nearest hundredth.

2. Let f be the function defined by

   $$f(x) = e^{4 - 2x^2} - 8.$$

   (a) Approximate any zeros of $f(x)$ to the three decimal places.

   (b) What is the range of $f(x)$? Give an exact answer. Justify your answer.

   (c) Find the equation of the line normal to the graph of $f(x)$ where $x = 1$. Justify your answer.

3. A particle moves along a horizontal line so that its velocity at any time $t\left(-\dfrac{\pi}{6} < t < \dfrac{\pi}{6}\right)$ is given by $(t) = \dfrac{1}{3} \tan(3t) + 2$ m/s. At time $t = 0$, the particle is 3 m to the left of the origin.

   (a) Approximate the acceleration of the particle when the particle is at rest.

   (b) Write an equation for the position, $s(t)$, of the particle.

IF YOU FINISH BEFORE TIME IS CALLED, CHECK YOUR WORK ON THIS SECTION ONLY. DO NOT WORK ON ANY OTHER SECTION IN THE TEST.

STOP

Section IIB

Time: 45 Minutes

3 Questions

Directions: For the three problems that follow in Section IIB, show all your work. Your grade will be determined on the correctness of your method, as well as the accuracy of your final answers. During Section IIB, you will be NOT be allowed the use of a calculator. During this section, you will also be allowed to return to questions 1–3 in Section IIA to continue working on those problems, but you will NOT have the use of a calculator.

4. A box in the shape of a rectangular prism has a square bottom and is open on top. The material for the sides of the box costs $18 per square foot. Find the dimensions of the largest box (by volume) that can be made for $360. Justify your answer.

5. Let f be the function defined by
$$f(x) = 3x^2 - 4 - \frac{x^3}{2}.$$

   (a) Find the exact x-coordinates of any point where $f(x)$ has a tangent line that is parallel to the line $y = -9x - 8$.

   (b) Find all points of inflection of $f(x)$. Justify your answer.

6. The function $f(x)$ is continuous on a domain of $[-4, 4]$ and is symmetric with respect to the origin. The first and second derivatives of $f(x)$ have the properties shown in the following chart.

x	$0 < x < 1$	$x = 1$	$1 < x < 3$	$x = 3$	$3 < x < 4$
$f'(x)$	positive	D.N.E.*	negative	0	negative
$f''(x)$	positive	D.N.E.*	negative	0	negative

*D.N.E. means "does not exist"

   (a) Find the x-coordinates of *all* relative extrema on the domain $[-4, 4]$. Classify them as relative maximums or relative minimums. Justify your answer.

   (b) Find the x-coordinates of any points of inflection on the domain $[-4, 4]$. Justify your answer.

   (c) Sketch a possible graph of $f(x)$, given that $f(0) = 0$ and $f(4) = -2$.

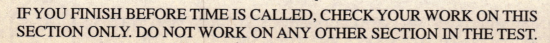

IF YOU FINISH BEFORE TIME IS CALLED, CHECK YOUR WORK ON THIS SECTION ONLY. DO NOT WORK ON ANY OTHER SECTION IN THE TEST. STOP

Practice Test 1 — AB

Answer Key for Practice Test 1 — AB

Section I: Multiple-Choice Questions

Section IA

1. C	8. C	15. B	22. E
2. B	9. B	16. D	23. B
3. D	10. D	17. C	24. E
4. C	11. A	18. B	25. E
5. A	12. E	19. C	26. C
6. A	13. A	20. B	27. C
7. C	14. A	21. C	28. A

Section IB

1. C	6. A	10. D	14. B
2. E	7. B	11. E	15. E
3. C	8. E	12. A	16. C
4. B	9. D	13. B	17. E
5. C			

Unanswered problems are neither right nor wrong, and are not entered into the scoring formula.

Number right   =   _____

Number wrong   =   _____

Section II: Free-Response Questions

Use the grading rubrics beginning on page 424 to score your free-response answers. Write your scores in the blanks provided on the scoring worksheet.

Practice Test 1 Scoring Worksheet

Section IA and IB: Multiple-Choice

Of the 45 total questions, count only the number correct and the number wrong. Unanswered problems are not entered in the formula.

_____ – (1/4 × _____) = _____
number correct   number wrong   Multiple-Choice
                                                              Score

Section II: Free-Response

Each of the six questions has a possible score of 9 points. Total all six scores.

Question 1 _____
Question 2 _____
Question 3 _____
Question 4 _____
Question 5 _____
Question 6 _____

TOTAL _____
Free-Response Score

Composite Score

1.20 × _____ = _____
Multiple-Choice Score   Converted Section I
                                       Score (do not round)

1.00 × _____ = _____
Free-Response Score   Converted Section II
                                       Score (do not round)

TOTAL = _____
of converted scores   round to the nearest
                              whole number

Probable AP Grade

Composite Score Range	AP Grade
65–108	5
55–64	4
42–54	3
0–41	1 or 2

Please note that the scoring range above is an approximation only. Each year, the chief faculty consultants are responsible for converting the final total raw scores to the 5-point AP scale. Future grading scales may differ markedly from the one listed above.

Answers and Explanations for Practice Test 1 — AB

Section I: Multiple-Choice Questions

Section IA

1. **C.** Realize that $\ln(x + 3)$ is a shift of 3 to the left of $\ln(x)$ and so has a vertical asymptote at $x = -3$ and a zero at $(-2, 0)$. Thus $\ln(x + 3) \geq 0$ if $x \geq -2$.

2. **B.** For symmetry with respect to the y-axis, $f(-x) = f(x)$.

   For I: $f(-x) = 2\cos(-x) = 2\cos x = f(x)$

   $\Rightarrow$ symmetric with respect to y-axis

   For II: $f(-x) = (-x + 2)^2 \neq f(x)$

   $\Rightarrow$ not symmetric with respect to y-axis

   For III: $f(-x) = \ln|-x| = \ln|x| = |f(x)$

   $\Rightarrow$ symmetric with respect to y-axis

3. **D.** $\sin 2\theta = 2\sin\theta\cos\theta$

4. C. $\displaystyle\lim_{b \to -\infty}\left(\frac{\sqrt{b^2+5}}{4-3b}\right)=\lim_{b \to -\infty}\left(\frac{\sqrt{b^2+5}}{4-3b}\right)\left(\frac{\frac{1}{\sqrt{b^2}}}{\frac{1}{\sqrt{b^2}}}\right)$

Because $b \to -\infty$, $b < 0$, so $\sqrt{b^2} = -b$

$$=\lim_{b \to -\infty}\left(\frac{\sqrt{1+\frac{5}{b^2}}}{(4-3b)\left(\frac{1}{-b}\right)}\right)$$

$$=\lim_{b \to -\infty}\left(\frac{\sqrt{1+\frac{5}{b^2}}}{\left(\frac{4}{-b}\right)+3}\right)=\frac{1}{3}$$

5. A. $\displaystyle\lim_{x \to 2^+}\left(\frac{3}{x-2}+x\right)=\lim_{x \to 2^+}\left(\frac{3+x(x-2)}{x-2}\right)$

$$=\lim_{x \to 2^+}\left(\frac{x^2-2x+3}{x-2}\right)=\left(\frac{3}{0+}\right)=+\infty$$

6. A. The function $y=\dfrac{\cos(t-1)-1}{t-1}$ is a shift of 1 to the right of $\dfrac{\cos t-1}{t}$. By the special trig limit,

$$\lim_{t \to 0}\left(\frac{\cos t-1}{t}\right)=0$$

$$\lim_{t \to 1}\left(\frac{\cos(t-1)-1}{t-1}\right)=0$$

Alternatively, L'Hôpital's rule may be applied:

$$\lim_{t \to 1}\left(\frac{\cos(t-1)-1}{t-1}\right)=\lim_{t \to 1}\frac{-\sin(t-1)}{1}=0$$

7. C. The only point of discontinuity in the function is at $x=5$, and the limit is being taken as x approaches 3, so just substitute.

$$\lim_{x \to 3+}\left(\frac{5x}{5-x}\right)=\frac{5(3)}{5-3}=\frac{15}{2}$$

8. C. $\displaystyle\lim_{x \to 0}\left(\frac{x}{\sin 2x}\right)=\lim_{x \to 0}\left(\frac{1}{2}\cdot\frac{2x}{\sin 2x}\right)$

$$=\lim_{x \to 0}\left(\frac{1}{2}\cdot\frac{1}{\frac{\sin 2x}{2x}}\right)$$

$$=\frac{1}{2}\cdot\frac{1}{1}=\frac{1}{2}$$

9. B. Simplify $f(x)$ first.

$$f(x)\begin{cases} \dfrac{x(x-1)}{x-1} & = \text{for } x \neq 1 \\ & \quad \text{for } x = 1 \\ b \end{cases}$$

For $f(x)$ to be continuous at $x = 1$,

$$\lim_{x \to 1} f(x) = f(1) \Rightarrow 1 = b$$

10. D. Because this is a multiple-choice problem, discontinuities can be found by just tracing the curve and looking for any points where you must pick up your pencil.

11. A. For $a = 1$, the one-sided limits are not equal, so the limit does not exist. For $a = 3$, the limit is positive infinity, $\lim_{x \to 3} f(x) = +\infty$, which also means that the limit does not exist. For $a = 2, 4,$ and 5, the limits are $1, 1,$ and $1/2$, respectively.

12. E. A function cannot be differentiable at any point of discontinuity, so $f(x)$ is not differentiable at $x = 1, 2, 3,$ or 4. In addition, at $x = 5$ there is a sharp turn, which means that the left-hand and right-hand derivatives are not equal, so $f(x)$ is also not differentiable at $x = 5$.

13. A. $y = \dfrac{3}{4 + x^2} \Rightarrow \dfrac{dy}{dx} = \dfrac{(4 + x^2)(0) - 3(2x)}{(4 + x^2)^2}$

$$= \dfrac{-6x}{4 + x^2}$$

14. A. Because both the base and the exponent contain variables, use log differentiation.

$$y = x^{2x}$$
$$\ln y = \ln(x^{2x})$$
$$\ln y = (2x)(\ln x)$$
$$\frac{1}{y} \cdot \frac{dy}{dx} = (2x)\left(\frac{1}{x}\right) + (\ln x)(2)$$
$$\frac{dy}{dx} = y[2 + 2\ln x]$$
$$\frac{dy}{dx} = x^{2x}[2 + 2\ln x]$$

15. B. $a(t) = v't$

$$= \frac{d}{dt}(t \ln t)$$
$$= t \cdot \frac{1}{t} + \ln t \cdot 1$$
$$= 1 + \ln t$$

16. D. $V = \dfrac{4}{3}\pi r^3 \Rightarrow \dfrac{dV}{dr} = \dfrac{4\pi}{3}3r^2 = 4\pi r^2$

$$\dfrac{dV}{dr}\bigg|_{r=3} = 4\pi(9) = 36\pi$$

17. C. Since $y = 3xe^{2x}$

$y' = (3x)(2e^{2x}) + (e^{2x})(3)$

$y' = e^{2x}(6x + 3)$

$y' = 0$ or y' does not exist

$6x + 3 = 0$

$x = \dfrac{-1}{2}$

Because y' changes sign at $x = -1/2$, y has a relative extremum at $x = -1/2$.

18. B. $y = 3\tan\dfrac{x}{2} \Rightarrow \dfrac{dy}{dx} = 3\left(\sec^2\dfrac{x}{2}\right)\left(\dfrac{1}{2}\right)$

$$= \dfrac{3}{2}\sec^2\dfrac{x}{2}$$

$$\dfrac{dy}{dx}\bigg|_{x=\pi/2} = \dfrac{3}{2}\left(\sec\dfrac{\pi}{4}\right)^2 = \dfrac{3}{2}\left(\sqrt{2}\right)^2 = 3$$

Thus $m_t = 3$.

Normal line is perpendicular to tangent line $\Rightarrow m_n = \dfrac{-1}{3}$.

$y = 3\tan\dfrac{x}{2}$ and $x = \dfrac{\pi}{2} \Rightarrow y = 3\tan\dfrac{\pi}{4} = 3$

so $\left(\dfrac{\pi}{2}, 3\right)$ is the point of tangency.

Apply the point/slope form.

$y - 3 = \dfrac{-1}{3}\left(x - \dfrac{\pi}{2}\right) \Rightarrow 3y - 9 = -x + \dfrac{\pi}{2}$

$$6y - 18 = -2x + \pi$$

$$2x + 6y = 18 + \pi$$

19. C. Sketch the parabola and rectangle as shown here.

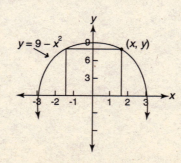

$$A = (\text{base})(\text{height})$$
$$A = (2x)(y)$$
$$= 2x(9 - x^2)$$
$$A = 18x - 2x^3$$
$$\frac{dA}{dx} = 18 - 6x^2$$
$$\frac{dA}{dx} = 0 \text{ or } \frac{dA}{dx} \text{ does not exist}$$
$$6x^2 = 18$$
$$x^2 = 3$$
$$x = \pm\sqrt{3}$$

x	$0 < x < \sqrt{3}$	$x = \sqrt{3}$	$\sqrt{3} < x < 3$
$\frac{dA}{dx}$	pos	0	neg
A	incr	rel max	decr

Thus $x = \sqrt{3}$ yields the maximum area of $A = 2\sqrt{3}(9 - 3) = 12\sqrt{3}$.

20. B. Sketch the cone. Show $h =$ height of pile, $d =$ diameter, and $r =$ radius. Find dh/dt when $h = 5$, given $dV/dt = 10$.

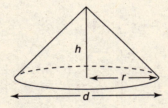

$$V = \frac{1}{3}\pi r^2 h \text{ and } h = \frac{1}{2}d = \frac{1}{2}(2r) = r$$
$$= \frac{1}{3}\pi(h)^2 h$$
$$V = \frac{1}{3}\pi h^3$$

$$\frac{dV}{dt} = \frac{\pi}{3} 3h^2 \frac{dh}{dt}$$
$$\frac{dh}{dt} = \frac{1}{\pi h^2} \cdot \frac{dV}{dt}$$
$$\left.\frac{dh}{dt}\right|_{h=5} = \frac{1}{25\pi}(10) = \frac{2}{5\pi} \text{ m/s}$$

21. C. $\displaystyle\int \frac{3}{x^2}\, dx = 3\int x^{-2}\, dx$
$$= 3\frac{x^{-1}}{-1} + C$$
$$= \frac{-3}{x} + C$$

22. E. $\displaystyle\int_0^\pi \cos\frac{x}{2}\,dx = 2\int_0^\pi \cos\frac{x}{2}\cdot\frac{1}{2}\,dx$

$$= 2\left[\sin\frac{x}{2}\right]_0^\pi$$
$$= 2[1-0]$$
$$= 2$$

23. B. $\displaystyle\int 3^{2x} = \frac{1}{2}\int 3^{2x}(2)\,dx$

$$= \frac{1}{2}\cdot\frac{1}{\ln 3}3^{2x}+C$$

Or, if you forget the formula,

$$\int 3^{2x}\,dx = \int e^{(\ln 3)(2x)}\,dx$$

$$= \frac{1}{(2)(\ln 3)}\int e^{(\ln 3)(2x)}\big[(2)(\ln 3)\big]\,dx$$

$$= \frac{1}{(2)(\ln 3)}e^{(\ln 3)(2x)}+C$$

$$= \frac{1}{(2)(\ln 3)}\cdot 3^{2x}+C$$

24. E. $\displaystyle\int_0^{1/2}\frac{2x}{\sqrt{1-x^2}}\,dx = (-1)\int_0^{1/2}\left(1-x^2\right)^{-1/2}(-2x)\,dx$

$$= (-1)\left[\frac{\left(1-x^2\right)^{1/2}}{\frac{1}{2}}\right]_0^{1/2} = -2\left[\sqrt{\frac{3}{4}}-\sqrt{1}\right] = -\sqrt{3}+2$$

25. E. $\displaystyle\int \frac{5}{\sqrt{9-4x^2}}\,dx = 5\int\frac{1}{\sqrt{9-4x^2}}\,dx$

$$= \frac{5}{2}\int\frac{2}{\sqrt{3^2-(2x)^2}}\,dx$$

$$= \frac{5}{2}\arcsin\frac{2x}{3}+C$$

26. C. $\displaystyle\int_1^{e^3}\frac{\ln x}{x}\,dx = \int_1^{e^3}\ln x\left(\frac{1}{x}\right)\,dx$

$$= \left[\frac{(\ln x)^2}{2}\right]_1^{e^3}$$

$$= \frac{1}{2}\left[\left(\ln e^3\right)^2-(\ln 1)^2\right]$$

$$= \frac{1}{2}\left[3^2-0\right]$$

$$= \frac{9}{2}$$

27. C. Sketch the region as shown.

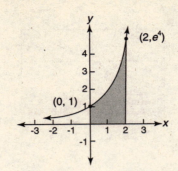

$$A = \int_0^2 e^{2x}\,dx = \frac{1}{2}\int_0^2 e^{2x}(2)\,dx$$
$$= \frac{1}{2}\left[e^{2x}\right]_0^2$$
$$= \frac{1}{2}\left(e^4 - e^0\right)$$
$$= \frac{e^4 - 1}{2}$$
$$= \frac{e^4}{2} - \frac{1}{2}$$

28. A. average value $= \dfrac{1}{b-a}\int_a^b f(x)\,dx$
$$= \frac{1}{4-0}\int_0^4 e^{3x}\,dx$$
$$= \frac{1}{4}\cdot\frac{1}{3}\int_0^4 e^{3x}\cdot 3\,dx$$
$$= \frac{1}{12}\left[e^{3x}\right]_0^4$$
$$= \frac{1}{12}\left(e^{12} - e^0\right)$$
$$= \frac{e^{12} - 1}{12}$$

Section IB

1. C. $f(x) = |x| = \begin{cases} x & \text{for } x \geq 0 \\ -x & \text{for } x < 0 \end{cases}$

$$\Rightarrow f'(x) = \begin{cases} 1 & \text{for } x > 0 \\ -1 & \text{for } x < 0 \end{cases}$$

Thus $f'(2) = 1$.

2. E. The expression $2e^6$ is a constant. The derivative of any constant is 0.

3. C. A calculator graph of the function is shown here, with the maximum value of $y = 0.685$ when $x = 0.866$.

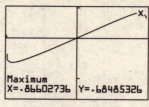

Domain: $-1 \le x \le 1$

4. B. Definition of the derivative at a point:

$$f'(c) = \lim_{x \to c} \frac{f(x) - f(c)}{x - c}$$

For this problem, $f(x)$ changes to $f(\theta) = \sin\theta$ and $c = \pi/3$.

$$f'\left(\frac{\pi}{3}\right) = \lim_{\theta \to \pi/3} \frac{\sin\theta / \sin\frac{\pi}{3}}{\theta - \frac{\pi}{3}} = \lim_{\theta \to \pi/3} \frac{\sin\theta - \frac{\sqrt{3}}{2}}{\theta - \frac{\pi}{3}}$$

5. C. A calculator graph of the function, displaying two different windows, is shown here. The two roots are approximately $x = 0.592$ and $x = 0.957$, yielding a sum of 1.55.

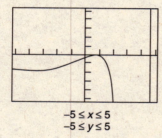

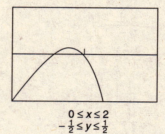

$-5 \le x \le 5$
$-5 \le y \le 5$

$0 \le x \le 2$
$-\frac{1}{2} \le y \le \frac{1}{2}$

6. A. Mean value theorem: $f'(c) = \dfrac{f(b) - f(a)}{b - a}$

$$f(x) = e^{(1/2)x} \Rightarrow f'(x) = \frac{1}{2}e^{(1/2)x} \quad f(0) = 1 \text{ and } f(2) = e$$

$$f'(c) = \frac{f(b) - f(a)}{b - a} \Rightarrow \frac{1}{2}e^{(1/2)c} = \frac{e - 1}{2 - 0}$$

$$e^{(1/2)c} = e - 1$$

$$\ln\left(e^{(1/2)c}\right) = \ln(e - 1)$$

$$\frac{1}{2}c = \ln(e - 1)$$

$$c = 2\ln(e - 1) \approx 1.083$$

7. B. A calculator sketch is shown here, displaying two different windows. To find the bounds of integration, find where the two curves intersect by finding the roots of $y = \ln x + 2 - 2x$. The roots are approximately $x = 0.203$ and $x = 1$. Use your calculator to find $\int_{.203}^{1} (\ln x + 2 - 2x)\, dx$

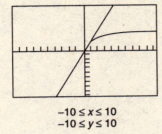

$-10 \le x \le 10$
$-10 \le y \le 10$

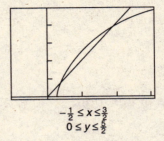

$-\frac{1}{2} \le x \le \frac{3}{2}$
$0 \le y \le \frac{5}{2}$

```
Y₁=In X+2
Y₂=2X
fnInt(Y₁-Y₂,X,.203,
1)
          .1619025079
```

8. E. $\displaystyle\lim_{n \to \infty} \sum_{i=1}^{n} \left[\left(1 + \frac{2i}{n}\right)^2 + 1 \right]\left(\frac{2}{n}\right) = \int_{1}^{3} \left(x^2 + 1\right)\, dx$

The Riemann sum inside the limit shows a function pattern of $x^2 + 1$, so choices (B) and (D) can be eliminated. The base of each rectangle is $2/n$ wide, which means the bounds of integration must be 2 units apart, so choice (C) is eliminated. The endpoint of the first rectangle (when $i = 1$) is given by $1 + 2/n$, which means that the lower bound of integration must be 1, so choice (A) can be eliminated. Thus only (E) fits all the requirements.

9. D. Do not try to integrate. Simply substitute z for the dummy variable x.

10. D. The slope of the tangent line is just the value of the derivative at that point.

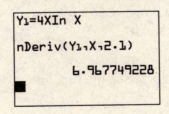

```
Y₁=4XIn X
nDeriv(Y₁,X,2.1)
          6.967749228
■
```

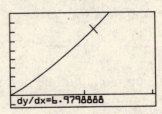

```
dy/dx=6.9798888
```

11. E. Separate the variables and find the antiderivative of each side.

$$\frac{dy}{dt} = \pi y \Rightarrow fy = \pi y \, dt$$

$$\int \frac{1}{y} \, dy = \pi \int 1 \, dt$$

$$\ln |y| = \pi t + C$$

$$y = e^{\pi t + C}$$

$$y = Ce^{\pi t}$$

and choice (E) is of this form.

12. A. $f(x) = \dfrac{x^3}{\sqrt[3]{x}} = \dfrac{x^3}{x^{1/3}} = x^{8/3}$

$$f'(x) = \frac{8}{3} x^{5/3} = \frac{8}{3} x \sqrt[3]{x^2}$$

13. B. Sketch the area and solid as shown.

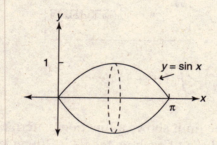

By discs, horizontal axis $\Rightarrow dx$.

Along the x-axis, region A extends from 0 to $\pi \displaystyle\int_0^\pi$.

$$V = \pi \int_a^b (\text{radius})^2 \, dx \Rightarrow \pi \int_0^\pi (\sin x)^2 \, dx = \pi \int_0^\pi \sin^2 x \, dx$$

14. B. Apply the definition of the derivative, where $f(x) = \sin x$.

$$\lim_{h \to 0} \frac{\sin (1 + h) - \sin 1}{h} = f'(1) = \cos 1 \approx 0.54$$

15. E. Find the least common multiple of the two piece of the function.

$$\left. \begin{array}{l} \text{For } y = \sin 3x, \text{ period} = \dfrac{2\pi}{3} \\ \text{For } y = \cos 2x, \text{ period} = \pi \end{array} \right\} \Rightarrow \text{L.C.M.} = 2\pi$$

or graph the function on your calculator and observe the length of the period.

16. C. Sketch $y = \ln x$ and show four circumscribed rectangles.

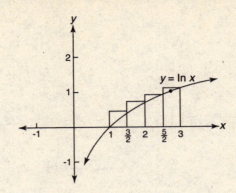

$$Area \approx \frac{1}{2}\ln\frac{3}{2} + \frac{1}{2}\ln 2 + \frac{1}{2}\ln\frac{5}{2} + \frac{1}{2}\ln 3$$
$$= \frac{1}{2}\left(\ln\frac{3}{2} + \ln 2 + \ln\frac{5}{2} + \ln 3\right)$$
$$\approx 1.557$$

17. E. $\displaystyle\int \sin x \cos^2 x\, dx = \int (\cos x)^2 \sin x\, dx$

$$= -\int (\cos x)^2 (-\sin x)\, dx$$
$$= \frac{-(\cos x^3)}{3} + C$$

Section II: Free-Response Questions

Section IIA

1. (a) Begin by sketching the area A.

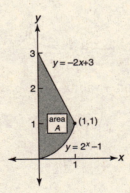

$$A = \int_0^1 \left[(-2x+3)-(2^x-1)\right] dx$$

$$= \int_0^1 \left(-2x+4-2^x\right) dx$$

$$= \left[-x^2+4x-\frac{1}{\ln 2}\cdot 2^x\right]_0^1$$

$$= \left(-1+4-\frac{2}{\ln 2}\right)-\left(0+0-\frac{1}{\ln 2}\right)$$

$$= 3-\frac{1}{\ln 2}$$

(b) Sketch the solid generated.

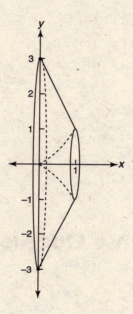

By washers horizontal axis $\Rightarrow dx$.

Area A extends from 0 to 1 along the x-axis $\Rightarrow \int_0^1$.

Washers: $\pi \int_0^1 \left(\text{outer radius}\right)^2 - \left(\text{inner radius}\right)^2 dx$

$$= \pi \int_0^1 \left[(-2x+3)^2-(2^x-1)^2\right] dx$$

(c) Sketch the solid generated. This problem can be done either by discs or by shells. Both solutions are shown here; either would be sufficient for the AP exam.

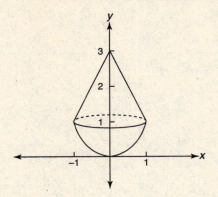

By discs, vertical axis $\Rightarrow dy$.

Area A extends from 0 to 3 along the y-axis, but two integrals are needed $\Rightarrow \int_0^1 + \int_1^3$.

$r_1 + x_1 \qquad r_2 = x_2$

Solve both equations for x in terms of y because the integral is dy.

$$y = 2^x - 1 \qquad\qquad y = -2x + 3$$
$$2^x = y + 1 \qquad\qquad 2x = 3 - y$$
$$x = \log_2(y+1) \qquad x = \frac{3-y}{2}$$

Discs: $\pi \int_0^1 (\text{radius})^2 \, dy + \int_1^3 (\text{radius})^2 \, dy$

$$\pi \int_0^1 \left(\log_2(y+1)\right)^2 dy + \pi \int_1^3 \left(\frac{3-y}{2}\right)^2 dy$$

By shells, vertical axis $\Rightarrow dx$.

Area A extends from 0 to 1 along the x-axis $\Rightarrow \int_0^1$.

Shells: $2\pi \int_0^1 \binom{\text{average}}{\text{radius}} \binom{\text{average}}{\text{height}} dx$

$$2\pi \int_0^1 (x) \left[(-2x+3) - (2^x - 1) \right] dx$$

Use a calculator to approximate the volume to the nearest hundredth.

$$\pi \int_0^1 \left(\log_2(y+1)\right)^2 dy + \pi \int_1^3 \left(\frac{3-y}{2}\right)^2 dy$$

$$= 2\pi \int_0^1 (x) \left[(-2x+3) - (2^x - 1) \right] dx \approx 3.33$$

$$Y_1=(\ln (X+1)/\ln 2)^2$$
$$Y_2=(1.5-.5X)^2$$

$$\pi(\text{fnInt}(Y_1,X,0,1)$$
$$+\text{fnInt}(Y_2,X,1,3))$$
$$3.325766843$$

or

$$Y_1=-2X^2+4X-X*2^X$$
$$2\pi\text{fnInt}(Y_1,X,0,1)$$
$$3.325766843$$

Grading Rubric

(a) 3 points $\begin{cases} 1: \text{integrand} \\ 1: \text{bounds of integration} \\ 1: \text{antiderivative and solution} \end{cases}$

(b) 3 points $\begin{cases} 2: \text{integrand} \\ 1: \text{bound of integration} \end{cases}$

(c) 3 points $\begin{cases} 1: \text{integrand} \\ 1: \text{bounds of integration} \\ 1: \text{calculator approximation} \\ \quad \text{to the nearest hundredth} \end{cases}$

2. (a) zeros: let $f(x) = 0$.

$$e^{4-2x^2} - 8 = 0$$

A graphing calculator shows the zeros to be approximately $x = \pm\, 0.980$

(b) $f(x) = e^{4-2x^2} - 8 \Rightarrow f'(x) = -4xe^{4-2x^2}$

$f'(x) = 0$ or $f'(x) = $ does not exist

$\quad x = 0$

x	$x < 0$	$x = 0$	$x > 0$
$f'(x)$	pos	0	neg
$f(x)$	incr	rel max	decr

$f(0) = e^4 - 8$

To find the minimum value for y.

$$\lim_{x \to \infty}\left[e^{4-2x^2}-8\right]=\lim_{x \to \infty}\left[\frac{1}{e^{4-2x^2}}-8\right]=-8$$

Thus the range is $-8 < f(x) \le e^4 - 8$

(c) Normal at $x = 1$

$$f'(x) = -4xe^{4-2x^2} \Rightarrow f'(1) = -4e^2$$

Thus the slope of the tangent is $m_t = -4^{e2}$

$\Rightarrow$ slope of the normal is $m_n = \dfrac{1}{4e^2}$.

$$f(x) = e^{4-2x^2} - 8 \Rightarrow f(1) = e^2 - 8$$

Thus $(1, e^2 - 8)$ is the point of tangency.

Normal line: $y - (e^2 - 8) = \dfrac{1}{4e^2}(x-1)$

$$y + 0.611 = .034(x-1)$$

$$y = .034x - .645$$

Grading Rubric

(a) 2: 1 point for each zero

(b) 4 points $\begin{cases} 1: \text{differentiates } f(x) \\ 1: \text{finds critical numbers for } f'(x) \\ 1: \text{justifies maximum} \\ 1: \text{conclusion} \end{cases}$

(c) 4 points $\begin{cases} 1: \text{finding } \dfrac{1}{f'(1)} \text{ as slope of normal} \\ 1: \text{finding point of tangency} \\ 1: \text{equation of line} \end{cases}$

3. (a) "at rest" $\Rightarrow v(t) = 0$

A graphing calculator shows that $v(t) = 0$ when $t \approx -0.469$ seconds. To find the acceleration at this time, find the derivative of $v(t)$ when $t = -0.469$.

$$a(-0.469) = v'(-0.469) \approx 37.012 \text{ m/s}^2$$

```
Y₁=(1/3)tan 3X+2
A
          -.4685492165
nDeriv(Y₁,X,A)
           37.01210299
```

(b) $s(t) = \int v(t)\,dt \Rightarrow s(t) = \int \left[\frac{1}{3}\tan(3t) + 2\right]dt$

$$= \frac{1}{3}\int \tan(3t)\,dt + 2\int dt$$

$$= \frac{1}{3}\cdot\frac{1}{3}\int \tan(3t)(3)\,dt + 2\int dt$$

$$s(t) = \frac{-1}{9}\ln|\cos(3t)| + 2t + C$$

$$s(0) = \frac{-1}{9}\ln|\cos 0| + 0 + C = -3$$

$$\Rightarrow C = -3$$

Thus $s(t) = \frac{-1}{9}\ln|\cos(3t)| + 2t - 3$.

Grading Rubric

(a) 4 points
$$\begin{cases} 1:\text{indicates } v(t) = 0 \\ 1:\text{finds zero for } v(t) \\ 1:\text{indicates } a(t) = v'(t) \\ 1:\text{evaluates } a(-0.469) \end{cases}$$

(b) 5 points
$$\begin{cases} 1:\text{indicates } s(t) = \int v(t)\,dt \\ 2:\text{finds antiderivative, including constant } C \\ 1:\text{indicates } s(0) = -3 \\ 1:\text{finds } C \end{cases}$$

Section IIB

4. Sketch the box.

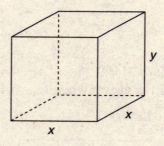

Let x = length of sides of base

y = height of box

Maximum volume: $V = x^2 y$

$$C = 6(4xy) + 18(x^2) = 360$$
$$24xy + 18x^2 = 360$$
$$y = \frac{360 - 18x^2}{24x} = \frac{60 - 3x^2}{4x}$$
$$V = x^2 y \Rightarrow V = x^2\left(\frac{60 - 3x^2}{4x}\right)$$
$$V = \frac{1}{4}(60x - 3x^3) \text{ Domain: } x > 0$$

$$\frac{dV}{dx} = \frac{1}{4}(60 - 9x^2)$$

$$\frac{dV}{dx} = 0 \text{ or } \frac{dV}{dx} = \text{ does not exist}$$

$$9x^2 = 60$$

$$x^2 = \frac{60}{9} = \frac{20}{3}$$

$$x = \frac{2\sqrt{15}}{3}$$

Justify maximum: $\dfrac{d^2V}{dx^2} = \dfrac{1}{4}(-18x)$

$$\frac{d^2V}{dx^2}\bigg|_{x=\frac{2\sqrt{15}}{3}} < 0 \Rightarrow x = \frac{2\sqrt{15}}{3} \text{ yields a maximum}$$

$$x = \frac{2\sqrt{15}}{3} \Rightarrow y = \frac{60 - 3\left(\frac{20}{3}\right)}{4\left(\frac{2\sqrt{15}}{3}\right)} = \sqrt{15}$$

Thus the base of the box is $2\sqrt{15}/3$ feet, and the height of the box is $\sqrt{15}$ feet.

Grading Rubric (9 points)

1: volume formula

1: cost equation

1: substitutes to write V as a function of a single variable

2: differentiates volume equation

1: finds critical number for differentiated equation

2: justifies maximum (first or second derivative test)

1: finds other dimension

5. (a) tangent parallel to $y = -9x - 8 \Rightarrow f'(x) = -9$

$$f(x) = \frac{-x^3}{2} + 3x^2 - 4 \Rightarrow f'(x) = -\frac{3}{2}x^2 + 6x$$

$$-\frac{3}{2}x^2 + 6x = -9$$

$$3x^2 - 12x - 18 = 0$$

$$3(x^2 - 4x - 6) = 0$$

$$x = \frac{4 \pm \sqrt{16 - 4(1)(-6)}}{2}$$

$$= \frac{4 \pm \sqrt{40}}{2} = 2 \pm \sqrt{10}$$

Thus $f(x)$ has tangent line parallel to $y = -9x - 8$ at $x = 2 - \sqrt{10}$ and $x = 2 + \sqrt{10}$.

(b) $f'(x) = -\frac{3}{2}x^2 + 6x \Rightarrow f''(x) = -3x + 6$

$\quad f''(x) = 0 \qquad$ or $\qquad f''(x)$ does not exist

$\quad x = 2$

x	$x < 2$	$x = 2$	$x > 2$
$f''(x)$	pos	0	neg
$f(x)$	cc up	POI	cc down

Thus $f(x)$ has a point of inflection at $(2, 4)$.

Grading Rubric

(a) 4 points $\begin{cases} 1: \text{derivative of } f(x) \\ 1: \text{sets derivative equal to 9} \\ 1: \text{solution of equation} \\ 1: \text{correct to 3 decimal places} \end{cases}$

(b) 5 points $\begin{cases} 1: \text{differentiates } f'(x) \\ 1: \text{finds zero of } f''(x) \\ 1: \text{uses some type of interval testing} \\ \quad \text{on } f''(x) \\ 1: \text{conclusion} \\ 1: \text{finds } y\text{-coordinates} \end{cases}$

6. You may want to begin with the graph of $f(x)$ first, although the graph cannot be used for the justification of the extrema in part (a). Try to fill in conclusions about $f(x)$ on the basis of the first derivative and the second derivative individually, and then translate to a graph.

(a) For the relative extrema:

x	$0 < x < 1$	$x = 1$	$1 < x < 3$	$x = 3$	$3 < x < 4$
$f'(x)$	positive	D.N.E.*	negative	0	negative
$f(x)$	increasing	rel max sharp turn	decreasing		decreasing

*D.N.E. means "does not exist."

Thus the relative maximum is at $x = 1$ and, by symmetry, the relative minimum is at $x = -1$.

(b) For points of inflection:

x	$0 < x < 1$	$x = 1$	$1 < x < 3$	$x = 3$	$3 < x < 4$
$f''(x)$	positive	D.N.E.*	positive	0	negative
$f(x)$	concave up		concave up	POI	concave down

Thus a point of inflection is at $x = 3$ and, by symmetry, also at $x = -3$ and $x = 0$.

(c) One *possible* graph is shown below.

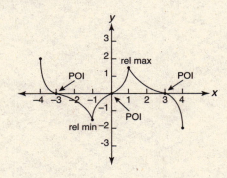

Grading Rubric

(a) 4 points $\begin{cases} \text{1: indicating a relative maximum at } x = 1 \\ \text{1: indicating a relative minimum at } x = -1 \\ \text{2: justification (change in sign of } f'(x) \\ \quad \Rightarrow \text{ relative extrema)} \end{cases}$

(b) 3 points $\begin{cases} \text{1: indicating a POI at } x = 3, x = -3, \\ \quad \text{and } x = 0 \\ \text{2: justification of POI} \end{cases}$

(c) 2 points: graph consistent with the above

Answer Sheet for Practice Test 2 — BC

(Remove This Sheet and Use It to Mark Your Answers)

Section IA
Multiple-Choice Questions

1 Ⓐ Ⓑ Ⓒ Ⓓ Ⓔ
2 Ⓐ Ⓑ Ⓒ Ⓓ Ⓔ
3 Ⓐ Ⓑ Ⓒ Ⓓ Ⓔ
4 Ⓐ Ⓑ Ⓒ Ⓓ Ⓔ
5 Ⓐ Ⓑ Ⓒ Ⓓ Ⓔ

6 Ⓐ Ⓑ Ⓒ Ⓓ Ⓔ
7 Ⓐ Ⓑ Ⓒ Ⓓ Ⓔ
8 Ⓐ Ⓑ Ⓒ Ⓓ Ⓔ
9 Ⓐ Ⓑ Ⓒ Ⓓ Ⓔ
10 Ⓐ Ⓑ Ⓒ Ⓓ Ⓔ

11 Ⓐ Ⓑ Ⓒ Ⓓ Ⓔ
12 Ⓐ Ⓑ Ⓒ Ⓓ Ⓔ
13 Ⓐ Ⓑ Ⓒ Ⓓ Ⓔ
14 Ⓐ Ⓑ Ⓒ Ⓓ Ⓔ
15 Ⓐ Ⓑ Ⓒ Ⓓ Ⓔ

16 Ⓐ Ⓑ Ⓒ Ⓓ Ⓔ
17 Ⓐ Ⓑ Ⓒ Ⓓ Ⓔ
18 Ⓐ Ⓑ Ⓒ Ⓓ Ⓔ
19 Ⓐ Ⓑ Ⓒ Ⓓ Ⓔ
20 Ⓐ Ⓑ Ⓒ Ⓓ Ⓔ

21 Ⓐ Ⓑ Ⓒ Ⓓ Ⓔ
22 Ⓐ Ⓑ Ⓒ Ⓓ Ⓔ
23 Ⓐ Ⓑ Ⓒ Ⓓ Ⓔ
24 Ⓐ Ⓑ Ⓒ Ⓓ Ⓔ
25 Ⓐ Ⓑ Ⓒ Ⓓ Ⓔ

26 Ⓐ Ⓑ Ⓒ Ⓓ Ⓔ
27 Ⓐ Ⓑ Ⓒ Ⓓ Ⓔ
28 Ⓐ Ⓑ Ⓒ Ⓓ Ⓔ

Section IB
Multiple-Choice Questions

1 Ⓐ Ⓑ Ⓒ Ⓓ Ⓔ
2 Ⓐ Ⓑ Ⓒ Ⓓ Ⓔ
3 Ⓐ Ⓑ Ⓒ Ⓓ Ⓔ
4 Ⓐ Ⓑ Ⓒ Ⓓ Ⓔ
5 Ⓐ Ⓑ Ⓒ Ⓓ Ⓔ

6 Ⓐ Ⓑ Ⓒ Ⓓ Ⓔ
7 Ⓐ Ⓑ Ⓒ Ⓓ Ⓔ
8 Ⓐ Ⓑ Ⓒ Ⓓ Ⓔ
9 Ⓐ Ⓑ Ⓒ Ⓓ Ⓔ
10 Ⓐ Ⓑ Ⓒ Ⓓ Ⓔ

11 Ⓐ Ⓑ Ⓒ Ⓓ Ⓔ
12 Ⓐ Ⓑ Ⓒ Ⓓ Ⓔ
13 Ⓐ Ⓑ Ⓒ Ⓓ Ⓔ
14 Ⓐ Ⓑ Ⓒ Ⓓ Ⓔ
15 Ⓐ Ⓑ Ⓒ Ⓓ Ⓔ

16 Ⓐ Ⓑ Ⓒ Ⓓ Ⓔ
17 Ⓐ Ⓑ Ⓒ Ⓓ Ⓔ

CUT HERE

Section I: Multiple-Choice Questions

Section IA

Time: 55 Minutes

28 Questions

Directions: The 28 questions that follow in Section IA of the exam should be solved using the space available for scratchwork. Select the best of the given choices and fill in the corresponding oval on the answer sheet. Material written in the test booklet will not be graded or awarded credit. Fifty-five minutes are allowed for Section IA. *No calculator of any type may be used in this section of the test.*

Notes: *(1) For this test,* ln x *denotes the natural logarithm of* x *(that is, logarithm of the base* e*).* *(2) The domain of all functions is assumed to be the set of real numbers* x *for which* f(x) *is a real number, unless a different domain is specified.*

1. If $g(t) = \dfrac{e^{\ln t}}{t}$, then $g(e) =$

    A. $\dfrac{e}{2}$

    B. e

    C. 1

    D. $\dfrac{1}{e}$

    E. 0

2. A particle moves along the curve $xy = 12$. If $y = 3$ and $\dfrac{dx}{dt} = 2$, what is the value of $\dfrac{dy}{dt}$?

    A. $\dfrac{-3}{2}$

    B. $\dfrac{-2}{3}$

    C. $\dfrac{2}{3}$

    D. $\dfrac{3}{2}$

    E. 6

3. What is $\lim\limits_{\theta \to 0}\left(\dfrac{3\theta}{\tan\theta}\right)$?

    A. $-\infty$

    B. 0

    C. 1

    D. 3

    E. $+\infty$

4. Evaluate $\lim\limits_{x \to \infty} e^{-x} \cdot \ln x$.

    A. -1

    B. $\dfrac{1}{e}$

    C. 1

    D. 0

    E. does not exist

GO ON TO THE NEXT PAGE

5. Given that $f(x) = \begin{cases} 3 - 4x & \text{for } x \le 0 \\ x^2 & \text{for } 0 < x < 2 \\ 3x - 4 & \text{for } x \ge 2 \end{cases}$

Find $\lim\limits_{x \to 2^-} f(x)$.

A. -5

B. 2

C. 4

D. 6

E. The limit does not exist.

6. If $x = t^2 - 1$ and $y = t^2$, then $\dfrac{d^2 y}{dx^2} =$

A. 1

B. $\dfrac{3}{4t}$

C. $\dfrac{-2}{9t^4}$

D. $\dfrac{9t^4}{2}$

E. $\dfrac{t^4}{\left(t^{3-1}\right)^2}$

7. $\dfrac{d}{dx}\left[\dfrac{\cos x}{\sin x + 1}\right] =$

A. $\sin x + 1$

B. $-\csc^2 x - \sin x$

C. $-\csc^2 x + 1$

D. $\dfrac{-\sin x}{\sin x + 1}$

E. $\dfrac{-1}{1 + \sin x}$

8. If $y = \sqrt{\ln 3x}$, then $y' =$

A. $\dfrac{1}{3x\sqrt{\ln 3x}}$

B. $\dfrac{1}{2x\sqrt{\ln 3x}}$

C. $\dfrac{1}{6x\sqrt{\ln 3x}}$

D. $\dfrac{1}{2\sqrt{\ln 3x}}$

E. $\dfrac{3}{2x\sqrt{\ln 3x}}$

9. $\displaystyle\int x \sin x \, dx =$

A. $-x^2 \cos x + c$

B. $-x \cos x + \sin x + c$

C. $\sin x + x \cos x + c$

D. $x \sin x - \cos x + c$

E. $\cos x + c$

10. If $y = \arctan(3x)$, then $\dfrac{dy}{dx}\bigg|_{x=1} =$

A. $\dfrac{1}{10}$

B. $\dfrac{1}{4}$

C. $\dfrac{3}{10}$

D. $\dfrac{1}{3}$

E. $\dfrac{3}{4}$

11. $\dfrac{d}{dy}\left[\log_3 4y\right] =$

A. $\dfrac{1}{4y \ln 3}$

B. $\dfrac{\ln 3}{y}$

C. $\dfrac{4}{y \ln 3}$

D. $\dfrac{1}{y}$

E. $\dfrac{1}{y \ln 3}$

12. The graph of $y = e^{-x^2}$ has a point of inflection at

 A. $x = 0$

 B. $x = \pm 2$

 C. $x = \pm \sqrt{2}$

 D. $x = \dfrac{\pm \sqrt{2}}{2}$

 E.   The graph has no points of inflection.

13. The radius of a circle is increasing at the rate of 3 meters per second. Find the rate, in square meters per second, at which the area of the circle is changing when the area is 16π m^2.

 A. 8π m^2/s

 B. 12π m^2/s

 C. 24π m^2/s

 D. 96π m^2/s

 E. $96\pi^2$ m^2/s

14. A particle moves along a horizontal path such that its position at any time $t\,(t \geq 0)$ is given $s(t) = t^3 - 4t^2 + 4t + 5$. The particle is moving right for

 A. $t > 2$ only

 B. $0 < t < \dfrac{2}{3}$ only

 C. $\dfrac{2}{3} < t < 2$

 D. $0 < t < \dfrac{2}{3}$ or $t > 2$

 E. $t > \dfrac{2}{3}$

15. Find the equation of the line that is tangent to the curve $xy - x + y = 2$ at the point where $x = 0$.

 A. $y = -x$

 B. $y = \dfrac{1}{2}x + 2$

 C. $y = x + 2$

 D. $y = 2$

 E. $y = -x + 2$

16. $\displaystyle\int 3xe^{2x}\,dx =$

 A. $3xe^{2x} e - e^{2x} + C$

 B. $6xe^{2x} - 4e^{2x} + C$

 C. $xe^{2x} - 3e^{2x} + C$

 D. $\dfrac{1}{2}xe^{2x} - \dfrac{1}{4}e^{2x} + C$

 E. $\dfrac{3}{2}xe^{2x} - \dfrac{3}{4}e^{2x} + C$

17. $\displaystyle\int \cot 3\phi\,d\phi =$

 A. $\dfrac{-1}{3}\ln|\cos 3\phi| + C$

 B. $\dfrac{-1}{3}\ln|\csc 3\phi + \cot 3\phi| + C$

 C. $-3\csc^2 3\phi + C$

 D. $\dfrac{1}{3}\ln|\sin 3\phi| + C$

 E. $3\sec^2 3\phi + C$

18. $\displaystyle\int \dfrac{2x}{\sqrt{x+5}}\,dx =$

 A. $x - 10\ln\sqrt{x+5} + C$

 B. $\dfrac{4}{3}\sqrt{x+5}(x - 10) + C$

 C. $\dfrac{2}{3}\sqrt{x+5}(x - 10) + C$

 D. $\dfrac{4}{3}\sqrt{x+5}(x + 20) + C$

 E. $2x^2\sqrt{x+5} + C$

GO ON TO THE NEXT PAGE

19. The integral $\int_1^2 \dfrac{dx}{\sqrt[3]{x-1}}$

   A. converges to $\dfrac{3}{2}$

   B. converges to 0

   C. diverges

   D. converges to -1

   E. converges to $\dfrac{-3}{2}$

20. Suppose that $f(x) = \begin{cases} 2x & \text{for } x \le 1 \\ 3x^2 - 1 & \text{for } x > 1 \end{cases}$

   Then $\int_0^2 f(x)\,dx =$

   A. 7

   B. 6

   C. 5

   D. 2

   E. 1

21. Find the area of the region bounded by the graphs at $y = \dfrac{x^3 + 2}{x}$, $y = 0$, $x = 1$, and $x = e$.

   A. $\dfrac{e^2}{2} - \dfrac{4}{e} - \dfrac{9}{2}$

   B. $\dfrac{9}{2} - \dfrac{e^2}{2} - \dfrac{4}{e}$

   C. $2\sqrt{e^9} + \dfrac{4}{e} - \dfrac{38}{9}$

   D. $\dfrac{-5 - e^3}{3}$

   E. $\dfrac{e^3 + 5}{3}$

22. The rate of decay of radioactive uranium is proportional to the amount of uranium present at any time t. If there are initially 54 grams of uranium present, and there are 42 grams present after 120 years, this situation can be described by the equation

   A. $y = 54e^{kt}, k = \dfrac{1}{120} \ln \dfrac{7}{9}$

   B. $y = 54e^{kt}, k = \dfrac{7}{9} \ln 120$

   C. $y = 42e^{kt}, k = \dfrac{1}{120} \ln \dfrac{7}{9}$

   D. $y = 42e^{kt}, k = \dfrac{7}{9} \ln \dfrac{1}{120}$

   E. $y = 42e^{kt}, k = 120 \ln \dfrac{7}{9}$

23. The average value of $\tan x$ on the interval from $x = 0$ to $x = \pi/3$ is

   A. $\ln \dfrac{1}{2}$

   B. $\dfrac{3}{\pi} \ln 2$

   C. $\ln 2$

   D. $\dfrac{\sqrt{3}}{2}$

   E. $\dfrac{9}{\pi}$

24. The region bounded by the graphs of $y = x^2 - 5x + 6$ and $y = 0$ is rotated about the y-axis. The volume of the resulting solid is

   A. 10π

   B. 52π

   C. $5\pi/6$

   D. $5\pi/3$

   E. $19\pi/3$

25. Let A be the region bounded by $y = \ln x$, the x-axis, and the line $x = e$. Which of the following represents the volume of the solid generated when A is revolved around the y-axis?

A. $\pi \int_0^1 \left(e^2 - e^{2y}\right) dy$

B. $\pi \int_0^1 \left(e^2 - e^y\right) dy$

C. $\pi \int_0^1 e^{2y} dy$

D. $2\pi \int_1^e \left(e^2 - e^{2y}\right) dy$

E. $\pi \int_0^1 e^2 dy$

26. Which of the following series diverge?

I. $\displaystyle\sum_{n=1}^{\infty} \frac{4}{3^{n+1}}$

II. $\displaystyle\sum_{n=2}^{\infty} \frac{(-1)^n}{n}$

III. $\displaystyle\sum_{n=3}^{\infty} \frac{3}{n^2 + 1}$

A. none

B. I only

C. II only

D. III only

E. All of them

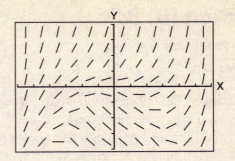

27. Above is the slope field for which of the following differential equations?

A. $\dfrac{dy}{dx} = \sin x$

B. $\dfrac{dy}{dx} = x^2 + y$

C. $\dfrac{dy}{dx} = 2x + 3$

D. $\dfrac{dy}{dx} = 3y - 2$

E. $\dfrac{dy}{dx} = \cos y$

28. A particle moves in the xy-plane so that at any time $t > 0$, $x = \dfrac{1}{4}t^4 - 3t$ and $y = \dfrac{1}{3}(3t - 5)^4$. The acceleration vector of the particle at $t = 2$ is

A. $\left(-2, \dfrac{1}{3}\right)$

B. $(5, 4)$

C. $(12, 36)$

D. $(12, 4)$

E. $\left(\dfrac{-52}{15}, \dfrac{1}{810}\right)$

IF YOU FINISH BEFORE TIME IS CALLED, CHECK YOUR WORK ON THIS SECTION ONLY. DO NOT WORK ON ANY OTHER SECTION IN THE TEST.

STOP

Section IB: BC

Time: 50 Minutes

17 Questions

Directions: The 17 questions that follow in Section IB of the exam should be solved using the space available for scratchwork. Select the best of the given choices and fill in the corresponding oval on the answer sheet. Material written in the test booklet will not be graded or awarded credit. Fifty minutes are allowed for Section IB. *A graphing calculator is required for this section of the test.*

Notes: *(1) If the exact numerical value does not appear as one of the five choices, choose the best approximation. (2) For this test,* ln x *denotes the natural logarithm function (that is, logarithm to the base* e*). (3) The domain of all functions is assumed to be the set of real numbers* x *for which* f(x) *is a real number, unless a different domain is specified.*

1. If a, b, and c are constants, what is $\lim_{z \to a}\left(bz^2 + c^2 z\right)$?

    A. $a^2b + ac^2$

    B. $az^2 + a^2z$

    C. $bz^2 + ac^2$

    D. $a^2b + c^2z$

    E. $bz^2 + c^2z$

2. The slope of the line normal to the curve $g(x) = \sin\frac{x}{2} + 3x$ at the point where $x = \frac{\pi}{7}$ is approximately

    A. -0.287

    B. 0.449

    C. 1.276

    D. 2.671

    E. 3.487

3. Given $\lim_{x \to 3^+} f(x) = 2$, which of the following MUST be true?

    A. $f(3)$ exists

    B. $f(x)$ is continuous at $x = 3$

    C. $f(3) = 2$

    D. $\lim_{x \to 3^-} f(x) = 2$

    E. None of these must be true.

4. A point of inflection for the graph of $y = x^3 + 4x^2 - x + 5\sin x$ has x coordinate

    A. -4.467

    B. -3.273

    C. -2.066

    D. -1.059

    E. $-.519$

5. If $y = x^{x-2}$, then $\dfrac{dy}{dx}\bigg|_{x=3} \approx$

    A. 2.358

    B. 3.761

    C. 4.296

    D. 4.553

    E. none of these

6. A right circular cylindrical can having a volume of $2\pi \text{ in}^3$ is to be constructed. Find the radius of the can for which the total surface area is a minimum. $\left(V = \pi r^2 h, A = 2\pi r^2 + 2\pi rh\right)$

  A. 1/4

  B. 1/2

  C. 1

  D. 2

  E. 4

7. If $g(x) = \frac{1}{2}\left|3 - x\right|$, then the value of the derivative of $g(x)$ at $x = 3$ is

  A. $\dfrac{-1}{2}$

  B. $\dfrac{1}{2}$

  C. 0

  D. 3

  E. nonexistent

8. $\displaystyle\int \frac{dx}{x^2 - x - 2} =$

  A. $-\dfrac{1}{3}\ln\left|\dfrac{x+1}{x-2}\right| + C$

  B. $\ln\left|\dfrac{x-1}{x+2}\right|^3 + C$

  C. $-\dfrac{1}{x} - \ln\left|x\right| - \dfrac{x}{2} + C$

  D. $\dfrac{1}{3} - \ln\left|\dfrac{x-1}{x+2}\right| + C$

  E. $\ln\left|\dfrac{x-2}{x+1}\right|^3 + C$

9. For the function $y = x^{100}$ find $\dfrac{d^{100}y}{dx^{100}}$.

  A. 0

  B. 100

  C. $(100!)x$

  D. $100!$

  E. $100x$

10. $\displaystyle\int_1^2 \sin^5 x \, dx \approx$

  A. 0.732

  B. 0.815

  C. 0.867

  D. 0.924

  E. 1.173

11. Which of the following is equal to the shaded area in the figure below?

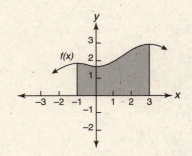

  A. $\displaystyle\lim_{n \to \infty}\sum_{i=1}^{n}\left(\dfrac{3}{n}\right)f\left(\dfrac{3i}{n}\right)$

  B. $\displaystyle\lim_{n \to \infty}\sum_{i=1}^{n}\left(\dfrac{4}{n}\right)f\left(-1+\dfrac{4i}{n}\right)$

  C. $\displaystyle\lim_{n \to \infty}\sum_{i=1}^{n}\left(\dfrac{3}{n}\right)f\left(-1+\dfrac{3i}{n}\right)$

  D. $\displaystyle\lim_{n \to \infty}\sum_{i=1}^{n}\left(\dfrac{4}{n}\right)f\left(\dfrac{4i}{n}\right)$

  E. none of these

12. What is $\displaystyle\lim_{h \to 0}\frac{e^{x+h} - e^{x}}{h}$?

  A. 0

  B. $\ln x$

  C. x

  D. e^x

  E. 1

GO ON TO THE NEXT PAGE

13. The average value of the function $f(x) = x \sin x$ on the closed interval $[1, \pi]$ is approximately

   A. 1.326

   B. 1.467

   C. 2.840

   D. 3.142

   E. 4.076

14. For what values of x will the series $\sum_{n=1}^{\infty} \dfrac{x^{n+1}}{(n+1)^2}$ converge?

   A. $(-1, 1]$

   B. $[-1, 1)$

   C. $(-1, 1)$

   D. $[-1, 1]$

   E. $(-\infty, +\infty)$

15. When the value of cos2 is approximated by using the fourth-degree Taylor polynomial about $x = 0$, the value of cos2 is

   A. $1 + \dfrac{4}{2} - \dfrac{16}{24}$

   B. $1 + \dfrac{4}{2} + \dfrac{16}{24}$

   C. $1 - \dfrac{4}{2} - \dfrac{16}{24}$

   D. $-1 - \dfrac{4}{2} + \dfrac{16}{64}$

   E. $1 - \dfrac{4}{2} + \dfrac{16}{24}$

16. A curve is described by the parametric equations $x = \dfrac{1}{4} t^4$ and $y = \dfrac{1}{3} t^3$. The length of this curve from $t = 0$ to $t = 2$ is given by

   A. $\displaystyle\int_0^2 \sqrt{\dfrac{t^8}{16} + \dfrac{t^6}{9}}\, dt$

   B. $\displaystyle\int_0^2 \sqrt{\dfrac{t^4}{4} + \dfrac{t^3}{3}}\, dt$

   C. $\displaystyle\int_0^2 \sqrt{\dfrac{t^{10}}{400} + \dfrac{t^8}{144}}\, dt$

   D. $\displaystyle\int_0^2 \sqrt{\left(t^3 - t^2\right)^2}\, dt$

   E. $\displaystyle\int_0^2 \sqrt{\left(t^6 - t^4\right)}\, dt$

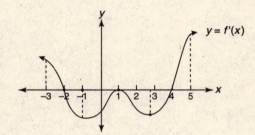

17. Above is the graph of $f'(x)$. On what interval (5) is the graph of $f(x)$ concave upwards?

   A. $-3 < x < 1$ and $1 < x < -1$

   B. $-2 < x < 1$ and $1 < x < 4$

   C. $-1 < x < 3$

   D. $-1 < x < 1$ and $3 < x < 5$

   E. $-3 < x < 1$

IF YOU FINISH BEFORE TIME IS CALLED, CHECK YOUR WORK ON THIS SECTION ONLY. DO NOT WORK ON ANY OTHER SECTION IN THE TEST.

STOP

Section II: Free-Response Questions

Section IIA

Time: 45 Minutes

3 Questions

Directions: For the three problems that follow in Section IIA, show your work. Your grade will be determined on the correctness of your method as well as the accuracy of your final answers. Some questions in this section may require the use of a graphing calculator. If you choose to give decimal approximations, your answer should be correct to three decimal places, unless a particular question specifies otherwise. During Section IIB, you will be allowed to return to Section IIA to continue your work on questions 1–3, but you will NOT be allowed the use of a calculator.

Notes: *(1) For this test, ln* x *denotes the natural logarithm function (that is, logarithm to the base* e*). (2) The domain of all functions is assumed to be the set of real numbers* x *for which* f(x) *is a real number, unless a different domain is specified.*

1. Let R be the first quadrant region enclosed by the graphs of $y = \sin x$ and $y = e\left(x^2 - 2\right)$.

   (a) Find the area of R.

   (b) Set up, but do not evaluate, an integral which represents the length of the boundry of the region R.

   (c) The base of a solid is the region R. Cross sections of the solid are semicircles perpendicular to the base and the x-axis, with their diameters on region R. Set up, but do evaluate, an integral which represents the volume of this solid.

2. Two particles move in the xy-plane. For time $t \geq 0$, the position of particle P is given by $x = t - 3$ and $y = (t - 2)^2$ while the position of particle Q is given by $x = 2t/3 - 5/3$ and $y = 2t/3 + 4/3$.

   (a) Find the velocity vector for each particle at $t = 2$.

   (b) Set up, but do not evaluate, an integral expression that represents the distance traveled by particle P from $t = 1$ to $t = 4$.

   (c) Find the exact time at which the two particles are at the same position at the same time.

   (d) In the viewing window at the top of the next page, sketch the paths of particles P and Q, from $t = 0$ until they collide. Indicate the direction of each particle along its path.

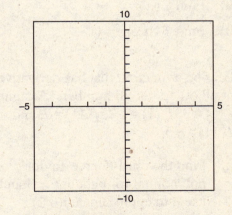

VIEWING WINDOW [-5,5] x [-10,10]

GO ON TO THE NEXT PAGE

3. Let $f''(x) = 10 \sin x - \left(e^x\right) \cos x$ for the interval $[-2.5, 5]$.

(a) On what intervals is the graph of $f(x)$ concave down? Justify your answer.

(b) Find the x-coordinates of all relative extrema for the function $f'(x)$. Classify the extrema as relative minima or relative maxima. Justify your answer.

(c) To the nearest tenth, find the x-coordinates of any points of inflection of the graph of $f'(x)$. Justify your answer.

IF YOU FINISH BEFORE TIME IS CALLED, CHECK YOUR WORK ON THIS SECTION ONLY. DO NOT WORK ON ANY OTHER SECTION IN THE TEST.

Section IIB

Time: 45 Minutes

3 Questions

Directions: For the three problems that follow in Section IIB, show your work. Your grade will be determined on the correctness of your method as well as the accuracy of your final answers. During Section IIB, you will NOT be allowed the use of a calculator. During this section you will also be allowed to return to questions 1–3 in Section IIA to continue working on those problems, but you will NOT have the use of a calculator.

4. Let $y = f(x)$ be a continuous function such that $\dfrac{dy}{dx} = 3xy$, $x \geq 0$, and $f(0) = 12$.

(a) Find $f(x)$.

(b) Find $f^{-1}(x)$.

5. Let f be a function that has derivatives of all orders for all numbers. Assume $f(1) = 3$, $f'(1) = -2$, $f''(1) = 7$, and $f'''(1) = -5$

(a) Find the third-degree Taylor polynomial for f about $x = 3$ and use it to approximate $f(3.2)$.

(b) Write the fourth-degree Taylor polynomial for g, where $g(x) = f\left(x^2 + 3\right)$ about 3.

(c) Write the third-degree Taylor polynomial for h, where $f(x) = \displaystyle\int_3^x f(t)\, dt$ about $x = 3$.

6. Let f be the function defined as

$$f(x) \begin{cases} 6x + 12 & \text{for } x \leq -2 \\ ax^3 + b & \text{for } -2 < x < 1 \\ 2x + \dfrac{5}{2} & \text{for } x \geq 1 \end{cases}$$

(a) Find values for a and b such that $f(x)$ is continuous. Use the definition of continuity to justify your answer.

(b) For the values you found in part (a), is $f(x)$ differentiable at $x = -2$? at $x = 1$? Use the definition of the derivative to justify your answer.

IF YOU FINISH BEFORE TIME IS CALLED, CHECK YOUR WORK ON THIS SECTION ONLY. DO NOT WORK ON ANY OTHER SECTION IN THE TEST.

Answer Key for Practice Test 2 — BC

Section I: Multiple-Choice Questions

Section IA

1. C	**8.** B	**15.** E	**22.** A
2. A	**9.** B	**16.** E	**23.** B
3. D	**10.** C	**17.** D	**24.** C
4. D	**11.** E	**18.** B	**25.** A
5. C	**12.** D	**19.** A	**26.** A
6. C	**13.** C	**20.** A	**27.** B
7. E	**14.** D	**21.** E	**28.** C

Section IB

1. A	**6.** C	**10.** B	**14.** D
2. A	**7.** E	**11.** B	**15.** E
3. E	**8.** A	**12.** D	**16.** E
4. C	**9.** D	**13.** A	**17.** D
5. C			

Unanswered problems are neither right nor wrong, and are not entered into the scoring formula.

Number right   =   _____

Number wrong   =   _____

Section II: Free-Response Questions

Use the grading rubrics beginning on page 460 to score your free-response answers. Write your scores in the blanks provided on the scoring worksheet.

Practice Test 2 Scoring Worksheet

Section IA and IB: Multiple-Choice

Of the 45 total questions, count only the number correct and the number wrong. Unanswered problems are not entered in the formula.

$$\underline{\hspace{3cm}} - (1/4 \times \underline{\hspace{3cm}}) = \underline{\hspace{3cm}}$$
$$\text{number correct} \qquad \text{number wrong} \qquad \text{Multiple-Choice}$$
$$\text{Score}$$

Section II: Free-Response

Each of the six questions has a possible score of 9 points. Total all six scores.

Question 1   _____
Question 2   _____
Question 3   _____
Question 4   _____
Question 5   _____
Question 6   _____

TOTAL   _____
Free-Response Score

Composite Score

$$1.20 \quad \times \quad \underline{\hspace{3cm}} \quad = \quad \underline{\hspace{3cm}}$$
$$\text{Multiple-Choice Score} \qquad \text{Converted Section I}$$
$$\text{Score (do not round)}$$

$$1.00 \quad \times \quad \underline{\hspace{3cm}} \quad = \quad \underline{\hspace{3cm}}$$
$$\text{Free-Response Score} \qquad \text{Converted Section II}$$
$$\text{Score (do not round)}$$

$$\text{TOTAL} \quad = \quad \underline{\hspace{3cm}}$$
$$\text{of converted scores} \qquad \text{round to the nearest}$$
$$\text{whole number}$$

Probable AP Grade

Composite Score Range	AP Grade
65–108	5
55–64	4
42–54	3
0–41	1 or 2

Please note that the scoring range above is an approximation only. Each year, the chief faculty consultants are responsible for converting the final total raw scores to the 5-point AP scale. Future grading scales may differ markedly from the one listed above.

Answers and Explanations for Practice Test 2 — BC

Section I: Multiple-Choice Questions

Section IA

1. C. Simplify first.

$$g(t) = \frac{e^{\ln t}}{t} = \frac{t}{t} = 1$$

2. A. $xy = 12$

$$\frac{dx}{dt} \cdot x + \frac{dy}{dt} \cdot = 0$$

$$2 \cdot 3 + \frac{dy}{dt} \cdot 4 = 0$$

$$\frac{dy}{dt} \cdot 4 = -6$$

$$\frac{dy}{dt} = \frac{-3}{2}$$

3. D. $\lim\limits_{\theta \to 0}\left(\dfrac{3\theta}{\tan\theta}\right) = \lim\limits_{\theta \to 0}\left[\left(\dfrac{\theta}{\sin\theta}\right)(3\cos\theta)\right] = (1)(3)(1) = 3$

or use L'Hôpital's rule:

$$\lim_{\theta \to 0}\left(\frac{3\theta}{\tan\theta}\right) = \lim_{\theta \to 0}\frac{3}{\sec^2\theta} = \frac{3}{1} = 3$$

4. D. $\lim\limits_{x \to \infty} e^{-x} \cdot \ln x$

$= \lim\limits_{x \to \infty} \dfrac{\ln x}{e^x}$ of the form $\dfrac{\infty}{\infty}$

using L'Hôpital's rule:

$= \lim\limits_{x \to \infty} \dfrac{\frac{1}{x}}{e^x}$

$= \dfrac{0}{\infty}$

$= 0$

5. C. The one-sided limit is approaching 2 from the left, so use the "middle" part of the piece function.

$\lim\limits_{x \to 2^-} f(x) = \lim\limits_{x \to 2^-} \left(x^2\right) = 4$

6. C. $x = t^3 - 1 \quad y = t^2$

$\dfrac{dx}{dt} = 3t^2 \quad \dfrac{dy}{dt} = 2t$

$\dfrac{dy}{dx} = \dfrac{dy}{dt} \cdot \dfrac{dt}{dx} = 2t \cdot \dfrac{1}{3t^2} = \dfrac{2}{3t} = \dfrac{2}{3}t^{-1}$

Then $\dfrac{d^2 y}{dx^2} = \dfrac{dy^1}{dx} = \dfrac{dy^1}{dt} \cdot \dfrac{dt}{dx} = \dfrac{-2}{3t^2} = \dfrac{1}{3t^2} = \dfrac{-2}{9t^4}$

7. E. $\dfrac{d}{dx}\left[\dfrac{\cos x}{\sin x + 1}\right] = \dfrac{(\sin x + 1)(-\sin x) - (\cos x)(\cos x)}{(\sin x + 1)^2}$

$= \dfrac{-\sin^2 x - \sin x - \cos^2 x}{(\sin x + 1)^2}$

$= \dfrac{\left(-\sin^2 x + \cos^2 x\right) - \sin x}{(\sin x + 1)^2}$

$= \dfrac{-1 - \sin x}{(\sin x + 1)^2}$

$= \dfrac{-1}{1 + \sin x}$

8. B. $y = \sqrt{\ln 3x} = (\ln 3x)^{1/2}$

$\dfrac{dy}{dx} = \dfrac{1}{2}(\ln 3x)^{-1/2}\left(\dfrac{3}{3x}\right)$

$= \dfrac{1}{2x\sqrt{\ln 3x}}$

9. B. $\int x \sin dx$ Using integration by parts,

$= \int u\,dv$ let $u = x$ and $dv = \sin x$

$= uv - \int v\,du$ Then $du = dx$ and $v = -\cos x$

$= x(-\cos x) - \int(-\cos x)\,dx$

$= -x\cos x + \sin x + C$

10. C. $y = \arctan(3x) \Rightarrow \dfrac{dy}{dx} = \dfrac{3}{1+(3x)^2}$

$\left.\dfrac{dy}{dx}\right|_{x=1} = \dfrac{3}{1+3^2} = \dfrac{3}{10}$

11. E. $\dfrac{d}{dy}\big[\log_3 4y\big] = \dfrac{1}{\ln 3} \cdot \dfrac{4}{4y} = \dfrac{1}{y\ln 3}$

12. D. To find a point of inflection, find the second derivative and do interval testing.

$y = e^{-x^2} \Rightarrow y' = \left(e^{-x^2}\right)(-2x)$

$\quad y'' = \left(e^{-x^2}\right)(-2) + \left(-2x\left[e^{-x^2}(-2x)\right]\right)$

$\quad\quad = -2e^{-x^2} + 4x^2 e^{-x^2}$

$\quad\quad = e^{-x^2}\left(-2 + 4x^2\right)$

$y'' = 0$ or y'' or does not exist

$4x^2 = 2$

$x^2 = \dfrac{1}{2}$

$x = \dfrac{\pm\sqrt{2}}{2}$

x	$x < \dfrac{-\sqrt{2}}{2}$	$x = \dfrac{-\sqrt{2}}{2}$	$\dfrac{-\sqrt{2}}{2} < x < \dfrac{\sqrt{2}}{2}$	$x = \dfrac{\sqrt{2}}{2}$	$x > \dfrac{\sqrt{2}}{2}$
y''	pos	0	neg	0	pos
y	concave up	POI	concave down	POI	concave up

Thus there are points of inflection at $x = \dfrac{\pm\sqrt{2}}{2}$.

13. C. Sketch the circle; r = radius and A = area.

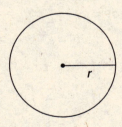

Find dA/dt when $A = 16\pi$, given $dr/dt = 3$.

$A = \pi r^2$

$\dfrac{dA}{dt} = \pi 2r \dfrac{dr}{dt}$ $A = 16\pi \Rightarrow r = 4$

$\left.\dfrac{dA}{dt}\right|_{r=4} = 2\pi(4)(3) = 24\pi\,\text{m}^2/\text{s}$

14. D. "moving right" $\Rightarrow v(t) > 0$

$$v(t) = s'(t) \Rightarrow v(t) = 3t^2 - 8t + 4$$
$$v(t) = (3t - 2)(t - 2)$$
$$v(t) = 0 \Rightarrow t = \frac{3}{2} \text{ or } t = 2$$

pos   neg   pos

0    $\frac{2}{3}$ 2 $\rightarrow v(t)$

Thus $v(t) > 0$ for $0 < t < \frac{2}{3}$ or $t > 2$.

15. E. Use implicit differentiation.

$$xy - x + y = 2$$
$$\left[x\frac{dy}{dx} + y(1) \right] - 1 + \frac{dy}{dx} = 0$$
$$\frac{dy}{dx}[x + 1] = 1 - y$$
$$\frac{dy}{dx} = \frac{1 - y}{x + 1}$$

$xy - x + y = 2$ and $x = 0 \Rightarrow y = 2$

Thus $(0, 2)$ is the point of tangency.

$$\left. \frac{dy}{dx} \right|_{x = 0} = \frac{1 - 2}{0 + 1} = -1 \Rightarrow m_t = -1 \text{ is slope of tangent}$$

Use the point/slope form.

$$y - 2 = (-1)(x - 0) \Rightarrow y = -x + 2$$

16. E. Use integration by parts: $\int u\, dv = uv - \int v\, du$

$$u = x \quad dv = e^{2x}$$
$$du = dx \int dv = \int e^{2x}\, dx$$
$$\int dv = \frac{1}{2} \int e^{2x}(2)\, dx$$
$$v = \frac{1}{2} e^{2x}$$
$$\int 3xe^{2x}\, dx = 3 \int xe^{2x}\, dx$$
$$= 3 \left[x \left(\frac{1}{2} e^{2x} \right) - \int \left(\frac{1}{2} e^{2x} \right) dx \right]$$
$$= \frac{3}{2} xe^{2x} - \frac{3}{2} \int e^{2x}\, dx$$
$$= \frac{3}{2} xe^{2x} - \frac{3}{2} \cdot \frac{1}{2} \int e^{2x}(2)\, dx$$
$$= \frac{3}{2} xe^{2x} - \frac{3}{4} e^{2x} + C$$

17. D. $\int \cot 3\phi\, d\phi = \frac{1}{3} \int \cot 3\phi\,(3)\, d\phi$

$\qquad\qquad = \frac{1}{3} \ln|\sin 3\phi| + C$

18. B. Use u-substitution. Let $u = \sqrt{x+5}$

$$u^2 = x + 5$$
$$x = u^2 - 5$$
$$dx = 2u\,du$$

$$\int \frac{2x}{\sqrt{x+5}}\, dx = 2 \int \frac{u^2 - 5}{u} 2u\,du$$

$$= 4 \int \left(u^2 - 5\right) du$$

$$= 4 \left[\frac{u^3}{3} - 5u\right] + C$$

$$= 4 \frac{u}{3}\left[u^2 - 15\right] + C$$

$$= \frac{4}{3}\sqrt{x+5}\left[(x+5) - 15\right] + C$$

$$= \frac{4}{3}\sqrt{x+5}\,(x - 10) + C$$

19. A. The integral $\int_1^2 \dfrac{dx}{\sqrt[3]{x-1}}$ has a discontinuity at its lower limit of integration, 1.

$$\int_1^2 \frac{dx}{\sqrt[3]{x-1}} = \lim_{c \to 1^+} \int_c^2 (x-1)^{-\frac{1}{3}}\, dx$$

$$= \lim_{c \to 1^+} \left[\frac{3}{2}(x-1)^{\frac{2}{3}}\right]_c^2$$

$$= \lim_{c \to 1^+} \left[\frac{3}{2}(1) - \frac{3}{2}(c-1)^{\frac{2}{3}}\right]$$

$$= \frac{3}{2} - 0$$

$$= \frac{3}{2}$$

20. A. $\int_0^2 f(x)\, dx = \int_0^1 2x\, dx + \int_1^2 \left(3x^2 - 1\right) dx$

$$= \left[x^2\right]_0^1 + \left[x^3 - x\right]_1^2$$

$$= [1 - 0] + \left[(8 - 2) - (1 - 1)\right]$$

$$= 1 + 6 = 7$$

21. E. $\text{area} = \int_1^e \dfrac{x^3 + 2}{x}\,dx$

$$= \int_1^e \left(x^2 + \dfrac{2}{x}\right)dx$$

$$= \left[\dfrac{x^3}{3} + 2\ln x\right]_1^e$$

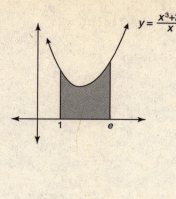

$$= \dfrac{e^3}{3} + 2\ln(e) - \left(\dfrac{1}{3} + 2\ln(1)\right)$$

$$= \dfrac{e^3}{3} + 2 - \dfrac{1}{3} - 0$$

$$= \dfrac{e^3}{3} + \dfrac{5}{3}$$

$$= \dfrac{e^3 + 5}{3}$$

22. A. The phrase "rate of change proportional to amount present" translates into

$\dfrac{dy}{dt} = ky$

Solving this differential equation yields

$y = Ce^{kt}$

(For this work, see the differential equations section on page 292.)

"54 grams present initially" $y = 54$ when $t = 0$

$54 = Ce^0 \Rightarrow C = 54$

Thus $y = 54e^{kt}$

"42 grams after 120 years" $\Rightarrow y = 42$ when $t = 120$

$42 = 54e^{120k}$

$\dfrac{7}{9} = e^{120k}$

$\ln\dfrac{7}{9} = 120k$

$k = \dfrac{1}{120}\ln\dfrac{7}{9}$

Thus $y = 54e^{kt}$, $k = \dfrac{1}{120}\ln\dfrac{7}{9}$

23. B. $\text{average value} = \dfrac{1}{b-a}\int_a^b f(x)\,dx$

$$= \dfrac{1}{\dfrac{\pi}{3} - 0}\int_0^{\pi/3} \tan x\,dx$$

$$= \dfrac{3}{\pi}\left[-\ln|\cos x|\right]_0^{\pi/3}$$

$$= \dfrac{-3}{\pi}\left[\ln\dfrac{1}{2} - \ln 1\right]$$

$$= \dfrac{-3}{\pi}\ln\dfrac{1}{2}$$

$$= \dfrac{-3}{\pi}\ln 2^{-1}$$

$$= \dfrac{3}{\pi}\ln 2$$

24. C. $y = x^2 - 5x + 6$

$0 = (x-2)(x-3)$

$x = 2 \quad x = 3$

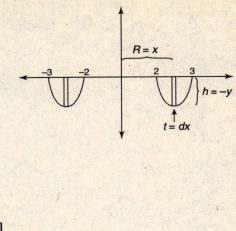

$V_{shell} = 2\pi Rht$

$V = 2\pi \int_2^3 x(-y)\,dx$

$= 2\pi \int_2^3 x(-x^2 + 5x - 6)\,dx$

$= 2\pi \int_2^3 x(-x^3 + 5x^2 - 6x)\,dx$

$= 2\pi \left[\frac{-x^4}{4} + \frac{5x^3}{3} - 3x^2\right]_2^3$

$= 2\pi \left[\left(\frac{-81}{4} + 45 - 27\right) - \left(-4 + \frac{40}{3} - 12\right)\right]$

$= \frac{5\pi}{6}$

25. A. Sketch the area and solid as shown.

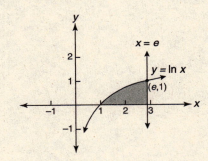

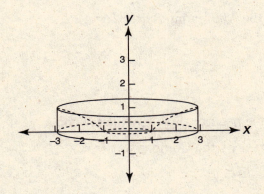

By washers, vertical axis $\Rightarrow dy$.

Area A extends from $y = 0$ to $y = 1$ along the y-axis $\Rightarrow \int_0^1$.

Washers: $\pi \int_a^b \left[\left(\dfrac{\text{outer}}{\text{radius}} \right)^2 - \left(\dfrac{\text{inner}}{\text{radius}} \right)^2 \right] dy \Rightarrow$

$$V = \pi \int_0^1 \left(e^2 - e^{2y} \right) dy$$

26. A.

I. $\displaystyle\sum_{n=1}^{\infty} \frac{4}{3^{n+1}}$

$\displaystyle\lim_{n \to \infty} \left| \frac{u_{n+1}}{u_n} \right|$

$= \displaystyle\lim_{n \to \infty} \left| \frac{4}{3^{n+2}} \cdot \frac{3^{n+1}}{4} \right|$

$= \displaystyle\lim_{n \to \infty} \left| \frac{1}{3} \right| = \frac{1}{3} < 1$

So series converges by the Ratio Test.

II. $\displaystyle\sum_{n=1}^{\infty} \frac{(-1)^n}{n}$

$= \displaystyle\sum_{n=2}^{\infty} (-1)^n \cdot \frac{1}{n}$

with $u_n = 1/n$,

i) $u_n > 0$

ii) $u_{n+1} < u_n$

and

iii) $\displaystyle\lim_{n \to \infty} u_n = 0$

So series converges by the Alternating Series Test.

III. $\displaystyle\sum_{n=3}^{\infty} \frac{3}{n^2 + 1}$

$= 3 \displaystyle\sum_{n=3}^{\infty} \frac{1}{n^2 + 1}$

Compare this series to the p-series. $\displaystyle\sum_{n=3}^{\infty} \frac{1}{n^2}$, which is convergent ($p > 1$). Since $\dfrac{1}{n^2 + 1} < \dfrac{1}{n^2}$, given series also converges by the Comparison Test.

$\Rightarrow$ So none of the series diverge.

27. B. In general for slope fields:

i) if the columns of slopes are the same

$$\left(\underset{\diagup}{\overset{\diagdown}{\equiv}} \quad \underset{\diagup}{\overset{\diagdown}{\gtrsim}} \quad \overset{}{\underset{}{\equiv}} \quad \text{etc} \right)$$

then the differential equation depends on just x — as in A and C

ii) if the rows of slopes are the same

$$\left(\begin{array}{c} \backslash\backslash\backslash \\ |\ |\ | \quad \text{etc} \\ /\ /\ / \end{array} \right)$$

then the differential equation depends on just y — as in D and E

iii) otherwise, depends on x and y — as in Graph B

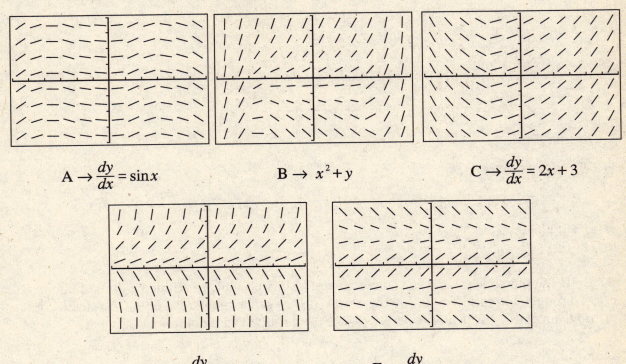

$$A \to \frac{dy}{dx} = \sin x \qquad\qquad B \to x^2 + y \qquad\qquad C \to \frac{dy}{dx} = 2x + 3$$

$$D \to \frac{dy}{dx} = 3y - 2 \qquad\qquad E \to \frac{dy}{dx} = \cos y$$

28. C.
$$\begin{aligned}
x(t) &= \tfrac{1}{4}t^4 - 3t & y(t) &= \tfrac{1}{3}(3t-5)^4 \\
x'(t) &= t^3 - 3 & y'(t) &= \tfrac{4}{3}(3t-5)^3 \cdot 3 \\
x''(t) &= 3t^2 & &= 4(3t-5)^3 \\
x''(2) &= 3 \cdot 2^2 & y''(t) &= 12(3t-5)^2 \cdot 3 \\
x''(2) &= 12 & &= 36(3t-5)^2 \\
& & y''(2) &= 36(6-5)^2 \\
& & y''(2) &= 36
\end{aligned}$$

Since acceleration vector is $(x''(2), y''(2))$ desired vector is $(12, 36)$.

Section IB

1. **A.** The limit is to be taken as z approaches a. Because a, b, and c are constants, the argument is just a polynomial function with z as the independent variable, so substitute a into the function for z.

$$\lim_{z \to a}\left(bz^2 + c^2 z\right) = b(a)^2 + c^2(a) = a^2 b + ac^2$$

2. **A.** The slope of a normal line is the negative reciprocal of the slope of the tangent line. Find $-1/g'(\pi/7)$ with your calculator. Let $y_1 = \sin(x/2) + 3x$

```
nDeriv(Y₁,X,π/7)

              3.487463936
-1/Ans
           -.2867413164
```

or find $g'(x)$

first: $g(x) = \sin\dfrac{x}{2} + 3x$

$g'(x) = \dfrac{1}{2}\cos\dfrac{x}{2} + 3$

and now find $\dfrac{-1}{g'\left(\dfrac{\pi}{7}\right)}$.

3. **E.** By finding one (or more) counterexamples, it is possible to eliminate each of choices A through D in turn. The following graph shows such a counterexample. The stated condition, $\lim\limits_{x \to 3^+} f(x) = 2$, is true, whereas choices A through D are not true.

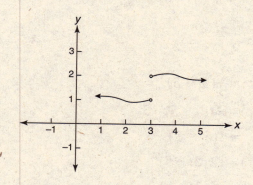

4. **C.** The graph is shown on the next page. Note that choices A and D approximate zeros of the function; B a relative maximum, and E a relative minimum. Choice C −2.066 best approximates where the graph changes its concavity — in this case from concave downward to concave upward.

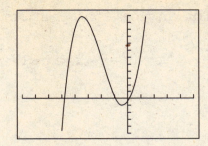

5. C. Use a calculator to find the derivative at a point.

```
nDeriv(X^(X-2),X,3)
               4.295839398
```

6. C. $V = \pi r^2 h$

$2\pi = \pi r^2 h$

$\dfrac{2}{r^2} = h$

$A = 2\pi r^2 + 2\pi rh$

$A(r) = 2\pi r^2 + 2\pi r\left(\dfrac{2}{r^2}\right)$

$\qquad = 2\pi r^2 + \dfrac{4\pi}{r}$

$\qquad = 2\pi r^2 + 4\pi r^{-1}$

$A'(r) = 4\pi r - \dfrac{4\pi}{r^2}$

$0 = 4\pi r - \dfrac{4\pi}{r^2}$

$0 = 4\pi r^3 - 4\pi$

$0 = 4\pi\left(r^3 - 1\right)$

$r = 1$

7. E. A quick sketch of the graph (with or without a calculator) shows a sharp turn at $x = 3$, so the derivative at that point is nonexistent.

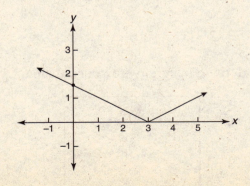

8. A. Using integration by "partial fractions," first separate the integrand into its component parts.

$$\frac{1}{(x+1)(x-2)} = \frac{A}{x+1} + \frac{B}{x-2} \Rightarrow \text{Note: } x^2 - x - 2 = (x+1)(x-2) \text{ multiplying by}$$

$(x+1)(x-2)$ gives:

$$1 = A(x-2) + B(x+1)$$

when $x = -1$ $\quad 1 = A(-3) + B(0)$

$$\left\langle -\frac{1}{3} = A \right\rangle$$

when $x = 2$ $\quad 1 = A(0) + B(3)$

$$\left\langle \frac{1}{3} = B \right\rangle$$

Then $\displaystyle\int \frac{dx}{(x+1)(x-2)}$

$$= \int \left(\frac{-\frac{1}{3}}{x+1} + \frac{\frac{1}{3}}{x-2} \right) dx$$

$$= -\frac{1}{3} \ln|x+1| + \frac{1}{3} \ln|x-2| + C$$

$$= -\frac{1}{3} \left(\ln|x+1| - \ln|x-2| \right) + C$$

$$= -\frac{1}{3} \ln\left| \frac{x+1}{x-2} \right| + C$$

9. D. Find the first few derivatives and look for a pattern.

$$y = x^{100}$$

$$\frac{dy}{dx} = 100x^{99}$$

$$\frac{d^2 y}{dx^2} = 100 \cdot 99 x^{98}$$

$$\frac{d^3 y}{dx^3} = 100 \cdot 99 \cdot 98 x^{97}$$

$$\frac{d^4 y}{dx4} = 100 \cdot 99 \cdot 98 \cdot 97 x^{96}$$

$$\vdots$$

$$\frac{d^{100} y}{dx^{100}} = 100 \cdot 99 \cdot 98 \cdot 97 \cdots 3 \cdot 2 \cdot 1 x^0 = 100$$

10. B. Find the value of the definite integral with your calculator.

```
Y₁=(sin X)^5

fnInt(Y₁,X,1,2)
          .814956842
```

11. B. The shaded area is equivalent to the definite integral.

$$\int_{-1}^{3} f(x)\,dx$$

The base of the area is 4 units, and if this base were divided into n equal subintervals, each subinterval would have a width of $4/n$. Thus the right-hand endpoint of the ith rectangle is given by $-1 + 4/n$.

Thus $\int_{-1}^{3} f(x)\,dx = \lim_{n \to \infty} \sum_{i=1}^{n} \left(\frac{4}{n}\right) f\left(-1 + \frac{4i}{n}\right)$

12. D. The question is in the form of the definition of the derivative, using h instead of Δx where $f(x) = e^{x}$.

$$f'(x) = \lim_{h \to 0} \frac{f(x+h) - f(x)}{h}$$
$$f(x) = e^{x} \Rightarrow f'(x) = e^{x}$$

13. A. By the definition of average value, use a calculator to find

$$\frac{1}{\pi - 1} \int_{1}^{\pi} x \sin x\,dx$$

```
fnInt(Xsin X,X,1,π)
        2.840423975
Ans/(π-1)
        1.326313839
```

14. D. Using Ratio Test: $\sum_{n=1}^{\infty} \frac{x^{n+1}}{(n+1)^{2}}$

$$\lim_{n \to \infty} \left| \frac{u_{n+1}}{u_n} \right| = \lim_{n \to \infty} \left| \frac{x^{n+2}}{(n+2)^{2}} \cdot \frac{(n+1)^{2}}{x^{n+1}} \right| = \lim_{n \to \infty} \left| x \cdot \frac{(n+1)^{2}}{(n+2)^{2}} \right|$$

$$= |x| \cdot \lim_{n \to \infty} \left| \frac{(n+1)^{2}}{(n+2)^{2}} \right| = |x| \cdot 1 = |x|$$

This ratio will be less than 1 when $|x| < 1 \Rightarrow -1 < x < 1$

Testing the endpoints:

   i) when $x = -1$: series becomes $\sum_{n=1}^{\infty} \frac{(-1)^{n+1}}{(n+1)^{2}}$ since $0 < |u_{n+1}| \le |u_n|$ and $\lim_{n \to \infty} u_n = 0$,

     alternating series test indicates series is convergent $\Rightarrow$ include $x = -1$

   ii) when $x = 1$: series becomes $\sum_{n=1}^{\infty} \frac{1}{(n+1)^{2}}$ since $\frac{1}{(n+1)^{2}} < \frac{1}{n^{2}}$ is a convergent p series,

     comparison test indicates series is convergent $\Rightarrow$ include $x = 1$ $\therefore$ interval of convergence is $-1 \le x \le 1$ or $[-1,1]$

15. E.
$$f(x) = \cos x \qquad f(0) = 1$$
$$f'(x) = -\sin x \qquad f'(0) = 0$$
$$f''(x) = -\cos x \qquad f''(0) = -1$$
$$f'''(x) = \sin x \qquad f'''(0) = 0$$
$$f^{iv}(x) = \cos x \qquad f^{iv}(0) = 1$$
$$T_3 f(x) = f(0) + \frac{f'(0)x}{1!} + \frac{f''(0)x^2}{2!} + \frac{f'''(0)x^3}{3!} + \frac{f^{iv}(0)x^4}{4!}$$
$$= 1 + 0 - \frac{1x^2}{2} + 0 + \frac{1x^4}{24}$$
$$= 1 - \frac{x^2}{2} + \frac{x^4}{24}$$
$$f(2) \approx 1 - \frac{2^2}{2} + \frac{2^4}{24} = 1 - \frac{4}{2} + \frac{16}{24}$$

16. E. For a curve described by parametric equations, arc length $= \int_{t_1}^{t_2} \sqrt{\left(\frac{dx}{dt}\right)^2 + \left(\frac{dy}{dt}\right)^2}$

$$x = \frac{1}{4}t^4 \qquad y = \frac{1}{3}t^3$$

$$\frac{dx}{dt} = t^3 \qquad \frac{dy}{dt} = t^2$$

so arc length $= \int_0^2 \sqrt{(t^3)^2 + (t^2)^2}\ dt$

$$= \int_0^2 \sqrt{t^6 + t^4}\ dt$$

17. D. For a function $f(x)$, its graph is concave upward if its slope is increasing on an interval.

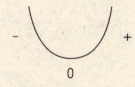

For graph of some $f(x)$, slope changes from negative (–), to zero (0), to positive (+) when the graph is concave upward. On the given graph of $f'(x)$, slope is increasing (in this case, y-coordinate is changing from negative to zero to positive) on the intervals $-1 < x < 1$ and $3 < x < 5$.

Section II: Free-Response Questions

Section IIA

1. (a) (see graph below)

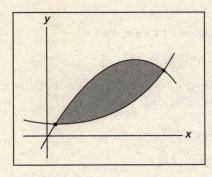

$\sin x = e^{x^2 - 2}$

Using calculator to find (x), $x = 0.138394$ or $x = 1.40959$

Let $a = .0138394$, let $b = 1.30959$

area $= \int_a^b \left(\sin x - e^{x^2 - 2} \right) dx = .401$

(b) boundary length $= L$

$$L = \int_a^b \sqrt{1 + (\cos x)^2}\, dx + \int_a^b \sqrt{1 + \left(\left(e^{x^2 - 2} \right) 2x \right)^2}\, dx$$

For $y = f(x)$ from $x = a$ to $x = b$, arc length is $\int_a^b \sqrt{1 + \left[f'(x) \right]^2}\, dx$

(c)

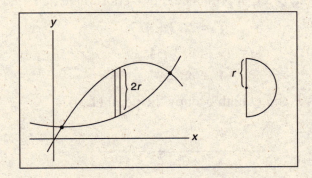

$r = \left(\sin x - e^{x^2 - 2} \right)/2$

area of cross section $= \left(\pi r^2 \right)/2 = (\pi/8)\left(\sin x - e^{x^2 - 2} \right)^2$

so volume $= (\pi/8) \int_a^b = \left(\sin x - e^{x^2 - 2} \right)^2\, dx$

Grading Rubric

(a) 3 points 2: correct integral

　　　　　　1: limits of integration

　　　　　　1: correct integral

　　　　1: answer

(b) 3 points 1: correct derivatives of sinx and e^{x^2-2}

　　　　　　1: correct arc length integral

　　　　　　1: correct limits of integration and sum of integrals

(c) 3 points 1: correct radius

　　　　　　1: correct integral

　　　　　　1: correct constant ($\pi/8$)

2. (a) $V_P = (dx/dt, dy/dt) = (1, 2t - 4)$ at $t = 2$, $V_P = (1, 0)$

　　$V_Q = (2/3, 2/3)$ at $t = 2$, $V_Q = (2/3, 2/3)$

(b) $\text{dist} = \int_1^4 \sqrt{(dx/dt)^2 + (dy/dt)^2}\, dx$

　　　$= \int_1^4 \sqrt{1^2 + (2t - 4)^2}\, dx$

(c) 　$X_P = X_Q$

　　$t - 3 = 2t/3 - 5/3$

　　$3t - 9 = 2t - 5$

　　　$t = 4$

at $t = 4$ both P and Q are at points having x-coordinate of 1

　　$Y_1 = (t - 2)^2$　　　　　$Y_2 = 2t/3 + 4/3$

$t = 4, Y_1 = (4 - 2)2$　　$t = 4\ Y_2 = 8/3 + 4/3$

　　$Y_1 = 4$　　　　　　　$Y_2 = 4$

at $t = 4$ particles P and Q both occupy the point $(1, 4)$

(d) see graph below

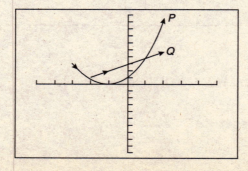

Grading Rubric

(a) 2 points 1: correct derivatives

1: correct vectors

(b) 2 points 1 correct integral

1: limits of integration

(c) 3 points 1: sets $X_P = X_Q$, or $Y_P = Y_Q$

1: correct solution for t

1: other coordinate shown to be equal

(d) 2 points 1: graph and direction for P

1: graph and direction for Q

3. (a) $f(x)$ is concave down when $f''(x)$ is negative

The graph of $f''(x)$ is shown below from the calculator with a window of X[–2.5, 5] and Y[–10, 30].

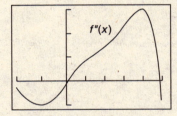 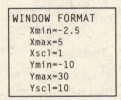

The zeros of $f''(x)$ are $x = 0.11$ and $x = 4.61$, and from the graph, $f''(x) < 0$ when $-2.5 < x < 0.11$ and $4.61 < x < 5$, so these are the intervals where $f(x)$ is concave down.

(b) $f'(x)$ will have relative extrema when its derivative, $f''(x)$, changes sign. From the graph in part (a), this occurs when $x = 0.11$ and $x = 4.61$. At $x = 0.11$, $f'(x)$ has a relative minimum, since $f''(x)$ changes from negative to positive. At $x = 4.61$, $f'(x)$ has a relative maximum, since $f''(x)$ changes from positive to negative.

(c) By definition, a function has points of inflection where concavity changes and the tangent line exists. A function is concave up when its derivative is increasing; a function is concave down when its derivative is decreasing. So, $f'(x)$ will have points of inflection where its derivative, $f''(x)$, changes from increasing to decreasing or decreasing to increasing, that is, where $f''(x)$ has relative extrema. From the graph in part (a), $f''(x)$ has relative extrema when $x = -1.6$ and $x = 3.8$, thus these are the inflection points of $f'(x)$.

Grading Rubric

(a) 3 points 1: indicates need for $f''(x)$ negative

1: finds zeros of $f''(x)$ via calculator

1: correct intervals

(b) 4 points 2: correct x-coordinates

2: justification: sign change in $f''(x)$

(c) 2 points 1: correct x-coordinates

1: justification: relative extrema of $f''(x)$

4. (a) Solve the differential equation by separating the variables.

$$\frac{dy}{dx} = 3xy$$

$$\frac{1}{y}\,dy = 3x\,dx$$

$$\int \frac{1}{y}\,dy = \int 3x\,dx$$

$$\ln y = \frac{3}{2}x^2 + C_1$$

$$e^{(3/2)\,x^2 + C_1} = y$$

$$e^{(3/2)\,x^2}\,e^{C_1} = y$$

$$C_2 e^{(3/2)\,x^2} = y$$

$$f(0) = 12 \Rightarrow x = 0 \text{ when } y = 12$$

$$C_2 e^{(3/2)(0)} = 12 \Rightarrow C_2 = 12$$

Thus $f(x) = 12e^{(3/2)\,x^2}$

(b) To find the inverse, interchange x and y.

$$12e^{(3/2)\,x^2} = y$$

$$12e^{(3/2)\,y^2} = x$$

$$e^{(3/2)\,y^2} = \frac{x}{12}$$

$$\frac{3}{2}y^2 = \ln\frac{x}{12}$$

$$y = \pm\sqrt{\frac{2}{3}\ln\frac{x}{12}}$$

But y must be greater than or equal to 0, so

$$f^{-1}(x) = \sqrt{\frac{2}{3}\ln\frac{x}{12}}$$

Grading Rubric

(a) 6 points $\begin{cases} 1: \text{separates the variables} \\ 2: \text{integrates correctly} \\ 2: \text{finds correct } C \\ 1: \text{expresses} f(x) \end{cases}$

(b) 3 points $\begin{cases} 1: \text{interchanges } x \text{ and } y \text{ on } f(x) \\ 1: \text{solves for } y \\ 1: \text{expresses} f^{-1}(x) \end{cases}$

5. (a) $P_3(f)(x) = f(1) + \dfrac{f'(1)(x-3)}{1!} + \dfrac{f''(1)(x-3)^2}{2!} + \dfrac{f'''(1)(x-3)^3}{3!}$

$\qquad = 3 - 2(x-3) + (7/2)(x-3)^2 - (5/6)(x-3)^3$

$\qquad f(3.2) \approx 3 - 2(0.2) + (7/2)(0.2)^2 - (5/6)(0.2)^3$

$\qquad\qquad \approx 2.733$

(b) $P_4(g)(x) = P_2(f)(x^2 + 3)$

$\qquad = 3 - 2\big((x^2+3)-3\big) + 3.5\big((x^2+3)-3\big)^2$

$\qquad = 3 - 2x^2 + 3.5(x^4)$

(c) $P3\,(h)(x) = \displaystyle\int_3^x \big(3 - 2(t-3) + (7/2)(t-3)^2\big)\,dt$

$\qquad = \Big[3t - (t-3)^2 + (7/6)(t-3)^3\Big]_3^x$

$\qquad = 3x - (x-3)^2 + (7/6)(x-3)^3 - \Big[3(3) - 0 + 0\Big]$

$\qquad = 3(x-3) - (x-3)^2 + (7/6)(x-3)^3$

Grading Rubric

(a) 4 points 3: correct $P_3(f)(x)$ <–1> for each error

$\qquad\qquad\quad$ 1: correct approximation for $f(3.2)$

(b) 2 points 2: correct $P_4(g)(x)$ <–1> for each error

(c) 3 points 1: correct set up

$\qquad\qquad\quad$ 1: correct antiderivatives

$\qquad\qquad\quad$ 1: correct answer

6. (a) For $f(x)$ to be continuous, $y = ax^3 + b$ must contain the points $(-2, 0)$ and $(1, 9/2)$.

$\left.\begin{array}{l} 0 = -8a + b \\[4pt] \dfrac{9}{2} = a + b \end{array}\right\} \Rightarrow \begin{array}{l} a = \dfrac{1}{2} \text{ and } b = 4 \\[4pt] \text{will guarantee continuity} \end{array}$

$f(x) = \begin{cases} 6x + 12 & \text{for } x \le -2 \\[6pt] \dfrac{1}{2}x^3 + 4 & \text{for } -2 < x < 1 \\[6pt] 2x + \dfrac{5}{2} & \text{for } x \ge 1 \end{cases}$

Justification:

$f(x)$ is continuous at $x = a$ if $\begin{cases} f(a) \text{ exists} \\[4pt] \lim\limits_{x \to a} f(x) \text{ exists} \\[4pt] \lim\limits_{x \to a} f(x) = f(a) \end{cases}$

At $x = -2 : f(-2) = 0$

$$\lim_{x \to -2^-} f(x) = \lim_{x \to -2^-} (6x + 12) = 0$$

$$\lim_{x \to -2^+} f(x) = \lim_{x \to -2^+} \left(\frac{1}{2} x^3 + 4 \right) = \frac{1}{2}(-8) + 4 = 0 \left. \begin{array}{c} \\ \\ \end{array} \right\}$$

$$\Rightarrow \lim_{x \to -2} f(x) = 0 = f(-2)$$

Thus $f(x)$ is continuous at $x = -2$.

At $x = 1 : f(1) = \frac{9}{2}$

$$\lim_{x \to 1^-} f(x) = \lim_{x \to 1^-} \left(\frac{1}{2} x^3 + 4 \right) = \frac{9}{2}$$

$$\lim_{x \to 1^+} f(x) = \lim_{x \to 1^+} \left(2x + \frac{5}{2} \right) = \frac{9}{2} \left. \begin{array}{c} \\ \\ \end{array} \right\} \Rightarrow \lim_{x \to 1} f(x) = \frac{9}{2} = f(1)$$

Thus $f(x)$ is continuous at $x = 1$.

(b) $\quad f(x) \begin{cases} 6x + 12 & \text{for } x \le -2 \\ \frac{1}{2} x^3 + 4 & \text{for } -2 < x < 1 \\ 2x + \frac{5}{2} & \text{for } x \ge 1 \end{cases}$

$f'(x) \begin{cases} 6 & \text{for } x \le -2 \\ \frac{3}{2} x^2 & \text{for } -2 < x < 1 \\ 2 & \text{for } x \ge 1 \end{cases}$

$$\left. \begin{array}{l} f'(-2^-) = 6 \\ f'(-2^+) = 6 \end{array} \right\} \Rightarrow \text{differentiable at } x = -2$$

Justification:

$$f'(c) = \lim_{x \to c} \frac{f(x) - f(c)}{x - c}$$

$$f'(-2^-) = \lim_{x \to 2^-} \frac{(6x + 12) - 0}{x - (-2)} = \lim_{x \to 2^-} \frac{6(x + 2)}{x + 2} = 6$$

$$f'(-2^+) = \lim_{x \to 2^+} \frac{\left(\frac{1}{2} x^3 + 4 \right) - 0}{x - (-2)} = \lim_{x \to 2^+} \frac{\frac{1}{2}(x^3 + 8)}{x + 2}$$

$$= \lim_{x \to -2^+} \frac{\frac{1}{2}(x + 2) - (x^2 - 2x + 4)}{x + 2} = \frac{1}{2}(12) = 6$$

Thus $f(x)$ is differentiable at $x - 2$.

$$\left. \begin{array}{l} f'(1^-) = \frac{3}{2} \\ f'(1^+) = 2 \end{array} \right\} \Rightarrow f(x) \, x \text{ is not differentiable at } x = 1$$

Justification:

$$f'(c) = \lim_{x \to c} \frac{f(x) - f(c)}{x - c}$$

$$f'(1^-) = \lim_{x \to 1^-} \frac{\left(\frac{1}{2}x^3 + 4\right) - \frac{9}{2}}{x - 1} = \lim_{x \to 1^-} \frac{\frac{1}{2}\left(x^3 - 1\right)}{x - 1}$$

$$= \lim_{x \to 1^-} \frac{\frac{1}{2}(x - 1)\left(x^2 + x + 1\right)}{x - 1} = \frac{3}{2}$$

$$f'(1^+) = \lim_{x \to 1^+} \frac{\left(2x + \frac{5}{2}\right) - \frac{9}{2}}{x - 1} = \lim_{x \to 1^+} \frac{2(x - 1)}{x - 1} = 2$$

Thus $f(x)$ is not differentiable at $x = 1$.

Grading Rubric

(a) 3 points $\begin{cases} 1\text{: finds values of } a \text{ and } b \\ 2\text{: justifies with the definition of continuity} \end{cases}$

(b) 6 points $\begin{cases} 1\text{: determines differentiability at } x = -2 \\ 2\text{: justifies with definition of derivative,} \\ \quad \text{including one-sided limits} \\ 1\text{: determines differentiability at } x = 1 \\ 2\text{: justifies with definition of derivative,} \\ \quad \text{including one-sided limits} \end{cases}$

Appendix: Calculus Dictionary

English	Calculus
domain of $\sqrt{s(x)}$	$s(x) \geq 0$
domain of $\dfrac{1}{s(x)}$	$s(x) \neq 0$
domain of $\ln\left[s(x)\right]$	$s(x) > 0$
zeros or x-intercepts	$f(x) = 0 \text{ or } y = 0$
y-intercepts	$x = 0$
symmetry with respect to y-axis or even function	$f(-x) = f(x)$
symmetry with respect to the origin or odd function	$f(-x) = -f(x)$
symmetry with respect to x-axis	$g(-y) = g(y)$
vertical asymptote (x = a)	$\lim\limits_{x \to a} f(x) = \pm\infty$
horizontal asymptotes (y = a)	$\lim\limits_{x \to \pm\infty} f(x) = a$
continuity	$\lim\limits_{x \to a} f(x) = f(a)$
definition of derivative	$f'(x) = \lim\limits_{\Delta x \to 0} \dfrac{f(x + \Delta x) - f(x)}{\Delta x}$ $f'(c) = \lim\limits_{x \to c} \dfrac{f(x) - f(c)}{x - c}$
instantaneous rate of change of y with respect to x	$\dfrac{dy}{dx}$
slope of a curve f(x) at x = c	$f'(c)$
slope of tangent to f(x) at x = c	$f'(c)$
slope of normal to f(x) at x = c	$\dfrac{-1}{f'(c)}$
critical numbers	$f'(x) = 0 \text{ or}$ $f'(x) \text{ does not exist}$
f(x) increasing	$f'(x) > 0$
f(x) decreasing	$f'(x) < 0$
f(x) concave up	$f''(x) > 0 \text{ or } f'(x) \text{ increasing}$
f(x) concave down	$f''(x) < 0 \text{ or } f'(x) \text{ decreasing}$
point of inflection	change in concavity; tangent line exists

English		Calculus
P.V.A.		
	position function	$s(t) = \int v(t)\,dt = \int \left[\int a(t)\,dt \right] dt$
	velocity function	$s'(t) = v(t) = \int a(t)\,dt$
	acceleration function	$s''(t) = v'(t) = a(t)$
	particle moving right	$v(t) > 0$
	particle moving left	$v(t) < 0$
	particle at rest	$v(t) = 0$
	particle changes direction	$v(t)$ changes sign
	total distance t_1 to t_2	$\left\| s(t_1) - s(t_c) \right\| + \left\| s(t_c) - s(t_2) \right\|$ where t_c = time particle changes direction
Newton's method		$x_{n+1} = x_n - \dfrac{f(x_n)}{f'(x_n)}$
rate of change of y proportional to amount of y present		$\dfrac{dy}{dt} = ky$ or $y = Ce^{kt}$
definition of definite integral		$\displaystyle \lim_{n \to \infty} \sum_{i=1}^{n} f(c_i)\,\Delta x_i$
trapezoidal rule		$\dfrac{b-a}{2n} [f(x_0) + 2f(x_1) + 2f(x_2)$ $\qquad + \cdots + 2f(x_{n-1}) + f(x_n)]$
area between curves		$\displaystyle \int_{\text{left}}^{\text{right}} (\text{top} - \text{bottom})\,dx$ $\displaystyle \int_{\text{lower}}^{\text{upper}} (\text{right} - \text{left})\,dy$
average value of $f(x)$ on $[a, b]$		$\dfrac{1}{b-a} \int_a^b f(x)\,dx$

Notes

CliffsNotes

LITERATURE NOTES

Absalom, Absalom!
The Aeneid
Agamemnon
Alice in Wonderland
All the King's Men
All the Pretty Horses
All Quiet on the Western Front
All's Well & Merry Wives
American Poets of the 20th Century
American Tragedy
Animal Farm
Anna Karenina
Anthem
Antony and Cleopatra
Aristotle's Ethics
As I Lay Dying
The Assistant
As You Like It
Atlas Shrugged
Autobiography of Ben Franklin
Autobiography of Malcolm X
The Awakening
Babbit
Bartleby & Benito Cereno
The Bean Trees
The Bear
The Bell Jar
Beloved
Beowulf
The Bible
Billy Budd & Typee
Black Boy
Black Like Me
Bleak House
Bless Me, Ultima
The Bluest Eye & Sula
Brave New World
The Brothers Karamazov
The Call of the Wild & White Fang
Candide
The Canterbury Tales
Catch-22
Catcher in the Rye
The Chosen
The Color Purple
Comedy of Errors…
Connecticut Yankee
The Contender
The Count of Monte Cristo
Crime and Punishment
The Crucible
Cry, the Beloved Country
Cyrano de Bergerac
Daisy Miller & Turn…Screw
David Copperfield
Death of a Salesman
The Deerslayer
Diary of Anne Frank
Divine Comedy-I. Inferno
Divine Comedy-II. Purgatorio
Divine Comedy-III. Paradiso
Doctor Faustus

Dr. Jekyll and Mr. Hyde
Don Juan
Don Quixote
Dracula
Electra & Medea
Emerson's Essays
Emily Dickinson Poems
Emma
Ethan Frome
The Faerie Queene
Fahrenheit 451
Far from the Madding Crowd
Farewell to Manzanar
Fathers and Sons
Faulkner's Short Stories
Faust Pt. I & Pt. II
The Federalist
Flowers for Algernon
For Whom the Bell Tolls
The Fountainhead
Frankenstein
The French Lieutenant's Woman
The Giver
Glass Menagerie & Streetcar
Go Down, Moses
The Good Earth
The Grapes of Wrath
Great Expectations
The Great Gatsby
Greek Classics
Gulliver's Travels
Hamlet
The Handmaid's Tale
Hard Times
Heart of Darkness & Secret Sharer
Hemingway's Short Stories
Henry IV Part 1
Henry IV Part 2
Henry V
House Made of Dawn
The House of the Seven Gables
Huckleberry Finn
I Know Why the Caged Bird Sings
Ibsen's Plays I
Ibsen's Plays II
The Idiot
Idylls of the King
The Iliad
Incidents in the Life of a Slave Girl
Inherit the Wind
Invisible Man
Ivanhoe
Jane Eyre
Joseph Andrews
The Joy Luck Club
Jude the Obscure
Julius Caesar
The Jungle
Kafka's Short Stories
Keats & Shelley
The Killer Angels
King Lear
The Kitchen God's Wife
The Last of the Mohicans

Le Morte d'Arthur
Leaves of Grass
Les Miserables
A Lesson Before Dying
Light in August
The Light in the Forest
Lord Jim
Lord of the Flies
The Lord of the Rings
Lost Horizon
Lysistrata & Other Comedies
Macbeth
Madame Bovary
Main Street
The Mayor of Casterbridge
Measure for Measure
The Merchant of Venice
Middlemarch
A Midsummer Night's Dream
The Mill on the Floss
Moby-Dick
Moll Flanders
Mrs. Dalloway
Much Ado About Nothing
My Ántonia
Mythology
Narr. …Frederick Douglass
Native Son
New Testament
Night
1984
Notes from the Underground
The Odyssey
Oedipus Trilogy
Of Human Bondage
Of Mice and Men
The Old Man and the Sea
Old Testament
Oliver Twist
The Once and Future King
One Day in the Life
   of Ivan Denisovich
One Flew Over the Cuckoo's Nest
100 Years of Solitude
O'Neill's Plays
Othello
Our Town
The Outsiders
The Ox Bow Incident
Paradise Lost
A Passage to India
The Pearl
The Pickwick Papers
The Picture of Dorian Gray
Pilgrim's Progress
The Plague
Plato's Euthyphro…
Plato's The Republic
Poe's Short Stories
A Portrait of the Artist…
The Portrait of a Lady
The Power and the Glory
Pride and Prejudice
The Prince
The Prince and the Pauper

A Raisin in the Sun
The Red Badge of Courage
The Red Pony
The Return of the Native
Richard II
Richard III
The Rise of Silas Lapham
Robinson Crusoe
Roman Classics
Romeo and Juliet
The Scarlet Letter
A Separate Peace
Shakespeare's Comedies
Shakespeare's Histories
Shakespeare's Minor Plays
Shakespeare's Sonnets
Shakespeare's Tragedies
Shaw's Pygmalion & Arms…
Silas Marner
Sir Gawain…Green Knight
Sister Carrie
Slaughterhouse-Five
Snow Falling on Cedars
Song of Solomon
Sons and Lovers
The Sound and the Fury
Steppenwolf & Siddhartha
The Stranger
The Sun Also Rises
T.S. Eliot's Poems & Plays
A Tale of Two Cities
The Taming of the Shrew
Tartuffe, Misanthrope…
The Tempest
Tender Is the Night
Tess of the D'Urbervilles
Their Eyes Were Watching God
Things Fall Apart
The Three Musketeers
To Kill a Mockingbird
Tom Jones
Tom Sawyer
Treasure Island & Kidnapped
The Trial
Tristram Shandy
Troilus and Cressida
Twelfth Night
Ulysses
Uncle Tom's Cabin
The Unvanquished
Utopia
Vanity Fair
Vonnegut's Works
Waiting for Godot
Walden
Walden Two
War and Peace
Who's Afraid of Virginia…
Winesburg, Ohio
The Winter's Tale
The Woman Warrior
Worldly Philosophers
Wuthering Heights
A Yellow Raft in Blue Water